The Politics of English

Conflict, Competition, Co-existence

This book is part of the series *Worlds of English* published by Routledge in association with The Open University. The three books in the series are:

English in the World: History, Diversity, Change
(edited by Philip Seargeant and Joan Swann)

ISBN 978-0-415-67421-8 (paperback)

ISBN 978-0-415-67420-1 (hardback)

ISBN 978-0-203-12456-7 (ebook)

Communicating in English: Talk, Text, Technology
(edited by Daniel Allington and Barbara Mayor)

ISBN 978-0-415-67423-2 (paperback)

ISBN 978-0-415-67422-5 (hardback)

ISBN 978-0-203-12454-3 (ebook)

The Politics of English: Conflict, Competition, Co-existence
(edited by Ann Hewings and Caroline Tagg)

ISBN 978-0-415-67424-9 (paperback)

ISBN 978-0-415-67425-6 (hardback)

This publication forms part of the Open University module U214 *Worlds of English*. Details of this and other Open University modules can be obtained from the Student Registration and Enquiry Service, The Open University, PO Box 197, Milton Keynes, MK7 6BJ, United Kingdom (Tel. +44 (0845 300 60 90, email general-enquiries@open.ac.uk).

www.open.ac.uk

The Politics of English

Conflict, Competition, Co-existence

Edited by Ann Hewings and Caroline Tagg

Guide - unit 20
Leave Africa out
  DVD - 1 clip 19.1 and 2
  Chapter 4, 23, 6 - if time

Routledge
Taylor & Francis Group

Published by

Routledge
2 Park Square
Milton Park
Abingdon OX14 4RN

in association with

The Open University
Walton Hall
Milton Keynes MK7 6AA

Simultaneously published in the USA and Canada by

Routledge
711 Third Avenue
New York, NY 10017

Routledge is an imprint of the Taylor & Francis Group,
an informa business

First published 2012

Edited and designed by The Open University.

Typeset by The Open University.

Printed and bound in the United
Kingdom by Latimer Trend &
Company Ltd., Plymouth.

British Library Cataloguing in Publication Data:
A catalogue record for this book is available from the
British Library.

Library of Congress Cataloging-in-Publication Data

The politics of English : conflict, competition, co-
existence / edited by Ann Hewings and Caroline Tagg.

p. cm. -- (Worlds of English)

ISBN 978-0-415-67425-6 (hardback) -- ISBN 978-0-
415-67424-9 (pbk.)   1.   English language--Political
aspects--English-speaking countries 2.   Language and
languages--Political aspects. 3.   Intercultural communication. 4.   Language policy--English-speaking countries.
I. Hewings, Ann. II. Tagg, Caroline.

PE2751.P65 2012

306.44'90917521--dc23

2011037887

ISBN 978-0-415-67424-9 (paperback)

ISBN 978-0-415-67425-6 (hardback)

1.1

Contents

CMA-

Series preface

The books in this series provide an introduction to the study of English, both for students of the English language and the general reader. They are core texts for the Open University module U214 *Worlds of English*. The series aims to provide students with:

- an understanding of the history and development of English, and a critical approach to its current global status and influence
- skills and knowledge to use in analysing English-language texts
- an appreciation of variation in the English language between different speakers and writers, and across different regional and social contexts
- examples of the diversity of English language practices in different parts of the world
- an understanding of how English is learned as a first language or as an additional language, and of its role as a language of formal education around the world
- an appreciation of how media, from print to the internet, have affected the English language and contributed to its position in the world today
- an understanding of how English is promoted around the world and the controversies surrounding the politics and economics of such decisions and its impact on other languages and the people who speak them
- informed reflections on the likely future role of English.

The readings which accompany each chapter have been chosen to exemplify key points made in the chapters, often by exploring related data, or experiences and practices involving the English language in different parts of the world. The readings also represent an additional 'voice' or viewpoint on key themes or issues raised in the chapter.

Each chapter includes:

- **activities** to stimulate further understanding or analysis of the material
- **boxes** containing illustrative or supplementary material

- **key terms** which are set in coloured type at the point where they are explained; the terms also appear in colour in the index so that they are easy to find in the chapters.

The other books in this series are:

Seargeant, P. and Swann, J. (eds) (2012) *English in the World: History, Diversity, Change*, Abingdon, Routledge/Milton Keynes, The Open University.

Allington, D. and Mayor, B. (eds) (2012) *Communicating in English: Talk, Text, Technology*, Abingdon, Routledge/Milton Keynes, The Open University.

Ann Hewings
Series Editor

Biographical information

Daniel Allington

Daniel Allington is Lecturer in English Language Studies and Applied Linguistics at The Open University, although he has also worked as an illustrator and taught English in the UK and abroad. His research into the production and consumption of culture has appeared in major journals and edited collections, and he is part of an international team of scholars writing a history of the book in Britain.

Guy Cook

Guy Cook is Professor of Language and Education at The Open University. He has published extensively on various aspects of applied linguistics. From 2004–2009, he was co-editor of the journal *Applied Linguistics*. He is Chair of the British Association for Applied Linguistics (2009–2012) and is an Academician of the Academy for the Social Sciences. His books include *Translation in Language Teaching* (2010), Winner of the International House Ben Warren Prize.

John Gray

John Gray is Senior Lecturer in TESOL Education at the Institute of Education, University of London. He is the author of *The Construction of English: Culture, Consumerism and Promotion in the ELT Global Coursebook* (2010) and co-author (with David Block and Marnie Holborow) of *Neoliberalism and Applied Linguistics* (2012).

Ann Hewings

Ann Hewings is Senior Lecturer in Language and Communication at The Open University. She has taught English in a variety of countries to children, young people and adults. Her research and teaching interests focus on academic literacy in English and interdisciplinary and global perspectives on English language. Her publications include *Grammar and Context* (2005, co-edited with Martin Hewings).

David Johnson

David Johnson is Senior Lecturer in the Department of English at The Open University. He is the author of *Shakespeare and South Africa* (1996) and *Imagining the Cape Colony* (2012), as well as principal author of

Jurisprudence: A South African Perspective (2001) and co-editor of *A Historical Companion to Postcolonial Literatures in English* (2005).

Naz Rassool

Naz Rassool is Professor of Education in the Institute of Education at the University of Reading. She has published widely within the fields of the political economy of language in education; literacy and development; language relations within the global cultural economy; 'new managerialism' in education; and the sociology of technology in education. Her books include *Global Issues in Language, Education and Development: Perspectives from Postcolonial Countries* (2007). She has published numerous articles in refereed international academic journals.

Philip Seargeant

Philip Seargeant is Lecturer in Applied Linguistics in the Centre for Language and Communication at The Open University. He is author of *The Idea of English in Japan: Ideology and the Evolution of a Global Language* (2009) and *Exploring World Englishes* (2012), and editor of *English in Japan in the Era of Globalization* (2011). He has also published several articles in journals such as *World Englishes*, the *International Journal of Applied Linguistics*, *Language Policy*, *Language Sciences*, and *Language & Communication*.

Caroline Tagg

Caroline Tagg is Lecturer in Applied Linguistics in the Centre for English Language Studies at the University of Birmingham. Her research interests include the application of discourse analysis and corpus linguistics to digital interaction, particularly text messaging and social network sites. She is author of *The Discourse of Text Messaging* (forthcoming) and has published articles in journals such as *World Englishes* and *Writing Systems Research*.

General introduction

Ann Hewings and Caroline Tagg

This book takes as its starting point the understanding that all language use is political in nature. That is, language is not a neutral medium of communication, but plays a significant role in the negotiation of power relations – relations of conflict, competition and cooperation – between individuals and between communities. It is the primary means by which power relations are organised and reinforced, as is evidenced at state level by the writing and enactment of national policies and laws, and at the individual level in the myriad ways in which people relate to others in their everyday interactions. In other words, the management of political, diplomatic and social relations requires or uses language.

However, as explained in Chapter 1, politics can also be about language. Language regulation – that is, a society's rules about what someone can say, and how and when they can say it – is a constant and universal feature of social life. On the one hand, language can be officially regulated, and examples of official regulation include a state's pronouncements regarding free speech and censorship, or its decisions about what the country's official or national language (or languages) are to be. Language can also be formally regulated through the codification and dissemination of linguistic norms via educational institutions. On the other hand, language regulation can also happen on a more local and informal level, through people's judgements about appropriate or correct language use – think of people's attitudes towards swearing, 'sloppy' speech or politically incorrect language – and through the impact which such evaluations can have on people's own as well as others' language use.

These formal and informal language judgements and policies can have complex effects on how members of a society use language, and they can determine the role that different languages play in the negotiation of power relations within that society. What this means is that language is intricately bound up with the social behaviour of the individuals and communities who use and regulate it, and their ideas about the place of language – or a particular language – in society.

All languages play a role in power relations within certain contexts. However, English now has a global reach like no other language, given its history of colonialism, its association with global capitalism, its multiple forms and varieties, and the huge number of English language learners. Its role as a global lingua franca means that it is particularly likely to form a part (alongside other languages) of people's language practices, to be implicated in their language value systems, and to feature in language policies across the world, in English-dominant countries and elsewhere. That is, the English language may play a particularly significant role in global politics and power relations. And how it is used in relations between particular groups will depend on a number of contextual factors, including the ideas that the people involved have about the language. Ideas about English vary across the many contexts in which it is used, so that while to some people English appears as the language of opportunity, economic prosperity, mobility and freedom, to others it may be a symbol or tool of repression, disadvantage and cultural supremacy. People may also distinguish between varieties of English, according certain forms greater prestige or attractiveness than others. These ideas about English shape people's language practices and their behaviour towards others and, on an official level, they feed into the policies that regulate language and society. This book explores the complex and varied interplay of the English language with values, practices and policies in a range of local and global contexts.

The focus and structure of the book

The focus of this book, then, is on the political nature of the use of English alongside other languages, and how language policies are shaped both by language practices and by people's ideas about language. The structure is as follows: the first chapter expands on the arguments outlined above, setting out the general themes and propositions of the book. The following six chapters develop these arguments by looking at how policies and practices involving the English language are realised in a range of globally relevant areas. These include the dominance of English in international contexts of migration (Chapter 2); in educational institutions and policies across the world (Chapter 3); in international teaching, testing and publishing industries (Chapter 4); in the writing and dissemination of Anglophone literature, primarily in Britain's ex-colonies (Chapter 5); and in the global media (Chapter 6). Chapter 7 considers the role of translation as a counterpoint to the use of English as a lingua franca, and explores how the dominance of English has shaped the nature of translation practices. Each of these chapters looks not only at the way in which the English language both sustains, and is sustained by, an emerging status quo, but also at the way in which people contest and subvert the policies that regulate the use of language in their societies. Chapter 8 then returns to consider in greater depth the connection between language policies involving English, and the values and ideas that people have with respect to English and other languages. In particular, it looks at the way in which people's ideas about English are often bound up with concern for correctness and 'standards'; and at how judgements about language tend to be judgements about the people who use that language, with consequent social and political implications.

English is undeniably a force in the early twenty-first century world, be it a force for good or a force for ill. For how long, however, will it retain its status as a global lingua franca, what forms will the language take and what functions will it fulfil? In the Afterword, discussion focuses on the future of English, and the extent to which language policies and other attempts to regulate language use can in fact shape the future development and status of the language in ways intended by their proponents. Of course, what the arguments in this book suggest is that, given the complexity of policies, practices and language values in local and global contexts, the only way to really know what will happen is to wait and see.

1   The politics and policies of global English

Philip Seargeant

1.1   Introduction

Politics is the practice and theory of how groups organise and regulate themselves, and how power is achieved and used in public life. In many modern societies the term is often synonymous with 'electoral politics', and is used to refer to the activities of professional politicians who are involved in the work of government. In its wider sense though – as being to do with power relations of all types – it can be applied to the private as well as the public sphere. The phrase 'the personal is political' (Hanisch, 1970), made popular during the feminist movement of the 1960s and 1970s, was used to highlight the fact that power relations extend into our personal lives and relationships. The roles people are assigned and take up in society (in the workplace, in the family, in their personal relationships); the way they are expected to behave, to dress, to speak – all this is part of a larger pattern of interpersonal organisation which constitutes society, and which is sustained by relations of power between individuals and the groups in which they live. In the last few decades there has been a great deal of scholarship exploring the various ways in which relations of power shape all social interaction (e.g. Foucault, 1977, 1998; Bourdieu, 1984), and suggesting that power relations are responsible for the very existence of society. According to this view, we would not be able to operate as social beings – to make mutual decisions, to collaborate, to get things done – without relations of power; and in this respect, politics is a fundamental part of our everyday lives.

Allow about 10 minutes

Activity 1.1

If politics in the sense described above is a fundamental part of all aspects of our social lives, in what ways do you think it is related to or affects issues of language?

Comment

The part that language plays in expressing and reinforcing power relations within society is immense. Let's take the example of its role within the legal system of any country. When, for instance, an offender is sentenced for a crime, what actually happens is that the judge utters a particular speech act ('I sentence you to 300 hours of community service', for example) which has the effect of committing the offender to undergo the punishment. This speech act is backed, of course, by a whole institutional system of power (the police force, the probation and prison services, etc.), which can physically enforce the sentence. But it is the utterance of these particular words which legally decides the matter. And it is speech acts of this sort which organise all relations between individuals and the state, and which thus bind society together (Searle, 1996).

Speech acts are discussed in another book in this series: Allington and Mayor (eds) (2012), Chapter 1.

Yet language isn't only related to politics in this way; it can also itself be the focus of political debate and action. That is to say, politics doesn't only use language; it can also be about language. In fact, the regulation of language – the regulation of what one can say, of how and when one can say it – is something that happens constantly in social life. For example, in many countries the notion of 'free speech' is a central tenet of the nation's political identity. In such communities, a citizen's right to speak freely and without censorship is inscribed in the constitution or otherwise protected by law (see, for example, Figure 1.1). This, therefore, is a form of political sanction for a particular aspect of language use. Yet, even in communities which see this idea as an essential aspect of their cultural identity, there are always also proscriptions about what it is and isn't acceptable to say. These proscriptions can either be explicit laws or they can be social and cultural norms (e.g. they can be beliefs about what normally counts as bad or abusive language), but either way they act so that the individual's language use continues to be regulated at some level at all times.

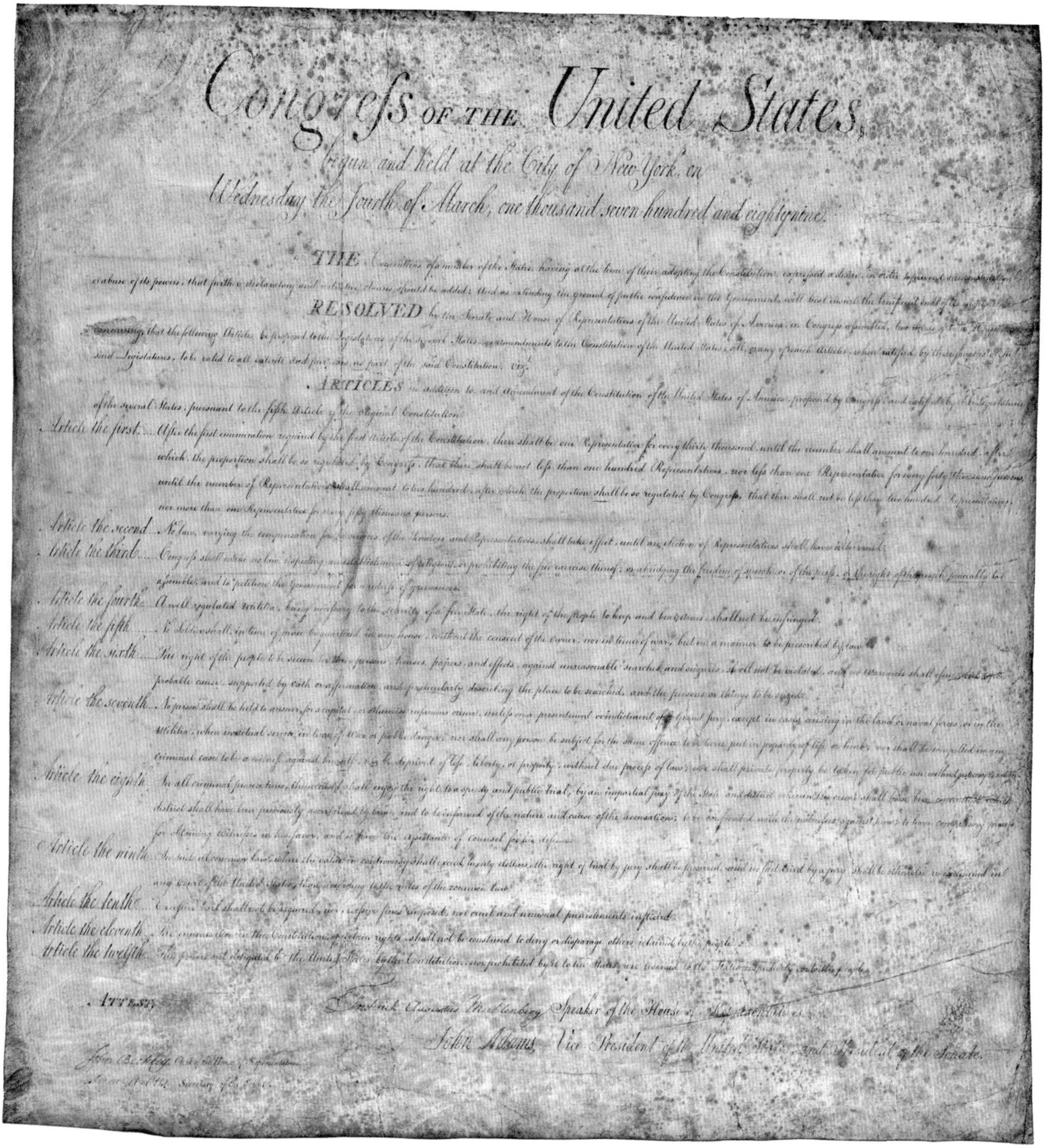
Congress of the United States,
begun and held at the City of New-York, on
Wednesday the fourth of March, one thousand seven hundred and eighty nine.

Figure 1.1 The First Amendment of the US Bill of Rights, prohibiting laws 'abridging the freedom of speech'

Figure 1.2(a) Evidence of language conflict on a school-crossing sign highlighting strong beliefs about the use of English in Wales

Figure 1.2(b) Another example of language conflict in Wales on a 'Give Way' sign

EMA

Further discussion of language policy and planning – especially as it relates to multilingual societies – can be found in another book in this series: Seargeant and Swann (eds) (2012), Chapter 6.

Debates about what an individual says and how he or she says it are often part of larger discussions concerning the place of language – and specific languages – in society. **Language policy** – the way a state or an organisation determines how language is to be used in society – is often concerned with the way that language relates to other political issues, especially those to do with cultural identity, equality and the ability of citizens to communicate both within their own community and with people from other communities. English – with its global reach, its history rooted in colonialism, its contemporary association with global capitalism, its multiple forms and varieties, and its status as one of the most taught languages around the world – is easily implicated in manifold political debates, and as such exists as a focus for language policies around the world, in English-dominant countries and elsewhere. The ways in which it features in the politics of communities around the world is the subject of this chapter. In particular, I will address the following questions:

- What impact does the spread of English have on people and societies around the world?
- What actions are people taking in response to the spread of the language and to the impact this spread is having?

These questions relate to politics, to policy and to issues of **language planning**. That is, they concern the role that English plays in the power relations that organise society, the way that people aim or attempt to regulate this role, and the specific measures (the language planning) that people employ to do this. To put it another way, the discussion will consider why and how English is implicated in contemporary political debates, and what strategies people are devising to ensure that the current status of English across the globe contributes to the cultural harmony and prosperity of the world rather than creating divisions and inequalities among its population.

1.2   Global English: a problem or a solution?

Let's begin by considering the differing attitudes that people have towards English in different contexts. Much language policy is based on general beliefs and opinions about language use, and so examining how such beliefs are framed can help in understanding what structures the politics of the language.

Activity 1.2

Allow about 20 minutes

Have a look at the two extracts below. They both express opinions about English, and about the influence it can have on societies around the world. Yet they express very different views. While reading them, consider first what their respective judgements on the English language are; and second, why it is that they offer such different characterisations of the same language.

Extract 1

The English language, like football and other sports, began here [in the UK] and has spread to every corner of the globe. Today more than a billion people speak English. It is becoming the world's language … the pathway of global communication and global access to knowledge. And it has become the vehicle for hundreds of millions of people of all countries to connect with each other, in countless ways. Indeed, English is much more than a language: it is a bridge across borders and cultures, a source of unity in a rapidly changing world. …

But there are millions of people in every continent who are still denied this chance to learn English – prevented from enjoying many of the benefits of the internet, commerce and culture. And I believe that no one – however poor, however distant – should be denied the opportunity that the English language provides. So I want Britain to make a new gift to the world – pledging to help and support anyone, whatever their circumstances, to have access to the tools they need to learn or to teach English.

(Prime Minister's Office, 2008)

Extract 2

Languages are possibly the most complicated structures the human mind has ever invented but, tragically, our species' most impressive creations are dying. According to the British linguist David Crystal, an indigenous language currently disappears every two weeks. By the end of the century, it is projected, 5,500 of the current 6,000 languages now spoken will join Latin and Greek as 'dead languages'. Those, of course, were once two of the world's top languages. Sic transit, as they used to say. What we are witnessing is linguicide. A language massacre. …

There's no mystery about the root cause of the linguistic holocaust that we're living through. Take a holiday anywhere in the world. Your airline pilot will, as you listen to the safety instructions (in English), be communicating with ground control in English. Signs in the airport, whatever country you're in, will be duplicated in one of the world's top 20 languages – most likely English. You'll see Coca-Cola logos. MTV will be playing on the screens. Muzak will be crooning out Anglo-American lyrics as you walk through the concourse to baggage reclaim. At the hotel, the desk clerk will speak your language, as will, probably, the bellhop. …

The spread of English is the product of naked linguistic superpower. If anyone anywhere wants to get ahead nowadays, an ability to speak English is obligatory. We take it for granted. …

How did this happen? How did a dialect, spoken by a backward, semi-literate tribe in the south-eastern corner of a small island in the North Sea spread, like some malign pandemic virus, across the globe? Should we feel guilty that our way of speaking is obliterating so many other tongues? Is it not a more sinister kind of colonialism than that which we practised a hundred years ago? Once we just took their raw materials. Now we invade their minds, by changing the primary tool by which they think: 'their' language.

(Sutherland, 2002)

Comment

The first extract is from a speech made by Gordon Brown in 2008 when he was British Prime Minister. He was announcing a development initiative to promote the teaching of English across the globe. The view of English and its role in the world that is expressed in this speech is entirely positive – so much so that the speech advocates that this role should be further promoted. This positive judgement stems from the way that English is characterised in the rhetoric of the speech, and from associations that are made between the language and other elements of social life. Specifically, Brown equates knowledge of English with the ability to communicate successfully at a global level. But he goes further and also suggests that knowledge of English is a prerequisite for full access to the benefits of the 'internet, commerce and culture', that it acts as a tool of 'opportunity' for people from all parts of the globe, and that it can play a role in bringing about 'unity in a rapidly changing world'.

The second extract is from an article titled 'Linguicide: the death of language' by the writer John Sutherland, which was published in the British newspaper *The Independent* in March 2002. The global spread of English is here addressed from the perspective of the impact it can have on other languages and cultures. Both in the examples Sutherland gives of the global presence of English, and the explicit comments he makes about this, the view is a negative one in marked contrast to Gordon Brown's speech. The examples are of cultural homogenisation – Coca-Cola logos, MTV and the way that English is not just a facilitator of unity but something that produces a 'sameness' in diverse cultural contexts. As with Extract 1, the explicit comments about English relate it to other elements of social and political life. Its spread and promotion is described as 'the product of naked linguistic superpower', likened to colonialism, and blamed for killing off other languages and cultures. The word **linguicide** – a neologism modelled on concepts such as homicide, fratricide and regicide – is a term used in certain parts of the academic literature, and is often linked to the idea of a 'killer language' (e.g. Phillipson, 1992; Skutnabb-Kangas, 2000). In this characterisation, English is responsible not only for creating a bland global 'monoculture' – variously described as the 'McDonaldization' (Ritzer, 1996), 'Disneyization' (Bryman, 2004), or even 'Coca-Colonization' (Wagnleitner, 1994) of the world – but for actually killing other languages and, by extension, other cultures.

The views expressed in these two extracts are explicitly political. The first is part of a political speech and the second repeats ideas and research from academics, who are themselves involved in political activism (e.g. Skutnabb-Kangas et al., 2003). Before considering the overt politics associated with the spread of English, however, we need to clarify a few theoretical issues. It is important to note from the very beginning that what we are talking about here is not the English language itself, but the language as it is bound up with the societies that use it, the social and cultural practices these societies have, and the beliefs they hold about the role that language plays in their lives. In other words, as intimated above, beliefs about language are central to the politics of language; and beliefs about a particular language (e.g. English) are rarely, if ever, about that language alone, but instead about the associations that are made in society between the language and a variety of other social issues and practices (Woolard, 1998).

The association between language and other social issues is discussed further in Chapter 8.

One of the ways in which these associations are created is through the use of metaphors for describing language. Geoffrey Harpham argues that 'when it comes to language, metaphors are truly indispensable … [A]ny description that attributes to language a particular character, nature, or function will necessarily have the status of a metaphor' (Harpham, 2002, pp. 34–5). What he means by this is that when we describe either language in general or a particular language (e.g. English, Spanish, Japanese), we often do so in a metaphorical way. The reason for this is that language is such an all-pervasive and complex aspect of human life that it becomes difficult to explain its nature and use without likening it to other things. Yet in likening it to other phenomena in the world, we also create a particular perspective from which to view – and evaluate – its existence.

Allow about 15 minutes

Activity 1.3

Look back at the two extracts in Activity 1.2 and note any metaphors that are used to describe the English language and to talk about its role and influence in the world. What effect do you think the use of these metaphors has in terms of providing particular perspectives on the role of English in the world?

Comment

Both these extracts rely strongly on metaphor for their discussion of English. Extract 1 has a string of metaphors revolving around the way language can connect people. English is described as a 'PATHWAY of global communication', a 'VEHICLE for hundreds of millions of people of all countries to connect with each other', 'a BRIDGE across borders and cultures'. As well as this, it's referred to as 'a SOURCE OF UNITY', and is even likened to 'football and other sports'. In each case, the metaphor acts to highlight particular qualities or attributes of the language; and, in this speech, these attributes are specifically positive ones.

Extract 2 is equally metaphorical, but uses a very different pattern of imagery. Many of the metaphors here are based around ideas of death and killing. Other languages are said to be 'DYING' or already 'DEAD'. This is a result of 'LINGUICIDE'; it is a 'language MASSACRE', if not a 'linguistic HOLOCAUST'. The cause of all this is the spread of English, which is 'like some malign pandemic virus'. There are other metaphors as well: the spread of English is likened to a 'sinister kind of COLONIALISM', it is 'OBLITERATING' other languages and 'INVAD[ING the] minds' of people from non-Anglophone cultures. These metaphors thus highlight a specific consequence that can result from language contact, whereby the language practices of one community are greatly affected by those of another. But they do so in an evaluative and emotive way.

Both patterns of imagery are also an important part of the way that the extracts discuss not simply the English language itself, but its role in social life. In effect, neither passage is just about English, but is also about the ways in which different societies interact. The first calls for communication and collaboration between people across the globe; the second decries the way that diverse world cultures can become overwhelmed by the practices and values of globally dominant societies. In both cases, therefore, a discussion of language is used as a vehicle for a discussion about the state of modern global society and the way in which different communities interact with each other.

Before we leave this issue, there is one final metaphor worth mentioning. It is used in both extracts, and is the notion of a language as an object that can 'belong' to certain groups of people and, by extension, not belong to others. Extract 1 talks of 'the world's language' – that is, English as being the possession of the whole population of the world; while Extract 2 refers to different cultures as each having 'their' own language. This is a very common metaphor in everyday usage – so much so that you may not even notice it as being a metaphor. But it's a key element in the politics of language, and as such is one I return to in Section 1.5 below.

We have, then, a picture of English as always being characterised in particular ways and being associated with other aspects of social life. An important point we can thus make is that the impact English is having in diverse world contexts is a result both of actual linguistic issues (i.e. the way people use the language around the world) and of the beliefs and ideologies people have about the language. The importance of noting this is that what people think about the nature and spread of the language can then translate into what people do about the language, and that these actions in turn constitute the policies people devise and enact in order to regulate the shape and positioning of English in society. In Sections 1.3 and 1.4, I look at how different types of associations with the language lead to different programmes of action.

Ideology

The discussion so far has referred at various times to what people *think* about the English language, to their *beliefs* about and *attitudes* towards the language, and to the *associations* that are made between the language and other aspects of social life. To an extent, these various terms have been employed interchangeably in the chapter. None has been used in a particularly technical way; that is, with a delimited meaning specifically related to the discipline of linguistics (although some can, in certain contexts, adopt a specific technical sense). A term which encompasses much of what has been discussed in this respect, and that is often employed when examining the relationship between language and politics, is **ideology**. This word is used in popular or everyday contexts, but also operates as a technical term in academic discussions. In its technical sense it has a number of specific uses which are rather different from its popular use, and it is worth, therefore, dwelling a moment on its meaning.

The concept of ideology has a long and contested history in the political sciences, and, as is the case with many technical terms, can mean different things to different people. At its most basic it refers to systems of entrenched beliefs that people have about aspects of social life. But some traditions view these systems of belief in a negative way, while others see them in a neutral light, and this leads to differing definitions of the concept. For example, Marxist approaches consider ideology to be a form of 'false consciousness' or illusory thinking in society, which leads people to have a distorted view of the real nature of experience: and which is used by those in power (in Marxist terms: the ruling class) as a means of promoting their own agenda. In contrast to this is the 'total concept of ideology', associated with the sociologist Karl Mannheim (1936). Here ideology refers to systems of thought or belief that are shared collectively by the members of a community, and which constitute the basic principles, beliefs and values by which a particular society operates. Ideology in this sense is omnipresent, and is akin to culture – every society has such beliefs and thus, unlike the Marxist conception, ideology is never something one can get beyond.

With respect to language, different groups of linguists draw on both these traditions. In this chapter, I use the term in a predominantly Mannheimean sense, to refer to the way that there exist cultural conceptions of what constitutes language and of how it functions as part of social life. These conceptions, or **language ideologies**, can be both explicit and implicit (i.e. we can refer to them overtly, or they can unconsciously influence our behaviour), but in either case they constitute a shared belief system that influences the way in which we, as users of language, interact with language. In the words of Michael Silverstein, language ideologies 'are any sets of beliefs about language articulated by the users as a rationalization or justification of perceived language structure and use' (Silverstein, 1979, p. 193). Such patterns of belief are not static or unchangeable, of course – and much of the politics of language involves contesting or arguing about details of these beliefs – but they act as a framework against which we make sense of the role and value of language in society.

1.3 English as a positive resource

The extract from Gordon Brown's speech presented the idea of global English as pretty much a 'done deal'. It took for granted the status of English as the pre-eminent language for international communication in the world today, and on the basis of this, argued for the promotion of programmes of English language teaching (ELT) so as to allow more people access to this global dialogue. This was based on the conviction that, in the words of the linguist Randolph Quirk, 'the world needs an international language and … English is the best candidate at present on offer' (Quirk, 1990, p. 10). Yet, as we saw, the speech went further than this by drawing associations between competence in English and the ability to access various other resources, and presented the language as being key to full participation in modern global society. This section looks in greater detail at the type of arguments that are made for the promotion of English, at how these can translate into policies, and at the possible problems associated with such conceptions of the language.

Allow about
10 minutes

Activity 1.4

If you have ever learnt or wanted to learn another language, what motivated you to do so? What did you think (or hope) that knowledge of that language would allow you to do?

Comment

Motivations for learning a new language can be varied. They can be based on specific personal reasons, such as marrying into a family where that language is spoken. Or they can be based on more general, abstract ideas about the language, and beliefs about what knowledge of it will lead to. These general beliefs, if they are prevalent across society, may relate to the actual role that the language plays in that society, or to the perception people have of this role. One way of determining why English has such a high status around the world today, therefore, is to look at what motivates people to learn it, and to infer from these motivations the ideological beliefs that adhere to the language in different societies.

Figure 1.3 An advertisement for Gaba language school in Japan

We can illustrate the above contention with the following example. The advertisement in Figure 1.3 is for a chain of commercially run English-language schools in Japan (Seargeant, 2009). At the top of the advertisement is the reflective question: 'What would I do if I could speak English?' Underneath this is a list of responses by members of the public outlining their motivation for learning English. Each response is just a sentence long, and is followed in brackets by the occupation of the respondent. The first eleven translate as follows:

1 'I would live in Hawaii with several dogs.' (*Newlywed*)

2 'I would go shopping in London's antique stores by myself.' (*Shop clerk*)

3 'I would eat all the desserts in the world!' (*Female university student*)

4 'I would buy aromatherapy materials and prepare them myself.' (*Flower arranger*)

5 'I would open a shiatsu massage parlour for celebrities in Hollywood.' (*Apprentice masseuse*)

6 'I would scold noisy foreigners on the train.' (*Car salesroom owner*)

7 'I would bring up my children in America: one as an artist, the other as a computer programmer.' (*Pastry chef*)

8 'I would start a dental practice for foreigners.' (*Dentist*)

9 'I would run a surfing store on the Gold Coast.' (*Graduate student*)

10 'I would live in a house where I could wake up and dive straight into the pool.' (*Internet company manager*)

11 'I would increase my salary one hundred times.' (*Bank worker*)

TMA 5

The idea behind the advertisement is to illustrate a range of exciting life-opportunities to which the learning of English can provide access. At first glance, the rationales given by the participants seem rather esoteric, and few have anything much to do with communication, let alone English. What they have in common, however, is that they are related to ideas of aspiration, and English is thus presented by association as an agent of change in people's lives.

If we look closely at the various responses we can see certain specific patterns of association, and from these infer something about the ideological beliefs regarding English in Japan. Many of the answers, for example, are related to ideas of internationalism and a desire for geographical mobility (to move to the USA [5 and 7] or Australia [9]). There are also several which refer to forms of consumption (shopping

TMA 5

in antique stores [2]; eating all the desserts in the world [3]), to financial gain (increasing salary one hundred times [11]), or to career prospects (starting up one's own surfing shop [9] or dental practice [8]). Others include more general images of freedom and independence, either in everyday life (diving straight into the pool [10]), or at work (preparing aromatherapy materials [4]). The overall impression, then, suggests that English ability is viewed as a way of transcending one's normal life and gaining access to an alternative future. While at first glance these ambitions may seem non-political, they indirectly associate the language with particular values (consumerism, entrepreneurialism, etc.) which, in many instances, are quite culturally specific and related to the West.

The status of English in Japan, and of the nature of Expanding Circle Englishes more generally, is discussed in another book in this series: Seargeant and Swann (eds) (2012), Chapter 5.

Japan is what Braj Kachru has described as an Expanding Circle country (Kachru, 1992); that is, one in which English has no official status, and instead is learnt as a foreign language or for lingua franca purposes (i.e. for communication with speakers of other languages). Generally speaking, English is not an essential part of everyday life in Japanese society. Yet it is still greatly desired by large numbers of the population, and there have been suggestions in the past – most recently in a report published in 2000 by the Prime Minister's Commission on Japan's goals in the twenty-first century (CJGTC, 2000) – about making it an official language so as to help with the ongoing economic development and international standing of the country.

This idea of English as being important for economic advantage and improving employment prospects is a widespread ideology in various countries. In the Japanese context, this motivation means that learning English becomes a lifestyle choice. However, for many people around the world it is often more of an imperative. As the Nigerian scholar Ayọ Bamgboṣe writes, the case for many people 'is not so much [one of] *wanting* to learn English because of the advantages it confers (though there is undoubtedly an element of this) as *needing* to learn it, because not learning English is not really a choice' (Bamgboṣe, 2009, p. 648). Mercedes Niño-Murcia, who has researched attitudes to learning English in Peru, echoes this opinion, and suggests that for many people 'English is seen as a requirement imposed by globalization and a global market' in that it often acts as a prerequisite for finding stable work and decent wages, especially for those for whom emigration to an English-speaking country is often seen as the only solution to severe economic deprivation (Niño-Murcia, 2003, p. 121). As one of the people she interviewed for her study comments, '"El inglés es como el dólar"

("English is like the dollar")' in that it acts as a currency for social and geographical mobility in today's world (Niño-Murcia, 2003, p. 121).

We have, then, a basic ideological association between English and economic advancement – and the association can have different meanings or consequences depending on the context in which it is encountered. In certain contexts this association can then form the basis of language policy. For example, this same idea (knowledge of English facilitates economic advancement) is a common rationale for international development projects which promote English education as a means of poverty reduction (Seargeant and Erling, 2011; and see Figure 1.4). For instance, the British Council's 'Project English', which was set up to train 750,000 English language teachers in India and Sri Lanka, explains its purpose as follows:

> High proficiency in English is seen to be essential for socio-economic development in India and Sri Lanka … The impact of globalisation and economic development has made English the 'language of opportunity' and a vital means of improving prospects for well-paid employment.
>
> (Project English, 2009, quoted in Seargeant and Erling, 2011, p. 3)

Figure 1.4 English as a language for international development in Bangladesh

This idea of 'linguistic capital' is looked at in more detail in Chapters 2, 4 and 8.

Assertions of this sort which are premised on the association between ability in a prestige language (in this case English) and economic opportunity have been theorised by the sociologist Pierre Bourdieu (1991) using the metaphor of **'linguistic capital'**. Bourdieu suggests that linguistic resources (e.g. competence in particular languages or registers, literacy skills, etc.) are differentially distributed among members of society (due to factors such as community environment and education), and that possession of certain linguistic resources (such as a prestige variety of English) gives access to improved social opportunity (such as employment opportunities) which can then be transferred into actual economic capital. In other words, if one 'invests' in the learning of English (Norton, 2000), this will allow one to gain access to better jobs which, in turn, provide a financial return on one's investment in terms of better pay. So in the current global system, English is, in this sense, a sort of commodity – one with a high value – and for this reason is much sought after.

A question prompted by this line of theorising, however, is whether beliefs about the relationship between English ability and economic benefit match the way things actually are. Is there any empirical evidence to indicate that fluency in English is indeed linked to better pay in particular contexts? At present, evidence of this sort is rather sparse, although a few studies have examined the issue. For example, the economist François Grin (2001) investigated workplaces in Switzerland and found that there was some form of correlation between rises in salary and increased competence in English. Also, a study by Kaivan Munshi and Mark Rosenzweig (2006), which took a comparative look at English-medium education and Marathi-medium education in Bombay, found that the former did appear to lead to statistically higher wage premiums. Both these studies provide results which must, however, be seen as specific to the contexts in which they were conducted, and thus it is not at present possible to make broad generalisations about the exact nature of the causal relationship between English and economic advancement, despite the prevalence of the ideology.

A further question about the association between English and economic benefit is whether this should necessarily be considered a positive thing. While many policies explicitly promote the language on the basis of its perceived advantages for economic development, thus championing the premise on which the association is based, for some scholars this relationship is the product of a particular pattern of cultural values and for this reason, they argue, it needs to be viewed from a more critical standpoint. 'Critical' in this sense refers to an evaluative rather than a negative standpoint. We look at one such critique in the activity that follows.

Activity 1.5

Now turn to Reading A: *English and ambivalence in a new capitalist state* by Catherine Prendergast. In this reading, Prendergast examines ways in which the learning of English in Slovakia in the post-communist era (i.e. since 1989) is perceived. She focuses on the cultural and political values that learners in Slovakia associate with the language, and how English learning is closely interleaved with political and social changes in the country – specifically those related to the rise of capitalism. While reading the article, consider the following questions:

- Why is English considered 'capitalism's first language'?
- What circumstances lead to the 'ambivalence' of English's position in society?

Comment

Both in the overview of the social situation before and after the collapse of communism, and in the life stories of the informants she interviewed, Prendergast illustrates the ways in which English is closely tied to the ideas and workings of capitalism in Slovakia. She notes how, prior to the Velvet Revolution, the associations made between English and the capitalist West meant that access to the language was severely regulated: its teaching was marginalised in the curriculum, and there was little presence of English in the media. Since 1989, this relationship between English and capitalism has been further forged in a number of different ways: not only is English now seen as an essential skill for working in businesses which have a global profile, but also the way the language is taught – and specifically the way it is presented in textbooks – is now based around a narrative of capitalism. In other words, capitalist ideas are taught via the materials that are used to teach English, and thus the status of the language and the political ideology of capitalism are inextricably linked in mainstream English language education.

Yet while the new political system might be embraced in many quarters, there is also a certain ambivalence about it. For example, capitalism is seen to have brought with it opportunity, but also an uncertainty, especially in the employment sector. This leads to a situation which, in Prendergast's words, 'reveals a paradox of global English as the language of capitalism [in Slovakia]: offering the path to betterment it had become the idiom for the anxiety of falling behind'.

The picture, then, is a complex one, where English is regularly associated in diverse contexts across the globe with economic development and prosperity – and on this basis is often promoted both in language policies and in social practices (e.g. the employment market in Slovakia). But evidence pointing to the exact nature of this relationship – that is, under what circumstances and to what extent there is a causal relationship between English proficiency and increased economic status – is sketchy, and is likely to be very context-specific (not everyone in the world who learns English can expect to see their economic prospects improve). Furthermore, this relationship can be viewed as part of a wider ideological value system related to global capitalism, and in this way the learning of English is, both symbolically and in practice, tied up with complex questions about global politics. It is ideas of this sort, and the critical response they have generated, to which I turn in the next section.

1.4   The hegemony of English

Explorations of English which look at the political circumstances that influence the role it plays in the world, and the cultural values associated with it, can be described as critical approaches. The concept of criticism, in its technical sociological sense rather than its everyday sense, refers to the process of uncovering hidden presuppositions and patterns of belief, and exposing the workings – and specifically the power relations which sustain these workings – of social practices or institutions. Critical theorists often engage in a topic with the purpose of altering the way things are, and improving social relations. Here they follow Marx's thesis that 'philosophers have only interpreted the world in various ways; the point, however, is to change it' (Marx, 1998 [1845], p. 574). Thus critically inflected theory and research is itself political, and intends to intervene in the scenarios it reports on.

Scholars who take a critical approach to the study of English and society consider the ways in which the language has a particular influence on societies around the world, and they investigate the power relations that lie behind this influence. An important study in this tradition is that by Robert Phillipson (1992), who argues that the worldwide spread of English has, in great part, been orchestrated by countries such as the United States and Britain as a means of furthering their own political and economic interests. He refers to this as **linguistic imperialism**, a process whereby the politics of language contribute to the ways in which certain 'centre' nations (e.g. the USA and the UK) exercise power over those in the 'periphery' (i.e. poorer, developing countries). Linguistic imperialism is, according to this line of argument, a subspecies of cultural imperialism, and leads to the establishment of various forms of inequality between English and other languages, which in turn contributes to political inequalities between different countries and different social groups. Inequalities are to be found in the way that institutions promote or teach English (i.e. the way it is favoured in language policies, or centrally positioned in school curriculums), as well as in the production and reproduction of positive ideologies about the language – such as those that associate it with social mobility and economic advancement. According to Phillipson, processes of this sort forcefully promote the English language to – and in some instances, impose it on – communities around the world, and in doing so, spread the cultural and ideological values of the 'centre' countries, thus allowing them to maintain a dominant position in the world.

Examples that Phillipson cites include the way the World Bank and the International Monetary Fund (IMF) have emphasised English education in developing countries as a means of furthering the aim of national development; and the way that agencies such as the British Council and the United States Information Agency (USIA) have also promoted English as a tool for international development, as well as running extensive ELT programmes, teacher training courses, and subsidised lessons across the globe (Phillipson, 1992). (The British Council is a non-departmental public body in the UK which promotes Britain's international cultural relations; the USIA was likewise devoted to supporting US foreign policy and national interests abroad, until it closed in 1999.) Such initiatives lead him to the conclusion that:

The British Council is discussed further in Chapter 4.

> In the *postcolonial* world, the expansion of English was not left to chance. It was a strategic concern of the US and UK governments, without whose blessing and funding the English as a Second Language (ESL) profession would not have come into existence in the trail-blazing form it took in the 1950s and 60s … Language promotion invariably interlocks with economic and political interests.
>
> (Phillipson, 1998, p. 102)

There have been various critiques of this thesis, either refuting its claims or tempering its central arguments. The broad thrust of Phillipson's argument is to suggest that linguistic imperialism was a distinct part of the imperialist project – that there were dedicated policies during the colonial era which had as their aim the spread of English for the purposes of political domination, and this same basic dynamic continues through present-day organisations such as the World Bank and the British Council. This thesis views the spread of English as a 'top-down' process, therefore, with the language being imposed on communities around the world and its uptake predominantly determined by this imposition rather than by the actions and wishes of local communities. Critics of Phillipson's position argue that evidence for the first of these premises (top-down imposition) is mixed, while evidence for the second (lack of agency on the part of local communities) is contested (e.g. Pennycook, 1994; Brutt-Griffler, 2002). For example, Janina Brutt-Griffler suggests that a close examination of British colonialist education policies doesn't indicate 'any concerted, consistent attempt to spread English on a wide basis' (Brutt-Griffler, 2002, p. 78). In fact, colonialist policies often attempted to limit the teaching of English to a small administrative elite, and to withhold it from the general populace. Furthermore, she suggests, the spread of English was actually as much a by-product of anti-colonial struggles as it was part of the apparatus of the imperialist project. For example, as Gibson Ferguson notes, nationalist leaders in countries such as Ghana, Kenya and Malawi used English as a means of bringing together linguistically and ethnically diverse communities in a united front against colonial rule (Ferguson, 2006).

A discussion of how colonial language policies often limited access to English education can be found in the reading on 'ELT and colonialism' by Alastair Pennycook in another book in this series: Seargeant and Swann (eds) (2012), Chapter 3.

The linguistic imperialism hypothesis, then, is not without its detractors; yet it does draw attention to the importance of critiquing the ways in which the spread of English can produce political inequalities in the global community, and for this reason has been highly influential. If one considers the **hegemony of English** as a rather more complex and nuanced process – that is, not orchestrated solely by an all-powerful 'centre', but instead operating for varied cultural, political and economic reasons – we then have a useful framework for examining the politics of English in the contemporary world.

Hegemony

GMA CON

The term **hegemony** refers to the power exerted by one group over others. The concept was notably used and developed by the Italian Marxist philosopher and activist, Antonio Gramsci, who focused on the important role that culture can play in the exercise of power (Gramsci, 1971). He describes the way that one group or class can achieve domination over another not solely by state force – that is, the use of the police force, the judiciary, etc. – but also by cultural ideological means, and specifically by winning the consent of those being dominated. In other words, if the ruling class is able to make people accept that its right to power is legitimate – is how things naturally should be – then it is able to exercise power without resistance from the general populace. Gramsci suggested that forms of domination achieved via consensus are as powerful, if not more so, than those achieved by force. The 'hegemony of English' thus refers to the way that English has attained a dominant position in relation to other languages in societies both practically and ideologically, and to the social, cultural and political effects this can have.

If it is too simplistic to say that the worldwide diffusion of English has advanced an 'imperialist' agenda on the part of politically powerful Anglophone countries, what then are the main criticisms of the effects of the global spread of English? Ferguson (2006, pp. 125–6) sees four areas where the hegemony of English has possible deleterious effects:

1 The use of English as an international language can lead to inequalities in communication between native and non-native speakers.

2 English contributes to socio-economic inequalities within and between societies.

3 The dominance of English is a threat to **linguistic diversity**.

4 The spread of English can be implicated in processes of cultural homogenisation.

In other words, the spread of English can be linked both to communicative and social inequalities, and can be seen as a threat to local languages and cultural practices.

As Ferguson notes in points 1 and 2 above, English's pre-eminence as an international language – along with the concomitant high status this affords it in many societies – privileges some groups or countries (e.g. native English-speaking communities), while having the effect of marginalising or disenfranchising others. For example, Bamgbọṣe points to the way that the propagation of English in many countries is sustained by the emergence of an educated elite:

> It so happens that this elite is privileged in terms of access to positions, power, and influence. And it is a self-perpetuating elite, since it ensures that the opportunities it has are transferred to its offspring, particularly in terms of privileged education.
>
> (Bamgbọṣe, 2009, p. 650)

That is, the social benefits that English can give are in practice limited to those who can afford good-quality English-language education, and so knowledge of the language operates as a form of linguistic capital which perpetuates the divide between haves and have-nots.

Ferguson's third point relates to the threat that the spread of English can have on linguistic diversity. This threat is clearly documented in statistical predictions such as those suggesting that, of the estimated 6900 languages spoken in the world today (Ethnologue, 2009), somewhere between 20 and 50 per cent are likely to become extinct by the end of this century (Krauss, 1992; and see Figure 1.5). (Other people give more alarming figures; see, for example, those cited in the article by John Sutherland in *The Independent,* which you looked at in Activity 1.2.) The phenomenon of **language death** is the process by which a language stops being spoken entirely, either because its speakers die out without passing it on to their children, or because the community which speaks it shifts to the use of another language. It occurs most often in contexts in which a **majority language** – that is, a language such as English which has high political and social status – takes over the roles that were previously played by a **minority language** – that is, one spoken by a small proportion, or politically less influential section, of the population – and thus speakers of the minority language shift to using the majority one (May, 2009). If one considers that, at the end of the twentieth century, 96 per cent of the world's languages were spoken by only 4 per cent of its population (Crystal, 1999), and that English is one of the pre-eminent majority languages in today's world, it seems very likely that the spread of English must take some responsibility for the demise of smaller languages. It is for this reason that some scholars describe English as a 'killer language' (e.g. Nettle and Romaine, 2000; Skutnabb-Kangas, 2000) and why John Sutherland (Activity 1.2) described English as 'obliterating' other languages.

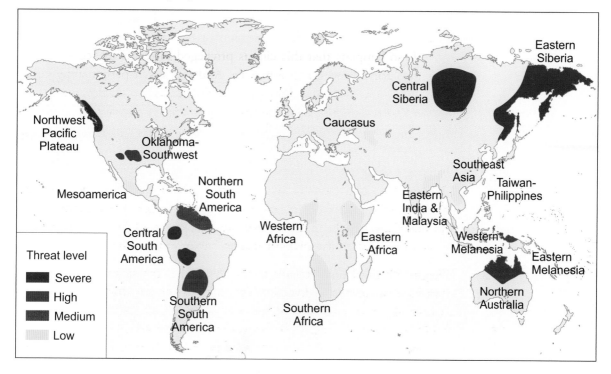

Figure 1.5 A map showing 'Language Hotspots', areas of the world where many languages are near extinction

One strategy for countering the threat to linguistic diversity caused by the spread of English is the notion of **linguistic rights.** This is the idea proposed by certain activists and policy makers that use of a particular language – especially the language of one's birth or community – is such a fundamental part of one's existence and identity that it should be considered a right, and be legally protected as such. As Grundy et al. (1998, p. 1) explain: 'When individuals or communities are denied the opportunity to learn and use their mother tongue and the official language of the country in which they live, a prima facie abuse of their rights occurs.' Provisions for linguistic protection of this sort are, for example, guaranteed in Article 2.1 of the United Nations Declaration of Human Rights (1948), which asserts that no one should be discriminated against on the basis of language. In 1996, a Universal

Declaration of Linguistic Rights was drawn up by UNESCO and a number of non-governmental organisations, stating its purpose as being to:

> correct linguistic imbalances with a view to ensuring the respect and full development of all languages and establishing the principles for a just and equitable linguistic peace throughout the world as a key factor in the maintenance of harmonious social relations.

> (UNESCO, 1996)

Language-related issues which are cited as the subject of rights in this and similar documents include: access to primary education based on language, the right of minority groups to preserve their language, and provision against enforced language shift (Skutnabb-Kangas, 2000).

The notion of linguistic rights, then, is promoted as one of the key ways in which policy can be used to counter effects of the hegemony of English and to try to ensure that the spread of English does not have a negative effect on societies around the world. The linguistic rights paradigm is criticised by some, however, for using a model of worldwide language distribution which relies too much on fixed links between particular languages and particular cultural or ethnic groups, and does not take full account of the complex ways in which languages are actually used, especially in multilingual societies. The activity that follows looks at one such critique.

Activity 1.6

Now turn to Reading B: *Locked in space: on linguistic rights* by Jan Blommaert. In this reading Blommaert outlines what he perceives as certain flaws in the way the debate about rights for minority languages is framed. He looks at how the notion of 'space' is conceptualised in approaches which focus on such rights, and suggests that an understanding of the relationship between a language and the community which uses it is of key significance for an appreciation of language politics in the era of globalisation. Of particular importance for his argument is the contrast between what are seen as local (or, as he occasionally refers to them, territorialised) languages, and global (or deterritorialised) languages. While reading Blommaert's argument, consider the following questions:

- What reasons does he give for saying that the discourse of minority language rights is misconceived?
- How does he critique the way that metaphors are used in the construction of the discourse of minority language rights, and how do the metaphors he identifies characterise the relationship between language and society?
- In what ways can the promotion of linguistic rights end up contributing to social inequality rather than combating it?

Comment

Blommaert identifies a number of ways in which the discourse about minority language rights obscures the linguistic politics that contributes to the marginalisation of certain languages. He notes, for example, that the threat to local languages does not always come from majority languages such as English – in some contexts it can come from other indigenous languages in a territory. Furthermore, English can often be a threat to other majority languages, such as French or Portuguese, rather than to local languages. As such, the simple formula which suggests that the dominance of English pushes out or overwhelms smaller languages does not always tally with the sociolinguistic realities of a given situation.

The main critique he makes, though, is that the linguistic rights paradigm is too tied to a sociolinguistics that sees languages being fixed to the communities and geographical localities with which they are associated. A key metaphor he draws attention to here is that of **language ecology**. This is the idea that different language systems and language practices exist in an ecology, as organisms do, and that they have complex relationships with the environment (the culture, belief systems, ways of life) in which they function. Drawing on this metaphor, the linguistic rights paradigm views indigenous languages as the natural means to express local cultural concerns, and suggests that if these languages die out, local cultures will also disappear. For this reason, according to advocates of the paradigm, people should have the right to keep their minority language (to have it protected in the workplace, in education, etc.), and in this way safeguard their local identity.

The counter-argument that Blommaert makes is that this sociolinguistic model can have the effect of tying people to their present circumstances, which isn't always desired. Majority languages such as English are languages of 'deterritorialisation' in that they are not tied to one locality, and are thus useful resources – both practically and symbolically – in a world in which mobility is so important. As Blommaert writes: '[t]he choice for English or French rather than indigenous languages in education is at the grassroots level often motivated by means of discourses of "getting out of here" and towards particular centres – metropolitan areas – where upward social mobility at least looks possible'. In other words, people often want mobility and the linguistic resources that give access to this; whereas, paradoxically, the linguistic rights paradigm often preserves hegemonic differences in society by representing people as tied to their locality.

1.5   Conclusion: appropriating English

The final point that Blommaert makes is that when analysing issues such as social inequality, we have to consider what people actually do with language. This means thinking about the politics of language not in terms of broad generalities – of a monolithic 'English' sweeping across the globe – but in terms of the actual linguistic resources people use: the different varieties, dialects and registers that people speak and write, and the status and affordances these have in different contexts. The idea that English in the contemporary world is multiplex – that it doesn't simply have one form and one identity – is key to the modern politics of the language, and again this is an issue which has both a practical and an ideological aspect: it concerns the different forms the language takes around the world and the different attitudes people have towards these forms.

As discussed in Reading B, the linguistic rights paradigm sets great store in the link between a given language and the place in which it is used. This idea has been mentioned earlier in the chapter. Particular languages are associated with particular cultures and are considered to be the rightful property of that culture – and are talked of as being 'owned' by a particular community. In the conclusion to this chapter, I want to return to this metaphor, and look at how it applies not to minority languages, but to English, and at the language ideologies that stem from this.

Allow about
10 minutes

Activity 1.7
- Who, in your opinion, could be said to own the English language today?
- What might be some of the aspects of ownership of a language?

Comment

The name of the language still suggests a significant relationship with the country of England, but, as has been discussed, this is a relationship that is increasingly complicated by the processes of globalisation. One important issue in this regard is that in today's world there are more non-native speakers of English than there are mother tongue speakers (Crystal, 2012). Given this fact there is, as Henry Widdowson says, a forceful case for the need to revise the old notions of ownership of the language:

> How English develops in the world is no business whatever of native speakers in England, the United States or anywhere else. They have no say in the matter, no right to intervene or pass judgement. ... The very fact that English is an international language means that no nation can have custody over it. ... It is a matter of considerable pride and satisfaction for native speakers that their language is an international means of communication. But the point is that it is only international to the extent that it is not their language. It is not a possession which they lease out to others, while still retaining the freehold. Other people actually own it.
>
> (Widdowson, 1994, p. 385)

For Widdowson, scholars and language professionals who share this view, the associations between English and the place of its historical origin and development are no longer relevant in the age of global English. One consequence of this is that native speaker norms for the language can no longer be promoted as the only 'correct' or authoritative varieties.

One way in which the ownership debate is being reformulated is through the idea of appropriation. This is the idea that various communities around the world now see the language as their own; they see the variety they speak as legitimate in its own right, and not something that needs to be compared (unfavourably) with standard varieties in the UK or USA. English has become a 'local' language for many communities around the globe, who adapt its form, functions and identity to fit in with their own culture.

A key issue here – and one that has been intimated throughout this chapter – is that the politics of English are closely tied to the politics of the societies and global institutions in which English is used. If our initial questions in this chapter were what type of influence does English have in the world today, and has its rise to become the pre-eminent global language of the contemporary era had a positive or negative effect on societies across the world, the answers we arrive at will depend on the circumstances in which the language is used. It is not possible to evaluate the spread of English in terms of a binary opposition: to ask simply whether English is either a force for good or a force for bad in the contemporary world. The actual picture of the language's influence is not an either/or issue; it is far more complex than that. It is dependent on the circumstances in which the language is used and learnt, on the way it is viewed in specific environments and at particular times in history, and on how it is regulated in domains ranging from education to the media to government. In the rest of this book, therefore, we look at the politics of the language as it is formulated, contested and played out in these various domains, and at the extensive ways in which English becomes a crucial site for the conflict, competition and cooperation which characterises today's world.

[handwritten: Translate ideas from here into what happened in Poland?) (GMA?)]

READING A: English and ambivalence in a new capitalist state

Catherine Prendergast

Source: Prendergast, C. (2008) '"We live and learn": English and ambivalence in a new capitalist state', *Globalisation, Societies and Education*, vol. 6, no. 1, pp. 91–5.

For Slovakia, a large part of the business of becoming a member of the capitalist world [in the years leading up to 2004 European Union accession] was learning capitalism's first language: English (Togneri 1999). There was much to learn. Before the Soviet Union's collapse, the communist government controlled the circulation of English (though did not completely censor it) because the language carried associations with the west. Although growing in global stature, English was nevertheless marginalised in the school curriculum during communism because every student was required to study Russian from primary school through high school. Bookstores did carry some English books, but very few people could afford them. One could buy a British newspaper from the newsstands, but it would be *The Daily Worker*. There were no English language TV stations. Opportunities to travel to English-speaking countries were rarely available. Accordingly, English was a language taught very much like Latin – a language one could learn but never really use.

Following Czechoslovakia's peaceful overthrow of the communist regime in the 'Velvet Revolution' of 1989, however, Slovakia over time became a hot spot for investment from the west and Slovaks began learning English *en masse*. Children faced increasing English requirements in their schools. Teachers of Russian, suddenly no longer in demand once the Soviet-backed requirement was abolished, were re-qualified to teach English in two-year courses at the state's expense. Employers hired English teachers to instruct their entire staff, and people seeking better employment flocked to the new private language academies that had opened when the state monopoly on education expired. Albeit these new schools offered courses in many of the major languages of western Europe, courses in English dominated and were often more expensive. One school in 2003, for example, charged 8200 Slovak crowns (then roughly $250) for 48 hours of business English, while charging only 3000 crowns for 50 hours of business German; such price disparities were a quick lesson in English's centrality to

As ~ Poland

capitalism. English, in short, had made the leap in Slovakia from *lingua non grata* to lingua franca.

In this [reading] I examine Slovak impressions of that rapid economic and linguistic transition, drawing on interviews and observations culled from a larger ethnographic study of English language learners I conducted in Slovakia during a five month period in the fall of 2003 (Prendergast, in press). Although reports from the western press have suggested that Slovakia has accomplished a somewhat uncomplicated transition out of communism, one brought about by the adoption of a slate of neo-liberal economic reforms including corporate tax breaks and loosened labor codes (see *Economist* 2005; Reynolds 2004; World Bank 2005) the stories of the individuals I spoke with in Slovakia who learned and used English in the midst of this transition belie this easy picture. They instead reveal the complexities of lives transformed in ways big and small by capitalism and its lingua franca. Far from intuitive, capitalism in practice had to do some work to establish itself as the 'common sense' of how to operate in the world (cf. Watkins 1998), and some form of English had equally to establish itself as the common sense of how to communicate in global capitalism. English lessons in post-communist Slovakia thus taught the rudimentary logic of capitalism: what a 'sale' is, where to park at the grocery store, and, most crucially, how to learn ever more English to keep your job. 'Father must learn English' one dialogue lesson in a Slovak-authored textbook proclaimed, in order to keep his job in the export division of his company (Zábojová, Peprník and Nangonová 2000, 47).

Yet although textbooks foreign and domestic introduced both English and capitalism as imperatives, the domestic ones did so with a bit more hesitation and hedging [...], registering their ambivalence about capitalism and the changes it effected. Many Slovaks were beginning to face capitalism's logic of built-in obsolescence, and they faced it in English. The dictates of the fast-moving information economy meant that in the process of learning and/or teaching English, Slovaks had to continually think and rethink what new brand of English – English for auto mechanics, au pairs, health professionals, were some of the offerings – could help them survive competition and stay afloat in a country where assurances of employment had disappeared. To keep up they had to multi-task, often learning English after their long days at work, or before their long days had begun. Tellingly, English was often used to describe the post-communist anxiety of job insecurity. In the fall of 2003, for example, an omnipresent ad in the bus stops and on billboards for life insurance featured the word 'Family' prominently in English with accompanying explanatory text of what life insurance was in Slovak. The text framed a photo of a young girl in swimming attire with three life preservers around her body. Life insurance, a new commodity in the post-communist era bespoke the privatisation of social security (Andrusz 2004). The branding of this new kind of security was achieved through English, as was the branding of a less easily commodified element of western capitalism, the new visible homeless population dubbed in young Slovaks' growing lexicon of Slovak–English slang as 'homelessak'.

As I spoke with people in post-communist Slovakia, I found the greatest anxiety was actually not that of winding up on the street, however, but rather the more modest fear of failing to capitalise on opportunities. This fear was the inevitable companion to the locutions of 'improvement' and 'bettering oneself' continually attached to English. It reveals a paradox of global English as the language of capitalism: offering the path to betterment it had become the idiom for the anxiety of falling behind. […]

English: a never-ending story

[…] When the revolution occurred midway through [Viola's] high school career, she and other students in her *gymnázium* in the moderate-sized city of Nitra quit taking the much resented Russian and demanded more – and different – lessons in English. [Viola] recalled her own and her fellow students' embrace [of] what they saw as real world English instruction – lessons on communication in 'real life' contexts drawn from British and American pop songs and CNN broadcasts. These communication skills didn't help her in college where she majored in biology, however, nor after graduation when she worked at the Slovak Academy of Sciences, for the most part taking notes from English language biology journals. Frustrated by the country-wide scarcity of funds to support laboratory research and struggling to survive on a scientist's salary in Bratislava where the rents had sky-rocketed, she decided to find a new profession. 'I told myself I'm young, I'm single, I have no children, so I have some time to do some career to improve myself'. […]

Young, female, single, and thus able to consider radically different career options (and surpass her peers in pay) Viola was part of a demographic that had emerged in Slovakia after 1989. Before then, there had been great incentives to marry early, generally to get one's own apartment and a shorter military service for one's spouse. Since the 1990s, Slovakia experienced a sharp decline in both the marriage and the birth rate and an increase in the age of first-time mothers (Bútorová et al. 2003). Nevertheless, the newfound social freedoms were accompanied by newfound skyrocketing real estate prices that made it difficult for young people to afford housing, particularly in Bratislava. Whereas before 1989, young people could receive a state flat, no such guarantees existed after rampant privatisation.

Viola speculated that if she had finished college before 1989 and embarked on her career back then, 'Maybe I would be satisfied to be a biologist, to have the salary according to some rules because the others would be in the same situation'. Her comment about how she might have done in relationship to others suggests that the economic transformation provoked her to change careers not only to fulfill needs, but to keep up with or surpass a newly stratifying set of peers. She saw her avenue for advancement in a job ad for a sales position with [a biotechnical firm run by a man named Goran]. One of the requirements of the job was that she 'speak English fluently'. She promised Goran that although she didn't speak very well, she would 'improve'. Once on the job she had little time to make the promised improvements before she was embroiled in situations that would tax her narrow reading knowledge of English. She was faced with 'business English'. As she put it, 'It was another type of words'. Her unfamiliarity with this 'type of words' left her unable to communicate with the firm's burgeoning American and British clientele. She emphasised to me the anxiety of her adjustment to business English: 'I was not able to say one word! ... I was shaking every time the phone started to ring'. Finally in 2001 she engaged the services of a private tutor (at her own expense and on her own time) and learned to speak the words of global economic parlance. In this way she followed Goran's philosophy of the imperative of English to commerce and competition: 'No other way', Goran explained of the need for his staff to learn English. 'I don't know who can change it. It will be the international language or second language for everybody'. Goran, the most traveled of the company, had come to view Slovakia as being in the grip of international forces, with no other choice than to keep up.

I now turn to Iveta, who also found herself swept up after graduation from college by the growth of corporate hunger for English instruction, though as a teacher, not as a student. Iveta, like Viola, had begun her study of English during the communist regime, but earlier, at the age of

11. She could only start taking English classes because some other students had left their spots in an accelerated curriculum that included English language instruction. She explained: 'It was not just English, but it was the opportunity to be better in some way, because the class was considered to be elite in the school. ... It was a bonus, something extra I could get'. Against the formal ideologies of equality, such special classes existed; Iveta saw a rare chance to get something 'extra' and grabbed it.

Later in life Iveta would, with similar rapidity, adapt to the new economic terrain. She had studied English and biology in a teacher-training course at a university in central Slovakia. After graduation she left biology far behind and sought work teaching English exclusively in a private language academy serving companies. She had expected to be hired as a full time employee, but she encountered instead the new rules of flexible labor arrangements and decreasing job security. The academy asked [her] to get her own license so she would be self-employed, paid only for the classes she taught. 'I was kind of forced into that', she said of the arrangement. She nevertheless prospered, given there was no shortage of companies needing her services. Noting the new imperative to learn English for many of the employees that were her students, she observed, 'With some of them it was a precondition to speak English to stay in their positions. ... For some of them it was really difficult, so they would give up, and would have to start again'. It was, she added ruefully, a 'never ending story'. The irony here of course is that Iveta, a master of English with no job security, found herself repeatedly at the front of a class full of students hoping to secure their own jobs by learning the English she proffered. Meanwhile Iveta hoped to find a more secure position by starting a private English immersion secondary school – a niche market not yet flooded by others, she considered.

As I sat talking with Iveta in her flat on the outskirts of Banská Bystrica, in a block style apartment building with a view of grazing sheep and the mountains beyond, I had to note that the most telling feature of how English had come to permeate the lives and job prospects of so many in Slovakia came most clearly from her kitchen. English expressions had been scribbled in black marker on almost every inch of her kitchen cupboards.

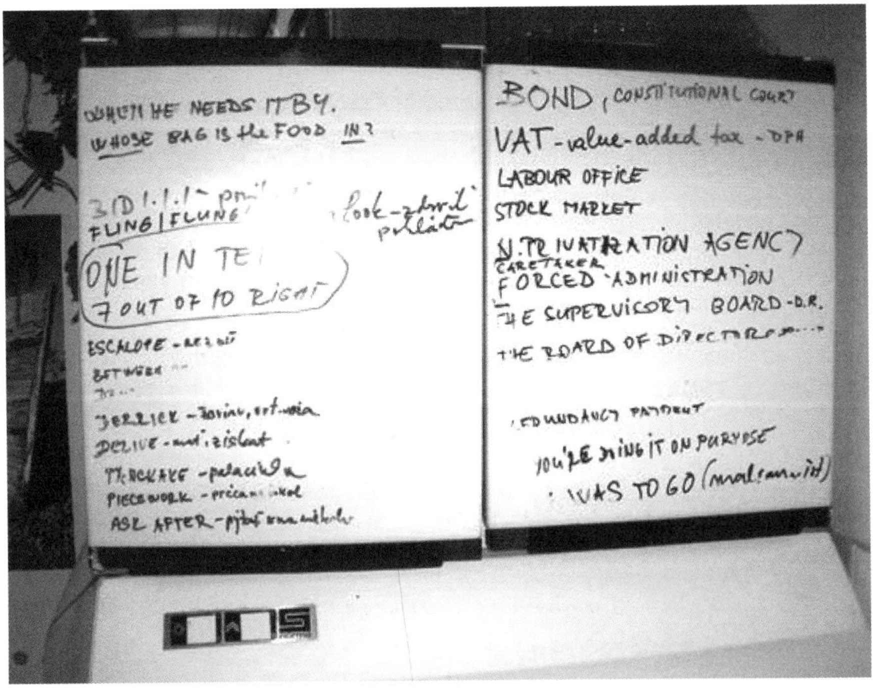

Figure 1 Iveta's cabinets. Photograph by Zuzana Ličková

The majority of expressions were economic, and many, like 'bond', 'stock market' and 'redundancy payment' were not accompanied by any Slovak translation. Apparently the scribbler was not Iveta, but her husband, a manager at one of Slovakia's many new supermarket chains. He listened to the BBC on the radio every morning during breakfast preparations and jotted down some of the phrases used on the program so he could learn them. 'He's hoping to get a better job some day', Iveta explained.

Iveta's cabinets embodied the belief in English as a pathway to economic betterment held by herself, her students, and her corporate partners. It spoke to the change in the kind of English people learned, an English that introduced people to economic liberalism. But it also spoke to how English had permeated not just the office, but through it, day-to-day living, such that the mundane activities of making coffee and doing dishes were now intermingled with learning English and capitalism. I tried to imagine the juggling her husband went through: How did he maneuver around the kitchen with both milk and marker in hand?

References for this reading

Andrusz, G. 2004. From wall to mall. In *Winds of societal change: remaking post-communist cities*, ed. Z. Nedovi-Budic, and S. Tsenkova, 21–42. Champaign: Russian, East European, and Eurasian Center at University of Illinois at Urbana-Champaign.

Bútorová, Z., J. Filadelfiová, O. Gyárfášosvá, J. Cviková, and K. Farkašová. 2003. Women, men, and equality of opportunities. In *Slovakia 2002: a global report on the state of society*, ed. G. Mesežnikov, M. Kollár, and T. Nicholson, 719–42. Bratislava: Institute for Public Affairs.

Economist. 2005. Transformed. *Economist* June 25: 8.

Prendergast, C. Forthcoming. *Buying into English: language and investment in the new capitalist world*. Pittsburgh: University of Pittsburgh Press.

Reynolds, M. 2004. Once a backwater, Slovakia surges. *New York Times* December 28, Business/Financial Desk late edition: 1.

Togneri, C. 1999. English – no longer a hobby. *The Slovak Spectator* February 8: 4.

Watkins, E. 1998. *Everyday exchanges: marketwork and capitalist common sense*. Palo Alto, CA: Stanford University Press.

World Bank. 2005. *Doing business in 2005: removing obstacles to growth*. Washington: World Bank.

Zábojová, E., J. Peprník, and S. Nangonová. 2000. *Angličtina I. pre samoukov a kurzy*. Bratislava: Vydavateľstvo Príroda, s.r.o.

READING B: Locked in space: on linguistic rights

Jan Blommaert

Source: Blommaert, J. (2010) *The Sociolinguistics of Globalization*, Cambridge, Cambridge University Press, pp. 43–7.

There is by now a well-entrenched and very respectable branch of sociolinguistics which is concerned with describing the world of globalization from the perspective of linguistic imperialism and linguicide (Phillipson 1992; Skutnabb-Kangas 2000), often based on particular ecological metaphors. These approaches start from a sociolinguistics of distribution and oddly assume that wherever a 'big' and 'powerful' language such as English 'appears' in a foreign territory, small indigenous languages will 'die'. There is, in this image of sociolinguistic space, place for just one language at a time. In general, there seems to be a serious problem with the ways in which space is imagined in such work. In addition, the actual sociolinguistic details of such processes are rarely spelled out – languages can be used in vernacular or in lingua franca varieties and so create different sociolinguistic conditions for mutual influencing; English sometimes 'threatens' other former colonial languages such as French, Spanish or Portuguese, rather than the indigenous languages (a phenomenon noted primarily in former exploitation colonies, and less prominent in former settlement colonies; see Mufwene 2005, 2008); or sometimes the 'threat' to indigenous languages can come from dominant local ('indigenous') languages rather than English [...]. So there are several major problems with the literature on linguistic rights.

One major problem is the way in which authors appear to assume the spatial 'fixedness' of people, languages and places. The discourse of minority rights is in general a discourse of strict locality, and the first lines of the UN Declaration on the Rights of Persons Belonging to National or Ethnic, Religious and Linguistic Minorities read: 'States shall protect the existence and the national or ethnic, cultural, religious and linguistic minorities *within their respective territories*, and shall encourage conditions for the promotion of that identity' (quoted in Skutnabb-Kangas and Phillipson, 1999). This Declaration is an agreement between states, which are here presented as territorially bounded entities in the space of which a particular regime can and should be developed with respect to 'minorities', defined in the same move as minorities within that particular ('state') territory. The rights granted by this Declaration are territorially bounded and organized rights, and distinctions between groups evolve along the classic Herderian triad of territory–culture–language (Blommaert and Verschueren 1998).

The Herderian triad is discussed further in Chapter 5.

This discourse of locality is usually couched in environmental–ecological metaphors: a particular place is characterized by specific features ranging from climate through biodiversity to people, cultures and languages. The relationship between these different components is seen as a form of synergy: it is through human variability that diversity in the environment is sustained, for the languages and cultures of local people provide unique views on this environment and help sustain it. See, for example, the point of view articulated by one of the most vocal advocates of linguistic rights, *Terralingua* (1999, from their website http://cougar.ucdavis edu/nas/terralin/learn.html):

> We know that a diversity of species lends stability and resilience to the world's ecosystems. Terralingua thinks that a diversity of

languages does the same for the world's cultures – and that these manifestations of the diversity of life are interrelated.

This diversity is invariably seen as something that needs to be preserved, consequently. It literally needs to be 'kept in place'. To go by the words of Skutnabb-Kangas and Phillipson (1995: 84): '[t]he perpetuation of linguistic diversity can … be seen as a recognition that all individuals and groups have basic human rights, and as a necessity for the survival of the planet, in a similar way to biodiversity' […].

There is a linguistic–ideological dimension to this, in which it is assumed that language functions in a community because it provides *local* meanings: meanings that provide frames for understanding the local environment, to categorize and analyse the (strictly) local world. References to the unique worldviews enshrined in these languages often revolve around local functionality as well: the worldviews are expressed in terms and grammatical relations that address or articulate a local decoding of the world. Let us return to Skutnabb-Kangas and Phillipson (1995: 89):

> Linguistic diversity at local levels is a necessary counterweight to the hegemony of a few 'international' languages. The 'World Languages' should, just as roads and bridges, be seen as tools for communication of ideas and matter, but the creation of authentic ideas and products (instead of mass-products) is in most cases necessarily best done locally.

The worldviews are invariably local (or territorialized) worldviews, linked to particular regional surroundings. A people's language localizes these people, it sets them within a particular, spatially demarcated ecology.

It is this view of local functionality that underpins the strong claims, cited above, that the survival of minority languages is crucial for the survival of the planet, for with every language that disappears a uniquely functional local set of meanings about the environment is lost. Languages are seen as local repositories of knowledge, and such local forms of knowledge are essential for understanding the (local) world. Consequently, when people are moved into a different environment, the language may lose (part of) its functions. Conversely, when another language is introduced in a particular environment, it may as well be

CMA

dysfunctional for it does not articulate the particular local meanings required for the sustenance of this environment. This idea in turn underpins the idea of linguistic imperialism, invariably conceived as a non-local language (usually the ex-colonial language, and usually English) penetrating or invading local spaces and disturbing the ecological balance that existed between people, their language and culture, and their environment (Skutnabb-Kangas 2000; Skutnabb-Kangas and Phillipson 1995, 1999 and Heugh 1999 provide examples).

In sum, what we see here is how language functions are territorialized, tied to particular local environments apparently constructed as static. Language apparently works excellently in its own, original place, and it loses functions as soon as the stable, original, 'autochthonous' (or 'native', 'aboriginal') link between language and place is broken. Consequently, a programme aimed at stimulating or promoting these local languages (invariably mother tongues of apparently inherently monolingual and monocultural people) ties the speakers of these languages to a place and reinforces the presumed fixed connection between people and their environment [...].

All of this sounds more or less acceptable, at least when some aspects of reality are conveniently overlooked. A rather disturbing aspect of contemporary reality, as we know, is *mobility*. In contemporary social structures, people tend to move around, both in real geographical space and in symbolic, social space. And all of these processes of mobility appear to display complex connections with language (Rampton 1995, 1999), including language attitudes and language planning.

Language as a social thing, i.e. something in which people have made investments and to which they have attributed values, seems to have awkward relations to space, the main axes of which are those of territorialization and deterritorialization. Territorialization stands for the perception and attribution of values to language as a local phenomenon, something which ties people to local communities and spaces. Customarily, people's mother tongue (L1) is perceived as 'territorialized language', alongside orality and the use of dialects. All of these forms of language emanate locality. Conversely, deterritorialization stands for the perception and attribution of values to language as something which does not belong to one locality but which organizes translocal trajectories and wider spaces [...]. Second or other languages (L2) as well as lingua francas and diaspora varieties, standardized varieties and literacy are seen as 'deterritorialized language', language that does not exclusively belong to one place (Jacquemet [...] 2005; Maryns and Blommaert 2001).

Language variation allows, defines and organizes spatial trajectories. Literacy allows a text to be moved, both physically across spaces in the world, as well as symbolically, across social spheres and scales. A standard variety of a language allows moving to adjacent places where people speak similar dialects, as well as across social spaces, into the elite. International languages such as French or English allow insertion in large transnational spaces and networks as well as access to the elites. The different 'types' of languages, in short, allow access to different scales. All of these scalar patterns of mobility are real, they revolve often around life-chances and opportunities, and consequently people often articulate relations between language or code choices and spaces. The choice for English or French rather than indigenous languages in education is at the grassroots level often motivated by means of discourses of 'getting out of here' and towards particular centres – metropolitan areas – where upward social mobility at least looks possible.

Moving through the various levels of education often involves moving through layered, scaled regimes of language, each time seen as enabling deterritorialization and hence social as well as geographical mobility. Senses of belonging to a particular community conversely often go hand in hand with the creation (or re-creation) of particular varieties that tie people to that community while at the same time indexing displacement and deterritorialization. 'Gangsta' English, for instance, is widespread in African urban centres as a language of the townships and the slums, where particular, often imaginarily violent youth cultures develop [...]. Such linguistic ideologies connecting language varieties to dynamics of locality and mobility, active both at the folk and at institutional levels, often foster resistance to the promotion of indigenous, minority languages [...].

Although one might deplore this, the reasons are usually sound enough. Symbolic marginalization is often just one correlate of real, material marginalization (Fraser 1995; Stroud 2001); L1 promotion is a form of symbolic upgrading of marginalized resources, and resistance is often based on an acute awareness of the persistence of real marginalization. If performed within a monoglot strategy (i.e. a strategy aimed at constructing 'full monolingualism' and rejecting bilingualism as a road to language attrition or language death), L1 promotion, is thus seen as an instrument *preventing* a way out of real marginalization and amounting to keeping people in their marginalized places and locked into one scale-level: the local. Imagine a family in the very marginalized and poor north-eastern parts of South Africa, speaking Venda. Education in Venda is likely to be perceived as keeping people in the marginalized region, as long as good, white-collar jobs and higher education are in effect concentrated in places like Johannesburg – and require access to English and/or Afrikaans. If the family wants to offer its children upward social mobility, then, it needs to offer them geographical mobility and consequently linguistic mobility as well. Language shift, under such conditions, is a strategy for survival. In the eyes of the speakers, the upgrading of marginalized symbolic goods may still be seen as less empowering than the creation of access to the real prestige goods. Mufwene (2002: 377) captures the core of this 'wicked problem' well: '[i]t sometimes boils down to a choice between saving speakers from their economic predicament and saving a language'.

The crux of the matter is that we need to think of issues such as linguistic inequality as being organized around concrete resources, not around languages in general but specific registers, varieties, genres. And such concrete resources follow the predicament of their users: when the latter are socially mobile, their resources will follow this trajectory; when they are socially marginal, their resources will also be disqualified. In both cases, the challenge is to think of language as a mobile complex of concrete resources. If we fail to do that, we risk drawing a caricature of social realities and becoming very upset about that caricature rather than about an accurate replica of social processes. This, needless to say, is a pointless exercise. The matter is of fundamental importance and is easily misunderstood, and this is why I am emphatic about it. [It is thus vital to view issues related to linguistic rights in terms of] the mobility of concrete semiotic resources (not 'languages') in a globalized context. There is always a tension between an ideologically perceived 'language' and sociolinguistically perceived 'resources'; [and] globalized economic forces exacerbate and exploit such tensions.

References for this reading

Allington, D. and Mayor, B. (eds) (2012) *Communicating in English: Talk, Text, Technology*, Abingdon, Routledge/Milton Keynes, The Open University.

Blommaert, J. and Verschueren, J. 1998. *Debating Diversity*. London: Routledge.

Fraser, N. 1995. From redistribution to recognition: dilemmas of justice in a 'post-socialist' age. *New Left Review* 212: 68–93.

Heugh, K. 1999. Languages, development and reconstructing education in South Africa. *International Journal of Educational Development* 19: 301–313.

Jacquemet, M. 2005. Transidiomatic practices: language and power in the age of globalization. *Language and Communication* 25(3): 257–277.

Maryns, K. and Blommaert, J. 2001. Stylistic and thematic shifting as narrative resources: assessing asylum seekers' repertoires. *Multilingua* 20(1): 61–84.

Mufwene, S. 2002. Colonization, globalization and the plight of 'weak' languages. *Journal of Linguistics* 38: 375–395.

Mufwene, S. 2005. *Créoles, Ecologie sociale, Evolution linguistique.* Paris: L'Harmattan.

Mufwene, S. 2008. *Language Evolution: Contact, Competition and Change.* London: Continuum.

Phillipson, R. 1992. *Linguistic Imperialism.* London: Oxford University Press.

Rampton, B. 1995. *Crossing: Language and Ethnicity Among Adolescents.* London: Longman.

Rampton, B. 1999. 'Deutsch' in Inner London and the animation of an instructed foreign language. *Journal of Sociolinguistics* 3(4): 480–504.

Skutnabb-Kangas, T. 2000. *Linguistic Genocide in Education – Or Worldwide Diversity and Human Rights?* Mahwah NJ: Lawrence Erlbaum.

Skutnabb-Kangas, T. and Phillipson, R. 1995. Linguicide and linguicism. *Rolig Papir* 53, Roskilde Universitetscenter, Denmark, 83–91.

Skutnabb-Kangas, T. and Phillipson, R. 1999. Language ecology. In Verschueren, J. *et al.* (eds.) *Handbook of Pragmatics,* 1999. Installment 1–24. Amsterdam: John Benjamins.

Stroud, C. 2001. African mother-tongue programmes and the politics of language: linguistic citizenship versus linguistic human rights. *Journal of Multilingual and Multicultural Development* 22(4): 339–355.

2 English and migration

Naz Rassool

2.1 Introduction

> I don't remember my country, I was born in Germany, but my
> parents came from Somalia. We left Germany before I was two
> years old so I can't speak German. I can speak Somali because my
> parents speak to me ... but I cannot read and write it. My parents
> talk a lot about home but for me Somalia is very far away, I can
> only imagine it when I listen to my parents talk about it ... when
> I look at the family photographs. For me home is where I am ...
> I have lived here now for 12 years and I think of London as
> my home.
>
> (14-year-old pupil in a London school, quoted in Rassool, 2004, p. 208)

The ways in which English is used, valued and regulated by various
groups around the world can only be understood in the context of
historical and contemporary migration – the movements of people or
groups from one country or area to settle in another. The English
language is bound up with patterns of migration in two main ways. On
the one hand, migration has shaped the structure and usage of English
language varieties. Possibly the most significant migration that facilitated
the spread and diversification of English was the expansion of the
British Empire, as new varieties of the language emerged as a result of
British settlement, colonisation and trade in North America, South East
Asia, East Africa, and so on. However, this predominantly one-way flow
from Britain to its colonies is only part of an increasingly complex
migration picture which has facilitated the global reach of, and
developments in, the English language. People from ex-British colonies
have brought new varieties of English back to the UK, or to other
Anglophone countries, and they have taken these English varieties with
them to parts of the world where English has no official status.

On the other hand, access to English increasingly determines who
migrates, why and where. English can facilitate migration (because of its
status as global lingua franca in situations such as that illustrated in the
quotation at the start of this chapter) and it may encourage migration –

people may actively choose to migrate to Anglophone countries because they already speak English, or in order to improve their English language skills. However, English can also be used as a tool with which to control people's movements and livelihoods, as is carried out not only through the citizenship and language tests that govern who may enter a country, but also through the institutional practices that control a person's access to services and jobs. Of course, depending on the country, other languages are also implicated in this 'gatekeeping' role. However, given the many countries in which English is spoken, and its use for much international communication, the English language plays a central part in the control of migration. Thus, English is instrumental not only in the bringing together of people through migration, but also in the negotiation of relationships often characterised by cultural difference, power inequality and conflicts of interests.

On an individual level, the way in which language and migration interact may seem straightforward – a person moves to a new country, taking their language with them and probably learning a new one – but, for those involved, the reality of adapting to a new culture and way of life is far from simple. The quotation at the start of this chapter, from a fourteen-year-old whose family migrated from Somalia to Germany and then to the UK, shows how people can have complex migration histories. Where people feel 'at home' – and the languages they feel at home in – depends on various personal, social and political circumstances, as well as demographic characteristics such as age and gender. People do not shed or replace identities as they move; rather, their sense of who they are becomes more complex, flexible and shifting as they interact with new people, cultures and languages. Rather than replacing one language with another – or choosing to integrate into or segregate themselves from a new society – migrants may carve out new multilingual and multicultural identities which reflect complex backgrounds.

In this chapter, I begin by looking at language as a factor behind decisions to migrate, before exploring the extent to which migrants are excluded from entering certain countries because of their lack of proficiency in the dominant language. I then focus away from policy and its impact on global trends to look at how migrants adapt, culturally and linguistically, to the situations which they create for themselves in new countries; and at how they often use their multilingual language skills as an important resource in their social and economic lives. Throughout this chapter, I focus not only on English as one example of the languages used by both migrant groups and people in the countries that receive them, but also on the special role that global English plays in the relationships of conflict, cooperation and competition that arise as a result of migration.

2.2   What is migration?

I would like to start by asking you to reflect on your own experience of migration, which requires first a consideration of what migration is. Above I defined migration in terms of 'space', in that it involves people crossing administrative boundaries (Kerswill, 2006). Migration can occur across boundaries within a country, but this chapter is mainly concerned with 'transnational migration' – that which involves movement between nations. Definitions based on length of stay are more problematic. We might suggest that migration 'implies a degree of permanence' (Kerswill, 2006, p. 8) – the United Nations (UN), for example, defines migration as a stay of one year or longer. But does this mean that a student studying abroad for nine months has not migrated, but someone on a two-year course has? Putting aside the UN definition, we can talk of short-term or long-term migration – short-term migrants may include students and seasonal workers; long-term migrants include, among others, the many Europeans who went to America around the turn of the twentieth century to start a new life. Often, whether someone has 'migrated' depends not only on official definitions and policies, but on the intentions and perceptions of individuals involved.

It is necessary to note that migration need not be, and never has been, a one-way, one-time displacement: migrants have always kept in touch with and often returned to countries of origin, and today this is perhaps more likely, given improved and cheaper transportation systems and communication technologies. It is also important to recognise that 'migrants' do not form one homogeneous group, but can be young, old, rich, poor, skilled or unskilled; they may migrate alone or with extended families and communities, and they may do so for a variety of reasons. Nor do migrants form a marginal group: in the beginning of the twenty-first century, around one in every thirty-five people can be classed as an international migrant (BBC News, 2011). The map in Figure 2.1 shows the complexity and diversity of migration flows in the early part of the twenty-first century.

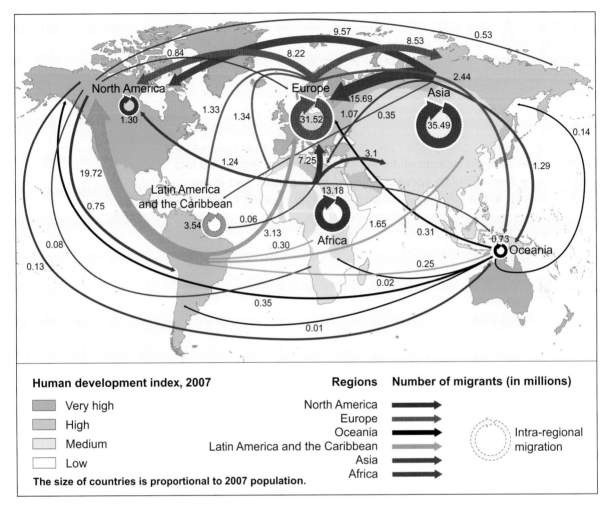

Figure 2.1 Migration flows in the world today (adapted from UNDP, 2009, p. 24, Map 2.1)

Allow about 10 minutes

Activity 2.1

Even if you have not migrated yourself, given the numbers who migrate either on a short- or a long-term basis, it is likely that you know somebody who has migrated away from where you live or into your community. What were their, or your, reasons for moving? What role did language play in the decision, and to what extent did the languages they, or you, speak facilitate the move? Remember that while our focus is on transnational migration, people also move within countries and face similar issues, so you can also focus here on domestic migration.

Comment

My family's history of migration is complex. My husband's and my grandparents migrated from India to South Africa during the mid- to late 1800s. The fact that my grandparents, who were Urdu speakers, had been educated through the medium of English played a major part in their decision to migrate to South Africa, and it meant that they were able to settle in their new country relatively quickly and set up businesses. During the 1970s my family and I migrated to the UK for political reasons related to the struggle against apartheid in South Africa. Again, the fact that we were fluent English speakers played an important part in the choice to settle in the UK. However, despite the role played by English in our decision, maintaining other languages (such as Urdu and Afrikaans, which I learnt in South Africa) remains important to me. This is a theme that I return to later in this chapter.

As you read the following discussion of language and migration, consider how your personal experience of migration fits into the wider picture.

It is possible to identify broad trends in migration patterns between the languages spoken by migrants and their destination countries. In this regard, migration flows between countries with languages that are closely related, such as the Bantu languages in sub-Saharan Africa, Germanic languages including German, Flemish and Dutch, or the Latin-based languages Spanish and Italian, tend to be larger than between countries where the languages spoken are very different (Belot and Ederveen, 2011). English, French and Spanish, because they spread to different countries during colonial migration, also play an important role in influencing global patterns of migration (Adsera and Pytlikova, 2010). English, like other ex-colonial languages, shapes migration patterns simply through its presence as an official language in so many countries.

However, English is now used within contexts characterised by migration in ways that reflect (and in turn sustain) its role as global lingua franca. The following exchange within a health clinic in Catalonia, Spain between a Pakistani patient (P) and two members of staff (S1 and S2) illustrates how English can be used for cooperation in situations where diverse people are brought together through migration.

1	P:	hola estoooo skin, esto, otro otro, skin
		[*hello thiiis skin, this, other other, skin*]
2	S1:	skin?
3	P:	ehhh, dermatologia la segunda?
		[*ehh, dermatology the second?*]
4	S2:	the second floor.
5	P:	second floor?
6	S2:	second floor.
7	P:	gracias
		[*thank you*]

(adapted from Moyer and Martín Rojo, 2007, p. 152)

This conversation shows how people negotiate interpersonal situations not only by using a dominant local language (in this case, Spanish), but by drawing on English, which the Pakistani patient has acquired through the colonial presence of Britain, and the clinic staff through subsequent globalisation. The practice above is unlikely to be an isolated occurrence, but is instead one repeated across the world, in situations where groups speaking different languages are brought together. The box below gives an indication of the nature of labour migration within Asia and to the Middle East, and we can presume that in many of these movements, English would play a role.

Migration status of Asian countries

1 Labour sending
   – *Bangladesh, China, Indonesia, Nepal, Philippines, Sri Lanka, Vietnam*

2 Labour sending and receiving
   – *India, Malaysia, Pakistan, Thailand*

3 Labour receiving
   – *Middle East, Brunei Darussalam, Taiwan (China), Japan, Republic of Korea, Hong Kong SAR, Singapore*

(Wickramasekera, 2002, p. 14, Box 3)

The desire to learn English is itself a motivating factor in decisions to migrate. The increased value attached to English language proficiency results in large flows of students from countries across the non-English speaking world to the UK, USA, New Zealand, Australia and South Africa, to attend English language courses or to learn English by immersing themselves in English-speaking countries. In South Korea the drive for English has given rise to the *kirogi* or 'wild goose family' phenomenon (wild geese migrate to better climates during winter) in which fathers, called 'goose dads', remain in Korea to work and send money for the maintenance and education of their children who are taken abroad by their mothers to study in English-speaking countries (Park, 2009).

The USA is the country of choice for the educational exodus, but other destinations include what Kachru (1982) refers to as Inner Circle English-speaking countries, such as New Zealand, Australia and the UK, as well as Outer Circle English-speaking countries, such as South Africa and Singapore. The drive for English which stimulates this migration is associated with status, prestige and improved employment prospects, and it demonstrates how migration may be directly influenced by people's perception of the importance of English and their desire that future generations of children acquire an identity as English speakers.

Kachru's Three Circles model is discussed in another book in this series: Seargeant and Swann (eds) (2012).

TMA 5

However, there are numerous reasons – environmental, economic and political – for which people may migrate, and (aside from cases such as the Korean 'goose families') language is not the only issue. These reasons include 'pull factors' (attractive factors which encourage people to move to a country) or 'push factors' (reasons to move away from somewhere). With regard to environmental factors, for example, people might choose to move to regions having a better climate and/or more arable land for agriculture (pull factors) – or of course they may *need* to migrate to areas with a better climate if they have experienced long periods of drought and soil erosion that have resulted in animal stocks dying and poor quality crop (push factors). Economic reasons involve migrations from rural to urban areas as people are attracted by employment opportunities, higher incomes and a better quality of life. Similarly, people from all over the world now migrate to countries such as the Gulf States in the Middle East where incomes are generally higher and untaxed. In many developing countries, intense poverty is a major factor pushing people to migrate. Indeed, most people who migrate do so to countries with a better standard of living than the country of origin (UNDP, 2009). Finally, sometimes people are forced to seek refuge abroad because of political factors such as ethnic, linguistic or religious discrimination and persecution which may be either tacitly or overtly supported by the state concerned. For example, the 1970s witnessed large-scale migration of political exiles fleeing oppressive regimes in countries including Chile, South Africa and parts of Eastern Europe, to settle in Western Europe, the USA and Canada (Rassool, 2000).

As the above suggests, one important way of categorising people's motivations is to distinguish 'forced' from 'voluntary' migration. People have varying levels of agency when they migrate, and their ability to choose is linked to their wealth and position in the country of origin and to how their status and resources transfer to the country they migrate to. For people who migrate voluntarily and with some ability to choose where to migrate to, there are many factors which they may consider. They are likely to feel that their ability to gain work and integrate into society depends on whether they can speak and are literate in the dominant language of the new country. They may also feel that their children will more easily adapt to schools and learning if they understand and/or are literate in the language of education in the adoptive country. Sharing a common language, therefore, is an important factor in making choices about the country of migration. At the same time, of course, parents might also be concerned about whether their children are able to continue learning a language that enables them to maintain links with their own cultural heritage. Where there are members of their particular language communities settled in the destination country, this becomes an important pull factor. (I look at 'chain migration' in greater depth in Section 2.5.) However, for refugees, the country to which they migrate is likely to be decided by international politics as well as by linguistic considerations.

multilingual experience

(EMA)

Communities and languages

It is usual to make a distinction between the **minority or community languages** of migrants (which may or may not be the languages spoken in the home) and the **dominant language** of the receiving society. For example, the Somali spoken in the UK by the fourteen-year-old girl from Somalia quoted at the beginning of this chapter can be considered a community language for her family, in a context where English is the dominant language. The term **heritage language** tends to be used more specifically in relation to second- or third-generation migrants who have shifted towards use of the dominant local language for most purposes but who may wish to acquire a deeper knowledge of their family's minority language. As we shall see, in actual practice, migrants can move between these languages in fluid ways.

See Chapter 1 for an exploration of the relationship between a language and the community which uses it.

2.3 Citizenship and language tests

Language fluency has become a major criterion for gaining residency and qualifying for citizenship. Citizenship tests have been used in the USA and Canada for many years, while in the UK and other European countries, New Zealand and Australia they came into being during the first decade of the twenty-first century – in reaction partly to external terrorist threats and partly to a perceived growth in, and concern over, ethnic diversity. These tests include those which are explicitly aimed at evaluating language proficiency but, in some countries, a certain level of competence in the language or languages of the receiving country is also required in order to sit tests assessing migrants' knowledge of national history, everyday life and culture. Migrants to the UK, for example, have to pass the *Life in the UK* test, which is offered in English (or, optionally, in Welsh or Gaelic for migrants to Wales and Scotland, respectively). Figure 2.2 gives three questions taken from the test. Those seeking permanent residence in the UK must memorise the answers given in the handbook and gain at least 75 per cent to pass. Unless you have (recently) taken the test yourself, I would wager that you would struggle to pass without studying the handbook, regardless of your familiarity with the UK – and that you would face a similar situation with a test about any country. (Answers are given at the bottom of the page.[1])

12. **When is Mother's Day?**
   - The Sunday, 1 week after Easter
   - The Sunday, 3 weeks before Easter
   - The Sunday, 2 weeks before Easter
   - The Sunday, 1 week before Easter

13. **What percentage of local authority expenditure is funded through the collection of council tax?**
   - 15%
   - 20%
   - 25%
   - 30%

14. **What percentage of the UK population is Buddhist?**
   - 0.3%
   - 0.4%
   - 0.5%
   - 0.6%

Figure 2.2 Example questions from the *Life in the UK* test (www.hiren.info/life-in-the-uk-test/10, accessed 1 June 2011)

The official aim of citizenship tests is to help migrants integrate into a receiving country by developing a common view and approach to life in society, and therefore to support social cohesion. Other political factors are put forward by the governments of receiving countries, including the need to screen out people who might be deemed to pose a threat to society. The English language requirement in general can be seen as fulfilling two purposes: first, to enable migrants to communicate with other citizens from outside their communities and therefore to integrate and become part of the broader community; and, second, to facilitate access to the labour market. Government statistics tend to suggest that the extent to which migrants are fluent in the main language of their country of adoption influences their ability to become employed within the mainstream labour market. For example, research commissioned by the Department of Work and Pensions in the UK reported that lack of proficiency in English and low educational qualifications were major barriers to employment for migrants from Bangladesh and Pakistan within the 45–64 age range and that fluency in English increases employability by 25 per cent (Tackey et al., 2006).

[1] 12. The Sunday, 3 weeks before Easter; 13. 20%; 14. 0.3%.

Activity 2.2

Look at the two extracts from Canadian and US English language tests given in the boxes below. In what ways do the two tests differ, and how effective do you think each is in testing the proficiency of potential migrants?

**Allow about
20 minutes**

Canadian English language test criteria

2. Your language abilities

The citizenship knowledge test and your interaction with CIC [Citizenship and Immigration Canada] staff will be used to assess if you have an adequate ability to communicate in either English or French. CIC staff will observe

- your ability to understand basic spoken statements and questions, and
- your ability to communicate basic information or respond to questions.

For example, as part of your interaction with departmental staff or as part of your written test or your interview with a citizenship judge, you will be expected to:

- answer simple questions on familiar topics, using short sentences;
- show that you know enough words for basic everyday communication;
- tell a simple story about everyday activities;
- speak about something you did in the past (or will do in the future);
- give simple everyday instructions and directions; and
- express satisfaction or dissatisfaction.

(Citizenship and Immigration Canada, 2011)

U.S. Naturalization Test: scoring guidelines for the English test

Section 312 of the Immigration and Nationality Act (INA) provides that most applicants for naturalization demonstrate an understanding of the English language, including an ability to read, write, and speak words in ordinary usage in the English language, as well as a knowledge of U.S. government and history (civics). This document provides a general description of how the English portion of the U.S. Naturalization Test is evaluated and scored by Officers of the U.S. Citizenship and Immigration Services (USCIS). These evaluation and scoring guidelines will not change with the implementation of the redesigned naturalization test.

SPEAKING: An applicant's verbal skills are determined by the applicant's answers to questions normally asked by USCIS Officers during the naturalization eligibility interview. USCIS Officers are required to repeat and rephrase questions until the Officer is satisfied that the applicant either fully understands the question or does not understand English. If the applicant generally understands and can respond meaningfully to questions relevant to the determination of eligibility, the applicant has demonstrated the ability to speak English.

READING: To sufficiently demonstrate the ability to read in English, applicants must read one sentence, out of three sentences, in a manner suggesting to the USCIS Officer that the applicant appears to understand the meaning of the sentence. Applicants shall not be failed because of their accent when speaking English. A general description of how the reading test is scored follows:

Pass:

- Reads one sentence without extended pauses
- Reads all content words but may omit short words that do not interfere with meaning
- May make pronunciation or intonation errors that do not interfere with meaning

Fail:

- Does not read the sentence
- Omits a content word or substitutes another word for a content word
- Pauses for extended periods of time while reading the sentence

- Makes pronunciation or intonation errors that interfere with meaning

WRITING: To sufficiently demonstrate the ability to write in English, the applicant must write one sentence, out of three sentences, in a manner that would be understandable as written to the USCIS Officer. An applicant shall not be failed because of spelling, capitalization, or punctuation errors unless the errors would prevent understanding the meaning of the sentence. A general description of how the writing portion is scored follows:

Pass:

- Has the same general meaning as the dictated sentence
- May contain some grammatical, spelling, punctuation, or capitalization errors that do not interfere with meaning
- May omit short words that do not interfere with meaning
- Numbers may be spelled out or written as digits

Fail:

- Writes nothing or only one or two isolated words
- Is completely illegible
- Writes a different sentence or words
- Written sentence does not communicate the meaning of the dictated sentence

According to regulation, applicants who fail the English literacy and/or civics test during their first examination will be rescheduled to appear for a second opportunity to take the test (8 CFR 312.5).

Comment

The Canadian test appears to test functional communicative skills – that is, the ability to interact in English and to perform key speech acts – to a greater extent than the US one; for example, a potential migrant to Canada must show their 'ability to understand basic spoken statements' while, to enter the USA, people must write dictated sentences. The focus in the US test is on an abstract notion of 'meaning', rather than how meaning is constructed between people through communication. As Tim McNamara and Elana Shohamy (2008, p. 93) put it, 'inferences about relevant real-world competence are difficult to draw from this highly constrained and artificial procedure'. The US test has the benefit of being more detailed than that of Canada, but both are vague in explaining how language proficiency is to be evaluated; for example, the US test requires candidates to read a sentence 'in a manner suggesting to the USCIS Officer that the applicant appears to understand the meaning of the sentence' – whatever this manner may be – while the Canadian test mentions 'simple questions on familiar topics' and knowing 'enough words for basic everyday communication', without (in this document at least) clarifying how 'familiar' topics are identified and what basic everyday communication entails. The extent to which the tests measure how somebody will cope in the particular situations in which they may find themselves is limited.

Furthermore, the very fact that the tests differ in detail and focus calls into question the validity of the construct they are designed to test. How can these tests be so necessary if they require very different competences from migrants? Why should countries have different requirements? One reason is that the tests are not required for functional or literacy reasons, but social and political ones. McNamara and Shohamy (2008) point out that high levels of language proficiency tend to be required in countries which have experienced intense debates over migration. As is evident from the test above, the USA does not require particularly high levels of language competence, while countries such as the UK, Australia and Denmark are steadily increasing the proficiency that migrants must demonstrate.

Language tests are also critiqued in Chapter 4.

As well as criticisms of ways in which some citizenship tests are designed, many linguists question the use of such tests in the first place. McNamara and Shohamy (2008, p. 93) highlight three main objections:

- First, people have the right to use a language of their choice and this right is violated when governments impose a language on them.
- Second, prior to migration, many migrants have no access to language classes or opportunities to learn.
- Third, migrants are capable of acquiring the language of the receiving society as and when the need arises, and of using other languages to fulfil social duties such as voting or working.

You read in Chapter 1 about problems connected with too straightforward a notion of linguistic rights, such as the assumption that people are tied to a particular community language. However, despite the benefits for migrants in learning the dominant language of a receiving society, the extent to which linguistic proficiency should be evaluated and enforced prior to entry is open to debate. One alternative is the better provision of language classes for migrants once they have arrived in their new country of settlement. This solution recognises the realities of language use in migrant communities; that migrants pick up the language skills they need in complex ways which directly relate to their own lives. Miller's (2010) study of migrants to the USA, all of whom had successfully set up their own businesses, shows how these migrants faced minimal linguistic demands, in part because their businesses tended to be in the service sector, but also because they served their own minority language community. Where they faced linguistic difficulties, they resorted to various strategies, one of which was to rely on other members of the language community. In other cases, as we shall see, migrants reach a high level of proficiency in the dominant local language and use it as an important resource alongside a community language (Martin-Jones, 2000). This practice challenges the principle of monolingualism which underlies citizenship tests – the idea that the population of one nation should, ideally, speak one language.

2.4   Multilingual resources in a global labour market

The previous chapter introduced the concept of linguistic capital – the idea that a person's language resources can translate into social opportunity and thus economic capital. What often happens when somebody migrates is that their linguistic abilities lose or gain in linguistic capital. In other words, a move between local contexts can effect a change in the value placed on particular linguistic resources. For example, groups who arrive in the UK with no or limited English language proficiency may find that their community language resources have no capital at all in the English labour market – refugees fleeing the war in East Pakistan (now Bangladesh) in 1971, for instance, many of whom came from rural areas and had limited levels of literacy (Haque, 2002), or the Vietnamese people who fled political instability via Hong Kong to the UK (Wong, 1991) and the USA (Tollefson, 1989). These groups lacked the necessary linguistic capital for immediate entry to the job market. On the other hand, migrants to the UK from ex-colonies during the 1940s and early 1950s were largely professional people, including university graduates, teachers and medical practitioners, as well as business people, seamen and ex-army personnel. As elite members of ex-British colonies, most were fluent in English and, given their English-based education, had good knowledge of Britain and British culture. Interestingly, most skilled migrants from the

Linguistic capital is also explored in detail in Chapter 4.

Caribbean during the 1970s and 1980s opted to settle in the USA and Canada where they felt they had better employment possibilities (Thomas-Hope, 2002). Again, being fluent English language speakers facilitated their absorption into the labour market as well as their settlement within American and Canadian society. In other words, the values associated with their linguistic resources in the Caribbean (where they form an elite group) were to an extent transferred to the UK and North American markets, enabling them to secure jobs. Nonetheless, some of these migrants experienced a decline in the value bestowed on the variety of English which they spoke. In a study conducted in 1997, a member of the Caribbean community who arrived in the UK during the 1950s stated:

> I consciously changed my accent because I felt so traumatized by comments such as 'Nigger, Nigger, pull the trigger, Bang! Bang! Bang!' Although in St Lucia I was regarded as a bright pupil, here they sent me to a remedial class because of my dialect ... after a long period of destructive rebellion I internalized my feelings and changed my speech register in order to belong.

> (interviewee, quoted in Rassool, 1997, p. 196)

So, somebody whose English is highly valued in the Caribbean may find that their variety of Caribbean English is evaluated negatively in comparison to standard British English in the UK. As this shows, such discrepancies can be an issue both when people are speaking different languages and when they are 'speaking the same language'.

Activity 2.3

Now turn to Reading A: *At the intersection of gender, language and transnationalism* by Ingrid Piller and Kimie Takahashi. The focus of the reading is on what the authors term 'reproductive work' which, as well as private housekeeping, includes roles in care and service sectors such as childcare and cleaning. These jobs are seen as reproducing the conditions required for 'productive work' – professional and manual work which contributes directly to the economy. Such work can also be defined in terms of the value placed on it by society: in relation to 'productive' work, jobs such as cleaning tend to be poorly valued, often part-time or temporary, and largely carried out by women (McElhinny, 2007). Increasingly, the women carrying out this kind of work are migrants. As you read, consider the following questions:

- In what ways – and to what extent – are the female migrant workers able to draw on their English language proficiencies as a positive resource?
- How may linguistic proficiency be used by employers to exclude migrant women, as in the case of British hoteliers described in the reading?

Comment

Female workers moving from countries where English is an official language – such as the Philippines – can find that their linguistic resources are greatly valued in a country – such as Taiwan – which may be financially richer but where the global lingua franca, English, is less widely spoken. English language skills can be an aspiration among Taiwanese employers, particularly for their children. The migrants' English is therefore a useful source of capital in obtaining work. It also becomes a valuable tool in resisting the inferior positions constructed for them in their position as 'reproductive' workers in a foreign country, and in building new identities in a receiving country in positive and affirming ways. One example in the reading is that migrant workers can consolidate as a group through jokes aimed at their employers' English. Ultimately, however, the value of their linguistic capital rests in the hands of their more powerful employers, who can choose instead to hire workers from other countries – such as Indonesia – whose lack of English is perceived as less threatening. Meanwhile, in British hotels, it is debatable whether enforcing linguistic criteria which works against migrant workers is justified on linguistic grounds or whether it can be perceived as discrimination against migrant workers, even if that is not the employers' intention.

The role of language in social discrimination is returned to in Chapter 8.

Reading A is important in counteracting the assumption often made – even, to an extent, elsewhere in this chapter – that migrant experiences are determined chiefly by one's national identity, and the social, cultural, economic and linguistic resources this bestows. In fact, the reading suggests that women of different nationalities may share migratory experiences with each other rather than with male counterparts, who may (in some cases) find 'productive', better-paid work in a receiving country. Similarly, Chinese students studying in Australia or the UK may share more characteristics with other international students – as members of urban elites with high levels of education and cosmopolitan outlooks – than they do with poorer Chinese migrants working in the restaurant industries of the same Anglophone countries.

Allow about
10 minutes

Activity 2.4

As a link between this section and the next, consider the way in which your language or your dialect is evaluated in different places. The way in which different values attach to language varieties can be seen not only in cases of migration, but whenever somebody moves between places – be it on a holiday or a trip to a nearby town. However extensively or little you have travelled, you are likely to have come into contact with people who make judgements about you because you speak differently from them. Think about a situation in which this has occurred. Was your language variety more or less highly valued? And to what extent did it change – if only momentarily – how you see yourself and the way you speak?

Comment

Although a fluent speaker of English when I arrived in the UK, I became aware that as a teacher my South African accent presented a communication barrier to learners whom I taught in London schools. They did not always understand my pronunciation of particular words. In order to become more clearly understood I learnt over time to adjust my accent to the local variety. On one occasion at a conference in Cape Town I was strongly criticised by a South African colleague (a leading academic in the field of language planning) for having changed my accent. He saw it as 'a denial of my roots', whereas for me it was just part of the process of adapting to my new environment and making myself intelligible to those whom I teach – while maintaining my multilingualism (my use of more than one language) and even improving my knowledge of Urdu.

2.5   Languages and multilingual identities in migrant communities

Migration almost always impacts on a person's sense of who they are, and this often involves some realignment between language and identity. One example of such realignment is that, in their countries of settlement, migrants have been seen to identify with a language variety that has a higher status in their country of origin rather than with their home or community language variety. For example, most Bangladeshis living in the UK originate from towns and villages in the Sylhet region.

Coming from different areas in the region they may speak different village, town and district language varieties. However, many Sylheti speakers settled in the UK, if asked, say that they speak Bengali, which has a higher status since it is the national language of Bangladesh. This self-selected identity has implications for research relying on self-report, where reported levels of literacy and language fluency in first languages are used to inform bilingual educational provision, or in studies focused on communication and health care provision.

Migration generally presents migrants with some tension between, on the one hand, maintaining heritage languages in order to safeguard cultural identity while, on the other hand, needing to become fluent and literate in the dominant local language as soon as possible in order to obtain jobs and become integrated members of the receiving country. In this section, I look at the complex ways in which these choices and negotiations are played out in the everyday lives of migrants in the process of settling in a new country.

For many migrants integrating into a new society, language maintenance is an active process, engaged in with the intention of holding on to a sense of where they come from. One example of this can be found in the community school movement set up in a number of countries to teach migrant children their heritage languages. However, the maintenance of cultural identity is often associated with a parallel tendency towards segregation. Various factors may encourage migrants to segregate themselves from mainstream communities. One issue is that migrants often settle in areas where there are established communities speaking the same language. 'Chain migration' describes the process of people migrating (sometimes from the same town or region) to a specific location because relatives or members of the same nationality previously migrated there. A variety of reasons can be cited for this practice, including the opportunity that it gives migrants to tap into existing community networks and the access they have to familiar cultural ways of doing and ways of living. Chain migration is a common occurrence in the migratory process: examples include the high numbers of Irish people settled in areas of north London; the clusters of Mexican migrants living in California, Texas and Chicago (Epstein and Gang, 2010, p. 3); and the Italian and Greek settlements found in the state of Victoria, Australia. You can probably think of examples in a town or city with which you are familiar.

Learning the language of the receiving country is seen by many migrants as representing a threat to their ability to maintain community languages. This is evident in Waxman's (2000) study of refugees to Australia from Afghanistan, Iraq and Bosnia and is also prevalent among the older generation in Somali refugee groups in the UK (Harding et al., 2007). At the same time, migrants may not fully integrate into mainstream society, not only because they live in ethno-linguistic clusters or 'ethnic enclaves', but because of their working conditions. Li Wei (1994) researched Chinese migrants who arrived in the UK during earlier waves of migration; that is, those who arrived as economic migrants from Hong Kong after the Second World War between the mid-1950s and mid-1960s, and political refugees who fled the Chinese Cultural Revolution between 1965 and 1976:

> [The] emigrants had had little formal education before they left for Britain, and spoke very little, if any, English. Their subsequent engagement in the family-based catering trade, which entails long working hours, has given them few opportunities to learn and use English. ... for most Chinese caterers there is hardly any social contact between themselves and the society at large, apart from the waiter–customer relationship. It is possible for a Chinese kitchen staff never to exchange a word with English-speaking people. ... Chinese waiters learn only enough to handle the menus and ... fewer than 20% of them are able to hold a simple conversation in English.
>
> (Wei, 1994, p. 58)

This was also the case in New York City, where half of all Chinese migrants were working in small businesses or family enterprises in the garment or restaurant industry by the end of the twentieth century, while many restaurants in Chinatown catered primarily to a Chinese clientele. Many Chinese migrants may feel it is not necessary to acculturate, given the tightly knit communities they maintain (Ong and Umemoto, cited in Au et al., 1998, p. 12). Moreover, across different communities, women in particular may not attend English language classes due to the lack of appropriate childcare, cultural factors and lack of access to transport (Waxman, 2000).

However, migrants also attach varying degrees of importance to the dominant language of the country of settlement, in enabling them to interact with society, to adapt and integrate, and to secure employment within the labour market. There is inevitably some shift between generations, whereby the migrating generation may gain only limited fluency in the dominant local language while, for second- or third-generation migrants (migrants' children or grandchildren), the dominant language becomes their main means of communication. As De Santis and Ugarriza explain in their study of Haitian and Cuban communities in the USA, '[c]hildren ... tend to adopt the dominant norms and values of the new host culture more rapidly than parents because of their enrolment in school, greater language facility, and friendship with children who are members of the new culture' (De Santis and Ugarriza, 1995, p. 354). According to Wei (1994) in a study of British-born Chinese in the UK, the younger generation is:

GMA

> perceived by the Chinese communities themselves as a major cause for concern. They are seen as lacking respect for traditional culture (e.g. authority structures of the family ...), which is often expressed through their Anglicised social behaviour (e.g. speaking English) ... Derogatory names such as 'bananas', meaning 'yellow outside, white inside', have been used to refer to this generation ... reports of the communication difficulties between the British-born and previous generations of Chinese emigrants are becoming more numerous ...
>
> (Wei, 1994, p. 50)

This is not to say that all second- and third-generation migrants drift inevitably from their heritage languages and cultures (Blackledge and Creese, 2010). A study I carried out in London highlights the value that children of migrants can place on their linguistic heritage (Rassool, 2004). The twelve- to fourteen-year-olds who participated in the research were from six comprehensive schools in south-east England, each of which had large intakes of children from different parts of the world whose parents had either settled there or who hoped to find asylum in the UK. Many spoke of their desire to learn their heritage language:

My family speak Tamil. Although I spoke it when I was small, I've lost it now and want to speak to my family and friends in India on the phone, or when I visit them.

…

I want to learn to speak Chichewa so that I can communicate with my Dad's side of the family. If I don't I will never get to know them properly, I'll always be different.

(schoolchildren interviewed in Rassool, 2004, p. 208)

What was also evident in their responses was that heritage languages were not only being used in an attempt to cling to past lives. Instead, some children expressed the wish to learn other minority ethnic languages so that they could communicate better with friends. For example, an Urdu speaker stated that 'I want to learn Bengali because I've got lots of friends who speak it.' Another, a Punjabi speaker of mixed cultural heritage, said 'I'd like to learn Portuguese so that I can communicate with my grandparents. Urdu to communicate with the guy of my dreams!' (quoted in Rassool, 2004, p. 209). For these young people, then, what were minority languages in the UK did not only represent the countries their parents had left behind, but also granted them access to new social networks in their country of settlement.

Thus, for most migrants, migration does not lead to a straight choice between two languages (and two ways of life), but to a more flexible and dynamic adoption of new, bilingual identities. That is, the everyday negotiation between different aspects of identity leads to the development of **hybrid identities** – complex, multilingual, multicultural identities – which involves adopting English while at the same time maintaining important cultural aspects of their lives in previous countries. As one pupil in my study put it:

Well, my language is very important to me because it is a part of who I am. But you've also got to know English very well in today's world … to get a good job, get promotion … and fit in better. If you don't know English today you'll have a hard time getting ahead.

(quoted in Rassool, 2004, p. 209)

This pupil's perspective provides an example of a self-defined hybrid identity articulated as a source of strength, highlighting an awareness of the need to adapt, while retaining important elements of their own culture. In everyday practices, this hybrid identity is realised not only in the ability to switch between languages in different contexts, but also in creative displays of code-mixing.

Code-mixing and creativity are discussed in another book in this series: Allington and Mayor (eds) (2012), Chapter 5.

In one study, Wei (2011) interviewed three young British-Chinese undergraduates in London. He found that they talked about themselves in highly creative ways that mixed Chinese and English. In this example, Wei has asked the interviewees what they plan to do after graduating from university:

Chris:　　以后工作就当"白领狗"，给人公司打工！
　　　　　(In future (I will) work as a "white-collar dog", working for someone's company.)

Lawson and Roland both laugh.

Roland:　　You are already *bilingual*!

Lawson:　　Good one.

Chris:　　That's what I mean.

(Wei, 2011, p. 1226)

The utterance 'white-collar dog', which Chris said in Chinese, can be attributed different meanings in English and Chinese. In British English, a 'white-collar' worker would include somebody working in banking and finance, where a new employee might initially work like a 'dog'. In Chinese the phrase is pronounced as 'bai ling gou', which sounds like the English word, 'bilingual'. The phrase is a pun – used spontaneously – which works not only by invoking two languages but by mixing them, so that 'bai ling gou' can be understood as 'bilingual'.

As such practices show, **codeswitching** – the use of more than one language within a conversation – is an important resource to these particular individuals in their sense of themselves, and how they make sense of the world and people around them. In terms of their national identity, the students saw themselves as neither Chinese nor British, but as global citizens who were unattached to a particular place:

Lawson:	I think one day we'll end up in different places, like Australia, America. Singapore, Hong Kong, Japan. Maybe China. Yeah, why not. But that doesn't mean we belong to China. We'll get used to it.
LW:	What about Britain then? Do you feel we belong to Britain?
Chris:	I do now. But that's because I'm here right now. When I finish uni, who knows? I could be anywhere.
LW:	Some people say once a Chinese always a Chinese. Do you agree?
Chris:	I don't know. Are we Chinese? We are Chinese, aren't we?
Roland:	But we are not Chinese Chinese.
Lawson:	Yeah. We are not Chinese from China. We belong to the world.
Chris:	Oh how grand. I like that. We belong to the world.
Roland:	Sounds like you are homeless.
Chris:	Yeah, homeless but happy, and proud of it.
	(All laugh.)

(Wei, 2011, p. 1233)

Nor did they see themselves as either Chinese-speaking or English-speaking. Instead they saw being bilingual as a central part of their identity:

Our parents think we speak too much English. My friends and teachers think we only speak Chinese, because we look Chinese. Nobody seems to understand who we are. We speak both Chinese and English. That's a fact. It's easy to understand, isn't it? Why don't people just leave us alone and let us speak whatever we can speak! You told us we are bilinguals. I like that. I really want to be bilingual and I want to be treated like a bilingual. I don't speak Chinese only; I don't speak English only; I speak both! That's who I am. That's who we are.

(Lawson, quoted in Wei, 2011, p. 1228)

As Li Wei (2011, p. 1228) concludes, this multilingualism 'does not mean to know all the languages fully and separately. They want to be able to pick and mix amongst the languages they know at various levels'.

In summary, research has shown that migrants can develop complex language repertoires and become flexible, multilingual language users. Their rich linguistic repertoires reflect their vibrant cultural experiences across space and time; and they contain memory traces of past migrations – we saw this with the London schoolgirl whose family had previously migrated from Somalia to Germany. Their migratory histories can mean that people develop hybrid identities which allow them not only to adapt to local expectations within formal mainstream situations and to revert to distinct cultural identities when at home or in a minority ethnic community, but also to create bilingual identities through creative codeswitching. This flexibility enables them to fracture the idea of fixed 'homelands' and 'belonging' and to redefine their place within their everyday environment. Within this process, migrant groups define their own language needs and aspirations to establish their place in the receiving society.

2.6 Multilingual space and linguistic landscapes

As, say, a tourist in an unfamiliar city, to what extent is it possible to know anything of the ethnic and linguistic backgrounds of the communities who live in each neighbourhood? One clue lies in people's impact on the public spaces in which they live – that is, the signs, posters, shop fronts and graffiti around them. The study of public signage in global contexts – the **linguistic landscape** – is now seen by linguists as important in understanding the role of language in global societies, particularly in urban environments. Signs are produced and displayed by people for other people, and their language choices reflect the values and practices of the immediate society, the migratory picture of the region and the country's language policies. Unsurprisingly, there is growing evidence that English occurs in signage around the world (e.g. Shohamy and Gorter, 2009). In this section, I look at the roles that English can play in the linguistic landscapes of Outer and Expanding Circle countries, and what this role tells us about the use of English – alongside other languages – in these contexts. I also look at the impact that migrants have on the linguistic landscapes of Anglophone countries.

In some cities, particularly in Outer Circle countries, the use of English in the linguistic landscape emerges clearly as the imposition of the language of a dominant group. Colonial dominance enabled English language and cultural mores to be inscribed into the cultural fabric of society in Australia, the USA, the Caribbean, South Africa, India and other British colonial countries. During the period of British colonialism new linguistic landscapes were created, including road signs and the naming of towns and buildings, which reflected the power of conquest. Buildings such as the Raffles Hotel in Singapore, built in 1887 (Figure 2.3) and named after Sir Stamford Raffles, who established a post there for the British Crown in 1819, were important cultural markers to the British.

Figure 2.3 The Raffles Hotel, Singapore

Figure 2.4 shows a plaque erected to mark the British conquest of Newfoundland, Canada. The commemorative plaque, marking conquest, makes particularly clear that the construction of cultural and linguistic landscapes is linked to power and status. It is also evident that signs have symbolic as well as instrumental value; that is, the plaque in Figure 2.4 is not simply designed to provide details of the British landing in Newfoundland but, instead, it also symbolises the British dominance at the time and serves to inscribe the history of the British Empire into the landscape of Newfoundland. It is a powerful linguistic marker of occupation.

Figure 2.4 Commemorative plaque of the conquest of Newfoundland

Activity 2.5

English alongside other languages in the visual landscape is not just a matter of colonial influence, but is also evident in countries where English as a 'global language' may play a role, such as that of lingua franca between migrants and the majority community.

Turn to Reading B, which you will be asked to read next, and look at Figure [2]. The 'Sun shine livs' sign depicted is located in a street in Malmö, a city in the south of Sweden. It juxtaposes the English word 'sunshine' (written as two words in the sign) with the Swedish word 'livs' (which roughly translates as 'foodstuffs'). Both these terms are transliterated into Arabic and Persian script at the bottom of the sign. How would you explain the use of English in this sign?

Now read Reading B: *Ecological linguistic landscape analysis: a Swedish case* by Francis M. Hult. The study follows a conventional practice which involves systematic analysis of the frequencies with which different languages are employed on the signage in a carefully delimited area (often, as in this case, a street or streets). The study goes on to discuss the signs and relate them to policies and practices in the neighbourhoods.

As you read, consider the following questions:

- According to Hult, what roles do Swedish and minority languages play in the street signage, and why might these be 'noteworthy for what they may suggest about bilingualism' in this Swedish context?

- What does Hult conclude about the use of English signs in Sweden (such as in the Sun shine store), and what does this suggest about English in the world?

- How effective do you find the analysis and what might the limitations be?

Comment

Swedish appears from Hult's study to be instrumental; that is, it functions to convey information between the various groups that make up this multilingual society. The same is true for minority languages in Möllevången. Of course, it is not surprising that Swedish is a national lingua franca, given its dominant role in Sweden, nor that minority languages would be used for communication in a linguistically diverse area. However, the instrumental use of these languages suggests that a functional bilingualism operates in the linguistically diverse parts of the city. That is, migrants to the area are not abandoning their minority languages for Swedish, but nor have they been segregated from society. Bilingualism is itself valued.

Furthermore, this linguistic landscape challenges the assumption made elsewhere that English in global contexts is always or necessarily used as a lingua franca for instrumental purposes. In the particular signs explored by Hult, English is used instead in a 'metaphorical' or symbolic sense; that is, rather than being used for communicative purposes, it is used in this case to index economic and cultural values associated with globalisation. Other writers call this use of the language 'display English' (Curtin, 2009), where the effect of the sign comes not so much from what is said but the fact that it appears in English (or simply in a romanised script) and the image this invokes. In the predominantly Chinese-speaking city of Taipei, for example, shop signs written in English (or other European languages) might symbolise high quality, a 'vogue cosmopolitanness', foreign fashions and personal freedom (Curtin, 2009, p. 228).

Of course, in most cases, language choices on public signage can be seen as fulfilling both functions at once: as an instrument for communication and a symbolic marker. In the case of the touristic Algarve (Figure 2.5), for example, signs in English serve both to reach a foreign, non-Portuguese-speaking tourist market while also promoting an 'image of the place as tourist-friendly and cosmopolitan' (Torkington, 2008, p. 125).

Figure 2.5   Tourism billboards in the Algarve, Portugal (from Torkington, 2008)

Conclusions based on analysis of public signage must of course be treated cautiously. In some cases, researchers may talk to shop owners, but otherwise they depend on their own interpretations of the meaning and impact of each sign. While counting the distribution of languages across signs can reveal interesting differences between regions, caution must also be exercised – the practice assumes that signs and languages can be isolated and neatly distinguished from other signs and languages, and it assumes that what the researcher captures with their camera approximates to what the intended audience finds salient.

These brief snapshots of varied linguistic landscapes show that English is used in signage around the world for various reasons: as a vestige of its colonial dominance; as a lingua franca, particularly in tourist areas; and by business enterprises trying to index certain values. As such, we can see that signs tell us much about how English is produced, consumed, valued and regulated in these global contexts.

Of course, primarily Anglophone countries also see their linguistic landscapes altered by migration, and the growth in (often multilingual) public signage reflects deeper changes – or tensions – in Anglophone societies. In the process of adapting to their new lives, migrant groups recreate aspects of their homelands and their cultures in their new environments in order to generate a sense of 'home' and 'belonging'. This includes maintaining cultural traditions, customs and beliefs through the clothes that they wear, places of worship, shops selling familiar foods and clothing, community centres and festivities such as annual street carnivals, as is the case with the celebration of the Chinese New Year in Chinese migrant communities across the world. In doing so, they create new cultural markers such as temples, mosques and churches built in styles of architecture found in their home countries, and written signs within the new communities in which they come to live. Migration to English-speaking countries has also altered the cultural and linguistic landscapes through signs (see Figure 2.6) and shopfronts (see Figure 2.7). However, bearing in mind the fact that linguistic landscapes embody symbolic as well as instrumental uses of language, these linguistic landscapes can be seen as serving as collective identity markers as well as informational markers (Ben-Rafael, 2009).

Figure 2.6 Sign in English and Hindi on the Southall train station, Southall, London

Figure 2.7 Chinatown in Manhattan, New York

What do these landscapes tell us about migrants? The multilingual signs offer a vivid illustration of the way in which migrants construct and display multilingual identities, often resulting in signs which juxtapose dominant and minority languages. These migrant landscapes – multilingual spaces created within English-speaking countries – also show how migrants actively respond to and shape the physical and cultural landscapes of places in which they settle. What such street scenes show is that migration is never a one-way process: it is not simply a question of migrants adjusting to a new society and a new language – receiving societies must also adapt to new arrivals and the rich linguistic and cultural resources they bring.

2.7 Conclusion

The focus of this chapter has been on English in contexts shaped by migration, and the importance of the language both for migrants moving to Anglophone countries and for those relying on English as a lingua franca in encounters with people speaking various languages. You have seen how English, as a global lingua franca, is used both in relationships of cooperation, as migrants access services in Expanding Circle countries, for example; and in relationships of competition and conflict, where language is used as a tool for exclusion and discrimination.

However, it is also necessary to highlight the importance of multilingual practices in situations of migration. For example, when moving to a new country, migrants may maintain their heritage languages for a variety of reasons, while adopting the dominant language of the receiving population. Although there is inevitably a shift towards the dominant language over generations, the often transitory and short-term nature of much migration suggests that, in a globalised world where around one in thirty-five people may be a migrant, multilingualism should increasingly be seen as the norm. Migration challenges the principle of monolingualism to which many nation states adhere, and which is evident in their notion of the language element of citizenship as well as their education policies (Moyer and Martín Rojo, 2007, p. 137). In everyday practices, many migrants not only move flexibly between the languages available to them depending on where they are and who they are talking to, but they also draw on creative code-shifting, and these practices define them as cosmopolitan, bilingual individuals.

READING A: At the intersection of gender, language and transnationalism

Ingrid Piller and Kimie Takahashi

Source: Piller, I. and Takahashi, K. (2010) 'At the intersection of gender, language, and transnationalism' in Coupland, N. (ed.) *The Handbook of Language and Globalization*, Oxford, Wiley-Blackwell, pp. 540–4.

Introduction

In this [reading] we explore the ways in which language and transnationalism play out on the terrain of gender and sexuality. We are particularly concerned with the gendered nature of transnational migration and the unequal distribution of access to economic and social capital, to which language holds the key. Contemporary gender theory is informed by the idea that […]:

> […] gender is not always constituted coherently or consistently in different historical contexts, and […] gender intersects with racial, class, ethnic, sexual and regional modalities of discursively constituted identities. As a result, it becomes impossible to separate out 'gender' from the political and cultural intersections in which it is invariably produced and maintained. (Butler 1990: 3)

Thus our concern is with the ways in which gendered identities are produced and maintained in transnational contexts and the ways in which they are intersected by linguistic ideologies and practices. It is the aim of our enquiry to establish how social exclusion or inclusion is achieved at the intersections of gender, language, and migration. […]

From 'women's work' to 'migrant women's work'

Recent years have seen a significant expansion of the care and service sectors. Reproductive work – that is, traditional women's work – has undergone significant transformations both in qualitative and in quantitative terms. Qualitatively, reproductive work such as child-care, aged-care, cooking, or cleaning used to be predominantly domestic work. However, in many developed countries there has been a significant shift to outsource such work outside the home, to childcare centers, aged-care facilities, catering businesses, or cleaning chains. Quantitatively, the need for reproductive workers has increased substantially as women have taken on paid work outside the home and thus have less time to spend on unpaid reproductive work in the home. Furthermore, the expansion of the leisure and tourism industries has resulted in the creation of new types of reproductive work, or at least in a substantial expansion of work such as hotel cleaning. As a consequence of its transformation and expansion, reproductive work is no longer only women's work but has become migrant women's work – 'a structural relationship of inequality based on class, race, gender and (nation-based) citizenship' (Parreñas 2001: 73). In developed countries, migrant women have taken on a substantial share of reproductive work, often to the extent of dominating certain sectors. Migrant women may undertake reproductive work in domestic environments as maids or nannies (Anderson 2000; Chang 2000; Hondagneu-Sotelo 2001; Parreñas 2001; 2005) or in institutional environments as childcare workers, aged-care workers, or nurses (Francis et al. 2008; Isaksen 2007; Malawian nurses struggle 2008; Pulvers 2008) or as hotel cleaners (Adib and Guerrier 2003; Adkins 1995).

The experiences of migrant reproductive workers are profoundly embedded in linguistic and communicative inequalities. Anderson (1997) points out that migrant women who join the global care chain as domestics are neither likely nor expected to speak the language of the people they are serving. As Piller and Pavlenko (2007; 2009) suggest, limited or non-existent proficiency in the majority language may even work to the advantage of employers by creating 'the pretence of distance,' rationalizing reproductive workers' inferiority, and maintaining their unequal status – as in the case of a Filipina domestic worker in Toronto, who described her Canadian employers as follows: 'They think you're as stupid as your English is!' (England and Stiell 1997). Inability to communicate with the person whom the workers care for may also add psychological stress to an already strenuous domestic situation (Raijman et al. 2003).

At the same time, migrant women's linguistic backgrounds, or even a lack of proficiency in the local language, can be an asset in some contexts. For instance Filipina reproductive workers are more in demand than their counterparts from other countries of origin because of their ability to speak English, a highly privileged form of linguistic capital internationally (Piller and Pavlenko 2007; 2009). Lan's (2003) ethnographic study of foreign domestic workers in Taiwan demonstrates fascinating negotiations of power and identity between Filipina domestic workers and their newly rich Taiwanese employers on the terrain of

English language proficiency. Lan (2003; 2006) shows that it became trendy to hire Filipina domestic workers in Taiwan as the English learning boom there intensified (see also Chang 2004). Thus the ability to hire a Filipina domestic worker who can speak English and teach it to the employer's family boosts the social and class status of newly rich Taiwanese. Many of the Filipinas interviewed by Lan (2003; 2006), who had not been maids back home but often were college-educated and even had professional work experience, felt humiliated and conflicted about their position. However, they also capitalized on their English proficiency as a means of resistance against the positions in which they found themselves. One maid said of her employers: 'They have more money, but I can speak better English than most of them' (Lan 2003: 150). Lack of English proficiency on the part of the employers on the other hand clearly undermined their authority – they found it difficult to make requests of their employees in English, so much so that one employer ended up doing the work herself, while another had to invest time in improving her English in order to express dissatisfaction with her maid. The domestic workers also gained a sense of superiority over their Taiwanese employers either by correcting their English or by joking about their employers' poor English with their friends, as in this example:

> My employer called from the office and said, 'Luisa, twelve hours, don't forget to EAT my children!' She actually meant, 'twelve o'clock, don't forget to FEED my children!' [laugh]. [oh my God. Did you correct her?] No. Some employers don't like that. So I just answered, 'Don't worry! I already EAT your children!' (Lan 2003: 154)

While jokes may provide some temporary release (Constable, 2003), they act as a 'hidden transcript' (Parreñas 2001: 194), to be performed by migrant domestic workers only among fellow maids. In interactions with their employers, migrant domestic workers mostly follow the expected script of deferential performance and engage in linguistic resistance 'with disguise and caution' (Lan 2003: 154), for fear of losing their job. In fact, as Lan points out, Filipina domestic workers in Taiwan are rapidly being replaced by supposedly more 'docile' Indonesian workers, who are less capable of making demands due to their limited ability to speak English (or Chinese; ibid., p. 156). The author goes on to state that this phenomenon provides an aspect of the harsh reality where 'language becomes a means of symbolic domination to consolidate the employer's authority and silence the migrant workers.'

Because of the unregulated nature of domestic reproductive work, which often leaves migrant women at the mercy of their employers, many transnational migrants in the global 'care chains' aspire rather to institutional work. Lack of linguistic proficiency often becomes a key obstacle to such aspirations – despite the fact that not all institutional reproductive work calls for substantial linguistic skills. This is particularly true of cleaning work. In hotels, for instance, migrant women of color are often assigned the 'invisible' – and hence also unheard – positions of chambermaids (Adib and Guerrier 2003; Adkins 1995). Adib and Guerrier describe how women's work in hotels is stratified along their ethnic and national background: while receptionists' work – which also has an element of caring and is heavily feminized – is 'white women's work' in British hotels,

> […] ethnic minority and migrant workers are clustered in the lowest graded work in the hospitality industry […] and it is common to find that all the chambermaids in a hotel are drawn from the same ethnic minority or migrant group. While reception work is 'respectable' women's work, therefore, chambermaiding is not constructed merely as women's work, but as work to be undertaken only by certain groups of women. (Adib and Guerrier 2003: 420)

Access to 'respectable women's work' in such contexts is ostensibly a matter of skills, qualifications and experience. However, as Adib and Guerrier point out, 'front-line' reproductive work – in their study, receptionist work – is often also framed as 'white women's work,' and women of color face substantial barriers. In a context where racism has largely become invisible and a majority of white people consider themselves and their societies to be non-racist or post-racist (Hill, 2008), linguistic proficiency can sometimes substitute for racial or national discrimination. Racial and/or national discrimination are often illegal, and individual employers may genuinely feel themselves to be non-racists. Linguistic discrimination, however, is often a commonsense proposition, and it 'just so happens' that non-standard speakers – people 'whose English isn't good enough' – usually are minority members, and, even more importantly for our discussion, transnational migrants.

References for this reading

Adib, A., and Guerrier, Y. (2003) The interlocking of gender with nationality, race, ethnicity and class: The narratives of women in hotel work. *Gender, Work and Organization* 10(4): 413–32.

Adkins, L. (1995) *Gendered Work: Sexuality, Family and the Labour Market.* Buckingham: Open University Press.

Anderson, B. (1997) Servants and slaves: Europe's domestic workers. *Race and Class* 39(1): 37–49.

Anderson, B. J. (2000) *Doing the Dirty Work? The Global Politics of Domestic Labour.* London: Zed Books.

Butler, J. (1990) *Gender Trouble: Feminism and the Subversion of Identity.* New York and London: Routledge.

Chang, G. (2000) *Disposable Domestics: Immigrant Women Workers in the Global Economy.* Cambridge, MA: South End Press.

Chang, J. (2004) *Ideologies of English Language Teaching in Taiwan.* Unpublished PhD, University of Sydney, Sydney.

Constable, N. (2003) *Romance on a Global Stage: Pen Pals, Virtual Ethnography, and 'Mail Order' Marriages.* Berkeley, Los Angeles, and London: University of California Press.

England, K., and Stiell, B. (1997) 'They think you are as stupid as your English is': Constructing foreign domestic workers in Toronto. *Environment and Planning* A29(2): 195–215.

Francis, K., Chapman, Y., Doolan, G., Sellick, K., and Barnett, T. (2008) Using overseas registered nurses to fill employment gaps in rural health services: Quick fix or sustainable strategy? *Australian Journal of Rural Health* 16(3): 164–9.

Hill, J. H. (2008) *The Everyday Language of White Racism.* Malden, MA: Wiley-Blackwell.

Hondagneu-Sotelo, P. (2001) *Doméstica: Immigrant Workers Cleaning and Caring in the Shadows of Affluence.* Berkeley: University of California Press.

Isaksen, L. W. (2007) Gender, care work and globalization. In M. G. Cohen and J. Brodie (eds), *Remapping Gender in the New Global Order*, 45–58. London and New York: Routledge.

Lan, P.-C. (2003) 'They have more money but I speak better English!' Transnational Encounters between Filipina Domestics and Taiwanese Employers. *Identities: Global Studies in Culture and Power* 10(2): 133–61.

Lan, P.-C. (2006) *Global Cinderellas: Migrant Domestics and Newly Rich Employers in Taiwan.* Durham, NC: Duke University Press.

Malawian nurses struggle to cope with colleagues' overseas exodus (2008). *Nursing Standard* 22(33): 5. [no author].

Parreñas, R. S. (2001) *Servants of Globalization: Women, Migration and Domestic Work*. Stanford, CA: Stanford University Press.

Parreñas, R. S. (2005) *Children of Global Migration: Transnational Families and Gendered Woes*. Stanford, CA: Stanford University Press.

Piller, I., and Pavlenko, A. (2007) Globalization, gender, and multilingualism. In H. Decke-Cornill and L. Volkmann (eds), *Gender Studies and Foreign Language Teaching*, 15–30. Tübingen: Narr.

Piller, I., and Pavlenko, A. (2009) Globalization, multilingualism, and gender: Looking into the future. In L. Wei and V. Cook (eds), *Contemporary Applied Linguistics, Vol. 2: Linguistics for the Real World*, 10–27. London: Continuum.

Pulvers, R. (2008) Is aging Japan really ready for all the non-Japanese carers it needs? [electronic version]. *The Japan Times*. Available at: http://search. japantimes.co.jp/print/fl20080601rp. html (accessed on June 15, 2008).

Raijman, R., Schammah-Gesser, S., and Kemp, A. (2003) International migration, domestic work, and care work: Undocumented Latina migrants in Israel. *Gender and Society* 17(5): 727–49.

READING B: Ecological linguistic landscape analysis: a Swedish case

Francis M. Hult

Source: Hult, F. M. (2009) 'Language ecology and linguistic landscape analysis' in Shohamy, E. and Gorter, D. (eds) *Linguistic Landscape: Expanding the Scenery*, New York and Abingdon, Routledge, pp. 88–104.

Malmö, a city in the southern Skåne region of Sweden, is a rich multicultural and multilingual context. The third largest city in the country, it is home to a sizable and growing number of recent immigrants. The number of foreign-born inhabitants was 26 percent of the city's population in 2006 (City of Malmö 2006). These foreign-born inhabitants come from several continents: Europe (61 percent), Asia (28 percent), Africa (4 percent), South America (4 percent), North America (1 percent), and Oceania (0.27 percent) (City of Malmö 2006). The data drawn upon here were collected in the commercial areas of two different neighborhoods that are illustrative of this demographic diversity.

The first neighborhood, Centrum, is the dominant commercial and entertainment district of the city. The heart of the neighborhood is a long pedestrian shopping area, referred to as *Gågatan*, which includes major retailers, restaurants, bars, theatres, and cinemas. It is a primary tourism destination in the city as well as a space where local inhabitants of all ages and backgrounds congregate for shopping and entertainment. Accordingly, Gågatan is an ideal location for investigating how language use interacts with dominant commercial and entertainment activities.

The second illustrative neighborhood is known as Södra Innerstaden (Inner-city South). This neighborhood is noteworthy because it is the most diverse in terms of national origin. Some 31 percent of the people living in this neighborhood are foreign-born, and they come from 140 different countries (City of Malmö 2004). The heart of this neighborhood, which is contiguous with Centrum, is a shopping square known as *Möllevången*. Unlike the pedestrian shopping street in Centrum, Möllevången is characterized by shops and restaurants that specialize in a variety of ethnic minority foods, household goods, and discount products. This area, then, is an ideal setting in which to examine how language use takes shape in a space that reflects cultural diversity resulting from immigration.

Following other work in linguistic landscape analysis (e.g. Backhaus 2006; Ben-Rafael et al. 2006), I took comprehensive photography of public signage on Gågatan and in Möllevången. Using a 32 mm Canon Sure Shot BF camera with no zoom, I obtained images that approximated what would be visible at street level with the naked eye. Data analysis centered on storefronts. They represent what Ben-Rafael et al. refer to as 'bottom-up flows of LL [linguistic landscape] elements', which is to say 'those utilised by individual, associative or corporate actors who enjoy autonomy of action within legal limits' (2006: 10).

Linguistic landscape findings

Photography of storefronts ($n = 220$) on Gågatan and Möllevången yielded the results in Table [1] [...]. It is important to note that the data presented here are specific to these two locations and are not meant to be representative of either the city of Malmö or the country of Sweden as a whole. These data are meant only to be illustrative of aspects of multilingualism in Malmö and the discussion that follows should be interpreted accordingly.

Table [1]   Languages on storefronts by number and percentage

Language* combinations on storefronts	Number of storefronts in each location (%)	
	Gågatan	**Möllevången**
Swedish only	93 (60%)	28 (43%)
English only	25 (16%)	7 (11%)
Swedish and English	30 (19%)	4 (6%)
Swedish and minority language	2 (1%)	19 (29%)
English and minority language	0	1 (2%)
Swedish, English, and minority language	5 (3%)	6 (9%)
Total	155 (100%)	65 (100%)

* The term 'minority language' is used here to refer to languages other than English and the majority language Swedish. It is worth noting that English may also be considered a minority language in Sweden, as used by immigrants whose first language is English, for example. Since the focus of the original study was the relationship between English and other languages, English is treated separately.

The distribution of Swedish, English, and minority languages across the two spaces are suggestive of the niches of these languages. Figure [1] shows their distribution.

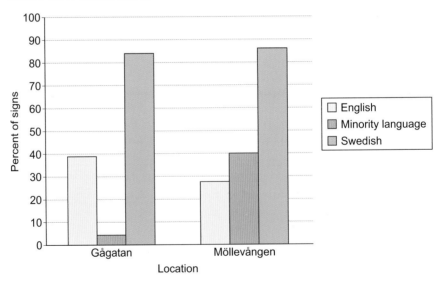

Figure [1]   Distribution of languages on storefronts

Both settings converge with respect to the use of Swedish. Swedish appears on 83 percent of storefronts on Gågatan and 87 percent of storefronts in Möllevången. As shown in Table [1], both areas include monolingual Swedish signs. There is a slight divergence in the use of English, which can be seen on 38 percent of storefronts on Gågatan but on 28 percent of signs in Möllevången. A further divergence is clear in Table [1], which shows that there are fewer monolingual English storefronts in Möllevången than on Gågatan. Gågatan also exhibits a greater number of Swedish-English bilingual signs. The two neighborhoods differ vastly in the use of minority languages. These appear on 40 percent of storefronts in Möllevången but only on 4 percent of storefronts on Gågatan. Where Gågatan has a high proportion of Swedish-English bilingual signs, Möllevången has a high proportion of Swedish-minority language bilingual signs. Only one example of an English-minority language bilingual sign was observed in Möllevången.

Superficially, the distribution of languages in these two settings is what one might expect. In a neighborhood with a great deal of ethnic diversity and markets featuring ethnic minority foods, it is not surprising to see minority languages strongly featured on the linguistic landscape. The heavy use of minority languages in Möllevången serves to construct this neighborhood as an ethnic minority community. Likewise, in a neighborhood that features national and international retail stores catering to tourists as well as people from throughout the city, one might expect to see a high proportion of both Swedish and English. The heavy use of these two languages on Gågatan serves to construct this neighborhood as a site of national and international commerce. The strong presence of Swedish in both settings is indicative of its place as the *de facto* national language of Sweden so it is not surprising that it is featured prominently either.

[…] After one year of conducting ethnographic field observations in the two linguistic landscape contexts and subsequently scrutinizing the photographic data set, it became apparent that the languages present in the linguistic landscape were used in functionally distinct ways. [...] Different functional uses of the languages in the linguistic landscape can be read as signs of beliefs about those languages. This becomes perceptible when language choices are examined in terms of situational and metaphorical code-switching.

Situational code-switching reflects instrumental communicative choices based on, for example, who interlocutors are and what the setting is (Blom and Gumperz, 1986: 424; Sridhar 1996: 56). Metaphorical code-switching reflects stylistic choices that are meant to evoke a certain idea or abstract concept that is associated with a given language (Blom and

Gumperz 1986: 425; Sridhar 1996: 56). In a basic sense, situational code-switching can be said to be *governed by* the situation whereas metaphorical code-switching contributes to *shaping* the situation (Bell 1997: 247).

This functional distinction [...] provides insight into the linguistic landscape because it provides tangible evidence of beliefs about language use that govern code choices. If English is perceived as an instrumental language of wider communication for tourists, for example, one would expect to find a high degree of situational English use on Gågatan. If minority languages are primarily perceived as markers of community identity, one might expect to find a high degree of metaphorical use of these languages in Möllevången. If Swedish is perceived as the main language of transaction in general, one might expect to see high degrees of situational Swedish use in both settings.

In order to examine code-switching, unique individual utterances on storefronts were isolated from the photographic data set. Schiffrin's definition of utterances was employed here, with an emphasis on the written form: 'units of language production (whether spoken or written) that are inherently contextualized' (Schiffrin 1994: 41). Only linguistic objects visible from a street vantage point were considered, not small signs visible only in close proximity to a store. Identical utterances that were repeatedly used on a storefront, such as a store's name or the word 'sale', were counted only once. This amounted to an average of 1.26 unique utterances per storefront on Gågatan and 2.09 unique utterances per storefront in Möllevången. Some stores, of course, were more verbally rich than others. The results are shown in Table [2].

Table [2]   Types of code-switching on Gågatan and in Möllevången by number and percentage

Type of code-switching	Number of utterances (%)	
	Gågatan	**Möllevången**
Situational Swedish	132 (67.35%)	81 (59.56%)
Metaphorical Swedish	–	–
Situational English	14 (7.14%)	5 (3.68%)
Metaphorical English	41 (20.99%)	18 (13.24%)
Situational minority language	3 (1.53%)	29 (21.32%)
Metaphorical minority language	6 (3.06%)	3 (2.21%)
Total	196 (100%)	136 (100%)

When Swedish is used, it is in a situational manner in both settings. Swedish seems to serve a basic communicative function rather than a symbolic one. Moreover, the relatively high proportion of Swedish seems to indicate that its niche in the linguistic ecosystem is as a common denominator language, a reflection of its dominant status. The ways in which minority languages are used on Gågatan is what one might anticipate, considering the limited presence they have there. When used, they most often serve a metaphorical function, generally to indicate a notion of foreignness. Indeed, the few instances of metaphorical minority language use were generally on restaurants that specialize in ethnic minority food. The scant situational uses appeared on currency exchange offices, with the exception of one restaurant which used minority languages in an extensive manner. The patterns of minority language use in Möllevången are noteworthy for what they may suggest about bilingualism. Minority languages appeared on storefronts rarely in a metaphorical manner. Nearly all tokens of minority language use appeared to be situational (21.32 percent of utterances).

Figure [2] Sunshine Market in Möllevången

In Figure [2], for example, the English word 'sunshine', morphologically expressed as two lexical items, is used as the store's name. English appears to be used metaphorically, as it communicates nothing specific about what is sold at the store. It is not evident from the context alone exactly what is metaphorically indexed by the use of the word sunshine in the store's name, though it is probably something the particular LL actor who commissioned this sign wished to associate with English. Swedish appears situationally in the word 'livs', which means roughly foodstuffs. Thus the instrumental function of communicating what the store actually sells is done using Swedish. Below these words, Arabic and then Persian are used in tandem to communicate both the name of the store and what it sells to shoppers who speak those languages.

This kind of usage on signs might suggest that minority languages are not perceived foremost as community indexicals but as languages of transaction within the community, at least with respect to the linguistic landscape. Of course, the prominent use of minority languages in certain social situations can itself be said to represent an in-group phenomenon (Zentella 1997: 84–85). One must be cautious about drawing firm conclusions from this data alone. Still, the strong situational use of minority languages in Möllevången, together with the situational use of Swedish, seems to be an indication that Swedish-minority language bilingualism is quite valued in this community. In comparison, as reflected in Table [1], English appears on storefronts almost as prominently on Gågatan (38 percent) as do minority languages in Möllevången (40 percent). This suggests that English may be as valued in the dominant community as are minority languages in the ethnic minority community, as far as the linguistic landscape is concerned.

The patterns of English use are also noteworthy since they point to some potential implications for further critical research. The general folk belief about English, and the belief most strongly held in *de jure* language policies, is that English serves primarily as a language of wider communication in Sweden (Hult 2007: 154–204). It is a functional language for reaching those who do not speak Swedish or for obtaining information produced by those who do not speak Swedish. While use of English in this way has been empirically demonstrated in the domains of media and higher education (Falk 2001), the present data about the interaction order in these two Malmö communities show that English in everyday life on the street appears to serve different functions.

While there were instances of situational English use in both settings (7.14 percent and 3.68 percent of utterances on Gågatan and in Möllevången, respectively), they were few in comparison to the metaphorical use of English.

This would suggest that English in the linguistic landscapes of these two areas is not used primarily as a *lingua franca* to communicate with those who do not speak Swedish (e.g., tourists or recent immigrants). Rather, it seems that it serves more of a symbolic purpose such as indexing values associated with globalization, as in Figure [3]. This indicates a need, as Phillipson (2006) argues, for researchers to look beyond English as a *lingua franca* when attempting to understand the position of English in European settings. English may be linked with, *inter alia*, discourses of the world economy (as a *lingua economica*), discourses of the cultural values of English-speaking countries (as a *lingua cultura*), and discourses of popular culture (as a *lingua emotiva*) (Phillipson 2006: 80).

Figure [3]   Symbolic use of English

References for this reading

Backhaus, P. 2006. Multilingualism in Tokyo: A look into the linguistic landscape, *International Journal of Multilingualism* 3(1): 52–66.

Bell, A. 1997. Language style as audience design. In: N. Coupland and A. Jaworski (eds) *Sociolinguistics: A Reader*, New York: St Martin's Press, pp. 240–250.

Ben-Rafael, E., Shohamy, E., Amara, M. H. and Trumper-Hecht, N. 2006. Linguistic landscape as a symbolic construction of the public space: The case of Israel, *International Journal of Multilingualism* 3(1): 7–30.

Blom, J-P. and Gumperz, J. J. 1986. Social meaning in linguistic structure: Code-switching in Norway. In: J. J. Gumperz and D. Hymes (eds) *Directions in Sociolinguistics: The Ethnography of Communication*, New York: Basil Blackwell, pp. 407–434.

City of Malmö 2004. *Malmöbor med utländsk bakgrund* [Inhabitants of Malmö with Foreign Backgrounds], City of Malmö: Office of Communication and Development.

City of Malmö 2006. *Malmöbor med utländsk bakgrund* [Inhabitants of Malmö with Foreign Backgrounds], City of Malmö: Office of Strategic Development. Online. Available: http://www.Malmö.se/download/ 18.293ce0691104a399cfe80004500/ Rapporten+i+sin+helhet++070125.pdf (accessed February 9, 2007).

Falk, M. 2001. *Språkpolitik initiativ och domänförändringar i Sverige* [Language Policy Initiatives and Domain Changes in Sweden]. Report to the Nordic Council of Ministers Language Policy Research Group. Online. Available: http://www.siu.no/c1256bd100399325.nsf/0/ 7b367fc353748c94c1256bca002a135e!OpenDocument andExpandSection=3,6andHighlight=0,domenetap (accessed April 30, 2006).

Hult, F. M. 2007. Multilingual language policy and English language teaching in Sweden, PhD dissertation, University of Pennsylvania.

Phillipson, R. 2006. Figuring out the Englishisation of Europe. In: C. Leung and J. Jenkins (eds) *Reconfiguring Europe: The Contribution of Applied Linguistics*, London: Equinox, pp. 65–85.

Schiffrin, D. 1994. *Approaches to Discourse*, Oxford: Blackwell.

Sridhar, K. K. 1996. Societal multilingualism. In: S. L. McKay and N. H. Hornberger (eds) *Sociolinguistics and Language Teaching*, Cambridge: Cambridge University Press, pp. 47–70.

Zentella, A. C. 1997. *Growing up Bilingual*. Malden, MA: Blackwell.

3 Learning English, learning through English

Ann Hewings

3.1 Introduction

For many of you reading this chapter, English will be a language you are very familiar with, possibly the only language you know. However, others reading and studying through English may still be fine-tuning and consolidating their knowledge of the language. The teaching of English to speakers of other languages (**TESOL**) from nursery level to universities and beyond has become a hugely profitable business and a political and ideological point of tension. In this chapter you will consider the impact on people of learning the English language and/or learning other subjects through the medium of English. What reasons are there for the use of English in education in non-English dominant countries? How do history and politics influence English learning in countries with an English-colonial heritage? What tensions does this give rise to? Why should places with no prior ties to the English language be investing in it? Lastly, what are some of the characteristics of English as a language of study at university level? As you read this chapter, keep in mind how you would be coping if you were trying to understand it in a language with which you were less familiar. Try to put yourself into (or perhaps back into) the place of the English language learner.

**Allow about
10 minutes**

Activity 3.1

The photographs in Figure 3.1 were taken in different countries where people learn the English language. In Chapter 1 you considered what motivated people to study English in Japan. What are the reasons these children and adults are studying in English? To what extent are their motivations personal and individual or the result of decisions by governments, employers, or other organisations? Think about your own situation. Would you cope, or are you already coping, in a second or third language in order to study?

(a)　　　　　　　　　　(b)　　　　　　　　　　(c)

(d)　　　　　　　　　　(e)　　　　　　　　　　(f)

Figure 3.1　Learning through English (3.1a Children learning science in Malaysia; 3.1b Adult migrants in Canada; 3.1c A level English literature class in Singapore; 3.1d Postgraduate students in the UK; 3.1e Children in a London primary school; 3.1f Children in an Indian secondary school)

Comment

The position of English as a global language relies on and encourages the teaching of the language in a variety of contexts, and may involve monolingual or multilingual students. The children and adults in these photographs are learning English in order to study through the medium of English, to live in an English-speaking country, and/or to work through the medium of English. For the young children learning English as new arrivals in England there is little choice if they are to succeed in a monolingual education system. For the adults, the motivation may be to improve chances of promotion, or because employers insist on their learning English. In some settings, where students have a variety of language backgrounds, English is used as an academic lingua franca.

Alternatively, governments or parents may view English as necessary for economic or social advancement and therefore insist that it be used in classroom settings. These are just some of the reasons for learning English and using English in the classroom. You may well have thought of many others, including perhaps your own experience of learning English in an academic setting.

This chapter deals with the use of English as a language through which study at school and university takes place. The range of situations in which English is used as the language of instruction is diverse. Examples include:

- classes in Inner Circle countries (e.g. New Zealand, USA, Australia) which may contain a mixture of monolingual speakers of English or speakers of English as a second or third language

- classes in Outer Circle counties (e.g. India, Sri Lanka, South Africa, Malaysia) with a British colonial heritage of using English in education

- classes in Expanding Circle countries (e.g. Finland, Chile) where there has been no colonial history of English, where English is a foreign language and most pupils share a first language (L1)

- schools in which pupils have different languages and in which English is used as the language of education (e.g. some international schools)

- universities in countries around the world that teach subjects through English to students with a variety of L1 backgrounds.

Braj Kachru (1992) developed an influential model of English usage which characterised countries as belonging to the Inner, Expanding or Outer Circles. This model is dealt with in detail in another book in this series: Seargeant and Swann (eds) (2012).

The roles of history, politics, economics and educational policy are threaded throughout the chapter. While you read about English in different schools and countries and at different educational levels, you should keep in mind both the similarities and the differences. Try to extend the attitudes and arguments illustrated in one context to the other contexts, or to contexts you are familiar with.

3.2 English-medium education in bilingual and multilingual settings

To start with, I want to consider classroom language and its importance in learning for all learners – children and adults, monolingual and multilingual. Before getting into details of language, try to recall your first few days at school. For me, growing up on the outskirts of London, learning to queue up in the playground before going into the building, eating school dinners, and making friends with new people come to mind. What I don't have much recollection of is learning to interact in the classroom like a pupil. I know that I was supposed to put up my hand if I wanted to ask or answer a question, and on reflection I now see this as an attempt to create order, and as an expression of the school hierarchy. I was learning to be a pupil in a particular culture and at a particular time, to communicate according to societal and school rules before I started to learn about things usually associated with school subjects. The importance of language in this process, and particularly of talk for learning, is made here by education researcher, Neil Mercer:

> As a teacher and a class engage, day by day, in various activities and interactions, they are gathering a resource of shared experience which they can use as the basis for further activity. This is where the role of language is crucial. Teachers and learners can talk about what they have done, what they are doing and what they will do next; and as they do so the talk can thread together experiences shared over long periods of time.
>
> (Mercer, 2007, p. 118)

For many pupils around the world, learning may be something they do in a language which is different from the one they speak at home or in their wider community. For some this will be one of a number of languages in a country, for others it may be English, perhaps chosen for or imposed on them. How does using a language which may be only one of two or three that you know, and perhaps not the one you know best, affect the creation of the shared experience described by Mercer? This is a question you should keep in mind as you read the rest of the chapter.

In the next section, you are going to read about the situation in Malaysia, a detailed illustration of the role of English in education in a postcolonial country. What becomes clear is the complexity of struggles around language in postcolonial societies. Many of the issues that arise in this Malaysian case study have echoes in other postcolonial contexts and in countries where English has risen to prominence as a result of more recent social and economic changes.

A postcolonial case study: Malaysia

Tear gas used on 3,000 rallying against use of English in schools

This headline from *The Straits Times* (8 March 2009), Singapore's most prestigious English language newspaper, reflects the contentious nature of language planning in relation to education and society more generally in the neighbouring state, Malaysia. There are three main ethnic groups in Malaysia: Malays, who make up 60 per cent and speak the Malay language; Chinese (25 per cent), who speak a variety of Chinese dialects; and Indians (7 per cent), who speak mainly Tamil or Panjabi (Hashim, 2009). The indigenous peoples of Sabah and Sarawak (see Figure 3.2) comprise many historically isolated communities with a variety of local languages, cultures and religions. Colonisation by the British in the late eighteenth and early nineteenth centuries primarily benefited the British and an elite minority of the Malay and Chinese communities who already had economic, social or political power. Power and prosperity were maintained in this small group partly through access to education in English, while for the majority of the population the status quo was maintained through education in their local language. There was at the time ambivalence on the part of the colonial power about education through English. On the one hand it was seen as a civilising force, allowing access to literature and culture, but on the other it was seen as a potential threat to indigenous cultures, and in the case of the Malays, to their lifestyle as farmers and fishermen (Pennycook, 1994).

At the time of independence from Britain in 1957, English and vernacular language schools existed side by side and all taught English to varying degrees. The new government, in what came to be called Malaysia in 1963, took the step of making Malay the national language

You can read more about colonial attitudes towards education through English in Malaysia in a reading by Alastair Pennycook in Chapter 3 of Seargeant and Swann (eds) (2012), another book in this series.

Best source of material for Malaysia

CMA.

in an effort to affirm the status of the dominant ethnic group and create a sense of national identity in this ethnically and linguistically mixed country (Gill, n.d.; Rappa and Wee, 2006). English was still a compulsory school subject, seen as essential for employment and higher education, and used as a medium of instruction in secondary schools. However, following riots between ethnic Chinese and Malays in 1969, the government instituted a new economic policy with greater affirmative action in favour of the Malays. The status of the Malay language in schools was reinforced and English was relegated to the status of a second language, not used as a medium of instruction.

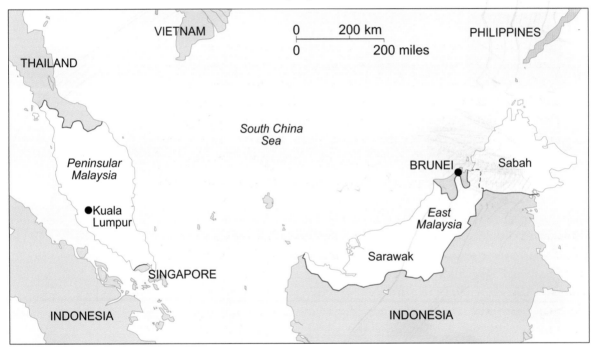

Figure 3.2 Map showing Peninsular Malaysia and East Malaysia (Sabah and Sarawak)

Changes in language policy influence access to political and economic power. Privileging Malay as a medium of instruction could be construed as disadvantaging those groups who were generally already proficient in English but perhaps less proficient in Malay, such as the Chinese business community located predominately on the West Coast and in the bigger cities, and Indian professionals such as teachers and lawyers. While the Malay language was accorded national status, the government also put additional resources into rural, predominantly Malay schools, to boost the level of English knowledge as this was seen as necessary to enable access to higher education and for the country's economic development. Through such interventions, it was hoped that Malays would take their place alongside the Chinese in the business and professional community. Proficiency in English continued to be associated with the Chinese, with Indian professionals, and now also with new urban middle-class Malays.

The person most associated with policies promoting the Malay language was the then Prime Minister, Mahathir Mohamad. He was also responsible for what was seen as a surprise reversal of the policy in 2002 when English was introduced in primary schools as the medium of instruction for maths and science. He linked this to changing technologies and economic development goals:

> To compete on equal terms with the world's most advanced countries, Malaysians – as well as most other Asian nationalities – still have some way to go. There are skills that must be learned and values that may yet have to change ... We do not become European simply because we wear a coat and a tie, speak English and practise democracy instead of feudalism. We have to learn the language of telecommunications, of computers, of the Internet ...
>
> (Mohamad, 1999, p. 40, quoted in Foo and Richards, 2004, p. 237)

Vernacular schools, such as those using Tamil and Chinese, were not obliged to follow the English for science and mathematics policy. Thus, primary school-aged Malays were more affected by this change, which again was aimed at redressing what was seen as an imbalance in educational opportunities and success. Presented as a six-year experiment, there was much disquiet over this policy, particularly in rural areas where children were, in effect, learning subjects through a completely foreign language. They were unlikely to have access to English language books; their parents, having been educated through Malay, would have little knowledge of English; and for teachers too it was often a struggle (Yasin et al., 2009). In addition, there were many who felt it was a return to the colonial times.

A Malaysian preschool

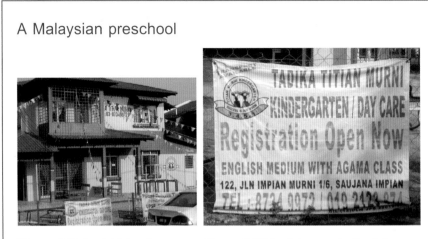

Figure 3.3(a)   A Malaysian preschool

Figure 3.3(b)   A banner in English outside a Malaysian preschool advertising that it is open for registrations

These photographs were taken outside a preschool in a suburb of the Malaysian capital Kuala Lumpur. The banners are in English and Malay and, as you can see, English-medium is the 'selling point'. The children being targeted are Malay speakers who would be expected to go to national schools where English was being used for part of the curriculum. It is interesting to note that alongside English, the other 'selling point' is that there is an 'agama class'; that is, a class teaching the Muslim religion. As being Malay and being Muslim are synonymous in Malaysia, the underlying message echoes that of Mahathir Mohamad and could be interpreted as 'learning English is important for your children, but it doesn't mean they are losing their national or religious identity'.

In 2009, the results of national tests at the end of primary school indicated that Malay children's performance in maths had declined over a three-year period, and for some this was attributed to the use of English as the teaching medium. This led to demonstrations on the streets of Kuala Lumpur. It united Malays, Chinese and Indians, but for different reasons, as the newspaper headlines in Figure 3.4 show.

Six years later, language debate rages on; Some want a return to mother tongue for teaching of subjects

16 January 2009, *The Straits Times*, Singapore

Maths and Science in English: Keep or scrap?

24 January 2009, *New Straits Times*, Malaysia

English policy a failure, claims union

10 February 2009, *New Straits Times*, Malaysia

English policy a success, say parents

14 February 2009, *New Straits Times*, Malaysia

Every language has a role to play

25 February 2009, *New Straits Times*, Malaysia

124 nabbed in huge KL protest; Tear gas used on 3,000 rallying against use of English in schools

8 March 2009, *The Straits Times*, Singapore

Figure 3.4 Newspaper headlines in 2009 on the use of English to teach maths and science in Malaysian schools

Educationalists in all communities stressed the advantages of learning at primary level in a child's main language. Others pointed to the lack of adequately trained teachers to undertake teaching through English. Additionally, certain groups saw this as an opportunity to reiterate their opposition to English, the colonial language, and to express fears that it would lead to the downgrading or eventual loss of the Malay language. Support for teaching maths and science through English, however, came from across the different ethnic communities, but was most associated with those from urban areas. Urban parents were among the most vocal supporters, as were pupils who already had access to English, certain higher education professionals, and many in business and the media. After some deliberation, the government decided to end the experiment, allowing pupils to learn in Malay or their own vernacular, while also placing emphasis on learning English as a foreign language.

What emerges from this story of colonial and postcolonial struggles around language is the complexity of the situation. The perception of the need for English conflicts with historical and contemporary feelings in relation to the colonists' language, Christian religion, Western economic power, disparities in wealth and opportunities, ethnic rivalries, and national politics. The competing pressures around the role of English must also be examined in relation to educational practices. Malaysia faces a shortage of teachers with the necessary English language skills to teach maths and science, a situation which the teachers and government are only too ready to acknowledge and which national and state governments have sought to rectify through initiatives such as the Project to Improve English in Rural Schools (e.g. Palmer and Jumiran, 2008). A further argument relating to the use of English to teach particular subjects focuses on the difficulty, particularly for younger children, of learning school subjects through what, to many, is a foreign language. For those, particularly in the rural areas, it creates another barrier to their educational success.

In the first reading for this chapter, Peter Martin, a researcher and teacher on language education with a particular interest in East Malaysia, examines how English is actually used in the classroom in an area with a multilingual heritage. Martin's research took place against the background of the Malaysian government's policy to use English as the medium of instruction in mathematics and science at a time when much media rhetoric criticised teachers if they made use of Malay in the classroom, reiterating instead the government line that subject knowledge should be taught monolingually through English. This reading is based on research involving two rural schools in different areas of Sarawak, on the island of Borneo (see Figure 3.2). Travel within jungle-covered Sarawak has traditionally been difficult, accomplished often by boat along its huge rivers. As a result, linguistic diversity has been maintained. Malay, therefore, is not the main language for many of the inhabitants, although as the national language it does have a lingua franca role. It is in this complex linguistic situation that Peter Martin observes what actually happens in the classroom. In Reading A he discusses a primary school only reachable along logging tracks in a community composed of a mixture of Sa'ben and Leppo' Ke' Kenyah peoples who mainly use the language Sa'ben. The teacher is ethnic Sa'ben, but also speaks another local language, Kelabit, as well as Malay and English.

Activity 3.2

Now turn to Reading A: *Tensions between language policy and practice in Malaysia* by Peter Martin.

Martin discusses the use of Malay in what is ostensibly an English lesson in terms of a 'safe' practice. As you read the piece, think about this question:

- What do you understand by his use of this word and do you think he means it to be a positive evaluation?

Then look again at Extracts 3 and 4. Notice which languages are used in codeswitching in the extracts of classroom interaction. Notice also how the teacher may initiate an exchange in English or Malay and switches between the two. Find two or three examples of the teacher using Malay or codeswitching. Can you suggest a reason for the change in language?

Reflecting on the situation in Malaysia from what you have read in this chapter and in Reading A, where do you stand on the use of English as a teaching language in the classroom?

Reading A is an edited version of a longer chapter and focuses only on Extracts 3 and 4 of the data from one of two classes observed.

Comment

I think Peter Martin views safe practices such as codeswitching as the pragmatic response to a situation where otherwise no learning would take place. The teacher may not know sufficient English to use it throughout the lesson, or to find ways of communicating meaning without translation. Translation using Malay as a lingua franca is also a speedy way to move the lesson along. Martin may also be implying 'safe' as being the easy way in this situation, a way that did not tax or challenge the learners or the teacher.

The extracts contain many examples of codeswitching, such as lines 57–67 in Extract 3 where the teacher is checking on the understanding of the colour 'brown'. Malay is used to ask a question in line 57 and from there on most of the interaction is in Malay in order to confirm the pupils' understanding of the word. In Extract 4, Malay is used extensively to make up for the cultural inappropriateness of the picture of the cook and cookbook. Students, too, in their responses, move between languages. And in the follow-up or feedback to students the teacher often confirms their answers in both English and Malay, but never in one of the local languages.

While the example from Sarawak indicates the challenges of using English in the classroom in a diverse linguistic context, there are many within Malaysia who argue that it is a necessity, as not being proficient in English might have negative consequences in education and employment for students in the future. Some, however, see the emphasis on English as part of American economic dominance, a view given credence by articles such as the one in *The New York Times* (9 July 2009) which characterised the move away from English-medium education negatively:

> The announcement on Wednesday … has raised concerns about whether English standards in the former British colony will slide and whether Malaysia's competitiveness as a destination for multinational companies may suffer.
>
> English has been the language of instruction for math and science in Malaysia since 2003, when former Prime Minister Mahathir Mohamad introduced the policy amid concerns that poor English skills were hindering students' job opportunities.
>
> Mr. Mahathir expressed sadness over the decision to revert to Bahasa Malaysia [the national language of Malaysia], saying that the decision would adversely affect children and make it difficult for them to keep abreast of scientific developments …
>
> (Gooch, 2009)

The difficulties faced by Malaysian pupils learning through English when they have little or no knowledge of the language, are faced by many other pupils around the world in a variety of different contexts. You can probably think of a number of examples. Ones that occur to me are: recently arrived migrant children in countries such as the UK, the USA and Australia; children in schools with a bilingual language policy which choose English as their second language (e.g. in a number of European countries); and children in predominantly multilingual schools, such as international schools which cater for the children of business people, diplomats and local families, where English language proficiency is highly valued so a decision to teach subjects through English has been made. Some of these are a result of local decisions by schools, or by parents in selecting particular schools, but arguably they also reflect the current dominance of the English language and propel that dominance into the next generation. In the next section, you will read about policies in Europe and their effect on language learning.

3.3   English in European education

The European Union (EU) has promoted the idea of individuals using two or more languages in addition to their mother tongue. Such 'plurilingualism' is viewed as important for integration within the EU both for economic reasons of 'the production, transfer, acquisition and application of knowledge, for employment and economic performance' (Mackiewicz, 2002, p. 3), and for cultural and political reasons to promote democratic citizenship (Breidbach, 2003). European plurilingualism seeks to protect smaller languages and to promote diversity, but in practice English has become the dominant language, often the first taught foreign language. In Nordic countries English use has become common particularly in higher education (Linn, 2010). In Denmark, for instance, English is introduced in schools at Grade 4, is obligatory at advanced levels, and is the medium of instruction for many courses at university. Other languages lag far behind and many Danes view English as sufficient because of its global status, a view tacitly supported at government level. However, Maarja Siiner (2010), whose research into Danish language policies illustrates the positive views of Danish-English bilingualism, also points out that there is an overall decrease in linguistic diversity and increasingly discriminatory attitudes towards minority languages spoken by immigrant communities.

Many European schools and other education institutions have taken up the practice of teaching some of their curriculum through the medium of a foreign language, and despite academic and political misgivings, this is commonly English. Such policies aim to promote both language learning and understanding and integration through **intercultural communication**: communication between people who have not just different languages, but different histories, social outlooks, values and behaviours. If you think back to the war-torn history of Europe in the twentieth century, it is easy to understand the motivations for this. The practice is referred to in Europe as **content and language integrated learning (CLIL)** and has been promoted through transnational agreements, particularly within the EU (Carrió-Pastor, 2009; Wiesemes, 2009). In targeting learning of a second or third language, the aim, though perhaps not the reality, is not to diminish the mother tongue but to improve overall oral communication skills and language awareness of both mother tongue and target language, while simultaneously developing positive attitudes towards language learning.

As in the case of Malaysia, there are significant problems in teaching through another language. The ability of teachers to satisfactorily develop pupils' curriculum knowledge and understanding, for example, requires significant investment in language training and support. Often help is provided by institutions such as the British Council or their equivalent in, say, France or Germany. This help by bodies funded by other governments could be seen as altruistic, or alternatively as a way of promoting their own national interest via language.

The role of the British Council in promoting English is examined further in Chapter 4.

A further concern related to CLIL policies is the increasing dominance of English as the main additional language learned. This reveals a tension in discussions around globalisation and language, where English represents positively valued internationalisation and the ability to 'improve one's market value' (Siiner, 2010, p. 48), while other languages are discounted.

3.4 English as an additional language in English-dominant countries

The dilemma over English in classrooms in Outer and Expanding Circle countries has both pedagogical and ideological aspects. Similarly, approaches to migrant education in Inner Circle, English-dominant countries have been subject to different political and educational forces. In the USA a shift towards 'English first' monolingual ideology has been blamed by teachers and researchers for low academic attainment among migrant groups. Ofelia García (García, 2009), an influential researcher in the field of bilingual education, has carried out extensive work with Latino (Spanish-speaking) communities where English is an additional language for many. Although many Latinos are proficient in both English and Spanish and use them in different contexts, their bilingualism is ignored. Monolingualism is viewed by many as the norm in the USA, and Spanish is seen only as a foreign language subject. This insistence on monolingualism in mainstream education contributes to the high failure rate of Latinos in US schools.

In Reading B, Frank Monaghan discusses the attitudes towards the languages other than English that children entering schools in countries such as England or the USA bring with them, and proposes a radical solution.

Activity 3.3

Now turn to Reading B: *English lessons* by Frank Monaghan. As you read, make sure you understand the concepts of **additive bilingualism** and **subtractive bilingualism**. Briefly reflect on how you think children who come to live in your country, but do not speak the dominant language(s), should be treated in school.

Do you agree with valuing children's mother tongues and promoting the use of those languages in the classroom? Are there disadvantages that Monaghan doesn't discuss?

Think of an example of using different languages with different levels of proficiency to communicate in a multilingual context; in other words, how you would, in García's terms, 'language' in a bi- or multilingual situation.

Comment

Subtractive bilingualism has been the norm in many English-dominant countries where integration with the English-speaking majority has been prioritised over the needs of recently arrived immigrant individuals and established immigrant communities. As you saw in the previous chapter, this can lead to loss of language, contact with relatives and culture. Additive bilingualism, on the other hand, is the potential outcome of educational programmes which seek to maintain both languages. However, in most English-dominant countries greater status is accorded to the dominant language of the country. This is often seen as part of a policy of assimilation. For many, this would seem a sensible way forward, as promoting the language of the host country would allow immigrants greater access to education, jobs and influence in the wider society. In

Australia, linguists such as Jim Martin, Frances Christie and Joan Rothery (1987) have long argued this way. Martin claims that lack of explicit teaching of English literacy skills disadvantages working-class, migrant and Aboriginal children whose homes do not provide them with models of writing, whereas, '[b]right, middle-class children learn by osmosis what has to be learned' (Martin, 1985, p. 61). If you are a member of a linguistic minority you may feel similarly, or perhaps have strong feelings about retaining your language and culture. So, while pragmatically responsible, additive bilingualism may ignore or downgrade the identities and skills that children bring into the classroom from their own language and culture. Monaghan argues for a much more profound shift in attitudes towards language, one which prioritises the ability to communicate over abilities relating to any one language. Problems with this approach that you may have thought of include: the number of languages that may be used within a classroom where children have arrived from many different parts of the world; the necessity of reading and writing at a sufficient level to pass examinations in the dominant language; understanding and using concepts which require careful explanation or definition.

An example of the benefits of being able to combine linguistic resources is exemplified by a British-educated friend of mine, born in Sarawak, Malaysia of Indian parents, who studied Spanish and French at university in the UK and who now works in the wine trade in London. She recently started working with Italians and visiting Italian winemakers and has drawn on her existing knowledge of the terminology of the wine industry in English, French and Spanish and her knowledge of how languages work, to enable her to move into her new role without first needing to take a course in Italian. Her existing language knowledge and the specified context mean that she is able to communicate adequately in order to transact business and is gradually expanding her language knowledge at the same time.

So far, you have read mostly about English in schools, but English learning and learning through English extends beyond compulsory education and is having a significant influence on higher education. Many of the issues around the dominance of English and the challenge for learners is similar across the educational levels, and you will be able to apply the arguments you have read already to English as a medium of instruction in universities.

3.5 English in higher education

Figures 3.5 and 3.6, from international universities in countries where English is not the dominant language, are indicative of university web pages worldwide. What they have in common is the use of the English language, often in addition to other local languages.

Activity 3.4

Look carefully at the images of university home pages in Figures 3.5 and 3.6. Is English used alongside other languages? Is it more or less prominent? Is this what you would have expected? What motives are there behind this use of English? What is the function of the home pages?

Allow about
5 minutes

Figure 3.5 University of Cape Town website

Figure 3.6 University of València website

Comment

You may have been surprised at the use of English home pages for universities in Spain and South Africa, although both pages also have tabs to other language versions. The status of English in the education systems in these countries is very different, yet it has been considered necessary or worthwhile to create home pages in English with hyperlinks to other pages, also in English. The function of university home pages is both **ideational** and **interpersonal**.

These concepts are further discussed in another book in this series: Allington and Mayor (eds) (2012), Chapter 1.

They are designed both to *supply information* about the university to present and prospective students, staff and others with an interest (ideational), and also to *attract* would-be students, donors or sponsors (interpersonal). The effort to be attractive can be seen in the pictures chosen for Cape Town and in the text for València. To me, Cape Town's main picture suggests a pleasant environment, but more importantly, the classical-style architecture calls to mind traditional European buildings on the lines of Greek temples. The message coming through is that Cape Town University follows in the footsteps and traditions of the great seats of learning of the past. The text for València is positive and modern, emphasising the range of facilities and courses on offer. It is personalised through the use of pronouns: '*our* University', '*your* future'. The main picture picks up modernity and students through soft focus superimposed images of people (students?) apparently talking or studying in a relaxed setting. The top right picture, however, like Cape Town, suggests solid, traditional architecture and, by implication, values and standards.

The use of English on university home pages and the layout of the pages are indicative of the position of the language in higher education and research contexts. As the figures for Australia in Table 3.1 indicate, universities have become international businesses, often juggling education for the local population with attracting overseas students who pay significantly higher fees. A survey of Australian universities illustrates the importance of international students studying on degree and non-degree courses.

Table 3.1 Numbers of international students studying in Australia

Sector	2008	2009	% growth
Higher education	174,713	196,007	12.2
Total (including non-degree courses)	433,918	491,565	13.3

(adapted from Australian Government, 2010)

The total of nearly half a million international students needs to be seen in the context of the overall Australian population of just over 22.5 million (Australian Bureau of Statistics, 2011). Students from China (31.2 per cent) and from India (13.5 per cent) were the largest groups, with Australia's northern neighbours Malaysia, Indonesia and Thailand also contributing strongly. In the UK in 2010 an estimated £2.5 billion was earned by universities through fees paid by international students, with an additional £2.5 billion going to local communities in exchange for housing and other goods and services (UK Council for International Student Affairs, 2010).

While economic considerations lead governments to encourage universities to attract international students, there are other significant benefits, as a report commissioned by Universities Australia indicates:

> international education enriches and changes Australian education and deepens relationships between nations. These social and cultural benefits are clearly of paramount importance in a world where international relations are undergoing rapid changes, and where Australia's future depends critically on its ability to establish diverse and productive international connections. ...
>
> We must identify and promote the many non-economic benefits of international education to Australia as a nation, to the individuals who benefit from it and to the regions around the globe from which they come.
>
> (Universities Australia, 2009)

As English has grown in importance as an international language, and international education has grown as a means of earning foreign currency, more universities in non-English dominant countries are also advertising themselves through English. Malaysia, for example, has ambitions to be a centre for higher education through the medium of English (Foo and Richards, 2004). In addition, countries which traditionally taught only in their own language or languages have started to move some or all of their curriculum into English. In Denmark, for example, many university courses are now taught through English (as discussed in Section 3.3), creating anxiety among some that Danish is under threat, especially in the domain of scientific research (Siiner, 2010). Analysis of how Danish and international students actually use language, however, indicates that in practice students codeswitch (Hultgren, n.d.) in much the same way as the school students in Reading B. For countries and institutions, then, the benefits of English are at least in part economic. But what of the motivations of students?

Activity 3.5

Allow about 15 minutes

Given the difficulties of learning through the medium of English for speakers of other languages, why do you think students are keen to take part in courses taught through English? A sample of the courses taught at the Nottingham Ningbo campus in China in 2011, listed below, might help to answer this question.

Architectural Environment Engineering	Finance Accounting and Management
Civil Engineering	International Business Management
Computer Science	International Economics and Trade
Environmental Engineering	International Studies
English Studies with International Business	Mechanical Engineering

(adapted from The University of Nottingham Ningbo, n.d.)

Comment

You may have noticed that many of the courses available at Nottingham Ningbo University are business, communication or science and technology orientated. This reflects the position of English in these spheres. Currently, it is recognised as the lingua franca of international business and of academic exchange, particularly in science and technology. Learning the skills and theory of business and management through English allows students to gain relevant academic, practical and language knowledge at the same time. The latest scientific research is circulated among members of the international academic community through journals which are largely English medium. While there are obvious problems for people having to learn another language in order to do their job, there are also benefits associated with having one globally dominant language. Doctors and researchers, for example, can use one language to access reports on drug developments, clinical trials and patient survival rates, attend international conferences in which the latest work is shared, and work in laboratories with people from all over the world.

Nottingham Ningbo is the first foreign partnership university approved by the Chinese Ministry of Education. Nottingham University also has a branch campus in Malaysia.

The global dominance of English in higher education has many critics. James Coleman (2006) outlined a number of concerns relating particularly to English-medium teaching in European universities. He highlights the dominance of English as a threat to policies of multilingualism in Europe, to cultural identity and to national education systems:

> What becomes of the famous *these-antithèse-synthèse* of a French academic essay? The distinctive approaches to lecturing in Italian, Spanish or German universities are part of the benefit of student exchanges, making young people question the narrowly ethnocentric, monocultural perspectives which too many of them take abroad, and a key element in developing their intercultural competence, their recognition that cultural norms are relative and not absolute, socially constructed and not given. How will they learn to look at their own culture in a new light if Anglo-American norms dominate a newly homogenized European academic discourse? If the only language on the PowerPoint slides is English?
>
> (Coleman, 2006, p. 10)

In universities which teach through English, recruiting academics with sufficient skill to lecture through English may create barriers for otherwise well-qualified staff and potentially an impoverished experience for students. The growth of English as the main language in much academic publishing means that researchers around the world need to write in English in order for their findings to reach a wide audience. It is not enough for scientists to be able to, for example, communicate via symbols and formulae; they need to be able to indicate the significance of their findings and how they fit into the bigger picture of research worldwide. A study of the professional literacy practices of academics in four continental European countries illustrated how they often rely on help with literacy in English and how this has a profound effect on the way in which research findings are disseminated around the world. In order to convey their research in a form likely to be accepted by English-language journals, many academics seek help from people who can assist in turning their texts into the appropriate form of writing for a scholarly English language publication. Put crudely, knowing the best person to help get research published in English may make the difference between ideas circulating largely in a national context or becoming known and possibly influential around the world (Lillis and Curry, 2010; Hewings et al., 2010). This brings us in the next section to a consideration of the type of English that is required in academic contexts.

3.6   English for academic purposes

The consequence of the dominance of English in the academic sphere is that many students need to acquire a command of English at institutions around the world. Universities in the UK, Australia and the USA, for example, have special departments that have been set up to assist students with **English for academic purposes (EAP)**, a specialist branch of the more general TESOL field. The assistance given in EAP classes may well be based on an analysis of the students' needs which takes into account when and where they will be using English, with whom, whether it is written or spoken, their current English language proficiency, and the disciplines or subjects being studied.

Activity 3.6   **Allow about**
                                                         5 minutes
Before reading on, consider the following questions:

- What do you think may be important features in 'academic' English? (Consider feedback that you have had on your academic work in the past.)

- If you have studied different subjects at university level, have you noticed different academic writing practices? If so, can you describe what they are?

- Who might benefit from being taught EAP?

Comment

You will look at the features of 'academic' English in the next activity and you will also compare different disciplines. If some of these features are new to you or surprising, then perhaps your answer to 'who might benefit' would be wider than just students for whom English is not their first language. In some institutions, EAP is no longer seen as only relevant to learners of English. The conventions, style and potential significance (passing examinations, getting work published) attached to academic writing mean that many native English speakers are also keen to benefit from EAP insights.

Specialists in any field develop common conventions and practices over time, and this includes writing in particular ways. For new members of any academic discipline these conventions need to be learnt: what procedures need to be followed, what are the relevant criteria for judging arguments and the validity of results, and what are the conventions of acceptable forms of argument?

Allow about 20 minutes

Activity 3.7

Read the following examples of specialised academic discourse. All three are extracts from the introductory sections of articles in research journals. As you read, focus on the following linguistic features: **lexis** (the particular words used, any specialised terminology) and overall **style** (e.g. whether they represent formal or informal, personal or impersonal ways of using language). Then consider:

* Which text is easiest for you to understand?
* What does reading them reveal about your own relationship to academic discourse communities?
* How do the texts differ?
* What, if anything, do they have in common in terms of style?

Example 1

As English continues its growth as a lingua franca, more and more speakers across the world find themselves in front of an audience that needs to hear the speaker's message in a language that neither speaker nor listener is entirely comfortable with. One reason for the discomfort can be traced to the extra time it takes to formulate one's message in a second language (L2). Slower English speakers in business meetings have inhibitions about taking the floor from native speakers (Rogerson-Revell, 2007), and international students may be frustrated by their inability to formulate responses quickly enough to contribute to classroom discussion (Jones, 1999). Though researchers have begun to explore the effect of L2 language use in interactive situations such as the meeting or the seminar, the ramifications of slower L2 speaking rates when holding an instructional monologue, such as a presentation or a lecture, have not been explored.

(Hincks, 2010, p. 4)

Example 2

In an essay published in the mid-nineteen-eighties Morton Bloomfield notes the sparseness of medieval English elegies. 'Elegies in the Middle English period tend to be incidental', he writes, 'with lamentation on someone's death occupying a small part of a longer poem. Chaucer's *Book of the Duchess* is, however, an elegy on the death of Blanche, wife of John of Gaunt.' Bloomfield then turns to the very different situation of Renaissance England: 'With the Renaissance, however, elegy enjoyed an exuberant growth which has never been explained, except perhaps with general reference to the revival of the classics, especially Latin. But this hardly accounts for the English Renaissance emphasis on elegy as a lament for a death. While there were some love elegies in the English Renaissance, the subject of most elegies was lamentation rather than wooing.'[1]

... What accounts for this change? ... Bloomfield's essay does not offer any alternative explanations. What is more, no subsequent study has focused in a sustained way on the issue he posed nearly twenty-five years ago.[3]

... What I propose is a sketch map for interpreting the development of the Renaissance English elegy.

(Wayland, 2009, pp. 429–30)

Example 3

The reductive deoxygenation of dimethyl sulfoxide to dimethyl sulfide is performed by bacteria from the genus *Rhodobacter*.[1, 2]

$$(CH_3)_2SO + 2H^+ + 2e^- \rightarrow (CH_3)_2S + H_2O \quad (1)$$

The enzyme responsible for this reaction is a mononuclear molybdoenzyme, which belongs to the DMSO reductase (DMSOR) family.[2–4] The two electrons in eq **1** are provided by the oxidation of the molybdenum center ($[Mo^{IV}] \rightarrow [Mo^{VI}]$). After the reduction of DMSO, for the molybdenum in the active site to return to the $[Mo^{IV}]$ state, the enzyme should go through a $[Mo^{V}]$ oxidation state.[2] ...

… Of special interest has been the temperature dependent dent MCD represented by the so-called C-term.(27) We shall here carry out DFT calculations on the MCD spectrum of [Mo^V] model systems to help in the interpretation of the experimental spectrum for DMSOR. Such a study should help with the understanding of the electronic structure of DMSOR-Mo[V].

(Hernandez-Marin et al., 2010)

Comment

My guess is that most readers of this book found Example 1 or Example 2 the easiest to comprehend, and Example 3 the hardest. Possible reasons for this are as follows.

The first example (which comes from the journal *English for Specific Purposes*) and the second (from *English Literary Renaissance*) include not only fewer specialised lexical items than the third (which is from the journal *Inorganic Chemistry*), but also fewer whose meaning is completely impenetrable to any reader who is 'outside' the specialised academic community of discourse. The meaning of technical terms such as *lingua franca*, *L2* (in Example 1), *elegy* and *English Renaissance* (Example 2) could perhaps be guessed at by educated 'outsiders' to the discourse of language study, if they drew on their general knowledge of English, but this is not possible for many of the terms in Example 3.

Examples 1 and 2 are both from fields of study (research into the learning of English in specific fields and English literature) which are relatively close to the subject matter of this book. Even if someone is not a 'full' member of the relevant research community, a reader of a book on the English language is more likely to have the kind of background knowledge required for making sense of an article on some aspect of English language teaching than for understanding the contents of *Inorganic Chemistry*.

The most obvious differences between the texts relate to their subject matter and the use of a different specialised lexis associated with a specific field of study. In chemistry this also involves conveying meaning through the additional code of mathematical symbols. Referencing conventions are also significantly different. Example 2 and Example 3 use numbers to reference the sources of their material. The numbers appear in colour in the online version of the article reproduced in Example 3 as they are hyperlinks to the full references. In Example 1, which is also reproduced from an online version, references are made using the name of the author. Again, in the online version the names appear in colour to indicate that they are hyperlinks to the full references.

The use of specialised lexis is itself a kind of similarity between the texts. But academic discourses have other characteristic features of style. One feature common to both Examples 1 and 3, which is typical of much writing in science and social science journals, is the lack or scarcity of overt references to the authors as individuals; they frequently disguise their personal opinions or agency through the use of passive constructions (*can be traced to, have not been explored*). Example 2, on the other hand, uses the pronoun *I*. In addition, the three examples have an obvious functional similarity: each introduces a report of research. John Swales (1990), an influential researcher in the field of academic writing, has suggested that the introductions to research articles often have a common basic structure, which reflects the aim of authors to claim a niche for themselves and their work in the research field in which they are involved. This is often done by indicating a gap in current knowledge (*... the ramifications of slower L2 speaking rates when holding an instructional monologue, such as a presentation or a lecture,* **have not been explored***; Bloomfield's essay* **does not offer** *any alternative explanations. What is more,* **no subsequent study has focused** *in a sustained way on the issue he posed nearly twenty-five years ago. ...* **What I propose is** *...;* **Such a study should help with** *the understanding of the electronic structure of DMSOR-Mo[V]*).

The idea of creating a niche is closely tied up with academic writing as argument, something that is designed to persuade the reader to agree with the findings or point of view put forward. You may already be aware of the difficulties in finding the right voice in academic writing, particularly one in which you can state your point of view. Someone who is a novice in a discipline may not feel able to direct a reader, such as a tutor marking their work, to do something or see something in a particular way or might feel uncomfortable using conventions such as referencing or impersonal constructions such as *it is important to,* or directives such as *note that*. Additionally, for students whose first language is not English, their own rhetorical traditions or those they have been taught are likely to influence their writing choices. For all students, learning to write within a discipline means that they are learning to write as a physicist, a geographer, a sociologist, and so on. They are taking on an identity within those disciplinary communities. For student writers working across a number of disciplines, the challenge is even greater. It does, however, start to explain why a student may be a successful writer in, say, anthropology but deemed unsuccessful in biology. Based on what we know of disciplinary discourse communities, it is unlikely that the writing practices associated with one discipline will transfer neatly across to another. The writing requirements of English literature, for example, are certainly different from those of English language. For higher education students then, like pupils starting school, learning the language of the discipline is one part of the learning of a new identity – as a linguist or a historian writing in English.

3.7 Conclusion

I started this chapter by asking you to put yourself in the place of someone learning through a language that was not their main language. You then read in detail about language policy in Malaysia and its relationship to the country's history, ethnic mix, and social and economic aspirations. You looked at statistics on the use of English in higher education institutions and examined the layout and function of university home pages. Extracts of academic articles formed the basis of activities investigating how English is adapted to the needs of academic disciplines. All this and more, you have accomplished using English. How well would you have coped in another language? Would you have expected teachers to take into account your existing linguistic knowledge and skills? Do you have sympathy with those who resent the dominance of English as they struggle to understand complex ideas in an unfamiliar language? Do you agree with those in charge of language policy and planning that knowledge of English is essential for personal and national advancement, or do you feel, rather, that the juggernaut of an international language ought to be resisted? Or could conflict between languages be resolved through policies designed to recognise and encourage languaging skills as a means to promote linguistic co-existence?

READING A: Tensions between language policy and practice in Malaysia

Peter Martin

Source: Martin, P. (2005) '"Safe" language practices in two rural schools in Malaysia: tensions between policy and practice' in Lin, A. M. Y. and Martin, P. W. (eds) *Decolonisation, Globalisation: Language-in-Education Policy and Practice*, Clevedon, Multilingual Matters, pp. 74–97.

Lesson A: (primary two, English)

This lesson was built around 'Unit 4: I'm Hungry' in the textbook *English 2* (Mutiara & Azly, 1996: 35), particularly the 'Listen and Say' activity, reproduced below:

> *Greg eats a green apple.*
>
> *Brian eats brown bread.*
>
> *The cook looks at the cook book.*
>
> *Glen holds a glass.*
>
> *There is salt and sugar on Tini's thumbs.*

The text is superimposed over a colour sketch of four children sitting at a table covered in a floral cloth. One boy is eating an apple, another boy is eating a piece of brown bread, and a third is holding a glass. A girl appears to be sifting salt and sugar through her hands and into two containers marked 'salt' and 'sugar'. Behind the table, a woman is stirring the contents of a pan on a raised stove. She is consulting a 'cook book'. The woman is wearing an apron and a chef's hat. Behind the woman is a shelf displaying dinner plates. [...]

[T]he pattern of discourse [used] in this classroom [...] includes reading through the text, jointly accomplished by teacher and pupils, and bilingual annotation of key words and concepts in the text. The teacher is able to establish, through the interaction that takes place, that the pupils understand the term 'green'.

The interactional strategies [...] continue throughout the lesson. The reading performance is jointly shared by the teacher and the students. The teacher then orchestrates the annotation of particular sections of text, using a range of pedagogical resources, and making use of both English and Malay. Noticeably, Sa'ben (a language common to all in the classroom) is not used as part of the lesson.

It is useful to look more closely at some of the linguistic resources used by the teacher. Extract 3 provides the next section of the lesson.

Extract 3 (lines 31–65)

Transcription conventions

T: Teacher
P: Pupil
Ps: Pupils
Plain font: English
Bold font: Malay
<*Italics*>:
<*English glosses*>
'brown bread': indicates reading from the textbook or other resource
'.': indicates a pause

	T:	aah . green . second one . 'Brian'
	Ps:	'Brian'
	T:	'eats'
	Ps:	'eats'
35	**T:**	'brown bread'
	Ps:	'brown bread'
	T:	where's Brian . **yang mana** Brian? <*which one is* Brian> . where's Brian? **yang mana** Brian? (*which one is* Brian> **dalam gambar** <*in the picture*> . look **dalam gambar** <*in the*
40		picture> . **apa yang dia makan itu?** <*what is he eating?*>
	P:	bread
	T:	bread . **apa itu?** <*what's that?*>
	P:	**roti** <*bread*>
	T:	**itu yang kita panggil** bread <*that's what's called* bread> .
45		**Bahasa Inggeris** <*English*> bread . **apa warna** bread **yang dia makan?** <*what's the colour of the* bread *he is eating?*> . what is the colour of the bread? ... what is the colour of the bread? what is the colour of the bread? . **apa warnanya?** <*what's the colour?*>
50	**P:**	brown
	T:	ah?
	P:	brown
	T:	brown
	Ps:	brown
55	**T:**	brown bread
	Ps:	brown bread
	T:	**dalam kelas ini apa yang** brown? <*in this class is there anything that's brown?*>
	Ps:	[inaudible]

60	**P:**	**roti** *<bread>*
	T:	**apa yang** brown? *<what's* brown?*>*
	P:	**muka** *<face>*
	T:	**ah muka kamu** brown **lah** *<ah your face is* brown*>*
	P:	**meja** *<table>*
65	**T:**	**itu warna yang dipanggil** brown *<that's the colour called* brown*>*
	P:	brown
	T:	**roti pun namanya** bread *<the name for* **roti** *is* bread*>*. 'the cook'

Focusing specifically on lines 37–46, it is clear that there are different ways in which the classroom participants organise the exchanges that form the building blocks of the lesson. The two IRF (Initiation-Response-Feedback) exchanges below, for example, show that the initiations (by the teacher) in both exchanges are made in Malay. The pupils' responses, though, are different, the first one being in English 'bread' and the second one in Malay '**roti**'.

Exchange 1:	I	**T:**	**apa yang dia makan itu**? *<what is he eating?>*
	R	**P:**	bread
	F	**T:**	bread

Exchange 2:	I	**T:**	**apa itu**? *<what's that?>*
	R	**P:**	**roti** *<bread>*
	F	**T:**	**itu yang kita panggil** bread *<that's what's called* bread*>*

The discourse in this classroom, then, allows for either English or Malay in the response slot, and I would argue that this is an important and pragmatic discourse strategy in this context. It is also 'safe' in that, potentially, it facilitates comprehension.

In Extract 4, where the particular section of text being discussed is 'the cook looks at the cook book', the teacher uses a different technique.

Extract 4 (lines 79–97)

	T:	tengok buku kamu *<look at your books>* .. OK **yang mana**
80		**yang** cook? *<which one is the* cook?*>*. **apa** cook **itu?** *<what is*
		a cook>. **tukang masak** *<cook>*. **di sekolah sini ada tukang**
		masak? *<in this school is there a cook?>*
	Ps:	**ada** *<yes>*
	T:	**apa nama dia?** *<what's her name?>*
85	P:	Rodiah
	T:	Rodiah . **siapa lagi?** *<who else?>*
	Ps:	Sepai
	T:	Sepai **jadi** . **tukang masak itu kami panggil** the cook *<so .*
		*we call the **tukang masak** the cook>*. **apa yang dia tengok**
90		**sana?** *<what is she looking at there?>*
	P:	**buku** *<book>*
	P:	**buku** *<book>*
	T:	**buku** . **apa warna buku itu?** *<what colour is the book?>*
	P:	**coklat** *<brown>*
95	P:	pink
	P:	brown
	T:	brown . ah . brown . [inaudible] .. OK the next one . 'Glen'

In this sequence, the teacher is not able to elicit the meaning of 'cook' from the pupils. The picture in the textbook shows a woman, wearing an odd-looking hat (in actual fact, a chef's hat), stirring a pan, and reading a book. It is rather a confusing image for the pupils in this particular context, as cooking and reading at the same time (indeed, the whole cultural concept of 'cook book' and 'recipe') would not be part of their cultural knowledge.

The pupils are not able to provide a response to the teacher's initiation '**apa** cook **itu?**' ('what is a cook?') in line 80. This is clearly an attempt from the teacher to get the pupils to provide the Malay equivalent, as he himself then provides the Malay gloss, **tukang masak** (line 81) in his next statement. That the pupils understand the concept of **tukang masak** ('cook') becomes clear as they provide the names of the two school cooks. As for any discussion about the 'cook book', the teacher focuses simply on the colour of the book. It is highly unlikely that the concept of 'cook book' (i.e. a book containing recipes) will be understood. [...]

What we can see in this lesson is a mixture of two languages: the language of the text, English, and the language of mediation, Malay. No use of Sa'ben was noted, not even in the introduction to the lesson. The pupils' responses were largely limited to single word labels, in either English or Malay. The language practices here, then, are 'safe' in that they allow the classroom participants to accomplish the lesson, albeit by using one school language, Malay, to teach the other school language, English. The juxtaposition of these two languages in the classroom, neither of which has any currency in the communities served by the school, shows the participants' pragmatic response to the policies imposed from above. One other striking feature of this lesson is the text and the accompanying sketch, both of which are culturally loaded. [...]

Tensions in classroom practices in the local/global context

[...] The clearest disengagement with language policy in the classrooms observed is that other linguistic resources are being used alongside the official language of the lessons. This is common practice in a large range of contexts, for example, Botswana (Arthur, 1996), Brunei (Martin, 1999, 2003), Kenya (Bunyi [2005]), and South Africa (Brock-Utne [2005]; Probyn [2005]), to name but a few. The use of a local language alongside the 'official' language of the lesson is a well-known phenomenon and yet, for a variety of reasons, it is often lambasted as 'bad practice', blamed on teachers' lack of English-language competence, or put to one side and/or swept under the carpet. In a [...] discussion of the impact of English as a global language on educational policies and practices in the Asia-Pacific region, for example, little mention is made of the way teachers switch between languages to accomplish lessons (Nunan, 2003). The prevailing rhetoric in the Malaysian context, as evidenced by [an] editorial from the major government-controlled English-medium newspaper [...], is how use of the local language is 'sabotaging' the language policy rather than, for example, helping to bail it out.

Several authors have referred to the hegemony of English, specifically where English is the medium of instruction, and the inequalities that arise. Of particular relevance to this study is the unequal access to English-language education in Malaysia between urban and rural areas. As noted by Toh (1984: 260, cited in Pennycook, 1994: 203), 'the formal educational system in Malaysia has been utilised more as a mechanism for the intergenerational transmission of economic status by high-status families rather than as a vehicle for the social advancement of the poor'. These high-status families are generally found in the urban areas. According to Tollefson (2000: 18), these inequalities can result in 'classes that are not meaningful to most children'. Braighlinn (1992: 21), with reference to the Brunei situation, makes a similar point, suggesting that the 'majority of non-middle-class youth receive virtually no education at all, because the medium of instruction [English] cannot be understood'. While not arguing with the sentiments expressed here, I would suggest that such statements are only partially true, as they do not take into account the often creative, pragmatic and 'safe' practices of the classroom participants in such contexts. One of the most significant of these 'safe' practices is 'code-switching' between the official language of the lesson and a language which the classroom participants have greater access to, usually a shared local language. In the classrooms in this study, the major language used to annotate the lessons is Malay, like English a language that is foreign to the two areas, albeit the official language of the nation, and a language in which the pupils have had the bulk of their education. I use the term 'safe' here after Chick (1996) and Hornberger and Chick (2001), but with my own slant, to refer to practices that allow the classroom participants to be seen to accomplish lessons. However, although the practices are 'safe' in that a language (or languages) in which the participants have greater access is used to annotate the lessons, there is little exploratory use of 'language' in the classroom.

The use of two or more languages, or 'code-switching', in the classroom creates its own tensions, particularly in the educational hierarchy outside the classroom. Language choice issues in the classroom are, in fact, much more complex than can be legislated for (cf. Merritt *et al.*, 1992). Several studies show how language planners, curriculum developers and school inspectors regard such bilingual practices as code-switching as a substandard form of communication in the classroom (for example, Lin, 1996; Martin, 2003). One reason for the lack of official recognition of or support for these practices might be the concern about the efficiency of a pedagogy that supports the switching between languages. But how much is actually known about this? [...] Another reason might be the pervasive influence of what Phillipson (1992: 185) has referred to as the 'monolingual fallacy', that is, the view that English is best taught monolingually [...].

The dynamics of the interaction for learning and teaching bilingually are under-researched. And yet we need to question whether bilingual interaction strategies 'work' in the classroom context. For example, are bilingual exchanges of the type shown in Excerpt 3 in this study in Malaysian classrooms useful for the students and do they facilitate learning? Can classroom code-switching support communication, particularly the exploratory talk which is such an essential part of the learning process? A corollary to this is whether teacher-training programmes (both pre-service and in-service), in multilingual contexts take into account the realities and pragmatics of classroom language use in such contexts. Questions such as these are critical in view of the fact that an increasing number of governments 'are introducing English as a compulsory subject at younger and younger ages, often without adequate funding, [and] teacher education for elementary school teachers' (Nunan, 2003: 591). […]

Conclusion

[…] [This] study purposely gives emphasis to the actual language practices in the schools, as […] it is fundamental that planners and policy-makers need to be aware of what is happening in the classroom, and how the participants in the classroom are putting policy into practice. The language practices […] are presented against a backdrop of the official policy, and the tensions inherent in the policy, as well as within a local, national, and global framework. […] In education and literacy (including electronic literacy), English and Malay predominate, and [students'] own languages are relegated to also-rans. The tensions between policy and practice in this study have led to what I refer to as 'safe' (but not necessarily pedagogically 'sound') practices in the classrooms. I conclude with the plea that as English is accepted as the contemporary global language, it is necessary to ensure that efforts are made to ensure equality of access to languages, including their own languages.

References for this reading

Arthur, J. (1996) Code-switching and collusion: Classroom interaction in Botswana primary schools. *Linguistics and Education* 8 (1), 17–33.

Braighlinn, G. (1992) *Ideological Innovation under Monarchy. Aspects of Legitimation Activity in Contemporary Brunei.* Amsterdam: VU University Press.

Brock-Utne, B. (2005) Language-in-education policies and practices in Africa with a special focus on Tanzania and South Africa – Insights from research in progress. In A.M.Y. Lin and P.W. Martin (eds) *Decolonisation, Globalisation: Language-in-Education Policy and Practice* (pp. 173–93). Clevedon: Multilingual Matters.

Bunyi, G. (2005) 'Language classroom practices in Kenya. In A.M.Y. Lin and P.W. Martin (eds) *Decolonisation, Globalisation: Language-in-Education Policy and Practice* (pp. 131–52). Clevedon: Multilingual Matters.

Chick, K. (1996) Safe-talk: Collusion in apartheid education. In H. Coleman (ed.) *Society and the Language Classroom* (pp. 21–39). Cambridge: Cambridge University Press.

Hornberger, N. and Chick, K. (2001) Co-constructing school safetime: Safetalk practices in Peruvian and South African classrooms. In M. Heller and M. Martin-Jones (eds) *Voices of Authority. Education and Linguistic Difference* (pp. 31–56). Westport, CT: Ablex Publishers.

Lin, A.M.Y. (1996) Bilingualism or linguistic segregation? Symbolic domination, resistance and code-switching in Hong Kong schools. *Linguistics and Education* 8 (1), 49–84.

Martin, P.W. (1999) Close encounters of a bilingual kind: Interactional practices in the primary classroom in Brunei. *International Journal of Educational Development* 19 (2), 127–40.

Martin, P.W. (2003) Bilingual encounters in the classroom. In J-M. Dewaele, A. Housen and Li Wei (eds) *Bilingualism: Beyond Basic Principles* (pp. 67–87). Clevedon: Multilingual Matters.

Merritt, M., Cleghorn, A., Abagi, J.O. and Bunyi, G. (1992) Socialising multilingualism: Determinants of code-switching in Kenyan primary classrooms. *Journal of Multilingual and Multicultural Development* 13 (1&2), 103–22.

Mutiara Hj Mohamad and Azly Abdul Rahman (1996) *English Year 2*. Kuala Lumpur: Dewan Bahasa dan Pustaka.

Nunan, D. (2003) The impact of English as a global language on educational policies and practices in the Asia-Pacific region. *TESOL Quarterly* 37 (4), 589–613.

Pennycook, A. (1994) *The Cultural Politics of English as an International Language*. London: Longman.

Phillipson, R. (1992) *Linguistic Imperialism*, Oxford: Oxford University Press.

Probyn, M. (2005) Language in the struggle to learn: The intersection of classroom realities, language policies and neo-colonial and globalisation discourses in South African schools. In A.M.Y. Lin and P.W. Martin (eds) *Decolonisation, Globalisation: Language-in-Education Policy and Practice* (pp. 153–72). Clevedon: Multilingual Matters.

Toh Kin Woon (1984) Education as a vehicle for reducing economic inequality. In S. Husin Ali (ed.) *Ethnicity, Class and Development: Malaysia* (pp. 224–64). Kuala Lumpur: Persatuan Sains Sosial Malaysia.

Tollefson, J. (2000) Policy and ideology in the spread of English. In J.K. Hall and W.G. Eggington (eds) *The Sociopolitics of English Language Teaching* (pp. 7–21). Clevedon: Multilingual Matters.

READING B: English lessens

Frank Monaghan

Specially commissioned for this book.

There is something about the teaching of English that has made it a lightning rod for politicians, journalists and some sections of civil society. Panics about the state of English often reflect a wider discomfort about the state of England (or America, or Australia ...).

What might the appropriate status of English be in a world where English has spread so widely across the globe while at the same time people from all over that globe are now settling in ever-increasing numbers in English-dominant countries, bringing with them their own languages and cultures?

Moral panics about language are discussed in detail in Chapter 8.

From discussions in Chapters 1 and 2 you will be familiar with the consequences of the spread of English to large parts of the world: that 'English' is a slippery thing to define and no longer 'belongs' to the English (or Americans, Australians, Canadians, etc.); that the consequences of its presence abroad are not always benign; that we would do well to consider the linguistic rights of others. This reading considers some of the consequences of that 'other' world turning up inside the classrooms of English-dominant settings.

Let's start with the notion of *the* English language, for example. There cannot ever be a definitive codification of it, in terms either of its grammar or of its vocabulary as these are subject to change over time and across space. Even if we agree to limit the description to standard English, there would then be the question of which standard English we are talking about. Unless we are prepared to accept the notion of American standard English being a separate language from British standard English or Indian standard English, we will have to accept that there is no one entity that can be identified as *the* English language. When we then take into account all the various mutually intelligible dialects and creoles that form the continuum that might be gathered under the English umbrella (or parasol for the sunnier varieties), it becomes clearer why some linguists do not regard the concept of discrete languages as a particularly useful one. Indeed, some linguists have argued that it is not even a necessary one. This, perhaps surprising, claim is at the heart of the notion of **languaging**, which proposes that people use a range of lexical and syntactic resources to communicate and that labelling them 'English' or 'Spanish', or indeed

'Scouse' or 'Patois', does not add much to our understanding – in fact it can get in the way. This is particularly the case in multilingual settings, which are increasingly becoming the norm. The 'language' as opposed to the 'languaging' approach is tied to a monolingual norm in which it is assumed that the target language (assuming it to be a fixed, stable and uncontested object) represents the ultimate learning goal and that we need to keep languages separate. This has had considerable consequences not only for classroom practices and underlying assumptions about the status of English in education, but also more broadly for the kind of society we live in.

In terms of education, there are those who believe that the second language should be kept out of the classroom so that the learners are exposed to English only. The outcome of this 'sink or swim' approach is termed **subtractive bilingualism**: the child's first language is effectively replaced with the second. Where there is an ostensibly positive attitude to bilingualism and where the aim is to add to the child's repertoire, the desired outcome is referred to as **additive bilingualism**. However, bilingual education is often limited to the idea that the home language is valuable in supporting the child's transition to the dominant language. In England, for example, the Department for Children, Schools and Families (DCSF) published a document entitled *The New Arrivals Excellence Programme Guidance*, which stated:

> They need to have their bilingualism (and sometimes multilingualism) recognised as a positive part of their intellectual development and *they need opportunities to use their home language to support their learning and development of English.*
>
> (DCSF, 2007, p. 37, my emphasis)

Ofelia García, a leading proponent of the languaging approach, has focused her research on bilingual learners in New York. She rejects the notions of subtractive and additive bilingualism on the grounds that both are essentially monolingual in orientation and argues that we should replace these essentially monolingual conceptualisations with what she terms **dynamic bilingualism**, a concept that acknowledges the reality that multilingual people in multilingual settings do not naturally keep their languages apart but operate in much more fluid and complex ways:

One of the things that language teachers would then have to contend with is that speakers and learners do not ever 'have' English or any other language but rather what we do with languages is we use them, we 'do' languages, that is why the term '*languaging*' has come into our profession.

The idea is that people use languages, do languages, have languaging, but they do not ever *have* language. We do language to negotiate situations ... we do not ever get students to really 'have' English or 'be' English speakers, but ... this language learning is used and learned through practice in very specific social contexts over the course of a lifetime. ... It's a continuum that never ends.

(García, 2010, pp. 4–5)

Some examples from her classroom-based research will help to illustrate the point she is making. In this first one, García describes how a child, Alicia, in an ESL (English as a second language) class, dialogues with herself to help make sense of what the teacher is trying to teach her:

I am sitting next to Alicia outside, and the teacher is going through some comparative exercise, 'this tree is bigger, that tree is smaller'. ... I am sitting next to Alicia and she is trying it out under her breath and she says 'this tree is grander', which is, of course, 'grande' from the Spanish ...

(García, 2010, p. 6)

Alicia has taken the morpheme 'er' (appropriate to form a comparative in English) and attached it to a Spanish adjective, which is not how the comparative is formed in that language. Under a more conventional approach to language teaching this would typically be treated as an error. Viewed from García's languaging perspective, this is evidence of the way people naturally use all the linguistic resources at their disposal to make meanings. This is a classic example of *doing* language rather than having a language.

In this next example García records an exchange between two children in a kindergarten class counting pumpkin seeds:

Herman: I have *veinticinco y* I need *dos mas*. No *tres*, look! (Counts to *veinticinco* in Spanish.) I only have *veintitres* now … *veinticinco*. I need *dos*!

[I have twenty-five and I need two more. No three, look! I only have twenty-three now … twenty-five. I need two!]

Rosaria: *Necesitas una? Toma ese … Yo tiene una mas.*

[You need another? Take this … I have another one.]

(adapted from García, 2010, p. 7)

The kindergarten operates on a 'two-way bilingual' model, whereby teachers and children officially spend half the day speaking and working in English and the other half in Spanish. Reality dictates otherwise, as the children 'language' using whatever linguistic resource best meets their communication purposes. García also provides fascinating insights into the children's individual backgrounds (Herman speaks Arabic at home, rather than English, and Rosaria's mother is American and English-speaking only and her father is Mexican and bilingual. Rosaria, she tells us, has some Spanish, 'it's not perfect, but it's enough' (García, 2010, p. 7). Enough, that is, to help Herman with his counting problem.

Children's languaging is not restricted to curriculum content, but covers all aspects of their efforts to make meaning. In the following example, García describes an English-speaking student who intervenes to ensure a newly arrived Spanish-speaking student is inducted into classroom routines:

Here we have Aristides, who is a translator – I've got millions of examples of Aristides. He always wants to make sure that everybody makes sense of what the teacher is saying. So, one day, the teacher is looking at Irene, who doesn't speak any English, and she is going: 'I'm getting angry at you!' and Aristides can't help it anymore, he gets up and he says: *Que tienes que escuchar a la maestra, Irene!* You have to listen to the teacher!

(García, 2010, p. 7)

Children don't only need to learn how to count or form comparatives, they have to learn how to be a student in a new environment and sometimes fellow students are best placed to help them with that.

As is clear from the above extracts, a striking feature of García's research is that she starts from the children, what they can and need to be enabled to do, rather than from a curriculum document and what it says they (and their teachers) should be able to do. It's also significant that she relates the children's specific biographies to their learning; this is because in this model:

> Bilingual education is much more than a technique or a pedagogy … it is also a way of equalizing opportunities. It rests on principles of social justice, and supports social practices for learning.
>
> (García, 2009, p. 386)

This larger vision leads to an equally large and challenging proposal:

> bilingual education should be the only option to teach all children in the twenty-first century in equitable ways.
>
> (García, 2009, p. 387)

That represents a significant challenge for top-down curriculum models and, in terms of teacher education, it also raises very significant issues about the kinds of attributes, skills, knowledge and understanding that teachers would need to have in order to work effectively. This would inevitably involve a great deal of change and investment in training and assumes that dynamic bilingualism rather than static monolingualism is the norm. Why should we do it?

Within English-dominant countries demographic changes have led to the establishment of large groups of people who do not have English as their first language, and it could be argued that the marketplace is responding to their multilingualism faster than is the education system or indeed society at large. In the USA, for example, Spanish speakers spend some US$400 billion a year, almost a quarter of the nation's purchasing power. In 1970, Spanish language advertising yielded US $14.3 million; thirty years later this had grown to US$786 million (García, 2009, p. 98). As of 2005, all prime-time TV shows on the ABC network (America's second largest) became available dubbed in Spanish. It has also been argued that Latinos, in certain regions of the United States, who are bilingual out-earn those who speak only English (Boswell, 2000). As more and more people are using languages other than English on the internet, for example, and digital technologies increasingly make the production of multilingual resources and communication ever more accessible (Edwards, 2004), it seems reasonable to conclude that the future is multi- rather than monolingual and this is evident in the make-up of modern schools.

In the Antipodes, North America and the UK, and in urban areas in particular, it is not surprising to find classrooms where anything between 30 per cent and 100 per cent of the students are learning English as an additional language and/or are from a minority ethnic group. This point is illustrated by the figures in Table 1 which show the percentage of pupils with English as an Additional Language in primary and secondary schools in England, based on statistics compiled by the Department for Education (2011).

Table 1 Percentage of pupils with English as an Additional Language in English schools 2005–2010

	Primary	Secondary
2005	11.5%	9.0%
2006	12.5%	9.5%
2007	13.5%	10.6%
2008	14.4%	10.8%
2009	15.2%	11.1%
2010	16.0%	11.6%

The evidence would suggest that increasing linguistic diversity is a trend that is set to continue into the future. Given such facts, is it fair or even practical for English (or indeed any national language) to carry on as if it were the only language in town? Quite apart from issues of social justice, it is also worth noting that there is a substantial body of research showing the positive advantages of bilingualism and of ensuring that bilingual learners maintain and develop their mother tongues alongside another language.

Jim Cummins, a leading researcher in this field, has identified six clear findings that have emerged from over 150 studies conducted over the last thirty-five years or so (Cummins, 2001):

1   Bilingualism has positive effects on children's linguistic and educational development. The German poet Goethe once wrote, *Wer fremde Sprachen nicht kennt, weiß nichts von seiner eigenen* ('To know no foreign languages is to know nothing of one's own'). This points to what has now been well established by research, that knowledge of other languages deepens understanding and flexibility of thought more generally.

2   The level of development of children's mother tongue is a strong predictor of their second language development. A solid foundation in a first language helps develop stronger literacy in a second. They are mutually supportive.

3   Mother tongue promotion in school develops not only the mother tongue but also children's abilities in the majority school language. This arises logically out of the previous two points. Similarly, where the mother tongue is neglected there is a strong risk of the child's personal and conceptual development being undermined.

4   Spending instructional time through a minority language in the school does not hurt children's academic development in the majority school language. When children study subjects through the medium of their own language, they do not just learn language but also concepts and intellectual skills which are then more easily transferred to a second language than acquired through it.

5   Children's mother tongues are fragile and easily lost in the early years of school. If children have limited access to their mother tongue, then they can lose their ability to communicate in it within two to three years. In general, we see a trend of language loss within two to three generations such that by the time many bilingual children reach adolescence there is a growing communication gap between them and their wider families, and they can become alienated from both their home and school cultures, with predictably negative consequences.

6   To reject a child's language in the school is to reject the child. If children feel that their cultural and linguistic identity is not valued by the school, then they are much less likely to be active and confident learners.

Cummins concludes:

> the cultural, linguistic and intellectual capital of our societies will
> increase dramatically when we stop seeing culturally and
> linguistically diverse children as 'a problem to be solved' and
> instead open our eyes to the linguistic, cultural, and intellectual
> resources they bring from their homes to our schools and
> societies.

(Cummins, 2001, p. 20)

García's invitation to us to make the conceptual shift from the idea of
inexpert second language use to one of children skilfully deploying the
full panoply of linguistic resources raises a fundamental question: in our
increasingly linguistically diverse schools is a monolingual English
approach an appropriate vehicle for preparing students, all students, for
life in an increasingly interconnected, interdependent, multilingual and
culturally diverse twenty-first century?

References for this reading

Boswell, T. (2000) 'Demographic changes in Florida and their importance for
effective educational policies and practices' in Roca, A. (ed.) *Research on Spanish
in the United States: Linguistic Issues and Challenges*, Somerville, MA, Cascadilla
Press.

Cummins, J. (2001) 'Bilingual children's mother tongue: why is it important for
education?', *Sprogforum*, no. 19, pp. 15–20; also available at
http://inet.dpb.dpu.dk/infodok/sprogforum/Espr19/CumminsENG.pdf
(Accessed 13 May 2011).

Department for Children, Schools and Families (DCSF) (2007) *The New
Arrivals Excellence Programme Guidance*, London, DCSF Publications.

Department for Education (DfE) (2011) *Schools, Pupils and their Characteristics*
[online], http://www.education.gov.uk/rsgateway/sc-schoolpupil.shtml
(Accessed 8 September 2011).

Edwards, V. (2004) *Multilingualism in the English-Speaking World: Pedigree of
Nations*, Chichester, Wiley-Blackwell.

García, O. (2009) *Bilingual Education in the 21st Century: A Global Perspective*,
Chichester, Wiley-Blackwell.

García, O. (2010) 'Reimagining bilingualism in education for the 21st century',
NALDIC Quarterly, vol. 7, no. 2, pp. 4–11.

4 English the industry

John Gray

4.1 Introduction

Since the 1980s, books aimed at the general reader that purport to tell 'the story' of English have become popular in the English-speaking world. Robert McCrum's (2010) *Globish: How the English Language Became the World's Language* is typical of the genre and, as the back cover blurb explains, the story is one of extraordinary success in terms of global reach:

> The English language has reached a point of no-return. More vivid and universal than ever before, English is now used, in some form, by approximately 4 billion people on earth, one third of the planet. ... Contagious, adaptable, populist and subversive, the English language has become as much a part of global consciousness as MS-DOS or the combustion engine. You could say that English plus Microsoft equals a new cultural revolution. The English language has, it seems, become a power in itself ...

But the story of English is a multifaceted one and not all aspects of the language's remarkable trajectory have received equal attention in either the popular or the academic literature. This chapter sets out to explore a frequently neglected aspect of this success story, namely the commercial dimension of the global spread of English. At the same time, it seeks to shed light on the suggestion made at the end of the blurb on McCrum's book that English can now be seen as a kind of agentive 'power in itself'.

You will recall the suggestion from Chapter 1 that in an increasingly globalised world English can be thought of as a kind of commodity, and that the French sociologist, Pierre Bourdieu, took the view that language functions as a form of capital in the modern economy. Before continuing, it is necessary to think about these economic metaphors in a little more depth and to consider their meanings more precisely. Let us begin with the concept of English as a commodity – a term which is normally applied to the products that can be bought and sold in the marketplace. On first view, English might seem an unusual candidate for commodity status as it is clearly not a product in the same way that a car or television is. To think about how such a term might be applied to language it is useful to begin by considering the economic model most closely associated with the current phase of globalisation. This is known as **neoliberalism** and it is based on the belief that an unfettered market economy is the best guarantor of human freedom and that the role of government is primarily to guarantee and extend the reach of the market. As the geographer and Marxist theorist David Harvey (2005, p. 166) explains, neoliberalism is also about 'putting a price on things that were never actually produced as commodities' – for example, entities such as culture, history and heritage. Neoliberal policies ultimately seek to incorporate as many aspects of human experience and activity as possible into the sphere of the economy and subject them to market forces. Below I consider some of the consequences of this.

In a globalised world, typified by economies based on neoliberal principles, the purpose of schooling and higher education is re-construed primarily in terms of servicing the needs of the economy. For example, a report commissioned by the UK government and published in 2010 made the point that, in today's world, education matters because 'it drives innovation and economic transformation' and because it 'helps to produce economic growth, which in turn contributes to national prosperity' (Browne, 2010, p. 14). In such a climate, the Canadian scholar Monica Heller (2002) suggests, languages and language learning are also viewed in largely economic terms – in the sense that some languages come to be seen as *worth* more than others. Bourdieu's concept of language as a form of capital is not dissimilar to this. He argues that utterances in the standard dialect of a language (e.g. standard British English), in contrast to those in a non-standard dialect (e.g. Glaswegian), are not simply 'signs to be understood and deciphered; they are also *signs of wealth*, intended to be evaluated and appreciated' (Bourdieu, 1991, p. 66).

<table>
<tr><td>**Allow about
10 minutes**</td><td>

Activity 4.1

Reflect on these economic metaphors and consider to what extent you agree that a price can be put on language. In what ways can language be seen as a commodity and a form of capital?

</td></tr>
</table>

Comment

In the current phase of globalisation those languages which may provide their speakers with a competitive edge in the job market are frequently packaged, promoted and sold in terms of the potential economic reward or the opportunities they can bring. The Japanese advertisement for English in Chapter 1 is a good example of language being packaged as a commodity. This can be seen as a departure from more traditional reasons for learning foreign languages, one of which is the potential they are said to offer learners to reflect on their worldview and thereby become, at least in theory, more informed, more culturally sensitive citizens. Furthermore, the ability to use certain languages (or certain varieties of language) in the neoliberal economy becomes part of a skill-set which employees can offer for sale in exchange for wages. It is in these senses that we can talk of language being subjected to a process of commodification or as a form of capital. From this perspective, socially legitimated forms of language and high-status foreign languages are seen as a kind of asset, and speakers with the ability to deploy them in the labour market are said to possess greater symbolic capital that can be converted into cultural or material advantages such as prestige, influence or employment.

TMA 5

You need to keep these ideas of commodification and capital in mind as you work your way though this chapter, which explores three key areas of activity within 'English the industry': commercial **English language teaching (ELT)**, English language testing, and academic publishing. As you will see, these three areas are closely related and can be thought of as overlapping in the manner of a Venn diagram (Figure 4.1). Let us begin with commercial ELT.

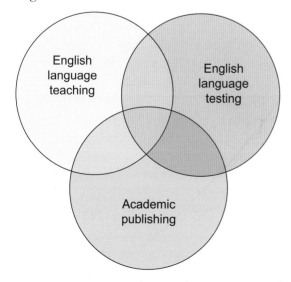

Figure 4.1   Key areas of the English language industry

4.2   Commercial ELT

Commercial ELT encompasses not only the teaching of English itself, but also the training of English language teachers and the production and dissemination of English language materials such as textbooks. Collectively, these activities constitute a global service industry which has grown massively since the 1970s when the current phase of globalisation may be said to have intensified. To understand how this industry operates, it is instructive to explore the manner of its expansion into the Eastern bloc following the collapse of communism in 1989 (Gray, 2002, 2010a). You will recall from Reading A in Chapter 1 that the move to a capitalist economy in Slovakia was followed by a dramatic rise in English language teaching and learning – something which was in fact mirrored across the region as a whole. In 1990, as the new post-Soviet world order was taking shape, the Economist Intelligence Unit (EIU), which styles itself as 'the foremost research and analysis resource in the world' (EIU, 2011), published a detailed report entitled *English in Eastern Europe* (McCallen, 1990). The report made it clear that English was a 'world commodity' and that UK service providers needed to act quickly to take advantage of the rapidly changing political and economic situation in the ex-communist countries.

The then dismal state of English language provision in the East European state school sector was seen as one of the potential advantages for the UK ELT industry, as the following quotation shows:

> As the state English language provision in several of the East European countries is low, or in some cases minimal, the potential for the private sector in each of these markets is considerable. The opportunities are particularly wide ranging in Poland, Hungary and possibly Czechoslovakia, where English language teaching in the state sector is limited. Also encouraging for the private schools in these countries is that, in the short term, there is little that the state sector can do to improve the situation. … *If these private schools can establish a reputation for high quality courses between now and when the state sector is able to provide and improve its English language teaching service, then the state education system may find it difficult to catch up.* The effect of this may be that the teaching of languages to

See P.33

schoolchildren in these two or three countries will be largely undertaken by the private schools.

(McCallen, 1990, p. 91, emphasis added)

And indeed, as has been shown (Thomas, 1999), the ELT industry lost no time in moving in. The provision of ELT across the region was facilitated by the intervention of the hedge-fund manager and philanthropist George Soros. His English Language Program (ELP) helped establish the private sector provision advocated by the EIU report. Altogether, US$5 billion were spent by Soros between 1993 and 2009 on 'democracy-building initiatives' in the Eastern bloc and beyond, in which English language teaching played a key part (Minett, 2009).

At the same time, as thousands of private schools and companies providing educational services are active globally in the promotion and dissemination of English, official bodies such as the British Council also play a key role. The British Council is a unique semi-state body. It is government funded and the British Secretary of State for Foreign and Commonwealth Affairs is answerable to the UK parliament for its activities; it is also a registered charity and it functions as a business. One of its key remits is to promote the English language globally. The introduction to its annual report for 2009–10 begins by pointing out that annual turnover for the year was £705 million – an increase of £60 million on the previous year's figures (British Council, 2010). In this way the revenue-generating role of the organisation is foregrounded for the readership (British Council annual reports are available for public scrutiny at www.britishcouncil.org).

Activity 4.2

Allow about 10 minutes

Look at the following extracts from the British Council's annual report for 2009–10 and pay particular attention to the choice of vocabulary. How does the British Council represent its activities? Why do you think this is so?

- 'In Afghanistan, we helped more than 10,000 English teachers develop their classroom skills' (page 15).
- 'We answered a call from President Kagame [of Rwanda] in 2008 to help his country make the change from French to English as the language of instruction in schools' (page 16).

- 'We are working with Colombia's Ministry of Education in their 23 teacher training programmes to help 7,000 English language teacher trainers across the country' (page 35).
- 'We are helping to assure the quality of Saudi Arabia's 58 universities and colleges' (page 36).

Comment

These examples reveal the repeated deployment of what might be called a discourse of 'help'. In fact they are only some of the many examples peppering the text. Why this choice of vocabulary? As you saw in Chapter 3, the perception that English-medium education caused some children to under-perform in maths and science led to civil unrest in Malaysia in 2009. Educational interventions in favour of English, at least in some settings, are thus potentially problematic and providers are often very aware of the need for careful presentation. In the case of the British Council there are two key constituencies to consider. The first is the British taxpayer. In fact the 2009–10 annual report addresses this group directly and seeks to reassure them by pointing out that it 'generated £2.50 for every £1 of public money received', adding that this 'represents good value for money' (British Council, 2010, p. 3). The second constituency is the wider global public for whom such interventions may have very real consequences. By describing its activities as 'help' or as a response to a request for 'help', the British Council represents its interventions as beneficial to recipients while simultaneously positioning itself in a positive light. Of course there is nothing unusual in this – most businesses seek to present their activities as being in the public interest, and commercial ELT is no different in this respect from any other enterprise. However, as we shall see, some such 'help' has given certain commentators pause for thought.

The example of the British Council helping President Kagame's country, Rwanda, to replace French with English as the medium of education in 2008 is a useful case study of the pressure to adopt English because of its global status, and the role of the 'help' that institutions like the British Council provide.

Case study: helping Rwanda

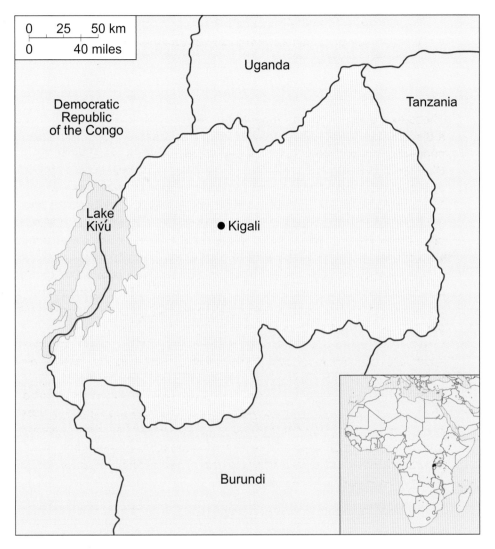

Figure 4.2 Rwanda and its neighbouring countries

The Republic of Rwanda, which became independent from Belgium in 1962, is a small sub-Saharan country bordering Uganda, Tanzania, Burundi and the Democratic Republic of Congo. According to the BBC country profile (BBC News: Africa, 2011), Rwanda has a population of 10.2 million and a life expectancy of fifty for men and fifty-four for women. Official languages are Kinyarwanda and (since 1996) English. During the 1990s ethnic tensions between majority Hutus and minority Tutsis led to genocide in which 800,000 people (mainly Tutsis) died. The ethnic conflict was brought to an end when the Tutsi-led army of the Rwandan Patriotic Front (RPF), many of whom had been in exile in Uganda, seized control of the country in 1994. Western powers were not entirely absent from this conflict. France supported the Hutus, at times directly with troops on the ground, while the USA and the UK indirectly supported the RPF with military training (Melvern, 2000).

In 2010, Paul Kagame (RPF), who had received military training in the USA, was re-elected president for a second term. During his first term the ethnic labels of Hutu and Tutsi were construed as divisive categories dating from the colonial period. Instead, the government posited a single Rwandan ethnicity based on Kinyarwanda, the common language of all Rwandans, and their largely shared religious and cultural practices. However, in 2006 France issued an international warrant for the arrest of President Kagame for his alleged role in triggering the genocide in the mid-1990s. This was followed by Rwanda's severing of diplomatic ties with France (restored in 2009) and the subsequent Rwandan charge that France had also been involved in the original genocide. At the same time, Rwanda joined the East African Community, a local Anglophone intergovernmental organisation, and was admitted to the Commonwealth in 2009, despite having no previous colonial links with the UK. This move ultimately represented a loss of French influence in the region and a concomitant rise in that of the UK, also a major provider of development aid (Smith, 2011).

In spite of some unease about the lack of freedoms in post-genocide Rwanda in certain sections of the Western media, President Kagame has the support of many Western governments, particularly on account of his willingness to restructure the Rwandan economy along neoliberal lines. The World Bank, which is a powerful force for globalisation, and the neoliberal economic measures imposed by it in return for loans, is also a key ally. Its *Doing Business Report 2010* noted that Rwanda is 'the world's top reformer of business regulation, making it easier to start businesses, register property, protect investors, trade across borders, and access credit. It marks the first time a Sub-Saharan African economy is the top reformer' (The World Bank, 2009).

Activity 4.3

What implications do you foresee for Rwanda and its peoples in adopting English as the language used for education? Given your assessment, how do you view the British Council's involvement?

Allow about 10 minutes

You might find it helpful to look back at the discussion of Malaysia in Chapter 3.

Figure 4.3   Rwandan primary school

Comment

Briefly, English has no colonial roots in Rwanda so the majority of teachers and students will have little background in it. Reading A, which you will be asked to look at in the next activity, explores the use of non-indigenous languages in African schools in more detail. In its 2009–10 annual report the British Council describes its intervention in this post-genocide situation as follows:

> We are working with the government of Rwanda and the UK's Department for International Development to bring English into the classroom as the country continues on its remarkable road to recovery. ...
>
> This decision will support the country's economic growth and provide opportunities for thousands of young Rwandans to participate in their country's development.
>
> The [Rwandan] Ministry of Education has to date, with our support, trained over 44,000 English teachers.
>
> (British Council, 2010, p. 16)

No explicit mention is made in the report of the political context in which the switch to English is being carried out. Rather, the focus is on providing support for a country in recovery.

Let us now explore some of the issues raised in Rwanda and elsewhere in Africa when English is used as the medium of instruction in schools, keeping in mind the commercial and political interests at stake in promoting the English language.

Activity 4.4

Now turn to Reading A: *Language policy, politics and development in Africa* by Eddie Williams. As you read make notes on:

- the reasons for and against using English as a medium of instruction in Rwanda. Are any or all of those reasons shared with other African countries?
- any points you see as being specifically relevant to the view of language as a form of capital useful for development
- the main criticisms made by Williams of the use of English or other colonial languages in schools.

Comment

Language policies favouring education through the medium of a European language are justified on the grounds of uniting linguistically diverse peoples without showing favouritism to particular vernacular language speakers. They are also favoured by many parents because European languages, and particularly English, are seen as a prerequisite to better employment opportunities. This is supported by statistics for Rwanda cited by the British Council which show the differences in salaries received by those with and without skills in English (Table 4.1).

help o support

Table 4.1 Salary differentiation in Rwanda: English skills vs no English skills

Job title	Professional salaries with English skills to at least intermediate level (gross salary/month, US$)	Professional salaries with no English skills (gross salary/month, US$)
Director	2,100	1,800
Senior Manager	1,750	1,580
Manager	1,420	1,350
Senior Analyst	1,050	920
Analyst	720	690
Secretary	510	450
Carpenter[1]	80	65
Electrician[1]	75	50
Plumber[1]	62	50
Receptionist	310	110

Source: Euromonitor International (starting salaries for 2010); self-employed and freelance are excluded.

Note: [1]Very few jobs of this type found.

(Euromonitor International, 2010, p. 74)

Williams, on the other hand, counters this with statistics on the failure of education in a foreign language to be *effective* education. Rather, the promotion of English favours a current elite who already have command of the language and are in a position to pass on this linguistic capital to their children. The intervention of the British Council in countries like Rwanda clearly involves much more than just 'helping'. Its intervention also contributes to the external repositioning of the country more firmly within the orbit of those countries that are part of the globalised economy where English has a significant presence. While this may be good for industries related to English, the sidelining of Kinyarwanda and French would suggest that the policy is politically and educationally risky. Current language policies in Rwanda and elsewhere have the effect of devaluing vernacular languages as an existing form of linguistic capital and it may be dangerous to assume that such devaluation will be without social consequences. Finally, it could also be argued that 'help' with education through English, even when solicited, and even if it were to succeed on its own terms, ultimately represents something of a lost opportunity for the development of genuine multilingual literacy, in which many languages have a role to play.

ELT publishing

Let us now turn to another aspect of English the industry, that of ELT textbook publishing, and four major UK companies which compete against each other and against indigenous publishing houses in countries around the world for a share of the lucrative global market. A successful course comprising a series of textbooks can be guaranteed decades of life; for example, the *Headway* course, published by Oxford University Press, which first appeared in 1986 and currently comprises books at elementary, pre-intermediate, intermediate, upper-intermediate and advanced levels. This is also the case if the course carries the imprimatur of a local Ministry of Education, if it is seen as preparing students for a high-stakes test (more on this later), or it is marketed successfully as embodying the latest in methodological thinking or technological innovation. A senior editor at a major UK publishing house responsible for textbooks aimed mainly at the Turkish secondary school market explained to me in interview how market research in such an environment is all-important:

> So what we do is we choose a lead country as a market and several subsidiary markets … the latest coursebook I've been doing, we've done main research in Turkey, we've done secondary research in Poland, in Greece, in Brazil, in Argentina, in Portugal, in Spain, in Hungary … we tend to agglomerate markets where you've got particular features, either a fast pace, or a particular methodology, or a particular set of teaching and learning circumstances, and we will go with that sort of thing … I get input from other markets, so I make it right for Turkey for instance, but I also check very closely with Poland *because they've been going through a reform* …
>
> (personal communication, 2000, emphasis added)

In this way, sales can be maximised and the risk of failure or under-selling in one segment of the overall market is reduced. The mention of educational reform, which was a recurrent feature in this interview, is also important. As language teaching curricula are reformed in more and more countries in ways which are congruent with a communicative (and generally English-only) methodology, UK ELT publishers are enabled to reap the benefits of what amounts to the creation of an increasingly standardised market. As a publishing manager in the same company explained to me, it is easier and more desirable to produce books for a single market, rather than for a number of diverse markets.

As the first decade of the twenty-first century drew to an end, the UK publishing industry's representative body, the Publishers Association, reported that a number of factors conspired to give the industry some cause for concern. These included: increased production costs, a 10 per cent rise in the price of paper in 2009, fluctuations in exchange rates which affected overseas printing, and the global financial crisis which began in 2007–08. Thus, the report noted that '[d]istributors in emerging markets, such as Eastern Europe, struggled to pay their bills on time, and markets reliant on parental purchase, such as Greece and Spain, undoubtedly experienced declines' (The Publishers Association, 2010, p. 49). The ELT market is almost entirely export led and the report underlined the importance of the sector for UK publishing exports overall. Altogether the ELT sector accounted for a hefty 17 per cent of all UK publishing export sales by the end of the first decade of the twenty-first century and the 2009 report showed that sales revenue grew by 26 per cent from £164 million in 2005 to £207 million in 2009 (as rising costs were passed on to customers) – despite being 14 per cent down in terms of volume for the same period. The report noted that a possible reason for the drop in sales, apart from the global financial crisis, could be the incursion of various types of digital media into the classroom and cited the Italian government's decision that all materials produced for state school education should be made available in paper *and* electronic formats. The report concluded that although worrying in the short term, ultimately the industry need not fear for its future as 'the push to introduce English into schools at an ever earlier age continues unabated, as does the requirement to demonstrate competency in English through high-stakes examinations' (The Publishers Association, 2010, p. 49) – something which, it suggested, should continue to fuel growth regardless of the materials format opted for by the market.

Allow about
10 minutes

Activity 4.5

At the end of this section on commercial ELT, let us pause and take stock of what the chapter has outlined so far. Think back to the introduction and the suggestion that the story of English is a multifaceted one. What have you learnt about the commercial facet of the story?

Comment

The main point to take away from this section is that the story of English, particularly from the second half of the twentieth century onwards, is also the story of a teaching industry which is active in the identification and capture of potential markets. Commercial ELT's move into Eastern Europe following the collapse of communism illustrates the rapidity of the industry's response to the emergence of a new world order. Demand for English clearly existed across the ex-Soviet Union, but it was the potential for the privatisation of provision (identified by the EIU report) which was viewed most favourably by the industry – and facilitated by powerful philanthropic capitalists such as George Soros. Today most of the major chains of language schools are found across the region, complemented by a host of smaller private sector providers. A second key point is the extent to which semi-state bodies such as the British Council are central to the export of English and the growth of the industry. However, Reading A served to question the wisdom of certain interventions and underline the way in which language policy, such as that in Rwanda, can have social and political ramifications that go beyond the provision of help with language teaching. Finally, the section has drawn attention to the fact that the sale of ELT textbooks is a multi-million pound enterprise which represents a significant portion of the UK's total book exports. Although the rise of digital publishing may have negative implications for the sale of books in the future, the industry takes the view that this is unlikely to impact negatively on the sale of English itself.

4.3 High-stakes tests

Let us begin this section with some terminology related specifically to testing. A **high-stakes test** is the term used to refer to an assessment instrument which has serious educational and social consequences for test takers, such as the citizenship tests discussed in Chapter 2. Two key terms of particular relevance to high-stakes tests are washback and impact. Although these are sometimes treated as synonyms, most scholars use 'washback' to refer to the effect of the test on teaching and learning, and 'impact' to refer to the effect of the test on society in general – for example, on individuals, groups and institutions.

Activity 4.6

Allow about 10 minutes

Think about any high-stakes test you have taken, in terms of 'washback' and 'impact' (e.g. a school entrance examination or your end of secondary school examinations). Consider the role of the test in teaching and learning prior to actually taking the test, and then reflect on the consequences of the test in your own life or its impact on society more generally.

Comment

Obviously your answers will vary depending on your age, your location and the kind of test you had in mind. In my own case, a high-stakes test I took was the 'Eleven Plus' which determined the kind of secondary school a child could attend. The small number of pupils who passed the test progressed with scholarships to prestigious academically oriented grammar schools, while the remainder went to varieties of less academic secondary schools. In terms of washback, I recall the period leading up to the test being dominated by preparation for the test. This is sometimes referred to as 'teaching to the test' whereby a testing regime determines completely the nature and content of classroom practice, and any content which is non-test related is sidelined. In terms of impact, the test allowed me to go to a grammar school which, in turn, facilitated later entry to university. But overall, the 'Eleven Plus' proved socially divisive. Many financially better-off parents were able to pay for extra coaching for their children, and schools in more affluent areas were often better able to prepare their pupils for the test. In this way, the test benefited children from more privileged backgrounds. Many children who failed felt stigmatised at an early age and, inevitably, grammar schools were seen as bastions of elitism, while the alternatives were viewed by many as second best.

As we shall see, high-stakes language tests are no less problematic. Indeed, the testing expert Elana Shohamy, whose work was also discussed in Chapter 2, argues that tests such as citizenship tests are not simply pedagogical tools, but are also social and political instruments which play a key role in 'shaping the definitions of language, in affecting learning and teaching, and in maintaining and creating social classes' (Shohamy, 2008, p. xiv). Furthermore, high-stakes language tests are also big business, and a small number of these are increasingly carried out on an industrial scale globally. These are issues to keep in mind as you read the remainder of this section.

OU. requirements?

TMA 5.

Personal experience?

IELTS, TOEFL and TOEIC

Let us now look at three high-stakes English language tests – the Anglo-Australian International English Language Testing System (IELTS), the North American Test of English as a Foreign Language (TOEFL) and Test of English for International Communication (TOEIC). All three tests are used by a wide constituency of higher education institutions, employers, professional bodies such as the UK's General Medical Council (GMC), and immigration authorities. All test reading, writing, speaking and listening and all are constantly monitored and modified by teams employed by the testing bodies with a view to improving their validity (the extent to which they test what they claim to test), reliability (the extent to which they give consistent results) and fairness (their overall equitability and absence of bias against different types of test taker). This ongoing work is clearly related to transparency and research into testing, but it is also used as part of each test's promotional apparatus, with studies being made available on their respective websites. The fact that these tests are *so* researched is in fact integral to the promotional claims made on their behalf. However, Tim McNamara (2008), who has carried out extensive research into testing, has questioned the extent to which those who are responsible for test design should also be responsible for test monitoring and evaluation.

Allow about 10 minutes

Activity 4.7

Let us begin by looking at the web pages for TOEFL and IELTS in Figures 4.4 and 4.5. In what ways do they promote the tests they advertise?

Figure 4.4   Extract from TOEFL web page

Figure 4.5   Extract from IELTS web page

Comment

As you can see, TOEFL and IELTS promote their products in terms of their global reach and the global possibilities they offer test takers. Note, for example, the way both web pages provide numbers for test takers and institutions which recognise the test. Note too the way in which the TOEFL web page engages the reader through the use of a photograph in which a smiling young woman, clearly identifiable as a student, meets the gaze of the imagined viewer. The image is also deliberately suggestive of East Asia where TOEFL has a strong presence in the market for high-stakes tests. This device, which is common in advertising, has been described by the sociologist Erving Goffman (1979) as a 'summoning look' in which the addition of a smile is used to connote social affinity (Kress and van Leeuwen, 1996). The image invites the viewer to identify with the young woman and people like her who have, as the map and the graffiti suggest, the freedom to 'go anywhere'. Precisely the same kind of summoning look pervades contemporary ELT textbooks aimed at the global market where students are similarly invited through artwork to feel membership of a global community of young, attractive, English-speaking cosmopolitans (Gray, 2010b).

The promotional claims made on the IELTS web page are also noteworthy. Let us start with the strapline – 'The world speaks IELTS', followed by the claim that IELTS is 'the test that sets the standard'. The implication of the strapline is that the kind of English which is tested by IELTS is the English spoken by the world and that this English is synonymous with IELTS. The second claim testifies to the power of the test to establish what the world standard is – presumably for both the test and for English (given their deliberate conflation). Both web pages also draw on travel metaphors – thus TOEFL is represented as a 'passport to study abroad' and IELTS as facilitating 'journeys into international education and employment'. This links back to the earlier discussion of commodification and symbolic capital. Both tests are in fact represented as travel documents allowing global freedom of passage to their bearers – a freedom which is based on the amount of symbolic linguistic capital the test takers are held to possess. The 'added value' aspect of such tests is spelt out even more explicitly on the TOEIC web page (www.ets.org/toeic) as follows:

> English is the language of global opportunity. The TOEIC® tests have helped many people throughout the world advance their careers and take advantage of the best employment opportunities. Your TOEIC scores can:
>
> - Make you a stronger candidate for job opportunities with leading global organizations that want employees who can speak and write in English
> - Demonstrate your ability to communicate across borders and cultures with co-workers and clients
> - Positively affect hiring decisions and other employment opportunities

- Help you to obtain new opportunities within a company

Today over 10,000 organizations in 120 countries around the world use the TOEIC tests to determine which candidates have the English-language skills to succeed in the global workplace. More than five million tests were administered last year. Take the TOEIC tests to give yourself a competitive advantage and advance your career.

(Educational Testing Service, 2011)

These promotional claims are high indeed. They are also clearly persuasive as the revenue generated by such tests shows. This is explored in the next section, along with some of the problems associated with high-stakes testing.

In terms of English the industry, testing is a particularly lucrative activity. As you have read in Chapters 2 and 3, it is closely linked to the population flows associated with globalisation (and the frequent use of English as a global lingua franca) and the internationalisation of education (in which English may be the medium of instruction). The British Council's 2009–10 annual report repeatedly draws attention to the importance of high-stakes tests such as IELTS in this respect. The introduction spells this out by linking IELTS with income generation overall and the growth of the higher education sector internationally:

The report looks in brief at how we are supporting the English language industry in the UK, which is worth £3–4 billion a year, and the success of the world's number one exam in its field, IELTS.

(British Council, 2010, p. 8)

The report also points out that 'more than 1.4 million people have taken IELTS this year alone' (British Council, 2010, p. 20). The figures for IELTS test takers also reveal a dramatic rise, as the 2008–09 annual report stated that 800,000 people had taken the test (British Council, 2009). The 2009–10 figures therefore show an increase of

75 per cent. In turn, this was reflected in the annual financial review, which reported an overall rise in profit on the previous year:

> This increase came principally from fees and income from services, including from teaching and examinations operations, which rose by £49 million (16 per cent) to £362 million. Examinations performed particularly strongly despite the economic downturn.
>
> (British Council, 2010, p. 58)

Seen from the perspective of test takers, the fees for English tests may appear high. The IELTS website states that the test has a set fee, £125 for 2012, and the website provides a link for prospective candidates to check how much this is in local currency. The TOEFL website explains that fees for their tests vary from country to country, but that candidates can expect to pay between US$160 and US$250. These are significant amounts of money – particularly for candidates in developing world countries.

You can read more about Suresh Canagarajah's influential views in the first book in this series: Seargeant and Swann (eds) (2012), Chapter 6.

Let's now build on the criticism of the high-stakes citizenship tests in Chapter 2, particularly the suggestion that tests do not always reflect the reality of what people will have to do with the language. It is ironic that this major concern stems from the sociolinguistic consequences of the global spread of English itself. Suresh Canagarajah (2006, p. 232), who has written about the implications of the global spread of English, makes the point that 'English is a heterogeneous language with multiple norms and diverse grammars' and that real proficiency in such a globalised language must be re-construed as multidialectal.

What exactly does this mean? Let us consider for a moment the case of a nurse or doctor coming to work in the UK's National Health Service (NHS) for whom English is a second or additional language. Clearly, a high level of proficiency is essential given that patients' lives may be at stake, and a high IELTS score for migrant health professionals is required. But is this all such professionals need in terms of language? In 2010, BBC Radio 4 featured a report on the way in which a hospital in a town near London tried to prepare its migrant health professionals by moving beyond the IELTS model of language. The hospital ran its own specialised language course which involved a focus on standard British English (more or less what IELTS tests), but also addressed the specific discourse of the NHS (clearly doctors and nurses need to understand and use the particular institutional and managerial terminology that goes with the job), and a focus on native speaker idiomaticity. The hospital pointed out that older native speakers in particular may use euphemisms such as needing 'to spend a penny' in preference to having 'to urinate', and that health professionals needed to be aware of such choices if they were to understand their patients. Although the hospital representative did not mention indigenous non-standard varieties (e.g. Cockney), World Englishes varieties (e.g. Nigerian English) or more recently emerging forms (e.g. Polish English), it is clear that many patients may describe their symptoms in a wide range of ways (particularly in multilingual metropolitan areas) and that proficiency in English in such a setting may entail a lot more than the ability to 'speak IELTS' – despite the website's suggestion that it is the world's English dialect of choice.

Canagarajah is not alone in suggesting that the testing industry needs to become more sensitive to the sociolinguistic realities of the multiplicity of ways in which English is used in today's world. He argues that, in a globalised world, varieties of English are no longer so geographically sealed off from one another. In turn, this means that proficiency in many settings entails some kind of 'shuttling' between dialects or ability to cope with plurality. What this means – think back to the hypothetical example of the NHS employee above having to respond to Cockney, Nigerian English, Polish English, and so on – is that many speakers need multidialectal competence (at least at the level of decoding).

For most scholars who are critical of the high-stakes testing regimes, the point is that such tests are perforce limited by their monodialectal focus. As the applied linguist Jennifer Jenkins (2006) points out, the high-stakes tests of the kind being considered here are in no way tests of international English, despite being marketed internationally as such. They are, and remain, tests of the standard varieties of sociolinguist Braj Kachru's (1985) Inner Circle countries where English is traditionally spoken as a native language by the majority of inhabitants. So where does this leave us with regard to these tests? Critical scholars such as Constant Leung and Jo Lewkowicz (2006) adopt a 'both and more' position. That is, they see a continuing role for tests of standard Inner Circle English, but they also argue that the concept of proficiency needs to be broadened to include the concept of multidialectal competence as the English of the Inner Circle is pluralised.

This is similar in many ways to the criticism of the monolingual focus of citizenship tests discussed in Chapter 2.

By way of conclusion to this section it is important to reiterate that high-stakes testing is closely associated with the activity of teaching and the sale of textbooks. In many cases textbooks are often written specifically to prepare students for such tests. However, although the tests are marketed on the basis that they purportedly test international English, a number of critical voices have been shown to question the veracity of such claims. Critics have suggested that the impact of increasing globalisation on English, and the pluralisation this has entailed, means that the concept of proficiency based on a single dialect is no longer feasible and that assessment is more complex than the testing industry suggests.

Interesting argument

4.4   Academic publishing

The third key area of activity within English the industry is academic publishing. Academic books emanate from two sources, university publishing houses (such as Oxford University Press (OUP), Cambridge University Press (CUP), Harvard University Press, etc.) and commercial publishers (such as McGraw-Hill, Pearson Education, etc.). Traditionally, the university presses dedicated their efforts to the publication of relatively small print-runs of scholarly monographs, while the commercial publishers specialised in the more lucrative university textbook market. Of course, there is a degree of overlap, and giants in the field, such as OUP and CUP, have always produced books of both types.

The sociologist John Thompson (2005), who has written extensively about the Anglo-American publishing industries, explains that a major problem facing academic publishers, which has been a constant since the 1980s, is the decline in sales of the monograph. The major buyers for this type of book are university libraries. However, the arrival of economic recession in the 1980s and the rise of neoliberal economic policies introduced in the USA and the UK throughout the 1980s meant that universities increasingly found themselves having to operate more thoroughly as businesses. Thompson points out that library budgets were increasingly squeezed, resulting in a decline in monograph purchases. At the same time, reduced amounts of money available had to be spread more thinly to cover investment in IT services (such as electronic catalogues and computers) alongside subscription to periodicals which began to proliferate in this period – particularly for science subjects. In the USA many small university presses did not survive. However, Thompson explains, spectacular economic vitality for some university publishing houses came as a result of activity in other parts of the English language industry:

> The ELT programmes at both OUP and CUP have been particularly successful and have served in many ways as the engines of growth for both organizations in the period since 1980.
>
> (Thompson, 2005, p. 89)

Unlike most university publishing houses, which have to be subsidised by their institutions, OUP and CUP actually transfer revenue to their hosts. Between 1998 and 2003, Thompson reports that OUP transferred a staggering £202 million to the university. In this way, the power of ELT publishing becomes apparent, not only as a lucrative activity in its own right, but also as a vital mechanism for sustaining other parts of the industry.

At the same time, the role of English in the delivery of higher education globally has expanded, with implications for university textbook sales to students. Linked to this expansion of English is an increasing homogenisation of curriculum content globally, particularly in subjects such as business, economics, engineering, ICT and science. This has been explained as being partly due to:

> the dominant role of the US in these subject areas, and partly because many young scholars go to the US for their graduate training and become familiar with the American curriculum, which they incorporate into their own teaching practices when they return to their home countries. This Americanization of the curriculum in some subject areas and some countries has helped to create and expand an international market for textbooks that were originally designed for US courses.
>
> (Thompson, 2005, p. 287)

In Europe it could be said that another kind of homogenisation has been under way since 1999. The 'Bologna process' is the name given to a European intergovernmental accord which has the stated objective of harmonising the architecture of the higher education sector through the creation of a European Higher Education Area (EHEA). This aims to facilitate the mobility of students and academics throughout the continent. Such a process indirectly encourages the use of English for course delivery to increasingly multilingual student cohorts. These two types of homogenisation clearly have implications for Anglo-American academic publishing, which is firmly focused on the international market and to a large extent determines the form university textbooks now take.

Nevertheless, the UK Publishers Association report for 2009 was cautious in its assessment of the sector's performance. This was deemed to be 'respectable' and 'helped significantly by price and, in part, by improving enrolments in higher education' (The Publishers Association, 2010, p. 1). The report noted that an estimated 62 million academic and professional books had been sold in 2009 to the value of £900 million. Sales were evenly divided between the home and the overseas market. Figures for the latter showed the top three sales destinations were mainland Europe, followed by East and South-east Asia and the USA, with the majority of overseas sales in non-English speaking countries. However, there was an overall drop of 4 per cent in the volume of sales between 2005 and 2009 – although hikes in pricing meant that revenue had actually increased by 18 per cent for the same period. This was explained by the fallout from the ongoing global financial crisis and cuts to university budgets in many countries.

At the same time, the report pointed out that sales for digital academic books had increased. Over 80 per cent of all ebooks sold in 2009 were in the academic and professional category – sales which generated a total of £77.4 million. Although this represented a 22 per cent rise on figures from 2008, the report urged caution in interpretation of the figures, as this was the first year for which digital figures were available and not all publishers may have recorded their data with the same degree of accuracy. At the time of writing (2011), it remains to be seen if this is the beginning of a major trend in academic publishing. Whatever the case, and whatever the long-term impact of the 2007–08 financial crisis on academic publishing, the particular role of the English language would appear to be secure given the ongoing internationalisation of the higher education sector.

This brings us to the end of the section on academic publishing. You will recall that the introduction to this chapter contained a Venn diagram which showed three key areas of English the industry overlapping in such a way as to suggest their mutual interdependence. The nature of this relationship has been underlined in this section. The sustaining power of ELT was shown to be crucial to the economic vitality of the industry as a whole and this leads into to the final reading on the topic in which the applied linguist Mark Pegrum explores the ways in which commercial ELT, the industry's most powerful driver, markets itself. Addressing language teachers and teacher educators, he analyses the recurring tropes in advertisements for ELT products (e.g. textbooks, dictionaries and tests), all of which are taken from publications aimed mainly at teachers and students.

Activity 4.8

Now turn to Reading B: *Selling English: advertising and the discourse of ELT* by Mark Pegrum. Before you begin it, though, think back to the way in which travel metaphors and the promise of employability were used to promote the high-stakes tests referred to earlier. What additional recurring promotional themes do you expect to find in this reading on the selling of English?

As you read, consider to what extent you agree with Pegrum's view that English is the language of international capitalism.

Comment

Pegrum's article draws much needed attention to the importance of advertising in the marketing of English. The products of the industry – language courses, teacher education courses, textbooks, dictionaries and tests are all commodities jostling for attention in the education marketplace. English too is just one of several major world languages a student might opt to study. In a consumer society commodities require branding and advertising if they are to be noticed. Branding is crucial in the creation of a set of associations for commodities – hence, as noted by Pegrum, the association of English in the industry's advertising with ideas of modernity, the good life and cosmopolitanism. The art critic John Berger, who has written illuminatingly about the power of advertising in contemporary society, makes the following observation:

> [Advertising] proposes to each of us that we transform ourselves, or our lives, by buying something more. ...

> Publicity persuades us of such a transformation by showing us people who have apparently been transformed and are, as a result, enviable.

> (Berger, 1972, p. 131)

Think of the image of the smiling, confident young woman on the TOEFL web page earlier. The transformation promised is the uninhibited freedom to travel which the test will bring. But as Berger goes on to argue, what the viewer really envies is not the figure in the advertisement, but the viewer's own dreamed-of self, transformed though purchase of the commodity being sold. In the case of the advertising surveyed by Pegrum it could be argued that what might be called the student's 'learning self' is encouraged to envy his or her future 'speaking self' and the world of opportunity it will become possible to inhabit. A second key issue raised by the article is the extent to which English can be seen as the language of international capitalism. You will recall that this was the view taken in Reading A in Chapter 1. There is no doubt that English is marketed by the industry as the language of capitalism in the direct sense that it is associated with success in business, and in the indirect sense that entrepreneurial values are repeatedly celebrated in the industry's advertising and in textbooks (Gray, 2010a). However, it would be incorrect to assume that these associations are in any way fixed or necessary. English may well be the language (or one of the languages) of international capitalism, but it is also the language of a host of global struggles which are often anti-capitalist in orientation. The frequent use of English by political demonstrators and campaigners for social justice around the world – in the blogosphere, on social network internet sites, or captured on television news programmes – is just one indication of this. It is important to remember that English is also a language of global resistance – but that is another story to be told elsewhere (see Chapter 6).

4.5   Conclusion

I began this chapter by suggesting that the story of English was more multifaceted than is sometimes suggested in the literature. My aim has been to show that one facet of the story is that of a multi-billion pound industry which exists primarily to make profit. In doing so, the chapter has shed light on the suggestion that English has reached a point of no-return and has become a 'power in itself'. Rather than seeing English in this way as somehow agentive, the chapter has shown that powerful forces propelled by human agents acting on behalf of commercial and governmental organisations are actively involved in promoting and sustaining the position of English in the world. At the same time, English is undoubtedly a form of symbolic capital capable of bringing benefit to those who have access to its socially legitimated forms. To think of restricting access to English is clearly not an option. This facet of the story of English is a complex one in which individual aspirations and hopes for a better life are mingled with neglect for mother tongues and inequalities among different kinds of speakers. It is also a story which unfolds against a background of ringing cash registers. As such, the chapter raises questions about how the practices of *English the industry* and the meanings it seeks to attach to the language can be contested by those (myself included) who continue to see the value of English – but who reject the values of the industry which disseminates it.

READING A: Language policy, politics and development in Africa

Eddie Williams

Source: Williams, E. (2011) 'Language policy, politics and development in Africa' (Paper 3) in Coleman, H. (ed.) *Dreams and Realities: Developing Countries and the English Language*, London, British Council, Teaching English Series, pp. 2–18.

Introduction

'Africa is the only continent where the majority of children start school using a foreign language,' observes a recent UNESCO report (Ouane and Glanz 2010). This [reading] will argue that this language policy is a significant contributory factor to the lack of development in the continent. [...]

[O]ne reason for the lack of positive impact of education in Sub-Saharan Africa is that what contributes to development is not simply 'education' in the sense of providing schools, teachers and materials for learners, but effective education, and that a crucial feature of much formal African education is precisely that it lacks effectiveness.

Language and education

[...]

It should come as no surprise that children [in primary classrooms who do not understand the teacher or the textbook] fail to achieve command of English adequate for academic purposes. Their weak command of English [...] is amply evidenced by test results from many quarters of Africa. [...] [I]n Rwanda [...] results of a study by Williams et al. (2004), who tested 251 Year 6 students in five primary schools indicated that only two (0.77 per cent) could read adequately for their studies in English at primary level. These findings suggest that the Rwandan government's current policy – that English should be the sole medium of instruction from Year 3 of primary schooling – is likely to face difficulties (although fewer than those arising from the policy in force from 2009 until 2011, which decreed that English should be the sole medium of instruction from Year 1).

Conversely, in educational contexts where African languages are taught and employed as media of instruction, students display considerable proficiency, as might be expected. [...] In Rwanda, testing in

KinyaRwanda of the same 251 Year 6 students concluded that the vast majority of students (over 90 per cent) could read independently in that language. These were students who, at the time of testing (2003), had experienced KinyaRwanda as a medium of instruction. [...]

The cognitive gains from investment in inadequate education are, as one would expect, negligible (Knight and Sabot 1990). Crucially then, it is effective education that enables individuals to acquire knowledge and skills, which in turn can contribute to development. The overwhelming case for educating children in a familiar language has been echoed, in the case of Africa, by repeated calls from educationists over the last hundred years [...]. Despite such views being widespread, governments have shown little will to change their policies, and their favouring of exoglossic languages [non-indigenous languages used as an official or second language] such as English is generally supported by local communities for whom 'English equals education'. Families see English as a 'strong' language, and primary school English as the first step towards the coveted white-collar job. Although simple conversational skills (exemplified by responses to banal questions such as 'What is your name?' 'How old are you?' posed by one-off visitors to African classrooms) may be acquired within a year or two, what governments and families appear not to appreciate is the considerable amount of time, effort and resource that is needed to learn a language to a point where learners are capable of using it for academic purposes – widely agreed to take five to seven years (cf. Cummins 2000).

Political motivations in language policy

Why is the solution advocated by so many, namely to use a known language (probably, but not necessarily the child's mother tongue) not implemented in primary schools? One important answer is that the political will is lacking. The reasons for this lack of political will are various, some being relatively obvious and explicit, others more subtle. African governments invariably cite the need for national unification and development as reasons for eschewing African languages. John Mwanakatwe, Minister of Education in post-independence Zambia, a country with some twenty different languages (Kashoki 1990), spelled out the motivation clearly:

Even the most ardent nationalists of our time have accepted the inevitable fact that English – ironically a foreign language and also the language of our former colonial master – has definitely a unifying role in Zambia.

(Mwanakatwe 1968)

Furthermore, the role of schools was crucial in promoting this unity through English:

For the sake of communication between Zambians whose mother tongues differ and in order to promote the unity of the nation, it is necessary for all Zambian children to learn the national language [i.e. English] as early as possible, and to use it confidently.

(Ministry of Education Zambia 1976, para. 47)

[...] While opting for English may have succeeded in preventing conflict in the educational arena between competing language groups, and while its dominance in the same arena is largely welcomed by the public, the language has, however, created division between, on the one hand, those who have good access to it, typically members of the reasonably well-off urban groups, and, on the other hand, those who do not, typically the members of poor urban and especially rural groups.

There is, however, a small but increasing proportion of pupils throughout Africa who gain access to high-quality English teaching through attending private fee-paying primary schools. Referring to this effect of English in Malawi, Kayambazinthu (1999:52) says that:

The dominance and limited access to English ... has created an élite group, [whose] proficiency in English is near-native ... these élites maintain and regularly use their knowledge of English in their professional environments, where they typically occupy the middle ranks of the political, administrative and academic institutions.

[...]

'Élite closure' is the term Myers-Scotton (1990) has coined for the process whereby a small dominant establishment in African countries ensures that they and their families have access to high standards of

English while inadequate education systems mean that this is largely denied to the majority. Perhaps the most extreme current example occurred in Rwanda where, following the massacres of 1994 and the intervention of the 'Anglophone' RPF (Rwandan Patriotic Front), political and economic power has tended to be concentrated in the hands of a relatively small English-speaking group, mainly educated in Uganda, who in 2009 introduced legislation to 'anglicise' Rwanda, with a 'straight for English' policy in primary education, accompanied by Rwanda joining the (ex-British) Commonwealth. This policy was modified in February 2011 such that KinyaRwanda became the medium of instruction for the first three years, with English as a subject. Nonetheless, since Rwanda is one of the few African countries where almost all inhabitants already share a common language (KinyaRwanda), this language policy does not seem to be focused on unification. It is therefore almost certain that Rwanda will generate a small English-proficient élite.

Likewise, as far as development is concerned, many governments look upon English as a vital tool. Yisa Claver (Director, Policy Planning at the Ministry of Education in Rwanda) commenting on Rwanda's 2009 decision to go 'straight for English' as a medium of instruction was clear on the role of the language in development:

> Really it is not choosing English for its own sake ... This is a way to make Rwanda to be equal, to use English ... English is now a world language, especially in trade and commerce. Rwanda is trying to attract foreign investors – most of these people are speaking English ... It's choosing English as a medium of instruction so we Rwandans of today, and tomorrow, will benefit.
>
> (Quoted in McGreal 2009)

To date, however, there is no doubt that in other countries in Africa, the dominant role of English in primary schools (the only level of education for the vast majority of people in poor countries) has proved to be a barrier to education, and hence to development, for the majority, since most students fail to acquire adequate academic competence in the language. It is no surprise then, that, whether one looks at development in terms of economic progress or of human needs, poor countries such as Malawi, Zambia and Rwanda that use

English or French as a means of 'accessing development' have not hitherto made great strides [...]

Governments, however, are not entirely to blame: they have strong support from the majority of parents, for whom 'education equals English'. [...]

Zambia provides clear evidence of this 'education equals English' attitude: in 1996, the year when the Zambian policy document *Educating our Future* was being drafted, and also a general election year in the country, politicians were worried that to promote Zambian languages as media of instruction at the expense of English would be a potential vote-loser. 'It proved not possible, for political reasons, to go as far as changing the medium of instruction to a local language' (Linehan 2004:7). Ruling politicians 'made clear to senior education officials that unless a non-contentious formula [for including local languages] could be found, the political preference would be for maintenance of the status quo, with English remaining in the same position as it had done from 1965' (Linehan 2004:7). The compromise position was, that initial literacy in year one should be in one of the seven 'educationally approved' Zambian languages, while English continued officially to be the medium of instruction. [...]

The obverse of this over-estimation of English is the under-estimation of African languages, and the negative impact of English on national self-esteem. An early expression of this came in 1969 from Kapepwe, at the time Vice President of Zambia, who said:

> We should stop teaching children through English right from the start because it is the surest way of imparting inferiority complex in the children and the society. It is poisonous. It is the surest way of killing African personality and African culture.
>
> (Cited in Serpell 1978:432)

Factors in development

One should not, of course, overstate the case for local languages in education; likewise, one should not overstate the case for education as a factor in development. Appropriate language policies are not the entire answer to poor quality education, and effective education is not the entire answer to human and economic development. [...]

Economic capital

In Africa, the framework of global economic structures within which countries have to operate renders economic growth problematic. [...]

Although the 21st century has seen partial debt relief for a number of African countries, whether this is sufficient to turn around African economies is open to question. Likewise, adverse conditions of trade (e.g. rich countries imposing tariffs on imports from developing countries, while subsidising their own exports), although showing signs of ameliorating (UN 2005:38–39), are not likely to undergo the kind of changes that will bring about significant benefits in Africa. In short, as far as economic capital is concerned, outside agency, largely Western, has hitherto lacked the will to help Africa, while African agency lacks the resource. For most children in Africa, the 'level playing field' will continue to look decidedly uphill: poor quality education is both a cause and an outcome of poverty, at household and national levels (cf. Kadzamira and Rose 2003, Colclough et al. 2000). It remains to be seen to what extent the considerable and ongoing Chinese activity in Africa, in terms of investments, loans and a growing Chinese diaspora in Africa (see Addis Fortune 2010, Foster et al. 2008) affects this economic scene, and indeed, the linguistic landscape in Africa.

[...]

Human capital

What is crucial in human capital is effective education. Although there is no simple causal connection from the language through which education is conducted to the well-being of the state, the weight of evidence suggests that literacy skills are more easily acquired in a language with which learners are familiar, leading to more effective education; in turn, effective education can contribute to poverty alleviation and development. It is abundantly clear that education in a language that few learners, and not all teachers, have mastery of, detracts from quality and compounds the other problems arising from economically impoverished contexts. [...]

While it is all very well to advocate that children be taught through their mother tongue, or at least a language with which they are familiar, an issue that cannot be avoided in this context is the choice of language of instruction. Sub-Saharan African countries are multilingual, some intensely so [...]

While practical solutions to this reality do not readily present themselves, one answer is to employ a language which is closely related to those spoken by all the learners, provided of course that they share related languages – thus the use of ChiChewa in Malawi does not seem to pose problems for speakers of other African languages in the country, according to research by Williams (2006:125–26). Where circumstances allow, this strategy offers a reasonable solution. Similarly, in urban contact areas where there is particularly intensive multilingualism, the most appropriate solution would seem to be to employ the language in which the learners communicate with each other outside the classroom. Such solutions require careful research and preparation, and are unlikely to be cost-free. Nevertheless, they arguably offer better value than using an ex-colonial language, where the learners' lack of proficiency in the medium of instruction means that there is massive wastage in the attempt to build human capital.

References for this reading

Addis Fortune 2010. *Africa: China's complex view of Africa. All Africa.com*, 8 June 2010. Available online at *http://allafrica.com/stories/201006100397.html*

Colclough, C., Rose, P. and Tembon, M. 2000. *Gender inequalities in primary schooling: The roles of poverty and adverse cultural practice. International Journal of Educational Development* 20(1), 5–29.

Cummins, J. 2000. *Language, Power and Pedagogy: Bilingual Children in the Crossfire. Clevedon: Multilingual Matters.*

Foster, V., Butterfield, W., Chen, C. and Pushak, N. 2008. *Building Bridges: China's Growing Role as Infrastructure Financier for Sub-Saharan Africa.* Washington, World Bank. Available online at *www.globalclearinghouse.org/infradev/assets%5C10/documents/Building%20Bridges. %20China %27s%20Growing%20Role%20as%20 Infrastructure%20Financier%20for%20Sub-Saharan%20Africa%20-%20Foster%20 % 282009%29.pdf*

Kadzamira, E. and Rose, P. 2003. *Can free primary education meet the needs of the poor? Evidence from Malawi. International Journal of Educational Development*, 23, 501–516.

Kashoki, M.E. 1990. *The Factor of Language in Zambia. Lusaka: Kenneth Kaunda Foundation.*

Kayambazinthu, E. 1999. *The language planning situation in Malawi. In R.B.Kaplan and R.B.Baldauf (eds), Language Planning in Malawi, Mozambique and the Philippines, 15–85. Clevedon: Multilingual Matters.*

Knight, J.B. and Sabot, R.H. 1990. *Education, Productivity and Inequality: The East African Natural Experiment. Oxford: Oxford University Press for the World Bank.*

Linehan, S. 2004. *Language of instruction and the quality of basic education in Zambia.* Paper prepared for UNESCO.

McGreal, C. 2009. *Why Rwanda said adieu to French. Guardian Weekly* 16 January 2009. Available online at *www.guardian.co.uk/education/2009/jan/16/ rwanda-english-genocide*

Ministry of Education, Zambia. 1976. *Education for Development: Draft Statement on Educational Reform. Mimeo. Lusaka: Ministry of Education, Zambia.*

Mwanakatwe, J.M. 1968. *The Growth of Education in Zambia since Independence. Lusaka: Oxford University Press.*

Myers-Scotton, C. 1990. *Élite closure as boundary maintenance: The evidence from Africa. In B.Weinstein (ed.), Language Policy and Political Development, 25–41. Norwood, NJ: Ablex.*

Ouane, A. and Glanz, C. 2010. *Why and How Africa Should Invest in African Languages and Multilingual Education. Hamburg: UNESCO Institute for Lifelong Learning.*

Serpell, R. 1978. *Some developments in Zambia since 1971. In S.Ohannessian and M. Kashoki (eds), Language in Zambia, 424–447. London: International African Institute.*

UN (United Nations). 2005. *The Millennium Development Goals. New York: United Nations.*

Williams, E. 2006. *Bridges and Barriers: Language in African Education and Development. Encounters Series. Manchester: St.Jerome.*

Williams, E., de Montfort-Nayimfashe, L., Ntakirutimana, E. and O'Sullivan, B. 2004. *Proficiency in French, English and KinyaRwanda in the Primary and Secondary Sectors of the Rwandan Education System. Unpublished report commissioned by CfBT Education Trust for the Department for International Development.*

READING B: Selling English: advertising and the discourses of ELT

Mark Pegrum

Source: Pegrum, M. (2004) 'Selling English: advertising and the discourses of ELT', *English Today 77*, vol. 20, no. 1, pp. 3–10.

Perceptions of English are influenced by many factors, not the least of which is advertising which, with its knowing, encouraging smile, not only helps to shape the public face of ELT and reinforce the trust of students within the industry, but also, importantly, serves to buttress the beliefs of teachers and planners about the nature of the service they are offering. While no advertising can be expected to present a completely fair or unbiased picture, it is instructive to examine its underlying presuppositions: that is, the discourses which it both feeds and – given

The language and techniques of advertising are covered in another book in this series, *Communicating in English: Talk, Text, Technology* (Allington and Mayor, eds, 2012, Chapter 6).

that they are pre-established in the minds of the target markets, whether industry practitioners, potential or current students, or the broader public – feeds *on*. […]

Keyword: *Native*

'English in England!' proclaims an advertisement for the London-based Evendine College, while the University of Nevada at Reno invites students to 'Study English and Live the Language …'. There is nothing atypical, apart from an initial decapitalised letter, about the advertising of a textbook entitled *natural English* by Oxford University Press, nor in the promotion by the same publisher of its dictionaries as 'The unbeatable collection for more natural, expressive English'. A 'natural' corollary of this focus on the English of native speakers is the appeal to tradition, particularly, though not unexpectedly, in the country with the longest English-speaking history: 'British Education, British Quality' declares an advertisement for member institutions of BASELT (the British Association of State English Language Teaching), while OUP stresses the heritage of 'The <u>original</u> and the best Advanced Learner's Dictionary', and concludes: 'Accept no imitations.'

What Phillipson (1992:185–199) has described as the monolingual and native-speaker fallacies – the demonstrably dubious and colonially-derived notions that English is best taught monolingually and by native speakers – are alive and well. To be fair, the same fallacies hold equally for other languages, so that elsewhere, for example, Evendine advocates learning Portuguese in Portugal. As broadly compatible as this idea may be with public perceptions of the learning of any language, it dovetails with a more English-specific problem.

Despite the work of Kachru (1985 & 1986, Kachru and Nelson 2001) and others (Crystal 1997, McArthur 1998) in problematising the 'ownership of English' (Widdowson 1994), Englishes from beyond the inner circle are generally silent, from an advertising point of view, in these publications from the heartland of ELT. Nowhere is there an invitation to learn Indian or Singaporean English which, despite their increasing codification, tacitly bow to exonormative standards, or at least do not compete in this arena; nowhere do the burgeoning Euro-English (McArthur 2003a, Modiano 2003) or ELF (English as a lingua franca: Seidlhofer 2001) find their way into this publicity. There is little room for the notion that most of those learning English today will rarely have occasion to use it with a native speaker (Kachru & Nelson 2001:18). Also conspicuously absent, after years of promotion of concepts of intercultural competence (Buttjes & Byram 1991, Byram 1997, McBride & Seago 2000, Byram, Nichols & Stevens 2001) and the intercultural speaker (Byram & Zarate 1997, Kramsch 1998), is any hint of the acceptability, much less the desirability, of the kind of hybridity, code-switching, and linguistic and cultural mobility which is the norm for multilingual populations (McArthur 1998, Canagarajah 1999 & 2002). [...]

Keyword: *Modernity*

In a turnabout on the trope of tradition, the majority of advertisers in fact prefer to look to the future, plugging into what Phillipson (1992:247) has called the association of English 'with the new gods of efficiency, science and technology, modernity, etc'. Most often, a mere sampling of lexis from the semantic field of novelty is sufficient to conjure up the requisite connotations, indicating how deep-rooted they are – as in the many advertisements for new/brand-new/modern dictionaries, by such publishers as Cambridge University Press and Macmillan, or a billing of LanguEdge Courseware as 'the future of TOEFL testing'.

Of particular note is Longman's ingenious series of advertisements for its *Dictionary of Contemporary English*, which foreground appropriate lexical items accompanied by definitions, thereby reinforcing particular semantic-ideational links between the English language and the publisher's product: one example takes its cue from the keyword 'innovation', defined as 'a new idea, method, or invention that is better than those that existed before' and illustrated by the phrase 'Recent innovations in English teaching'. In a similar vein, publicity for Longman's *Cutting Edge* textbook series borrows a definition from the above dictionary to elucidate the title's reference to 'the newest and most exciting stage in the development of something'.

While stressing novelty is a common device in advertising in many domains, in the context of ELT it is easily co-opted, knowingly or otherwise, into the shadowy service of powerful underlying discourses. The tendency, especially but not only in the developing world, to link English to Phillipson's 'new gods' and to hyperbolise the association of local languages with the old gods, with tradition and personal issues, risks establishing a diabolical dichotomy (Pennycook 1999:7) which at the very least may lead to linguistic atrophy in local languages [...]

Keyword: *Self-development*

Both 'development' and its prefixed form 'self-development' inform much of the advertising of ELT and both, on the face of it, have much to recommend them. Still, 'development' is linked to concepts of modernity and modernisation, and its automatic and unreflective association with English may entail similar liabilities, as Kashoki notes: 'Africans have been psychologically conditioned to believe that only European languages are structured to aid development' (cited in Phillipson 1992:286).

Perhaps the greatest hazard, however, lies in the slippage between the terms 'development' and 'self-development'. The positive potential of each notwithstanding, they are not the same; the latter may, and often does, imply 'individual or group escape rather than systemic change' (Pennycook 1999:2). The developmental promise of ELT often tacitly targets – and is best received by – those who wish to escape, as individuals, from limited and limiting life conditions. Small wonder that it appeals to able or advantaged individuals in poorer societies. [...]

'Go further' proclaims an IELTS advertisement, as does – coincidentally but significantly – an OUP advertisement for the *New Headway* textbook series. 'Get ahead' suggests the Study Group of institutions (providers of English language training along with other programmes). You can 'Study English and achieve your goals' through Kaplan International, while the English courses at Canada's Columbia International College offer 'Your Passport to the World', and the Australian Government's 'Study in Australia' campaign [...] promises 'Your future. Your world'.

Development schemes, if implemented collaboratively with full respect for local conditions, can bring many benefits; as can, in other ways, the personal endeavour towards self-development. But ensuring that 'self-development' feeds into and is seen in the broader context of 'development' is paramount, otherwise we are effectively promising access to the material benefits of capitalism for the few, while neglecting the many. English needs to be more than a privileged escape route. An advertisement for the Educational Testing Service (ETS) reads: 'Prepare your TOEFL and ESL students for their biggest challenge. Life'. Our challenge, as educators and planners, is to ensure that 'development' and 'self-development' remain – and are perceived by students as – compatible.

Keyword: *Life*

'Alive' is the keyword in another of Longman's series of advertisements for its *Dictionary of Contemporary English* [...]. In addition to 'going further' or 'getting ahead', enjoyment of life is a common Western goal at individual and societal levels, perhaps especially for the young. A customary notion in Western marketing, it is not surprising that it finds its way into ELT publicity, where it is often linked to the promotion of place. 'Have it all' says a Study Group advertisement with a full-page picture of a sweeping beachscape under an Australian flag. The Malta Tourism Authority promises 'English in a classroom of life, colour and culture!', while the British Council invites learners to 'Have a capital summer in London', and Berlitz advertises Intense Conversational English courses in Canada with the slogan: 'Learn it! Live it! Love it!'

The spirited, slightly hedonistic edge to such advertisements will certainly strike a chord in many – particularly Western and Western-influenced – milieux, which are arguably the target markets for some of the course types being advertised. However, their appeal may not be as universal, nor their promises as alluring, as they initially seem. Firstly, such publicity could well serve to alienate parts of the increasingly dominant markets, including those in East Asia, the new 'centre of gravity' of ESL (McArthur 2003b), which consist of students and their parents who see English – and self-development – instrumentally, and as a serious matter. [...]

Keyword: *Product*

For Naysmith (1987:3), English is 'the language of international capitalism', while Canagarajah (1999:173) describes it as 'a coveted linguistic capital'. Perhaps, given the role of economic power in maintaining a dominant language (Crystal 1997), and the linkage of English with the ongoing economic processes of globalisation, it is not surprising that the language itself has become the ultimate commodity, at least for those who are lucky enough to possess exportable quantities of this 'natural' resource.

The slogan 'Another job well done', accompanied by a large tick, advertises OUP's textbook *Business Vision*, while the University of Michigan Press announces: 'Academic success ... it's in the bag!' Language is portrayed as a discrete product which can be acquired 'Fast!', as Longman's advertisement for its *Powerbase* series indicates. Indeed, fast food springs to mind: 'one stop English' is promoted by Macmillan, while Longman announces 'No time? No problem!' – the reason being its *Language to go* series. Presumably this slogan would be equally appropriate for *Grammar Express*, advertised elsewhere by the same publisher.

Stylistically hip, this advertising plays on the image of a cash- and convenience-rich but time-poor stratum of society, its smooth patina designed to appeal to an affluent, upwardly-mobile demographic. However, just as fast food restaurants tend not to promote traditions of *haute cuisine* or enrichment of life through lingering appreciation of food, it downplays the richness of both native English traditions and intercultural communication in favour of a functional, instrumental, even 'material' approach to language, thus hooking up with the 'getting ahead' metaphor seen earlier. This is certainly one aspect of English which will catch the attention of potential students wishing to escape traditional societies and identities, but, on the other hand, such a strong message risks putting off those who are unsettled by the bland cosmopolitanism of neoliberal capitalism. [...]

Images of English

English is an asset belonging to its native speakers, who are free to market and sell it; it is an all but inevitable concomitant of modernisation, globalisation, self-development and a cosmopolitan enjoyment of life; it requires deference to Western ideals of individualism, open discussion and, ultimately, global citizenship: these are some of the key tropes of English to be found in the advertising examined in this article. While none is completely false or impossible, none is entirely or indisputably true, either. The peril inherent in the human tendency to structure reality linguistically and metaphorically lies always in what is hidden, in the propensity of discourses pretending to dominance to suppress other equally viable discourses, driving alternatives underground. [...]

While the discourses elucidated in this [reading] are particularly clear in advertising, they are not limited to it, but along with a number of variants broadly inform public and academic discussion about ELT. It is our responsibility as educators (to ourselves, our profession, and most of all our students) to ensure that commonplace tropes are closely examined to reveal both the value of all and the limitations of each. English does bring benefits. But these will be most clearly perceived by those who can deconstruct the discourses woven around it, to arrive at a balanced appreciation of what it gives, and what it may also take away.

References for this reading

Buttjes, D. & M. Byram, eds. 1991. *Mediating Languages and Cultures: Towards an Intercultural Theory of Foreign Language Education*. Clevedon: Multilingual Matters.

Byram, M. 1997. *Teaching and Assessing Intercultural Communicative Competence*. Clevedon: Multilingual Matters.

Byram, M., A. Nichols & D. Stevens, eds. 2001. *Developing Intercultural Competence in Practice*. Clevedon: Multilingual Matters.

Byram, M. and G. Zarate. 1997. 'Definitions, objectives and assessment of sociocultural competence.' In M. Byram, G. Zarate & G. Neuner, eds, *Sociocultural Competence in Language Learning and Teaching*, pp. 7–43. Strasbourg: Council of Europe.

Canagarajah, A.S. 1999. *Resisting Linguistic Imperialism in English Teaching*. Oxford: University Press.

Canagarajah, A.S. 2002. 'Globalization, methods, and practice in periphery classrooms.' In D. Block & D. Cameron, eds, *Globalization and Language Teaching*, pp. 134–150. London: Routledge.

Crystal, D. 1997. *English as a Global Language*. Cambridge: University Press.

Kachru, B.B. 1985. 'Standards, codification, and sociolinguistic realism: the English language in the outer circle.' In R. Quirk & H. Widdowson, eds, *English in the World: Teaching and Learning the Language and Literatures*. Cambridge: Cambridge University Press, 11–30.

Kachru, B.B. 1986. *The Alchemy of English: The Spread, Functions and Models of Non-Native Englishes*. Oxford: Pergamon.

Kachru, B.B. and C.L. Nelson. 2001. 'World Englishes.' In A. Burns & C. Coffin, eds, *Analysing English in a Global Context: A Reader*. London: Routledge, 9–25.

Kramsch, C. 1998. 'The privilege of the intercultural speaker.' In M. Byram & M. Fleming, eds, *Language Learning in Intercultural Perspective: Approaches through Drama and Ethnography*, pp. 16–31. Cambridge: University Press.

McArthur, T. 1998. *The English Languages*. Cambridge: University Press.

McArthur, T. 2003a. 'World English, Euro-English, Nordic English?' In *English Today* 73 (19:1).

McArthur, T. 2003b. 'English as an Asian language.' In *English Today* 74 (19:2).

McBride, N. and K. Seago, eds. 2000. *Target Culture – Target Language?* London: CILT.

Modiano, M. 2003. 'Euro-English: a Swedish perspective.' In *English Today* 74 (19:2), pp. 35–41.

Naysmith, J. 1987. 'English as imperialism?' In *Language Issues* 1(2), pp. 3–5.

Pennycook, A. 1999. 'Development, culture and language: ethical concerns in a postcolonial world.' Paper delivered at The Fourth International Conference on Language and Development, Hanoi; see <http://www.languages.ait.ac.th/hanoi_proceedings/pennycook.htm>.

Phillipson, R. 1992. *Linguistic Imperialism*. Oxford: University Press.

Seidlhofer, B. 2001. 'Closing a conceptual gap: the case for a description of English as a lingua franca.' In *The International Journal of Applied Linguistics* 11(2), pp. 133–158.

Widdowson, H.G. 1994. 'The ownership of English.' In *TESOL Quarterly* 28(2), pp. 377–388.

5 English literary canons

David Johnson

5.1 Introduction

In Chapter 4, the concept of the English language as a global industry introduced English-language publications as significant in the spread of English. Here, I explore what happens when literary texts, novels, plays and poems, in the English language, travel to and from non-Anglophone countries. In this chapter, I consider the body of literary works by writers in English from non-English dominant countries. Such literary works are a consequence of the global spread of the English language that accompanied the British Empire in the nineteenth century and the American Empire in the twentieth and twenty-first centuries. We discover that the economic, political and military conflicts that characterise the colonial and postcolonial histories of the British and American empires extend to the literatures and literary debates of former colonies. In order to appreciate these debates, I work through a number of case studies in a loosely chronological sequence. I begin in eighteenth-century Europe, and consider the original models of the national literary 'canon', those literary works valued most highly. I move next to consider how the English literary canon travelled to non-Anglophone countries under colonial rule, and contrast the case of English literature in India in the nineteenth century with that of English literature in Africa in the first half of the twentieth century. The next set of case studies focuses on literary canons in non-Anglophone nations in the postcolonial period, and I examine the cases of India, Kenya and South Africa. I conclude by considering the future of literary canons, addressing recent debates in the United States about the possibility of a canon of 'world literature'.

5.2 Models of the national literary canon

The concept of the literary canon has a long history, and I start by examining how it emerged in Europe in the eighteenth century, was consolidated in the nineteenth century, and continues to influence how we think about literature in the twenty-first century.

Relationship bet language and nationalism

General comment EMA

What is 'English literature'?

The answer to this deceptively simple question lies not in England, but in eighteenth-century Germany, where an influential generation of philosophers insisted on the connection between the rise of modern nation states, national languages and national literatures. Johann Gottfried Herder (1744–1803) (Figure 5.1) expressed the intimate bond between Nation-Language-Literature by posing the following rhetorical questions:

> How shall our [German] language be determined and regulated, if not through the best writers of our nation? How shall we acquire patriotism and love of our fatherland, if not through its language, through the most excellent thoughts and sensations, expressed in it like a stored-up treasure? Assuredly, we would not still be erring … if we only knew, from youth onwards, our best writers and elected them as guides.

> (quoted in Damrosch et al., 2009, p. 6)

Figure 5.1 Johann Gottfried Herder

Herder thus links 'the best writers of our nation', 'love of our fatherland' and the (German) 'language'. The 'thoughts and sensations' expressed in the German language by the nation's best writers represent a 'stored-up treasure', and they have the capacity to function as guides to the nation. Herder's challenge therefore was to forge an unbreakable bond between the German nation, the German language and German literature. Other European nations took up Herder's challenge for their respective languages and literatures, and strove to establish a defining bond between Nation-Language-Literature.

The cultural theorist Raymond Williams acknowledges the importance of Herder and his peers in explaining the history of the definition of 'English literature':

> That now common phrase, **English literature**, is itself part of a crucial development. The idea of a *Nationallitteratur* developed in Germany from the 1770s, and the following can be recorded: *Über die neuere deutsche Litteratur* (Herder, 1767); *Les Siècles de littérature française* (1772); *Storia della letteratura italiana* (1772). **English literature** appears to have followed these ... The sense of 'a nation' having 'a literature' is a crucial social and cultural, probably also political, development.
>
> (Williams, 1983, p. 185)

CMA.

The yoking of 'nation' to 'literature' in late eighteenth-century Germany was thus copied in England with the rise of 'English literature', in France with the rise of French literature and in Italy with the rise of Italian literature. All the literatures of Europe's nations were organised largely along national lines, and in the nineteenth century, the process was consolidated with the publication of further national literary histories. An important consequence, according to one literary historian, was that 'all literatures had been declared national, which is to say sealed off from each other behind national boundaries ... [and] national literary histories were composed and taught in such a way that they become closed in upon themselves' (Casanova, 2004, p. 105).

The eighteenth-century invention of national literatures and their nineteenth-century consolidation continues to exert a powerful influence today. The first activity in this chapter invites you to think about whether we have moved beyond the habit of thinking about literary works in terms of their nationality.

Activity 5.1

Imagine that you are responsible for the curriculum for English Literature in schools in England. Quickly write down the names of five writers

Allow about 10 minutes

(poets, novelists or dramatists) your think all pupils in England should read before leaving school.

Comment

My guess is that your list includes some of the following: William Shakespeare, John Milton, Jane Austen, William Wordsworth, Charles Dickens, Virginia Woolf. Depending on your formal education and your reading tastes, you might also have included: Geoffrey Chaucer, Christopher Marlowe, Daniel Defoe, Blake/Coleridge/Byron/Shelley/Keats, the Brontës, George Eliot or W. H. Auden. But it is very likely that certain considerations will have caused you to pause for thought. Can writers from Britain and Ireland, rather than England alone be considered? (Writers like Joyce, Burns, Dylan Thomas.) Can writers who produced literature in English, but lived between (for example) the United States and England, be included? (Writers like Henry James or T. S. Eliot.) Can writers from England who did not write in modern English be included – think particularly of the poets and dramatists of the Middle Ages? Can writers from Britain's colonies, such as Olive Schreiner or Katherine Mansfield, be included? Can writers from Britain's ex-colonies, such as Salman Rushdie or Linton Kwesi Johnson, be included?

These awkward questions suggest that implicit in any definition of 'English literature' lies a more fundamental question, namely: how do we decide which writers or literary texts should be included under the definition of 'English literature'? The writers who *are* included constitute what we term 'the canon of English literature' or 'the English literary canon', and my list above headed by Shakespeare might serve as a convenient shorthand for the English literary canon. The first step in this chapter is to appreciate that the English literary canon is the product of a lengthy and contested historical process. I turn now to look at the earliest stages in that process, the canonisation of Shakespeare as the exemplary canonical figure of English literature.

The canonisation of Shakespeare

The conventional wisdom is that Shakespeare's plays and poetry have always enjoyed universal acclaim. However, a more careful look at the history of Shakespeare's journey to the summit of the English literary canon suggests a more complicated and contradictory picture.

Figure 5.2   Statue of Shakespeare at Poet's Corner, Westminster Abbey, London

Three stages in Shakespeare's rise can be identified.

Stage one: successful playwright

During his own lifetime (1564–1616), Shakespeare enjoyed popularity as a playwright, but after his death, and especially in the final third of the seventeenth century, his reputation declined. During the English Civil War (1640–51), the London theatres were closed, but were reopened with the Restoration of the Monarchy in 1660. The Crown patronised the theatre directly, and the task of the royal theatre companies was to stage plays that would 'convince both Charles II and his theatre-going subjects that the English Revolution had indeed not taken place' (Dobson, 1992, p. 20). Shakespeare's plays were not especially popular with the royal court, and beyond the theatre companies attached to the Crown, Shakespeare's reputation was also modest: the open-air Red Bull theatre company included only four of his plays in its twenty-play repertoire in 1660, and the Phoenix Theatre in Drury Lane staged only one Shakespeare play in the same year – *Pericles*. By the end of the seventeenth century, Shakespeare was regarded as one of a number of talented English playwrights, and he contributed as one-among-many to English theatre companies' repertoires.

Stage two: national playwright

The eighteenth century saw a rise in Shakespeare's reputation, and by about 1750, he was established as the National Playwright. Two contexts were especially important in establishing Shakespeare's pre-eminence, namely the theatres, and the literary magazines and newspapers reviewing his plays. Theatre audiences expanded rapidly in the eighteenth century, as the number and size of the theatres increased. The link between 'nation' and 'literature' was especially strong in the theatres in moments of political crisis. For example, after the pro-Catholic Jacobite Rebellion of 1745, and again during the Seven Years' War (1756–63) against France, Shakespeare's plays most amenable to jingoistic interpretation were performed – *Henry V* was revived at Drury Lane, and a rewritten version of *King John* (*Papal Tyranny in the Reign of King John*) at Covent Garden.

As in the theatres, so too in the reviews, a strong sense of national pride is evident. Shakespeare was at least the equal of – if not better than – the classical Greek and Roman writers; in 1760, a Professor of Greek at Cambridge declared that the "'immortal and inimitable Shakespear [*sic*]'" surpassed 'the excellencies of Æschylus, Sophocles, and Euripides' (Taylor, 1990, p. 114). And Shakespeare could even serve as a secular religion, as Arthur Murphy explained in 1753: 'With us islanders, Shakespeare is a kind of establish'd religion in Poetry' (quoted in Dobson, 1992, p. 7). This applause for Shakespeare was reinforced by a number of complementary developments: Shakespeare's plays appeared in a scholarly edition for the first time in Nicholas Rowe's 1709 edition of his collected works; the first critical monograph on Shakespeare appeared in John Dennis's 1712 *Essay Upon the Writings and Genius of Shakespeare*; Shakespeare appeared for the first time in the education system (at Westminster School in 1728 and at Oxford University in 1750); monuments to Shakespeare were erected in places of national importance (e.g. at Poet's Corner in Westminster Abbey in 1741, shown in Figure 5.2); and Shakespeare's birthplace, Stratford-upon-Avon, became a site of secular pilgrimage after 1769. By the end of the eighteenth century, Shakespeare had become England's greatest literary asset, a source of unqualified national pride.

Stage three: Universal Genius

Shakespeare's stature was enhanced even further by intellectual developments in late eighteenth-century Germany. The German Romantics were involved in a bitter polemic with a conservative establishment that venerated the Greek and Roman classics and spurned all modern literatures in modern European languages. The establishment view was that *only* the literature of antiquity, and particularly Homer and Virgil, deserved the title of Universal Literature. The German Romantics attacked this view, and pressed the claims of modern literature, with Shakespeare thrust forward as the most persuasive example of a 'modern' writer worthy of the title Universal Genius. That Shakespeare wrote in the English language was no barrier to these young German critics recruiting him in their battle against literary-critical orthodoxy. The next generation of German Romantics shared Goethe's love of Shakespeare. A. W. von Schlegel, for example, described Shakespeare as 'a profound artist [who] has reflected, and deeply reflected, on character and passion, on the progress of events and human destinies, on the human constitution, on all the things and relations of the world' (von Schlegel, 1846 [1815], pp. 358–9). His only regret is that Shakespeare was not German. Bemoaning the fragmented state of the German people – 'we Germans … are in danger of disappearing altogether from the list of independent nations' (von Schlegel, 1846 [1815], p. 529) – von Schlegel cries out for a literary genius to promote Germany's regeneration. English Romantic poets and critics like Samuel Taylor Coleridge happily accepted German applause for Shakespeare, and popularised his ascension to the status of Universal Genius.

Activity 5.2

Do you agree that Shakespeare is England's greatest writer, even a Universal Genius? How did you reach your conclusion? To what extent did your education and upbringing influence your view of Shakespeare?

Allow about 10 minutes

Comment

These are deceptively difficult questions, and how you answer them will depend on any number of factors: whether English is your first or main language; whether your family and friends are Shakespeare-lovers; how many Shakespeare performances you have watched in theatres or on screen; and how much Shakespeare you studied at school or college. My own response to these questions oscillates between my experience of having goose-bumps in the theatre when watching particular scenes from Shakespeare performed well (when I would give him the title 'Universal Genius'), and my experiences as a teacher in Africa trying to help English school pupils whose first language wasn't English understand enough Shakespeare to pass their examinations (when I often felt part of a postcolonial education apparatus dedicated to enforcing Shakespeare's 'universality'). What these conflicting responses suggest to me is that no simple or dogmatic answer is possible.

5.3   The English literary canon and colonialism

Having examined the emergence of the English literary canon in Britain itself, we turn now to two episodes in the journeys of English literature to non-Anglophone nations under Britain's colonial empire (see Figure 5.3). The first is in India in the nineteenth century, and the second is in Africa in the twentieth century.

Nineteenth-century India

To analyse the travels of the English literary canon to non-Anglophone contexts requires both an appreciation of the affective power of literature, and an understanding of the social, political and educational mission of English literature beyond Britain's borders. British rule in India under Warren Hastings, the Governor-General from 1774 to 1785, was guided by an official policy known as 'Orientalism'. Dictated partly by expediency, Hastings was convinced that British colonial officials did not know enough about the India they ruled over, and he accordingly promoted their thorough immersion in Indian languages, cultures and traditions. In the words of one cultural historian, the goal of Orientalism was 'to train British administrators and civil servants to fit into the culture of the ruled and to assimilate them thoroughly into the native way of life' (Viswanathan, 1989, p. 28). With respect to British attitudes to Indian literatures, the late eighteenth century therefore represented a period of relative tolerance and cultural empathy on the part of the colonisers.

After the impeachment of Hastings on charges of corruption, and his replacement by Lord Cornwallis (1786–96), however, the policy of Orientalism was challenged and gradually superseded by the alternative policy of Anglicism. Anglicism reacted against Orientalism by advocating Western (and particularly British) culture at the expense of Eastern culture. Specifically, this meant that English literature was to be promoted over Indian literatures, a policy the Anglicists justified on two grounds. First, they argued that English literature was simply better than Indian literature, a sentiment vividly captured in Thomas Macaulay's 'Minute on Indian Education' (1835), in which he declared that 'a single shelf of a good European library was worth the whole native literature of India and Arabia' (quoted in Trivedi, 1993, p. 11). The second reason Britain's colonial administrators promoted English above Indian literature was to do with their need to educate and recruit Indians to serve in the lower reaches of the colonial bureaucracy.

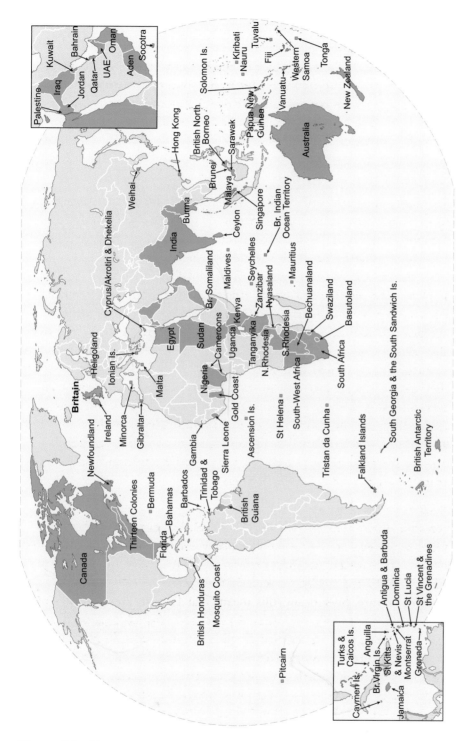

Figure 5.3 Map showing the extent of the British Empire

The British were unable to introduce the same Christian-based education package that served the purpose of educating junior bureaucrats in Britain because of the unshakeable hold of Hinduism. As an alternative, they introduced instead the teaching of English Literature as a substitute for Bible-based instruction. Administrators like Charles Trevelyan were convinced that 'without ever looking into the Bible one of those Natives must come to a considerable knowledge of it merely from reading English Literature' (Viswanathan, 1989, p. 94).

Figure 5.4   Hindu College, Calcutta, founded in 1817

Allow about
30 minutes

Activity 5.3

That the long-term impact of Anglicist policy on language and literature would ultimately be beneficial to India is explained in the words of the colonial official Charles Trevelyan in 1836. Read carefully Trevelyan's rationalisation for introducing the English language and English literature in India, and identify the following: (1) How does Trevelyan characterise Indian literature? (2) How does he characterise the impact of English language and literature? And (3) how does he see the future of India under British influence?

The vernacular dialects of India, will, by the same process [of introducing the English language and literature], be united among themselves. This diversity among languages is one of the greatest living obstacles to improvement in India. But when English shall everywhere be established as the language of education, when the vernacular literature shall everywhere be formed from materials drawn from this source, and according to models furnished by this prototype, a strong tendency to assimilation will be created. Both the matter and the manner will be the same. Saturated from the same source, recast in the same mould, with a common science, a common standard of taste, a common nomenclature, the national languages as well as the national character will be consolidated. ... We shall leave a united and enlightened nation where we found a people broken up into sections ... and depressed by literary systems, designed much more with a view to check the progress, than to promote the advance, of the human mind.

(quoted in Tharu, 1991, p. 166)

Comment

Trevelyan argues that before the coming of the British to India, India was frustrated by its many competing languages and literatures. India pre-British rule is characterised as a nation divided ('broken up into sections') and stagnating ('depressed by [its] literary systems'). Trevelyan's solution? Establish the English language and English literature as the 'source', 'models' and the 'prototype' for the Indian education system. The consequences of pursuing this policy will be positive, with the diverse Indian languages and literatures 'united', 'assimilat[ed]' and 'consolidated'. And ultimately the reward will be 'improvement' and 'progress', as the Indians – 'saturated' in the English language and English literature – will acquire a 'common' 'science', 'standard of taste' and 'nomenclature', and ultimately become 'a united and enlightened nation'. As we will return to these debates, it is useful to be clear about the stages in Trevelyan's argument: (1) a negative characterisation of Indian linguistic and literary diversity before British rule; (2) positive claims for the progressive effects of the English language and literature; and (3) a narrative of progress which insists on a journey from Oriental backwardness to Western modernity.

Notwithstanding their differences over language policy, the Orientalists and the Anglicists shared the same ambition: to recruit literate clerks and minor officials to administer the colonial civil service. Ultimately, the Anglicists like Macaulay and Trevelyan prevailed, and hence the teaching and examining of English literature was institutionalised. Satisfied that the Indian experiment was a success, British educators from the 1850s onwards also introduced English literature as an examination subject in Britain for candidates seeking entry into the civil service and the professions. Seventeen such examinations in English literature were in place by 1875, and they all demanded the memorising of set literary texts, with Shakespeare the most prominent author.

Twentieth-century Africa

Education policy in Britain's African colonies had proceeded up until the 1920s in laissez-faire fashion, with missionaries entrusted with the responsibility for education. However, the increasing demands of the expanding colonial economies, and the perceived failures of the existing education system to meet those demands, led to new initiatives. Guided by the policy of 'indirect rule', which claimed to respect African authority structures and to allow Africans to advance along 'their own lines', the educational policy makers in the 1920s committed themselves to greater investment in African education in pursuance of the following guiding principles: education should take into account the needs of Africans; vocational and industrial education should be expanded; teaching in vernacular languages should only be superseded at secondary level by English; religious and moral instruction should be at the centre of the curriculum; girls should have the same access to schooling as boys; and finally, a literary education should always be available to the minority 'who are required to fill posts in the administrative and technical services as well as … those who, as chiefs, will occupy positions of exceptional trust and responsibility' (HMSO, 1935, quoted in Watson, 1982, p. 21). In effect, the proposals for African education repeated substantially the nineteenth-century divide in England between utilitarian instruction based on the Bible for the masses, and a literary education for the rulers.

Allow about 45 minutes

Activity 5.4

In a similar spirit to the nineteenth-century British colonial officials in India, like Trevelyan, who promoted the English language and English literature, so too in Africa a century later, another generation of officials made plans for educating Africans. Read the passage below, written in the 1930s by Arthur Mayhew. As you do so:

1   Summarise in your own words his arguments about the place of the English language and literature in education for Africans.

2   Compare and contrast Mayhew's arguments for Africa with those of Trevelyan for India.

The first essential is to ensure those social and economic conditions without which there is no economic basis for cultural advancement. ... [We emphasise] the desirability of the [African] educated class keeping in touch with the masses of their countrymen. It may be that indigenous culture will be the link. In our African colonies the drift so far has been in the other direction, and it cannot be said that the product of higher education has in the past been in close touch with the various aspects of local and racial life.

In secondary and higher education English is the recognised medium of instruction. As a subject of instruction it occupies an important place in the curriculum. A working knowledge of the language is the main, though not the only, aim in the secondary course, with fuller scope for literary and cultural treatment in the post-secondary stages. The importance of the local languages and literatures ... is recognised, though a place for them cannot always be found in secondary and higher education courses. Where the vernacular languages are still in a primitive condition their development should be encouraged.

(Mayhew, 1938, pp. 52–3)

Comment

1   Mayhew registers that the necessary economic conditions must obtain before 'cultural advancement' can take place. Mayhew's opening sentence expresses the need to educate Africans so that they can function as members of an educated workforce in the British colonies in Africa. He also emphasises that Africa's school-educated elite must remain in touch with the African masses. He is unsure that the present dispensation meets this imperative, and considers ways of making adjustments. He notes that the existing education system for Africans is based on teaching them the English language and (in the 'post-secondary stages') English literature and culture. He acknowledges that this system of education has not been entirely successful: 'indigenous' African culture has been neglected, and school-educated Africans have been distanced from 'local and racial life'. He recognises further that 'local languages and literatures' are important, but that they have to date been subordinated within the curriculum to the teaching of the English language and literature. He argues too that the development of 'vernacular languages' (and presumably literatures) should be encouraged where they are 'still in

a primitive condition'. Let us tease out in a little more detail a couple of Mayhew's assumptions. First, he assumes that the English language and literature are superior to 'primitive' African languages and literatures, and that Africa's 'cultural advancement' can only take place under the tutelage of the British colonial administration. Second, Mayhew appears to treat the question of colonial education policy as one of strategy rather than of principle. In other words, his keen sense of the need to secure the colonial economy means that he is able to contemplate an education system based either on English or on African language(s) and literature(s). He is not committed to enforcing the English language and literature at all costs (although he believes it is superior); if teaching African languages and literatures achieves the required result, he appears prepared to accommodate such a concession.

2 Trevelyan and Mayhew are similar in their assumptions of British cultural superiority over Indians and Africans respectively, and in their convictions that a British education will inevitably lead them to 'progress' and 'advancement'. Based simply on the evidence of these two passages, Mayhew does, however, differ from Trevelyan in certain respects. First, he is more willing than Trevelyan to acknowledge the economic motives which underwrite British colonial education policies. Second, he is more willing than Trevelyan to concede that non-British languages and literatures have some value. Third, he is more strategic than Trevelyan, as he recognises the potential limitations of an exclusively Anglophone education model for Africans, and contemplates including elements of African languages and literatures in the curriculum. Mayhew is particularly concerned to avoid the opening up of a gulf between an English-educated and Anglophile African elite and the vast majority of Africans, as such a split might ultimately threaten British rule in Africa.

5.4   The English literary canon and postcolonialism

The military, political and economic anti-colonial struggles were accompanied by cultural resistance to British rule, and in the immediate aftermath of independence, there were efforts to replace the English literary canon with literary canons based on local writers and their work. Three case studies illustrate the different arguments which have dictated the constitution of postcolonial literary canons in India, Kenya and South Africa. In different but related ways, the writers from Britain's ex-colonies we discuss – Rajeswari Sunder Rajan and Ngũgĩ wa Thiong'o –

challenge the assumptions and arguments of colonial officials like Trevelyan and Mayhew.

Postcolonial India

Trevelyan's and Macaulay's plans for introducing an English education in India did not succeed in producing a docile pro-British Indian workforce to help run the colony. Instead, in the years to follow, there were successive waves of resistance to British rule, from the British-Sikh Wars of 1845–49 and the Great Indian Rebellion (the Indian Mutiny) of 1857–58, through Gandhi's all-India *satyagraha* ('non-violent resistance') campaign and the Jallianwalla Bagh (Amritsar) Massacre of 1919, to the 'Quit India' movement from 1942, which sought, through strikes, demonstrations and mass protests, to expel the British from India. India's protracted anti-colonial struggle ultimately culminated in independence from Britain in 1947.

Activity 5.5

Now turn to Reading A: *Writing in English in India*, by Rajeswari Sunder Rajan, a literary critic writing in one of India's national English-language newspapers *The Hindu*. *The Hindu* has circulation figures of 1.46 million, and Rajan contributes to ongoing debates about the place of the English language in India, the status of Indian literature in English vs Indian literature in Indian languages, and the relationship between Indian national identity and Indian literature. Rajan's arguments are compressed, so you might need to read the extract through two or three times, but as you do so, note down your answers to the following questions:

1   How does Rajan contrast the place of the English language in colonial and postcolonial India?

2   What alternatives does Rajan set out for assessing non-English writers writing in English?

3   What weaknesses have been apparent in the works of Indian writers writing in English?

4   From Rajan's paraphrase, summarise Salman Rushdie's view of Indian literature in English vs Indian literature in Indian languages.

5   What are Rajan's objections to Rushdie's arguments?

6   How does Rajan explain the relationship between Indian literature and Indian national identity?

Comment

(EMA)

1   Under colonialism, English was the language of the colonialist. It was introduced into the education system in order to create 'a babu class'; that is, a class of English-speaking civil servants who would serve the British colonial administration in India. (This is the argument for English in India you have already encountered in reading Trevelyan's blueprint.) The consequences of English serving British colonial interests in this direct fashion were that on one side, English was embraced by 'the comprador class' (the Indians who collaborated with the British), and on the other side, it was opposed by the anti-colonial Indian nationalists. This opposition was complicated by the fact that some anti-colonial nationalists read British radicals such as Tom Paine, and found support in their writings for Indian anti-colonial struggles. Under postcolonial rule, with language a divisive issue within a multilingual nation, and with Southern India especially strongly opposed to Hindi as the nation's official language, English has emerged as the 'pan-Indian and "link"' language for the whole nation. Accordingly, in postcolonial India, nationalists no longer argue for the removal of English from the education system or other forums of official, commercial or technological use. English is used by a small percentage of the population, and is characteristically the second language of the educated elite.

(EMA)

(EMA.)

2   There is an intimate connection between literary expression and choice of language. One line of argument contends that writing in a language other than the mother tongue – and especially writing in English, the language of the coloniser – fundamentally diminishes the authenticity of the literary work. James Joyce's character Stephen in *Portrait of the Artist as a Young Man* and the critic Ngũgĩ wa Thiong'o in *Decolonising the Mind* both produce compelling versions of this argument (you will encounter Ngũgĩ's argument in more detail in the next subsection). An alternative line of argument is that transcultural and translinguistic literary works demonstrate that identities are 'more fluid and constitutively mixed than they are fixed', and therefore national language barriers are no obstacle to literary achievement – acclaimed writers such as the Polish Joseph Conrad and the Russian Vladimir Nabokov exemplify this fluidity. A third alternative is the argument that certain writers, who no longer have the capacity to write in their native language, and have adopted a new literary language, have the ability to produce successful literary works. The character Sandeep's adoption of English in Amit Chaudhuri's *A Strange and Sublime Address* illustrates this alternative.

3   The influential argument of the critic Meenakshi Mukherjee is paraphrased. Mukherjee's argument is that Indian writers writing in English display an 'anxiety of Indianness'. Anxious that writing in

English diminishes the authenticity of their work, such Indian writers compensate by overstating or embellishing 'markers of "Indian-ness" to establish their "authenticity"'. This is reflected in 'ornate … writing, exoticism, nostalgic evocation of sensuous details' and 'glossing' details which non-Indian readers might not understand. Writers writing in Indian languages, by contrast, have no such anxieties, and therefore write in a much more natural way about India. Rajan has some sympathy for this generalisation, but notes that Salman Rushdie's *Midnight's Children* is an exception to this generalisation, as it displayed very little of such anxiety. Rajan argues that the more important issue is to understand the pressures exerted by two readerships – one in India and another in Britain and the United States. This split readership has produced an opposition between those Indian writers writing in English and focused on British and US readers and markets, and those Indian writers and critics writing in Indian languages and focused (inevitably) on Indian readers and markets.

4   Rushdie's argument is that Indian literature written in English (pre-eminently his own!) is 'a stronger and more important body of work' than all the literature produced in India's sixteen national languages. In making this claim, Rushdie casts Indian literature in English as 'cosmopolitan', and Indian literature in Indian languages as 'parochial'. Further, he attacks Indian critics hostile to his novels and those of other Indian writers in English for elevating political criteria above purely literary or aesthetic criteria in judging their literary work. Such critics are guilty of 'political correctness'. Rushdie proceeds to praise the work of the Anglo-Indian novelist R. K. Narayan (1906–2001), who goes beyond the specifics of 'the Indian condition' to reveal 'the human condition itself'.

5   Rajan claims that Rushdie's elevation of Indian writing in English at the expense of Indian writing in Indian languages is something that 'no literate Indian' takes seriously. Pointing to Rushdie's almost total ignorance of Indian writing in Indian languages, Rajan suggests that his fame, accompanied by his self-promotion, enables him to value his ignorance as 'worth more than anybody else's scholarship'. Regarding Rushdie's allegation that Indian writing in English was being persecuted by 'politically correct' critics, Rajan first highlights how persuasively Rushdie himself had contended in the past that literary 'criticism … must be political', and second, she argues in more general terms that '[t]he opposition between the aesthetic and the political as rigidly separate categories is bound to be a futile and false one'. Rajan rejects Rushdie's praise for Narayan as the perpetuation of yet another cliché, namely the opposition between the particular and the universal. Rushdie's universal is the 'mainstream

(western/white/male/bourgeois)', and his particular is the non-western/ the non-white/the female/the working class. (Rajan is relying here on the kinds of arguments covered in the earlier section on 'The canonisation of Shakespeare', namely that Shakespeare was 'made' universal at a particular historical moment.) By praising Narayan for overcoming 'the particular' and achieving 'the universal', Rushdie therefore reinforces a hierarchy that diminishes the 'national-Indian' and privileges a bogus universalism.

6   Since *Midnight's Children*, there have been a number of Indian literary works in English, which are unmarked by 'the anxiety of Indian-ness'; they have recorded and celebrated specifically Indian locales without trying to explain India to non-Indian readers. Crucially, this literary 'Indian-ness' is 'a construction, not the discovery and instatement of some pre-existing nationalist essence'. This construction in India is comparable to the processes 'the literatures in other countries have engaged in at specific historical conjunctures'. (Recall the examples at the beginning of the chapter: German literature in the German language for the German nation; English literature in the English language for the British nation.) In this case, we have the more complicated example of Indian literature in the English language for the Indian nation. Rajan's concluding remarks refer to the responsibilities of both writers and critics in relation to Indian literature in postcolonial India.

Postcolonial Kenya

Like Trevelyan's plans, Mayhew's education model for Africans failed to produce an obedient pro-British workforce, and in the 1940s and 1950s, resistance to colonial rule gathered momentum across the continent. In Kenya, the years after the Second World War were characterised by a sharp deterioration in living conditions for both the landless poor of the rural reserves and the badly paid and unemployed of the urban areas. Peaceful protest against British rule gave way to violent struggle in 1952 when the British governor declared a state of emergency and sanctioned the detention of 183 African leaders. The next four years saw an unequal war waged between the British military and the Kenyan insurgents of Inthaka na Wiyathi (Land Freedom Army, also known as Mau Mau). By 1956, over 10,000 Mau Mau had been killed, 590 British soldiers, 1819 Africans fighting for the British, thirty-two European settlers and twenty-six Asian civilians (Curtis, 2003, p. 323). Although violent opposition to British rule was much reduced with the suppression of the Mau Mau uprising, continuing anti-colonial resistance culminated in independence in 1963, with the Kenyan African National Union winning the first free elections, and then going on to hold power for the next thirty-nine years.

What did literature have to do with Kenya's colonial and anti-colonial histories? For the Kenyan writer Ngũgĩ wa Thiong'o (see Figure 5.5), literature was integral to the confrontation between the British coloniser and the Kenyan colonised. Ngũgĩ describes his own school and university education in 1940s and 1950s Kenya: 'The syllabus of the English Department … meant a study of the history of English literature from Shakespeare, Spencer and Milton to James Joyce and T. S. Eliot, I. A. Richards and the inevitable F. R. Leavis' (Ngũgĩ, 1986, p. 90). The consequences of such an education were that 'African children who encountered [English] literature in colonial schools and universities were thus experiencing the world as defined and reflected in the European experience of history' (Ngũgĩ, 1986, p. 93). For Ngũgĩ, such an education in the English literary canon therefore functioned as the cultural complement of Britain's political and economic domination of Kenyan society, and helped to create an African elite loyal to their British masters. In his own words:

The experiences of Ngũgĩ wa Thiong'o are discussed in more detail, including a reading by him, in another book in this series: Seargeant and Swann (eds) (2012), Chapter 1.

> the economic control of the African people was effected through politics and culture. Economic and political control of a people can never be complete without cultural control, and here literary scholarly practice … fitted well the aim and the logic of the system as a whole. After all, the universities and colleges set up in the colonies after the war were meant to produce a native elite which would later help prop up the Empire.
>
> (Ngũgĩ, 1986, p. 93)

For Ngũgĩ, 'literary scholarly practice', with the English literary canon headed by Shakespeare at its core, was therefore directly implicated in effecting the 'cultural control' of the Kenyan people that would 'complete' their economic and political subordination.

Figure 5.5 Ngũgĩ wa Thiong'o

Allow about
30 minutes

Activity 5.6

If Shakespeare and the English literary canon were the necessary cultural accompaniments of British colonial violence and exploitation in Kenya in the 1950s and 1960s, what Kenyan literary resources accompanied the anti-colonial struggles of Mau Mau? In 1968, Ngũgĩ and two colleagues at Nairobi University, Owuor Anyumba and Taban Lo Liyong, produced a manifesto which provided an answer. Read the following extract from their manifesto, and summarise the arguments.

We reject the primacy of English literature and cultures. The aim, in short, should be to orientate ourselves towards placing Kenya, East Africa and then Africa in the centre. All other things are to be considered in their relevance to our situation and their contribution towards understanding ourselves … In suggesting this we are not rejecting other streams, especially the western stream. We are only clearly mapping out the directions and perspectives the study of culture and literature will inevitably take in an African university. … We want to establish the centrality of Africa in the department. This … is justifiable on various grounds, the most important one being that education is a means of knowledge about ourselves. Therefore, after we have examined ourselves, we radiate outwards and discover peoples and worlds around us. With Africa at the centre of things, not existing as an appendix or a satellite of other countries and literatures, things must be seen from the African perspective.

… The study of the Oral Tradition would … supplement (not replace) courses in Modern African Literature. By discovering and proclaiming loyalty to indigenous values, the new literature would on the one hand be set in the stream of history to which it belongs and so be better appreciated; and on the other be better able to embrace and assimilate other thoughts without losing its roots.

(quoted in Ngũgĩ, 1986, pp. 94–5)

Comment

The manifesto argues that the colonial deference to English literature must be replaced with the postcolonial assertion of the primacy of Kenyan literature. Kenyan literature must no longer be merely a 'satellite' or 'appendix' of other countries and literatures. Rather, a Kenyan literary canon must be at the core of the Kenyan literary education, with successive layers of East African literature and African literature 'radiating' outwards. The 'streams' of Western literatures would be included within a Kenyan university literary education, but only as one among many literatures. Of particular importance in forging a postcolonial Kenyan literary education is the inclusion of the African oral tradition to supplement modern African literature. By transforming the Kenyan literary education along these lines, Kenyans will acquire a better knowledge of themselves, they will appreciate their own literature in its appropriate context, and they will remain connected with their pre-colonial roots.

It is worth pausing briefly to contrast Mayhew's plans for African education in the 1930s to Ngũgĩ's arguments fifty years later. It is clear that in the case of Kenya at least, Mayhew's proposals to moderate the entrenched English-centred linguistic and literary model of schooling had limited impact. Ngũgĩ's schooling under colonialism in the 1940s and 1950s remained steeped in the English language and English literature, with little evidence of Mayhew's gestures to linguistic and cultural accommodation. What is striking, however, is how prescient Mayhew's anxieties about the long-term effects of an English education under colonialism for Africa's elite might be: Kenya's elite remain Anglophile and out of touch with their own masses (according to

This situation has certain parallels with the position of English in the education system in Malaysia discussed in Chapter 3.

199

Ngũgĩ), and a strong culture of anti-colonial resistance (represented by Ngũgĩ) has flourished as a consequence of Britain's colonialist policies.

Postcolonial/post-apartheid South Africa

There are at least three complications to note at the outset in introducing the South African case study. Dating South Africa's transition to a 'postcolonial' society is complicated by its relatively large white settler population. In one sense, South Africa ceased to be a colony of Britain either in 1910 when it was declared the Union of South Africa, or in 1961 when it left the British Commonwealth to become the Republic of South Africa. In another sense, neither of these constitutional transitions amounted to 'independence' for the black majority, as they were denied basic political freedoms, and the white settler regime's policies of segregation and apartheid produced what became known as 'colonialism of a special type'. In this second sense, South Africa therefore only became 'postcolonial' in 1994 with the first free elections after the end of apartheid. A second complication is that English was not the only European language imposed in South Africa: the majority of white South Africans speak Afrikaans (derived principally from Dutch, but also influenced by French, German, indigenous and slave languages). Third, like India and Kenya, South Africa has numerous language groups and literatures within its borders, and arguments like Herder's discussed earlier, about the axiomatic bond between Nation-Language-Literature, must therefore be re-thought to accommodate such complexity.

The search for alternatives to the English literary canon began in the late nineteenth century, as certain scholars turned their attention to literatures in African languages, including oral literatures. A number of books and articles on African-language folklore and proverbs appeared, accompanied by reviews in newspapers of new works by African writers. The most wide-ranging study was Solomon T. Plaatje's *Sechuana Proverbs with Literal Translations and their European Equivalents* (1916), which included 732 proverbs, with English translations and their closest English equivalents. Plaatje described the object of the book as 'to save from oblivion, as far as this can still be done, the proverbial expressions of the Bechuana people' (quoted in Willan, 1984, p. 214), and the same ambition drove other such works, like Isaac Williams Wauchope's many articles on Xhosa proverbs and folklore in the newspaper *Imvo Zabantsundu* between 1889 and 1903, and Édouard Jacottet's two-volume *The Treasury of Ba-Suto: Being Original Se-Suto Text, with a Literal English Translation and Notes* (1908, 1911).

In the 1920s and 1930s, resistance to the exclusive elevation of the English literary canon headed by Shakespeare grew unevenly, and South African literary works were promoted in its stead. For example, when the Zulu intellectual Herbert Dhlomo argued that Shakespeare's blank verse 'comes naturally and without effort to the African writer [and] is native to our genius' (quoted in Johnson, 1996, p. 133), he was attacked by B. W. Vilikazi for failing to appreciate Zulu poetic models sufficiently. Despite their differences, both Dhlomo and Vilikazi expressed the desire for an independent South African literature. In 1923, a 'Special Correspondent' in an article 'Towards our own literature' in the newspaper *Ilanga Lase Natal* declared that a national literature should avoid a 'narrow or racial spirit', and seek rather to establish a 'brotherhood of the heart [through] the precision of Zulu and the elasticity of English' (2 December 1923, p. 4). Also indicative of a shift away from European religious and literary standards were Dhlomo's sympathetic critical introductions to black South African writers in the four issues of his small circulation periodical *The Reader's Companion* in 1938.

Figure 5.6   Stephen Biko, founder of the Black Consciousness Movement

Further impetus towards developing a South African literature independent of Afrikaans or English linguistic and literary models was provided in the 1970s by the Black Consciousness Movement. The leading theorist of black consciousness, Steve Biko (see Figure 5.6), emphasised the need to reverse European cultural imperialism and proclaim African culture. In a 1971 lecture titled 'Some African cultural concepts', Biko affirmed the need for a 'culture of defiance, self-assertion and group pride and solidarity. This is a culture that emanates from a situation of common experience of oppression. Just as it now finds expression in our music and our dress, it will spread to other aspects' (Biko, 1979, p. 46). Biko's ideas did indeed 'spread to other aspects', and especially to literature, as a number of writers and critics rejected Eurocentric aesthetic values. Writing in the context of the National Party's efforts to make Afrikaans the language of instruction at black schools, critics like Mothobi Mutloatse extended their political opposition to apartheid to their literary commitments: '[w]e are going to pee, spit and shit on literary convention before we are through; we are going to kick and push and drag literature into the form we prefer' (Mutloatse, 1980, p. 5).

With the escalation of the anti-apartheid struggle in the 1980s, deference to the English language and to English literature in South Africa diminished further, as critics made compelling cases for including the many South African literary traditions in a South African literary canon. These literatures included: the oral literatures of pre-colonial societies (Khoisan, Nguni and Sotho); English settler literature (headed by Olive Schreiner); Afrikaans literature; literature by black South Africans both in indigenous languages and in English or Afrikaans; literature by descendants of indentured labourers from India; and literature by 'Coloured' writers in English and Afrikaans.

With the release of Nelson Mandela and other political prisoners in 1990, and the first free elections in 1994, debates about constructing a new literature to serve the new nation intensified. The rhetoric of these debates was not always matched by actual changes in the teaching of literature in South Africa. For example, the extent of the changes to the South African literary canon was measured in 1992 by Bernth Lindfors, a University of Texas African Literature professor, who surveyed 139 course descriptions from the literature syllabuses of twenty-two South African universities, and drew the following rather negative conclusions:

> African literature on most campuses is still a marginalised step-daughter of traditional EngLit, which remains the queen mother of all its undernourished anglophone offspring. Moreover, in South Africa the battle for official recognition of indigenous literary legitimacy has only been half won, for native sons and daughters have crowded out most of the interesting foreigners from parts further north, the result being a kind of geographical apartheid in

which Africa above the Limpopo is underrepresented in the
pantheon of African letters.

(Lindfors, 1996a, p. 6)

In other words, Lindfors is convinced that African literature (literature
from north of South Africa's border – the Limpopo River) is shamefully
under-represented in the teaching of literature in South Africa. Several
South African critics disputed Lindfors's conclusions, arguing that they
not only fail to record accurately the number of South African and
African texts being taught, but also do not interrogate the very notion
of the literary canon. For Judith Coullie and Trish Gibbon, for example,
'the point is not "to create a separate canon" of women's or African
writing, but "to abolish all canons"' (Coullie and Gibbon, 1996, p. 17).
Lindfors's exclusive attention to the canon, they argue, 'is promoting a
deeply conservative view of literary studies that privileges the *content* of
the curricula over approaches and methodologies, and so elides any
examination of approach and its informing ideology' (Coullie and
Gibbon, 1996, p. 17). In other words, simply swapping Shakespeare for
Soyinka or Gordimer is not nearly enough; the centralising authority of
the literary canon itself – whether English, African or South African –
must be challenged.

Activity 5.7

Notwithstanding these salient criticisms, Lindfors reiterated his
commitment to the constitution of a literary canon for 'the rainbow nation'
of South Africa, and argued:

> South African university English departments can assist in this
> crucial process of self-definition by putting South African literature
> first and setting other African literatures on an equal footing with
> Western literatures. A rainbow nation deserves a rainbow
> education.

(Lindfors, 1996b, p. 29)

Reread this section on 'Postcolonial/post-apartheid South Africa', and
then consider both the appeal of Lindfors's concluding aspiration, and its
potential problems.

**Allow about
30 minutes**

Comment

The most obvious appeal of Lindfors's argument is that it repeats for post-apartheid South Africa Ngũgĩ's argument for postcolonial Kenya. As Ngũgĩ sought to forge a Kenyan literary canon to serve the postcolonial Kenyan nation, so Lindfors seeks to promote a 'rainbow' literature to serve post-apartheid South Africa. The shackles of the British colonial domination of South Africa's literary landscape should be broken, and a literary canon rooted in South African writing constructed. A second appealing aspect of Lindfors's dream of a rainbow literature is that the history of literature in South Africa has been a history of racial and linguistic compartmentalisation and conflict. From the early studies of African language literatures in the late nineteenth century to the debates between Dhlomo and Vilikazi in the 1930s, and the angry protests of the black consciousness generation of the 1970s, the pattern has been of literary historians making claims for the literatures of distinct racial and linguistic groups rather than making claims to represent a 'national literature'. What the post-apartheid political dispensation offers is the opportunity to imagine a national literary canon that represents the literatures of all the nation's racial and linguistic communities.

What are the potential problems with this aspiration? Lindfors hints at one when he identifies the 'geographical apartheid in which Africa above the Limpopo is underrepresented'. You will recall that one of the characteristics of the emerging eighteenth-century national literatures was that they swiftly became sealed off from each other behind national boundaries. Lindfors identifies such a danger with his observation that South African literature has already separated off from the literatures of the rest of Africa in South African university syllabuses. A second, related problem is the one identified by Coullie and Gibbon: are national literary canons by definition a good thing? Furthermore, does the fact that a literary canon is the product of an anti-colonial/anti-apartheid struggle automatically immunise it from installing new hierarchies, new forms of exclusion? If your answers to these questions are 'no', or even a more cautious 'maybe not', we might begin to consider arguments in favour of ditching national literary canons entirely, and start looking for alternative ways of organising our approach to the reading and studying of literature, whether in English or any other language. I take up these possibilities in the final section.

5.5   The future of the literary canons?

The concerns expressed about the exclusions inscribed in the South African national literary canon have also been expressed in relation to the literary canons of other nations. One important response in recent years has been to search for ways of configuring literary canons other than in relation to the nation and the national language(s). In the United States, the most powerful alternative proposed to the national literary canon has been the concept of a canon of 'world literature', and Reading B explores this possibility.

Activity 5.8

David Damrosch is an American literary critic, and he summarises recent arguments in the United States about literary canons. He is principally concerned with selecting literary texts for teaching in US universities so that students read beyond the traditional Western literary canon. Turn now to Reading B: *World literature in a postcanonical, hypercanonical age* by Damrosch, and as you read, note down the main points in his argument.

Comment

Damrosch's point of departure is the 1956 first edition of the *Norton Anthology of World Literature*, which contained no women writers and no writers from beyond the Western literary tradition. He contrasts the 1956 volume with the several world literature anthologies published since 2000, which provide a dramatically expanded range of writers, some with over 500 writers represented, and all including writers from dozens more countries. The positive conclusion one might draw from these developments is that the Eurocentric canon of world literature has been dismantled. But Damrosch looks more closely at the teaching of literature in the United States, and draws a more complicated conclusion. He compares the fate of the Western canon in the last ten to twenty years (the 'postcanonical age') to the fate of luxury motor cars (the 'postindustrial age'). With more sophisticated communication technology, instead of being superseded, the Lexus and Mercedes Benz have thrived and strengthened their hold on the market. In the same way, with more sophisticated critical theory, Shakespeare and Joyce have thrived and strengthened their standing in the canon of world, not just national, literature. Damrosch argues that whereas there used to be a two-tier model of organising literature into 'major' and 'minor' authors, there are now three tiers: a hypercanon (made up of the major writers); a countercanon (made up of writers from non-Western nations outside the literatures of the 'great-power languages'); and a shadow canon (made up of the former 'minor' authors, who have faded from prominence).

5.6   Conclusion

Damrosch's judgement on the fate of literary canons will certainly not be the last word on the subject. Viewed in historical perspective, the most striking aspect is the variety of ways in which literary canons have been constructed and understood: from the exclusionary national literary canons of Europe in the eighteenth century to the anti-colonial literary canons of the postcolonial period, and to the 'postcanonical' alternatives competing for ascendency in contemporary US universities. In all these different contexts, literature written in English has provoked conflicting opinions, and it continues to be at the heart of such critical debates.

READING A: Writing in English in India

Rajeswari Sunder Rajan

Source: Part 1 – Rajan, R. S. (2001) 'Writing in English in India, again', *The Hindu*, 18 February (available at http://www.hinduonnet.com/2001/02/18/stories/1318067m.htm).

Part 2 – Rajan, R. S. (2001) 'Dealing with anxieties', *The Hindu*, 25 February (available at http://www.hindu.com/thehindu/2001/02/25/stories/1325067a.htm).

[Part 1]

Does an Indian writing imaginatively in English cater to an elite audience that constitutes less than two per cent of the population? How authentic can such writing be? RAJESWARI SUNDER RAJAN looks at issues surrounding this debate, in the first part of a two-part essay.

Writers in English in India no doubt heartily wish that the issue of their writing in an 'other' tongue would go away, and cannot understand why it is resurrected periodically. That this should be happening at a time when Indian English fiction has 'come of age' (to use a favourite journalistic cliché), when, as writers, they have made it in the English-speaking west and are even being viewed as intrepid anti-colonialists 'writing back' to the empire, and when Salman Rushdie has announced their (and his) triumphant superiority to writers in all the other Indian languages put together in the post-Independence period – this must be annoying in the extreme. The bad blood between some (expatriate) Indian writers in English and their detractors, India-based critics, is turning out to be a literary quarrel of some seriousness. It covers a number of issues, some of which have been around for some time, but may nonetheless be worth rehearsing before I address the focal issue around 'Indianness' – a term of some political import in the present.

[**Figure 1**
Salman Rushdie]

The 'original' issue is about English in India. Why writing in English, studying in English, studying English literature, using English in the courts and offices is an issue still is because it hasn't remained the same issue. In British India, English was the language of the colonialist. As the language of rule and one that, further, was introduced in native curriculums explicitly as a means of producing a babu class, as Macaulay in his 1835 Education Minute made no bones about asserting, it was a force to reckon with. It was opposed by the nationalists and embraced by the comprador professional class, though the actual picture was more complicated than that: 'owning' the language of power also allowed the 'native' to put it and the study of its literature to subversive ends, and many nationalists read Tom Paine and John Stuart Mill and Ruskin with profit and pleasure. In independent India, when language became a major and divisive issue in a multilingual nation, with the southern states in particular opposing the imposition of Hindi as an official language, English rationalised its position as co-official language because it is a pan-Indian and 'link' language. Then, as earlier, it was a global language; today it is even more so (if something can be more global). Its influence can no longer be countered by nationalist or chauvinist demands for its removal from educational curricula or from other forums of official, commercial, or technological use. But 'literature', as we shall see, is a different matter.

The considerable role and status of English in India are therefore indisputable. But despite its long colonial history and its current global significance, English is used by less than two per cent of the population. (Overall literacy in India stands at only 52 per cent). English is the (usually) second language of a small elite class – unlike, say, English in a former British colony like Trinidad or Jamaica in the West Indies, where it is the first, i.e. 'native' language of the entire population of a region. This means (at least) two things: that, heterogeneous and numerically sizeable though an English-speaking population in India may be, they are broadly identifiable as a professional class, across regional differences. And two, the English they speak is less variable – less idiosyncratically 'indigenous' – than the varieties of patois that one is likely to find among native English speakers. 'Indianisms' can be found, of course, and now advertisers and television producers are giving currency to, even as they construct, a brand of Hindi-English, both class-marked as the usage of lower- and upper-class speakers, respectively. These have implications for the kind of writing that is produced in English by Indians.

The questions about doing creative or imaginative writing in English – using it 'literarily' – pop up for several reasons. Let us grant that the colonial history of the language is a remote one now, and that the time for nationalist arguments is past. But there remain those potent articles of faith, less critical than sentimental, that maintain that the intimacy of creative writing is permitted only in the mother tongue, and that a foreign language can alienate one from one's lived reality. The most famous expression of this angst is to be found in a writer's work, not a critic's. This is Joyce's Stephen Daedalus, in Portrait of the Artist as [a] Young Man, bemoaning the belatedness of the Irish writer:

> The language in which we are speaking is his [the Englishman's] before it is mine. How different are the words home, Christ, ale, master, on his lips and on mine! I cannot speak or write these words without unrest of spirit. His language, so familiar and so foreign, will always be for me an acquired speech. I have not made or accepted its words. My voice holds them at bay. My soul frets in the shadow of his language.

This is a theory of language-as-identity that perhaps we should refrain *Careful !* from universalising, still less establish as a critical standard about 'authenticity'. It is, all the same, a pervasive and fraught issue for writers in colonial and postcolonial situations: the Kenyan writer, Ngũgĩ wa Thiong'o's passionate polemic, Decolonising the Mind, is a well-known document in this debate. Other writers, equally, have expressed their comfort and facility in trans-cultural, trans-linguistic literary production, and gone on to prove their ability in it – and the examples are not only Indian writers, but the famous ones of the Polish Conrad and the Russian Nabokov. Identities are both more fluid and more constitutively mixed than they are fixed. Further, some Indians have the ability to write only in English, which has become virtually a literary first language: this from Amit Chaudhuri's A Strange and Sublime Address:

> Sandeep could hardly read Bengali. He could hardly write it. Brought up in Bombay, away from his own province, Bengal, he was one of the innumerable language-orphans of modern India. He was as illiterate in his language as … Chhaya and Saraswati.

So the answer to the question: can Indian writers write in English? must be 'yes', whether we mean by 'can' the empirical fact, or their ability, or their freedom to do so. (I shall return to this last point, about the freedom to write in English, shortly).

The question of how (well) they write (about India) nevertheless remains an interesting and contentious critical issue, no more settled once and for all than the language issue. Does the disjuncture between *struggle* the English language and a non-English reality impose certain kinds of constraints of subject-matter, style and fictional genre on the novelist? Meenakshi Mukherjee has suggested that it might produce in the contemporary writer a certain 'anxiety', perhaps more correctly a self-consciousness, reflected in an overplus of markers of 'Indian-ness' to establish their 'authenticity' as well as the intimacy of their knowledge of Indian culture and geography, if not necessarily to assert nationalist sentiments ('The Anxiety of Indianness'). These would show up as defects: ornate or too-descriptive writing, exoticism, nostalgic evocation of sensuous details, glossing. Mukherjee contrasts this with the greater self-confidence or 'naturalness' of writers in Indian languages.

Like many critical observations, this one is a generalisation rather than an unexceptionable fact. There is, however, another relevant consideration: Indian writers in English are positioned to look in two directions, towards their Indian English readers on one side, and their readers in the west in another, and in doing so, they could and sometimes do fail between explaining too much and explaining too little: hence the 'anxiety'. One of Salman Rushdie's great achievements in Midnight's Children, as readers in India were quick to notice and applaud, was how little of this anxiety he displayed. In other respects though, his text was craftily 'double-coded for different audiences' [...] with both costs and benefits from this strenuous 'play'.

The question of readership, then, becomes the crucial one. While it might be a mistake to argue that it absolutely determines what and how a novelist writes, to represent her solely as a spontaneous expressive artist – an artless koel pouring out her heart in song – is also a little thick. Writing with an audience in mind is one of the enduring characteristics of story telling [...]. And writing is a social practice: it takes place in the context of history and politics, the public and the domestic, war and commerce and love. The 'literary' is a space that includes a number of 'ancillary', if you like, activities: publishing, media and publicity, reviews, prizes and awards, circulation, the critical industry, educational syllabi. It also has an economic dimension: writers sometimes depend on it for a living, and books are bought and sold.

It is on this ground – the literary space of Indo-Anglian writing – that the quarrels between critics and (some) novelists have sprung up, some of the more serious aspects of which I would like to subject to some reconsideration here.

Given the small rewards of the literary profession in India and, for those writing in English, further, the inconsiderable size of an English readership, a negligible publishing industry, and virtually no literary infrastructure, it is understandable that many Indo-Anglian writers have sought markets in Britain or the United States. And lately those markets have sought them. The advances in some recently much-publicised instances – Rushdie's, Vikram Seth's, Arundathi Roy's, Pankaj Mishra's – have been spectacular by any standards. The Indian media, mainly the English-language newspapers, magazines and a few television chat-shows, have celebrated these, after all, entirely newsworthy achievements. Critical Indian voices have been sour in contrast, mainly because writers in the other Indian languages ('regional' writers) have languished far behind such fame or monetary rewards, denied, seemingly, their just desserts.

This isn't, or should not be, a contest, and it certainly isn't a contest of virtue. But a contest and contestation is now very much in the air. Its spirit was raised and the challenge posed by Salman Rushdie's infamous New Yorker article and special issue in 1997, subsequently enshrined in his Vintage Book of Indian Writing, in which he announced the result of this contest: 'prose writing – both fiction and non-fiction – created in this [post-Independence] period by Indian writers working in English, is proving to be a stronger and more important body of work than most of what has been produced in the 16 "official languages" of India, the so-called "vernacular languages", during the same time' (emphasis in original). He had no trouble admitting his own lack of access to most of this writing – he commands no Indian language, and translations into English are few and indifferent in quality. But he could bank on – correctly, as it has turned out – the importance of being Rushdie. His ignorance was worth more than anybody else's scholarship. Rushdie spectacularly made a virtue out of necessity. And in doing so, he (re)cast the English-'vernaculars' linguistic/literary situation in India as an opposition between a cosmopolitan against a parochial world view.

Almost no literate Indian takes Rushdie's valuation of regional language writing seriously. But his claims for English writing, which had long been amicably tolerated as a minor and minority literature, once again raised the questions about English-in-India with which I began.

Though Rushdie does not cite any Indian critic at length […] he does allude at length to 'Indian critical assaults'. Few of these, he complains, are 'literary in the pure sense of the word'. 'Rather, they are about class, power and belief. There is a whiff of political correctness about them …' This hoary opposition between the 'literary' and 'the political' from the man who, in successive novels, attacked the Emergency in

India, wrote a political fable about Pakistan, and drew upon himself the ire of the Ayotollah; and in his critical articles in the British press positively reeked of political self-righteousness on the subjects of racism, Empire and Thatcherism; who wrote the passionately polemical essay, 'Inside the Whale', in which he not only opposed the idea that politics and literature didn't mix, but insisted that criticism too must be political: 'it really is necessary to make a fuss about Raj fiction … If books and films could be made and consumed in the belly of the whale, it might be possible to consider them merely as entertainment, or even, on occasion, as art. But in our whaleless world, in this world without quiet corners, there can be no easy escapes from history, from hullabaloo, from terrible, unquiet fuss'; to whom the term 'pure' was at one time anathema!

The opposition between the aesthetic and the political as rigidly separate categories is bound to be a futile and false one because it simply renders the category of the aesthetic empty, degrades literature to mere sensibility and frisson, and refuses to grant the density of the social, historical and material matrix of texts. Rushdie would prefer to praise Narayan (patronisingly, one cannot help thinking) in terms of his 'art' – 'gentle, lightly funny' – rather than for any aspect of gender, class, region or nationalism in his fiction, as some recent criticism is interested in doing. We must ask whether this is a service to Narayan's reputation or the only properly critical way of acknowledging his work's worth.

Rushdie's praise of Narayan goes on to perpetuate another cliché, again one that circulates when the writers in question are women or minorities: Narayan, writes Rushdie, goes 'beyond' the 'heart of the Indian condition' 'into the human condition itself'. This opposition too, between the particular and the universal, hides the enshrining of mainstream (western/white/male/bourgeois) literature as the norm against which others are measured by their degree of overcoming of their particularities. Here it is the national-Indian limitation of his fiction that Narayan is praised for transcending.

[Part 2]

[…] The question of the Indianness of Indian English writing is a more problematic issue.

[…] Recent Indian fiction in English, following from Midnight's Children and its example, eschews the vague, unmarked terrain of much earlier fiction (Kamala Markandaya's novel of rural India, Nectar in A Sieve, for example, would be hard to place in any particular region of

Tamilnadu). In the fiction of Rushdie himself, and in that of Rohinton Mistry, Firdaus Kanga, even Shashi Deshpande (That Long Silence), and Chandra (Love and Longing in Bombay), it lovingly records and celebrates the city, its centre and suburbs (Bombay, in all these instances). Something like a regional Indo-Anglian fiction is indeed emerging […].

But, to return to the question of the 'anxiety of Indianness'. Why must it be so anxiously repudiated? […]

The construction of a literary 'Indian-ness' is, as I understand it, precisely understood as a construction, not the discovery and instatement of some pre-existing nationalist essence. It is an endeavour that the literatures in other countries have engaged in at specific historical conjunctures. All this is not to say, as I admitted earlier, that shrill nationalism does not operate in India in the fascistic mode […]. Books and films have been banned in India, protests against this or that negative representation of communities have been made, censorship has been heavy-handedly imposed.

But it is not left-liberal academics and critics who have been the agents of such repression; if anything they have been its victims. And in the past, it is they who have performed a watchdog function against such infringements on freedom. Even politically, it might be claimed that writers in India have had much greater freedom to write and publish their work than writers in many other parts of the non-West (or, if one includes McCarthyite America, even the west). […] [P]ost-Independence Indian writers have not been sent to jail or forced to go into exile for their political beliefs; this at least is a sign of Indian democracy's functioning. True, we might well need to celebrate this situation cautiously for it is a precarious one, as the experience of Emergency has taught us.

But part of the caution will also require that we not confuse criticism with censorship. If writers will write, critics will criticise, if they perform readings they will encounter questions – and these will be more or less intelligent, fair and responsible, and the writers will respond accordingly. These are the marks of a free and active cultural scene, not of repression. Left-liberal intellectuals and professors at Jawaharlal Nehru University are not the likely agents of cultural fascism in India. The expatriate writer, despite frequent visits home, is, perhaps understandably, out of touch with this intellectual scene. Or it may be that the self-representation of writers by and for themselves requires a certain aggrandisement of their travails. [...] Fiction is indeed where such fancies may be productively transformed or embellished.

READING B: World literature in a postcanonical, hypercanonical age

David Damrosch

Source: Damrosch, D. (2006) 'World literature in a postcanonical, hypercanonical age' in Saussy, H. (ed.) *Comparative Literature in an Age of Globalization*, Baltimore, MD, The Johns Hopkins University Press, pp. 43–6.

World literature has exploded in scope during the past decade. No shift in modern comparative study has been greater than the accelerating attention to literatures beyond masterworks by the great men of the European great powers. The tellingly titled *Norton Anthology of World Masterpieces* was content in its first edition of 1956 to survey the world through a total of only seventy-three authors, not one of whom was a woman, and all of whom were writers in 'the Western Tradition' stretching from ancient Athens and Jerusalem to modern Europe and North America. The numbers of included authors gradually expanded, and in the third edition of 1976, the editors finally found room for two pages of writing by a woman, Sappho. But the European and North American focus persisted into the early 1990s in the Norton as in most other 'world' literature anthologies and the courses they served.

This situation was just beginning to change at the time of the Bernheimer report, and Rey Chow was rightly concerned at the time that the early efforts to broaden the spectrum of world literature weren't so much dismantling the great-power canon as extending its sway by admitting a few new great powers into the alliance. As she said in her response to the Bernheimer report:

> The problem does not go away if we simply substitute India, China, and Japan for England, France, and Germany. ... In such instances, the concept of literature is strictly subordinated to a social Darwinian understanding of the nation: 'masterpieces' correspond to 'master' nations and 'master' cultures. With India, China, and Japan being held as representative of Asia, cultures of lesser prominence in Western reception such as Korea, Taiwan, Vietnam, Tibet, and others simply fall by the wayside – as

marginalized 'others' to the 'other' that is the 'great' Asian civilizations.

[Chow, 1995, p. 109]

To a very real extent, the expansion of our understanding of world literature has improved this situation during the past dozen years. The major anthologies (such as those now published by Longman, Bedford, and Norton itself) today present as many as five hundred authors in their pages, often with dozens of countries included. It is even possible to consider that the old Eurocentric canon has fallen away altogether. As Christopher Braider puts it [...], contemporary postcolonial scholars 'have not only completed the critical dismantling of the inherited literary canon but have displaced the European metropolis from the traditional center of comparatist attention' [Braider, 2006, p. 161].

This dismantling, however, is only half the story, and not only because it hasn't yet occurred in practice to the extent that it has been achieved in postcolonial theory. We do live in a postcanonical age, but our age is postcanonical in much the same way that it is postindustrial. The rising stars of the postindustrial economy, after all, often turn out to look a good deal like the older industries: Amazon needs warehouses of bricks and mortar; Compaq and Dell have built huge assembly-line factories, complete with toxic chemicals and pollution problems, as they crank out an ever-growing number of quickly obsolescing products to overburden our attics, basements, closets, and eventually the world's landfills. This recrudescence of old-style industrialization is compounded by a second factor: many of the established industries have proven to do quite well in our supposedly postindustrial age. Consider the automobile, icon and mainstay of the old industrial economy: far from going the way of the stage coach in the age of the Information Highway, the automobile is more ubiquitous than ever. Not only that: there are more *luxury* automobiles on the road than ever. The Lexus, the Mercedes, and their high-end friends have profited precisely by adding value in the form of dozens of microprocessors that do everything from improving fuel economy to remembering their drivers' preferred seating positions.

World literature presents a comparable situation, partly because, as has often been noted, literary theory stepped in to provide an alternate canon to fill the gap left by the literature it was busy deconstructing. If we no longer focus largely on a common canon of fictional, poetic, and dramatic masterworks that we can require our students to study and expect our readers to know, we need some alternate basis to work from. So, it's said, we rely on Butler, Foucault, Said, and Spivak to provide the common basis for conversations formerly underwritten by a common fund of knowledge of Shakespeare, Wordsworth, Proust, and Joyce.

But *have* these old-economy authors really dropped by the wayside? Quite the contrary: they are more discussed than ever, and they continue to be more strongly represented in survey anthologies than all but a very few of the new discoveries of recent decades. Like the Lexus, the high-end author consolidates his (much more rarely, her) market share by adding value from the postcanonical trends: the James Joyce who used to be a central figure in the study of European modernism now inspires ambitious collections of articles with titles like *Semicolonial Joyce* and *Transitional Joyce*. Undeniably, comparatists today are giving more and more attention to 'various contestatory, subaltern, or marginal perspectives,' as the Bernheimer committee hoped we would [Bernheimer, 1995], yet these perspectives are applied as readily to the major works of the 'old' canon as to emergent works of the postcanon.

How can this be? Something surely has to give. The number of hours in the day and the number of weeks in the semester haven't expanded along with the canon of world literature, yet we are definitely reading all sorts of works that are beyond the pale of the old 'Western Masterpieces.' We must be reading them in place of *something*: hence the frequent assumption, especially by the attackers of the recent expansion, that we're abandoning Shakespeare for Toni Morrison. But this is not so. Instead, just as in the postindustrial economy, what has happened is that the rich have gotten richer, while most others just scrape by or see outright declines in their fortunes. It's too simple to say that the old canon has vanished. Rather, the canon of world literature has morphed from a two-tiered system into a three-tiered one. Formerly, world literature could be divided into 'major authors' and 'minor authors.' Even in the heyday of the 'masterpiece' approach, a range of minor Western authors could still be found accompanying the major authors in anthologies, on syllabi, and in scholarly discussion: Apuleius and Petronius formed the frame from which Virgil and Ovid cast their radiance abroad to the world; the 1956 *Norton Anthology* included Aleksandr Blok along with its far more extensive selections from Tolstoy and Dostoevsky.

In place of this older, two-tiered model, our new system has three levels: a *hypercanon*, a *countercanon*, and a *shadow canon*. The hypercanon is populated by the older 'major' authors who have held their own or even gained ground over the past twenty years. The countercanon is composed of the subaltern and 'contestatory' voices of writers in languages less commonly taught and in minor literatures within great-power languages. Many, even most, of the old major authors coexist quite comfortably with these new arrivals to the neighborhood, very few of whom have yet accumulated anything like their fund of cultural capital. Far from being threatened by these unfamiliar neighbors, the old major authors gain new vitality from association with them, and only rarely do they need to admit one of them directly into their club. By 'they,' of course, I really mean 'us': it is we teachers and scholars who determine which writers will have an effective life in today's canon of world literature.

As we sustain the system today, it is the old 'minor' authors who fade increasingly into the background, becoming a sort of shadow canon that the older scholarly generation still knows (or, increasingly, remembers fondly from long-ago reading), but whom the younger generations of students and scholars encounter less and less. This process can be seen even within the national literatures, where pressures of time and range are much less pronounced than in the larger scale of world literature. Shakespeare and Joyce aren't going anywhere, and have actually added spacious new wings onto their mansions, but Hazlitt and Galsworthy are looking a little threadbare on the rare occasions when they're seen out and about. It may not be long until their cultural capital runs out and their ruined cottages are bought for a tear-down.

References for this reading

Charles Bernheimer, ed., *Comparative Literature in the Age of Multiculturalism* (Baltimore: Johns Hopkins University Press, 1995), 44.

Christopher Braider, 'Of Monuments and Documents. Comparative Literature and the Visual Arts in Early Modern Studies, or the Art of Historical Tact,' in *Comparative Literature in an Age of Globalization*, ed. Haun Saussy (Baltimore: Johns Hopkins University Press, 2006), 155–74.

Rey Chow, 'In the Name of Comparative Literature,' in *Comparative Literature in the Age of Multiculturalism*, ed. Charles Bernheimer (Baltimore: Johns Hopkins University Press, 1995), 109.

6 English and global media

Daniel Allington

6.1 Introduction

The M.V. *Summer* sails out of England with a cargo of military hardware. It becomes the target of men commanded by the highest South African authority determined in their mission to eliminate all anti-apartheid forces.

No one takes their threats seriously until the *Summer*, hijacked and loaded with two containers of deadly cargo sails right into the Lagos lagoon.

A gripping breathtaking story of international terrorism and remarkable insights.

Spectrum Books Limited
2nd Commercial Road
P.M.B. 5612
Ibadan

ISBN 978-246-072-9

Deadly Cargo!

Tony Marinho

Deadly Cargo!

Tony Marinho

MV SUMMER

KAYODE IPOWU

Figure 6.1 African author, African publisher: resisting the global media flow

Languages are used not only for communication between individuals, but for communication in what are called the mass media – publishing, radio, television, computer games, recorded music, etc. Only a very small proportion of the world's languages are employed in this way even on a national level. If we focus on the production of media for transnational distribution, we find ourselves looking at a still smaller group of languages. Although these media are consumed worldwide, they are produced within particular nation states and are to a great extent the product of national media industries and cultures. For historical reasons, some languages are more widely distributed than others, with the result that there is a greater potential market for media in those languages. Again for historical reasons, some languages are used by national media industries wealthy and powerful enough to reach out into and exploit their potential markets overseas. One of the defining features of global media culture is that the language with the largest international market is also the language used by the world's wealthiest and most powerful national media production industry, as well as by one of its closest runners up. I am talking, of course, about English, the US and the UK.

Notions such as linguistic and cultural imperialism do not adequately account for this situation: it might better be seen as the linguistic face of globalisation. Nonetheless, the historical roots of globalisation lie in the colonial period, and its effect has been to create a general flow of ideas and cultural products from developed nations in the global north to developing nations in the global south, and a general flow of capital in the opposite direction: the US produces almost all of the television content that it consumes, for example, while across Africa, television stations heavily rely on imported American and European content. As we shall see, however, these flows are not unchallenged.

6.2   The English-language media bloc

The English-language media bloc constitutes a vast export market for English-language media products – many of which can now be exported beyond the traditional bases of English in unchanged form, due to widespread proficiency in English throughout the world, and many more of which can also be exported in translated form. The British and American media industries have been producing for export to this market for a very long time, and have been able to create distribution networks and regulatory environments well suited to their exploitation of it.

Kachru's Three Circles model is discussed in another book in this series: Seargeant and Swann (eds) (2012).

Perhaps the key point of this chapter is that, with regard to media, what Braj Kachru (1988) calls the Inner Circle of English (countries where English is the main language) is constituted as a trading bloc that is almost entirely self-sufficient and that is overwhelmingly dominated by the US and the UK. It is a phenomenally lucrative market for media producers located within these countries, and it has provided them with a base from which to export media to the rest of the world. Yet it has remained relatively closed to products from what Kachru calls the Outer Circle (i.e. multilingual) countries where English plays an important role due to a history of British – or, in the case of the Philippines, American – colonialism.

The English language and the audience for popular music

To explore the relationship between media flows and the English language, I decided to compare the song download charts at iTunes.com (currently the leading internet music retailer) for the US, the UK, Australia and France – a country that I singled out because its music industry has been protected since 1994 by quotas that prevent French radio stations from neglecting French recording artists.

If we look at the top five song downloads for each of these countries at the time this chapter was first being drafted (29 May 2010), we find some very interesting relationships. As one might expect, the top five song downloads for the US are all in English, and all were recorded by American vocalists. The top five song downloads for the UK are all in English, and include two recorded by American vocalists, two by British vocalists and one by a vocalist from the British Virgin Islands signed to an American-owned record label. When we turn to Australia, we find that the songs being downloaded are very similar to those being downloaded in the UK and America. Of the top five, four are in English (we shall come to the odd one out in a moment), three of these having been recorded by American vocalists and one by a British vocalist. This illustrates the general flow of media – and language – within the Anglophone world, which is outwards from America first and the UK second.

Interestingly, this flow continues beyond the boundaries of the Anglophone world: only one of the top five downloads for France is entirely in French. The remaining four comprise three that are entirely in English (two recorded by British, and one by American, vocalists) and one that is sung by a French vocalist who alternates French verses with an English chorus. Ironically, the only non-English song currently in the top five downloads for Australia, the US and the UK is 'We no speak Americano' by the Australian DJs, Yolanda Be Cool & DCUP (2010). This is a novelty dance track whose only vocal is a sample from a song written in an Italian dialect but made internationally famous by two American films:

[handwritten margin note: Quote/ref here?]

> *It started in Naples* (Shavelson, 1960) and *The Talented Mr Ripley* (Minghella, 1999).
>
> A wider study would reveal that some countries with very large economies and populations exhibit a level of media self-sufficiency approaching that of the US, for example Japan, which has one of the three biggest music industries in the world. Despite this, no national music industry has the *global* dominance of the US music industry. Many US recording artists are 'big in Japan' – but the reverse is far from true.

As we shall see, there are signs that the situation may be changing – but it would not appear to be changing in a way that challenges the dominance of English-language media. Media scholar Jean Chalaby notes that French television channels were widely exported as recently as the 1990s, but their success has since declined – in large part for linguistic reasons:

> While English has become the world's lingua franca, knowledge of French has fallen off. The lack of a vast French-speaking market is not necessarily an obstacle ... but it remains a disadvantage. English-speaking channels have a much bigger natural constituency than their French counterparts; when they expand to non-English-speaking territories, they can get away with broadcasting in English for several years before starting to localize their feed. And should a channel broadcast in just one language that crosses several linguistic communities it can only be in English.
>
> (Chalaby, 2009, p. 158)

This is not the only reason for the difficulties faced by French-language television (Chalaby also points to policy mistakes by the French government), but it is one that leads to a vicious circle: lack of exposure to French-language media leads to unfamiliarity with French culture, which in turn reduces the marketability of French-language media products. For example, while American and (to a lesser extent) British media personalities are known around the globe, boosting the sales of almost everything that involves them, 'French film stars and entertainment celebrities ... [are] with a few exceptions ... absolutely unknown outside France' (Chalaby, 2009, p. 159).

There are thus considerable obstacles to the development of global media in languages other than English. This should not obscure the fact that the bulk of the global audience continues to prefer the products of national media industries outside the English-language media bloc. Admittedly, these media industries in many cases find it difficult to compete. This is the case where their potential audiences are relatively small, where they find it difficult to attract public or private investment, and where the media products in question are too expensive to produce in comparison to the cost of importing and translating 'foreign' equivalents (a notorious problem with cartoons). However, there are a number of transnational media blocs in existence besides the English-language media bloc. These are often linguistically defined, and tend to be dominated by national media industries that can out-compete the US and the UK on a regional level. For example, Joseph D. Straubhaar and Luiz G. Duarte (2005) have shown that US broadcasters have had great difficulty in exploiting North, Central and South American markets where the dominant languages are Spanish and Portuguese, since these are already well served by powerful media production industries – especially the Mexican television industry, which exports throughout the region. Straubhaar and Duarte also note that cultural differences reduce the appeal of US comedy, sport and music programming in Latin America, and that Latin American television companies have developed their own highly successful equivalent of the US soap opera: the telenovela. On the other hand, they observe that there are several kinds of programming in which English-language media producers retain an advantage even in Latin America. These include action-adventure films, cartoons and both documentaries and global news. We will return to the topic of news in detail below.

Activity 6.1

Make a list of all the media products you can remember encountering in the last twenty-four hours: everything from magazines to web pages to songs heard on other people's sound systems! For each one, make a note of what language or language variety was used, and also (as far as you can determine this) where it was produced and whether or not it was in translation. This chapter has suggested that people prefer to consume media products from within their own language market but that consumers within certain language markets – above all that represented by the Inner Circle of English – are less likely to consume media products that originated elsewhere. Does your own media consumption fit this pattern?

Allow about 15 minutes

Comment

Your answers will be personal. For comparison, I carried out the same activity while revising this chapter for publication. On that occasion, I made the following notes:

> All the media I have consumed in the last twenty-four hours were via the internet, with the exception of a number of children's books that I read with my son, an academic book that I made notes on for work purposes, and my current leisure reading, Karen Armstrong's *The Bible: A Biography* (2007). The latter text contains many non-English words and names, as well as frequent translated quotations. These originate, however, in ancient languages such as Aramaic rather than in contemporary competitors of English, and the book is fundamentally a product of the Anglophone publishing industry. Apart from Armstrong's book, I can recall consuming just two media products that were not wholly and originally in English. These were a Spanish-language Wikipedia page that I briefly scanned in search of basic information that was less readily available in English, and a bilingual English/Bengali children's book that caught my son's eye in the local library. The latter book was *Frog and the Stranger* by Max Velthuijs (2000): a translation from Dutch.

Reading through the notes above, I see that – had it not been for a gap in the English-language media (in the case of the Wikipedia page) and my son's love of animals (in the case of *Frog and the Stranger*) – my media consumption would have been still more overwhelmingly devoted to the Anglophone media industries. Given that the internet provides access to media in an immense range of languages, and that I live in a bilingual household, I am a little taken aback at my own insularity on this score. It fits the pattern almost too well!

While we tend to think of language and culture as immaterial things, a consideration of global media reminds us that they are economic and technological entities. Media are produced and distributed insofar as they bring some sort of a return (whether financial or political) on an investment, and that return is in large part determined by the world's organisation into markets defined to a great extent by language. In this chapter, I shall be exploring what that means for English. I begin with a consideration of the first global media industry: the book trade.

6.3   The international book trade

As discussed in Chapters 4 and 5, Britain took the lead in the globalisation of the publishing business. British printers and publishers made a great deal of money by producing texts for Britain's colonies (initially including much of what is now the United States), and in doing so they built up Britain's intellectual influence in the world. This influence has endured. In the mid-1960s, the UK was the world's largest exporter of books after the US, with the bulk of its exports going to British colonies and former colonies (Escarpit, 1966); in the early twenty-first century, the UK was claimed to have 'the largest exporting publishing industry in the world' (Holland, 2010, p. 5). One of the most linguistically significant consequences of this is that 'almost 50 percent of all [book] translations in the world are made from English into various languages, but only six percent of all [book] translations are made into English' (Kovač, 2002, pp. 49–50).

This has been a great advantage for Britain and the US, but smaller countries within the English-language bloc have been forced into a relatively marginal position. In the nineteenth century, British publishers produced special 'colonial editions' of books at such low prices that local publishers could not compete (Webby, 2006). In Australia, this, combined with the small size of the national market, meant that Australian writers needed to be published in Britain, with their work being 'adapted to the supposed demands and prejudices of non-Australian readers, who were assumed to form the bulk of its audience' (Webby, 2006, p. 56). Australia's response, in the early twentieth century, was to impose import restrictions on any book that was also available in an Australian edition, protecting the Australian publishing industry. To the reader, of course, this meant more expensive books, and so, when it was recommended that these import restrictions be lifted, some hailed it as '[a] win for Australian literacy, as downward pressure on book prices brings more books into homes and puts them within reach of youngsters' (Carr, 2009, p. 5). But many Australian authors were unhappy. One protested, 'I want to have a chance to see Australians reading their own stories in the original versions rather than, say, Americanised versions coming back here with several hundred changes and dumped into the market' (Nick Earls, quoted in ABC Premium News, 15 July 2009). In structural terms, the globalised English-language media industry thus bears more than a passing resemblance to the colonial book trade, with companies based within the largest, richest and most powerful English-speaking nations continuing to play the role of gatekeepers.

When it came to those parts of the British Empire where the English language was less widely spoken, the export of texts was initially motivated by religious, rather than commercial, considerations. Nineteenth-century book distributors in colonial Africa explicitly set out 'to bring good Christian literature to the natives ... *and to exclude* the trade in books not suitable for the minds and hearts of our people' (quoted in Newell, 2002, p. 9, emphasis added). In this, they appear to have been very successful: until the mid-1930s, the great majority of texts available to readers in British West Africa had been printed or imported by missionary organisations (Newell, 2002, p. 85). From the 1940s, however, a plethora of self-published pamphlets, so-called 'market literature', began to appear for sale first in the vast open-air marketplace of the Nigerian city of Onitsha, and later throughout Nigeria and Ghana (see Figure 6.2). But British publishers continued to dominate the book trade in English-speaking Africa, even after the period of decolonisation – when in fact, they were able to make larger profits than ever before, due to the newly increased demand for school textbooks.

The effects of this have been complex. Heinemann launched its African Writers Series of novels and plays in a bid to raise its profile as a publisher for the African educational market, but in doing so it played a key role in the establishment of a canon of African writing in English, publishing works by the Nigerian authors Chinua Achebe (who also played the role of editorial adviser) and Wole Soyinka. Oxford University Press launched a similar series, but researcher Caroline Davis argues that it regarded literary publishing as a way of diverting political attention from the money it was making, when 'in actuality [its] investment in African literature was insignificant in comparison with the considerable profits obtained from the African educational market' (Davis, 2005, p. 242). Macmillan published works of popular fiction in its Pacesetters series of African-authored paperback romances and thrillers, but Stephanie Newell suggests that these too were essentially a neocolonial phenomenon, being 'heavily edited, written in compliance with the publisher's generic specifications, printed and bound in Hong Kong, exported to African bookshops and advertised in Macmillan

Education's colourful, glossy catalogues which are produced in Basingstoke, Britain' (Newell, 2000, p. 93; see Figure 6.3).

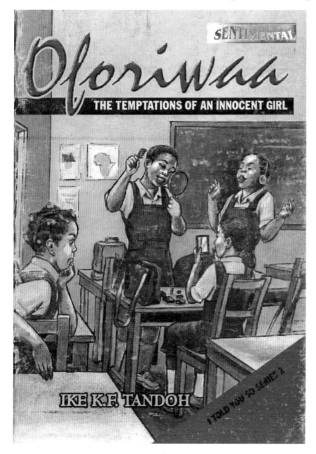

Figure 6.2 *Oforiwaa* by Ike Tandoh: an example of Ghanaian market literature

Figure 6.3 *Christmas in the City* by Afari Assan: a novel in the Macmillan Pacesetters series

Emphasising continuities with the colonial past can, however, lead us to neglect the ways in which the situation is still developing. Examining the situation in India, Sarah Brouillette (2007) finds that publishers such as Penguin and HarperCollins, which had formerly concentrated on selling to the Anglophone market, are beginning to exploit other language markets in countries such as India and China, where readership figures are expected to grow, in contrast to many Western regions. And returning to Africa, one can point to phenomena such as Spectrum Books: a publisher founded by the Dutch manager of a British educational publisher's Nigerian subsidiary, in partnership with a Nigerian entrepreneur. Spectrum has published an extraordinary range of material, from road maps to literary and popular novels by Nigerian authors (e.g. Tony Marinho's politically engaged thriller *Deadly Cargo!*; see Figure 6.1). Though its products are rarely seen outside Africa, Spectrum Books has had a huge influence on the Nigerian book trade, constituting a striking example of resistance to global media flows.

Activity 6.2

Now turn to Reading A: *Literary translation in current European book markets*, which contains extracts from a report by Miha Kovač and colleagues. The extracts selected focus on literary prizes, best-seller lists and translations as a means of exploring language and publishing trends across Europe. As you read, ask yourself what Kovač et al.'s research says about the place of the English-language book trade in relation to book markets across Western Europe. What is 'remarkable' about Kovač et al.'s findings, especially with regard to their Table [2]? What do they suggest might have been the expected state of affairs?

Comment

Kovač et al. suggest that West European book markets are generally closed to books originally written in non-European and East European languages. Books written in several West European languages seem to have the potential for high-volume sales across the region, but those written in English clearly have the greatest advantage in getting to market, since they are far more likely to be translated. On the other hand, Kovač et al.'s figures show that this does not necessarily lead to higher sales. It seems that readers do not always prefer what the book industry most willingly provides! Kovač et al.'s comment that Table [2] shows 'a more balanced distribution of languages, with English at the origin of only one out of three translations' emphasises the expectation that English would have been the origin of more than 'one out of three'. Within Europe, with its relatively large number of languages served by established book industries, the dominance of English is far from total.

In this section, you have explored the complex interactions of language, politics and economics with regard to the first global media industry. The following section looks at what is often seen as the most politically important facet of national and international media: the broadcasting of news.

6.4   TV and radio news

Throughout the 1920s, radio broadcasting developed differently in different national contexts, although in a manner substantially constrained by technical limitations, in particular the relatively small number of distinct frequencies that were available for broadcast. Hundreds of radio stations sprang up across the United States, financed by advertising, but until 1927, when the government intervened to impose order, they competed to be heard on the same frequencies, with the result that reception was often very poor. Many governments, by contrast, established radio stations under their own direct control, creating state monopolies. The British government took another path, providing the newly created BBC (British Broadcasting Corporation) with a monopoly and guaranteed income (via a licence fee paid by listeners), but at the same time granting it editorial independence.

The centralisation of broadcasting, with news at its heart, had important linguistic consequences for the Anglophone world outside the US. BBC radio combined regional programming with a National Service that was intended 'to be the vehicle of the "national" culture, which meant that it was the disseminator of the attitudes and values of the upper middle classes', and '[t]his was particularly true of the manner of speaking of those who contributed to it' (Davies, 1994, p. 86). This manner of speaking is generally known as received pronunciation (RP), and when the BBC began to broadcast to the British Empire as a whole in the 1930s, it continued to use the same high-prestige form of English. Radio services in the colonies offered their own programmes for re-broadcast by the BBC, and these were sometimes considered appropriate to broadcast throughout the colonies on the Empire Service – but were never broadcast to a British audience on the National or Regional Services (Potter, 2008).

Colonial culture, and colonial accents, could thus become part of the shared Imperial British culture broadcast by the BBC, but only through the gatekeeping of the BBC's London headquarters, and only for other colonial audiences. And when the Empire Service became the multilingual BBC World Service after the Second World War, a similar pattern was established: the core of World Service output consisted of world news and British culture in standard English with RP accents, with English-language content being translated for broadcast in a range of other languages. Today, the situation with regard to the BBC's

Accent is discussed in more detail in another book in this series: Seargeant and Swann (eds) (2012), Chapter 5.

international broadcasting is more or less the same, with the exception that cultural broadcasting has been curtailed.

For decades, international news broadcasting was undertaken only by state-funded organisations such as the BBC World Service (whose funding was withdrawn in 2010), and state-controlled organisations such as Voice of America. This was challenged by the 1984 launch of CNN International, a transnational satellite television channel offering news bulletins around the clock; together with BBC World News (founded in 1991), it is still one of the world's two most widely available news channels. These channels are global in terms of the audiences they reach. But as this chapter has argued, global media are the products of national media industries – and global news media are no exception. CNN and BBC World News may be news broadcasters to the world, but they emerged from – and are to a great extent sustained by – national news industries. CNN International grew out of a domestic US news channel, CNN, while BBC World News is a wholly owned subsidiary of the BBC. Accordingly, they present an American and a British perspective (respectively) on world events, and in linguistic terms, their programming is dominated by standard English pronounced in the accents that hold greatest prestige within the US and the UK. For example, one of the most familiar faces on BBC World News during the US-led invasion of Iraq was the Somali-born journalist Rageh Omaar – but, as one might expect from a 'public' (i.e. private) school-educated British citizen, he spoke with a perfect RP accent. Asked whether the BBC was a 'white man's club', he replied as follows:

> I suppose. It's the mentality. I'm in some ways guilty of this – I went to public school, I went to Oxford. I speak at a lot of schools with Somali kids and they say, 'How do I become a journalist? We may be from the same community, but I don't have your accent.' So it's a class thing rather than about being white necessarily.
>
> (Omaar, interviewed in Pool, 2007, p. 21)

Both CNN International and BBC World News are run on a commercial basis, but their main competitors today are state funded. (This is in contrast to the situation within their countries of origin, where their domestic sister channels compete with commercial news broadcasters such as Fox News and Sky News that are not treated as a source of information by significant international audiences.) The most successful of these state-funded competitors are the Arabic-language channel Al Jazeera (launched 1996) and its sister channel, Al Jazeera English (launched 2006), both of which are owned by the royal family of Qatar (see Figure 6.4). Al Jazeera's origins are unusual, however, in that it was not a product of Qatari media culture, since it was not spun off from Qatar's state television channel: in fact, a large proportion of its first employees were BBC trained, being staff made redundant when the original BBC Arabic channel had to be closed following the withdrawal of Saudi Arabian funding. Al Jazeera was not the first pan-Arab television station, and several more have been founded since its appearance, but it remains the most popular: according to Naomi Sakr, because it operates with much less 'day-to-day interference from owners and backers', 'represent[s] a noticeably wider range of opinion than its counterparts', and 'reject[s] … entrenched pan-Arab codes of journalistic submissiveness' to authority (Sakr, 2005, p. 89).

Figure 6.4   Headquarters of the Al Jazeera satellite news channel in Doha, Qatar

Al Jazeera's aim has been to speak to the Arab world, hence its use of Arabic. Al Jazeera English aims to address the world as a whole, hence its use of the English language, and its uniquely decentralised structure. This involves four editorially independent production centres, located in Qatar, London, Washington DC and Kuala Lumpur, with programming shifting between the four depending on the time of day. That is, half of its production centres are based within Kachru's Expanding Circle of English and the global south. Together with BBC World News and

CNN International, Al Jazeera English competes with several state-owned international English-language news broadcasters that operate with varying degrees of editorial independence: in particular, CCTV News (launched 2000), the transnational arm of the Chinese state broadcaster, which broadcasts only in English; Russia Today (launched 2005), owned and controlled by the Russian government, which broadcasts in English, Arabic and Spanish; and France 24 (launched 2006), which is funded by the French government but run by a public-private consortium, and which broadcasts in French, English and Arabic.

How are we to read this situation, in which English is confirmed as the primary language of global news by broadcasters funded by states where English is not an official language? The notion of linguistic imperialism is clearly inadequate to explain a situation where the governments of large and powerful nations with largely non-English speaking populations (and in the case of France, the avowed intention to oppose the media dominance of English) choose to finance overseas broadcasting in English. These governments do so in order to increase their influence in the world, and the English language provides a useful tool for that purpose, since it is widely spoken by the elite audiences they most want to reach. To reach the non-elite audiences would require broadcasting in a range of languages, a strategy that would be both expensive and of less direct political value.

In the early twenty-first century, we would thus appear to be witnessing a consolidation of English's status as the premier language of global news broadcasting. However, this is happening simultaneously with the emergence of the internet as a globally important disseminator of news and an alternative to broadcasting as a means of news distribution: global news broadcasters are looking towards a future in which the internet becomes their primary means of content delivery, particularly as mobile devices become widespread in all parts of the world, and not just in developed countries. The long-term consequences of such shifts are impossible to predict, although there are as yet no indications that it will lead to an increase in linguistic diversity.

6.5 News on the Net

In the early days of the web, it looked as if the online world was destined to be shaped by a myriad of small producers, and it is conceivable that news reporting in such a world might have been characterised both by a wider range of viewpoints and by the use of a wider range of languages and language varieties. Today, this model applies most closely to that part of the web that is called the **blogosphere**. This is the worldwide network of **blogs**; that is, 'frequently updated web site[s] consisting of personal observations, excerpts from other sources, etc., typically run by a single person, and usually with hyperlinks to other sites' (*Oxford English Dictionary*, 2003, 'weblog, n.', sense 2). There are millions of blogs in existence, and many of them do concern news. However, news bloggers are generally dependent on large news media corporations for their information, so it is arguable that the range of viewpoints represented has not been substantially increased. Moreover, news bloggers often use English in order to reach the widest possible audience. The classic example is perhaps Salam Pax, the 'Baghdad Blogger', whose blog *Where is Raed?* became an international hit when Pax's home country, Iraq, was invaded in 2003. Much of the 'news' on this blog was repeated from global media broadcasters, whose reports Pax commented on extensively. This is not surprising: in common with most 'citizen journalists', Pax lacked the resources to carry out any sort of investigative journalism and, being unaffiliated with any recognised news organisation, had difficulty gaining access to official press conferences. But his blog provided an Iraqi perspective on unfolding events and – crucially – was written in English. Even before Pax became famous thanks to mentions (and eventual publication) in the mainstream media, he recognised that he owed what international readership he had to his use of the English language and his referencing of American, rather than Arabic, media culture. In one of the earliest postings on *Where is Raed?*, Pax brought up this issue in an ironic discussion of what an Iraqi blog would have to be like if it were to avoid the sort of criticism that his 'western' style and use of English had laid him open to:

There is discussion of the role of the internet in relation to languages in another book in this series: Allington and Mayor (eds) (2012), Chapter 8.

SATURDAY, DECEMBER 21, 2002

…

Just after deleting [my previous] weblog I told Diane that I wish there was another Iraqi blogger. I have done a sort of a mental exercise on how that weblog would be:

To start with it would be in Arabic, and discuss as little politics as possible, if cornered would be very pro-Palestinian pro-Saddam. Just to stay on the safe side. It would also be filled with quotation from the Quran and Hadith [the sayings of Mohammad], or maybe Um-Kalthum [a popular Egyptian singer] songs. What I am trying to say is that most 'western' readers wouldn't get it because it would be so out of their cultural sphere.

… I got whacked for saying 'fuck you'. I should have said 'inachat khawatkum' no one would have understood. Just as most Iraqis don't understand most of what is being said by Americans. We would have smiled politely at each other and moved on.

(Pax, 2002)

It is unlikely that blogging will ever provide a real alternative to the mainstream media. However, recent developments have seen interesting relationships developing between the blogosphere and the mass media. For example, broadcasters often report on topics that are 'trending' (i.e. frequently mentioned) on the microblogging site Twitter. In this way, microbloggers can play a limited role in setting the agenda for news broadcasting, with national and global news broadcasters continuing to play a gatekeeping role. But in some cases, microbloggers appear to have used Twitter as a highly effective mass communication system. Following the contested Iranian election in 2009, for example, supporters of the opposition candidate Mir Hossein Mousavi used Twitter to send messages to one another and to the outside world describing government repression, and to criticise global news broadcasters for giving insufficient coverage to that repression. Moreover, the ability to use mobile phone technology to shoot video clips and transmit them via the internet has enabled new forms of participatory news gathering to develop, and this has proved especially important in locations where global news broadcasters are unable to maintain an official presence. For example, when BBC journalists were expelled from Iran in the aftermath of the 2009 election, the collation, filtering and verification of information and video clips provided by ordinary Iranians became central to its production of news on the country: a process to which it was able to allocate considerable resources thanks to the launch of the BBC Persian TV satellite channel the same year.

Activity 6.3

Allow about
10 minutes

Do you take an interest in news? Through what language(s) and media do you usually get to hear of events in your area and in the wider world? Do you think it matters what language the news is communicated in? Consider that news broadcasts typically feature a range of voices besides that of the newsreader or 'anchor'.

Comment

Once again, your answers will be personal. But it is important to think carefully about the significance of language. The assumption that it is enough to communicate in English alone, since it is understood by elite opinion formers, may be dangerous: one of the reasons why the original Al Jazeera is so influential is that it is *popular*; that is to say, it is viewed by many ordinary people in West Asia and North Africa. This would not be the case if it were broadcast in English.

A further point is that English-language broadcasters tend to favour interviewees who can speak to the camera in English, requiring no interpreter to mediate between them and the audience. This means that the views of non-users of the language are less likely to be heard in the global news media.

6.6   The movies

In contrast to books and the news, the market for motion pictures is comprehensively dominated by America, and by American English (hence my use here of the term 'movies' in the section title when a British English speaker might ordinarily prefer to say 'films'). Some developing world nations – in particular, Nigeria and India (which I shall be looking at in detail below) – produce large numbers of films, and reach large audiences, but the *economic* dominance of the US-centred English-language motion picture industry is currently unchallenged. In this section, I look at some of the reasons why this is so, and also investigate some of the linguistic characteristics of international Indian film making.

Hollywood movies are a tremendously successful export commodity. This is in large part thanks to the sheer size and efficient exploitation of the domestic market: films that can cover their production costs through ticket sales at home can be sold for lower prices abroad, undercutting competitor products produced for comparable sums of money. Moreover, two factors have ensured that the lucrative US home market was effectively closed to studios outside the US. The first of these was the language barrier, and the hostility of English-speaking audiences in the US and elsewhere towards films not in English: Paul Swann (2000, p. 35) observes that '[v]irtually all dubbed and subtitled films have historically performed poorly in general exhibition in the U.S.'. In this, Anglophone cinema resembles the Anglophone book trade, since it forms a largely self-sufficient bloc from which movies are exported but not imported. However, it differs from the book trade with regard to the second factor, which is Hollywood's control over film distribution: in contrast to the bipolar world of English-language book production, the English-language movie industry is effectively monopolar. This has generally prevented English-language films produced outside Hollywood from making inroads into the largest English-language market. As Swann (2000, p. 31) explains, '[m]ajor studios generally did not distribute British films, which found their way into mainstream cinemas only by circuitous and usually unprofitable routes. In 1947, for example, *Bedelia* (1946) … earned more than $100,000, but the British producer received less than $100'.

If anything, this is more the case today, now that mergers have subsumed the major Hollywood studios into global multimedia corporations with holdings in cable and satellite television, publishing, internet services and computer software. These entertainment giants, such as Disney, Time-Warner and News Corporation, have achieved control of the entire life cycle of their products, from production through distribution to sale. The contemporary Hollywood system revolves around the production of hugely expensive blockbuster movies that are released with massive multimedia advertising campaigns and are able to generate income not only through exhibition in cinemas (and later, DVD or Blu-Ray sales, downloads and television broadcasts), but also through franchising, with the licensing (and in some cases also the production) of tie-in books, music, fast food, toys and computer games. No other national film industry seems likely to acquire this capacity in the near future. The sheer scale of the economic difference between Hollywood and the rest of the world can be seen from *Businessweek*'s comparison between the US and the world's next largest movie industry by revenue, India (*Businessweek*, 2002). These show that the Indian film industry produced 1013 films in 2001, in contrast to just 739 produced in the US, and that it sold 3.6 billion tickets in comparison to the 2.6 billion tickets sold for American films. However, worldwide revenues for the Indian film industry were only $1.3 billion in 2002, while the US film industry generated $51 billion worth of revenue in the same period.

The Indian film industry is far less centralised than the US film industry, in large part because India itself is so linguistically diverse. While Hollywood produces films for consumption throughout the US, films are produced in a range of centres for the largest Indian language communities. The Indian constitution gives Hindi the status of India's primary national language, and the Hindi-language film industry, based in Mumbai and popularly known as 'Bollywood', is widely regarded as India's national cinema. Like the old Hollywood musicals that provided them with their initial generic template, Bollywood films are characterised by extravagant song-and-dance routines. They are subtitled or dubbed into more languages than Indian films in other languages (Dudrah, 2006), and they receive a higher proportion of their profits from overseas distribution (Rai, 2009, p. 34). Intriguingly, their increasing orientation towards overseas markets has been accompanied by an increasing propensity to feature characters who codeswitch between Hindi and English, a language behaviour known as 'Hinglish'.

Hinglish is now an established part of Indian popular culture, familiar from television shows and works of popular fiction. It is particularly prominent in those Indian films that are produced primarily for Western audiences, such as Mira Nair's film *Monsoon Wedding* (2001), which diverges from the Bollywood genre in numerous ways. For example, while Bollywood song-and-dance routines may be scoffed at in the West for their lack of realism (see Gopal and Sen, 2008), *Monsoon Wedding*'s single dance routine appears not as an interruption of the narrative but as an integral part of it with a realistic explanation: two characters rehearse a dance to perform at a wedding, but one of them drops out and the other has to find a stand-in. Moreover, *Monsoon Wedding*'s version of Hinglish is so heavily dominated by English that Jigna Desai and Rajinder Dudrah (2008, p. 15) have classified it as an English-language Bollywood spin-off. However, in the US and the UK, it was linguistically exotic enough to be nominated for the Golden Globe award for the Best *Foreign* Language Film and the BAFTA award for the Best Film *Not* in the English Language, showing that its 'Englishness' may be relative.

The heavy use of English in *Monsoon Wedding* must be interpreted in the context of its co-production with companies based in Europe and the US as well as in India. But that is not all that it signifies, since English use within the film is systematically associated with particular characters. The two characters whose wedding ceremony is the focus of the film's main storyline – Aditi, who works in Indian television, and Hemant, a computer programmer resident in the United States – speak primarily in English. But the film's other love story involves two characters – Aditi's maid, Alice, and the organiser of her wedding, P.J. Dubey – who never speak English. In this film, English thus seems to be associated with high social status. On the other hand, a minor theme of the film concerns Indian identity, and here language choice can be seen to play a different role:

Ayesha: Please, I'm begging you, I really need your help.

Rahul: I can dance, but – it's not a nightclub in Melbourne, you know. I can't dance to this music.

Ayesha: You're such a bloody firangi.

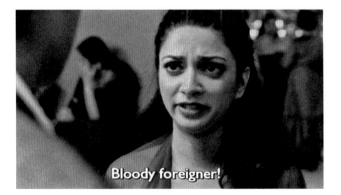

Figure 6.5   Still from *Monsoon Wedding*

As the subtitle shown in Figure 6.5 makes clear, 'firangi' means 'foreigner'. Although Ayesha's lines are mostly in English, this Hindi word is interjected to emphasise her point that if Rahul cannot dance to 'this music' (a Bollywood-style song), then – unlike her – he is not really Indian. When it turns out that Rahul can in fact dance to 'this music', the sub-plot ends happily; Indianness, the film suggests, is not about rejecting Anglophone global culture (the English language; nightclubs in Australia), but about embracing it along with symbolic elements of Indian culture (Hindi words; Bollywood song-and-dance). Bollywood represents a challenge of sorts to the domination of the global cinema industry by US-based producers, but even here English plays a role, both in attracting international audiences and in indexing a 'global' identity for upper-middle-class Indians.

As already noted, India is the world's second largest movie industry by revenue. However, it is not the most prolific producer of films. That is Nigeria, whose straight-to-video movie industry – unsurprisingly dubbed 'Nollywood' – has enjoyed incredible growth since the success of Chris Obi Rapu's pioneering film, *Living in Bondage* (1992). Nollywood films are produced on ultra-low budgets in a variety of languages and are enthusiastically watched across Africa and throughout the Nigerian diaspora, with those shot in English probably reaching the widest market. Reliable figures for Nollywood's output do not exist, but given that its films appear to reach combined audiences of hundreds of millions (Lobato, 2010), it is clearly generating large amounts of revenue. Indeed, Chukwuma Okoye has described Nigeria's film industry (in implied comparison to its vast but notoriously corrupt oil industry) as the country's 'most economically thriving industry which produces wealth for the populace rather than the thieving few' (Okoye, 2007, p. 27).

Like the Indian and Latin American media industries, Nollywood challenges the domination of global media by rich, English-speaking nations. Interestingly, Nigeria seems to have achieved its success in the world of film not by refusing the products of more powerful media producers, but by consuming them illicitly. Nigerians have long had a taste for US and Indian movies, but for many years, these have had no official distribution in Nigeria. In consequence, a massive black market network has developed in order to manufacture, distribute and retail pirate copies of Hollywood and Bollywood films on video cassette and (later) video CD. As Brian Larkin's (2004) extensive research has shown, it is exactly the same network that now manufactures, distributes and retails legal copies of Nollywood films, thus financing Nigerian film production. Thus, it may be that the secret of Nollywood's success lies in Nigeria's isolation from the official global media economy. Indeed, it seems a quintessentially African achievement:

> This wandering over the lines that separate the legal from the nonlegal has been a common experience for urban Africans, who have been progressively disembedded from the infrastructures linking them to the official world economy and instead have poured energy into developing informal networks – equally global

> – that facilitate traffic in economic and cultural goods outside the established institutions of world trade ...

> (Larkin, 2004, p. 290)

Allow about
5 minutes

Activity 6.4

What for you is a 'foreign' movie? Do you think of foreign movies as something that you enjoy? Why do you think that is?

Comment

Your answer will depend on who you are. Within English-dominant countries, a 'foreign film' usually means a film that was not made in English, rather than a film made in another country: few British viewers regard American movies as 'foreign', for example. Foreign-language films are typically regarded as a specialist or even an intellectual interest. Outside the Anglophone world, audiences tend to be far more tolerant of dubbing and subtitling, and far more likely to watch films made in languages they do not speak, so there is less of an assumption that 'foreign' films will be a minority taste.

6.7   The global consumer

Radio and terrestrial television broadcasts can be jammed, satellite dishes can be banned, and internet access can be restricted and controlled. But without such extreme measures, national boundaries cease to be very meaningful when it comes to media consumption in the contemporary world – and this can make it very difficult for national governments to impose media-related language policies. Overt resistance to cultural authority is, however, relatively rare, and most consumers appear to choose media products from among those that are most readily available. On the basis of statistics regarding translations between languages, Claire Squires argues as follows:

> UK and US audiences, unless they read in foreign languages and make the effort to acquire foreign-language editions, have a very limited access to texts created beyond their own cultures. ... [Non-Anglophone] European nations typically have access to a large number of books translated from English, but also a percentage from other languages that is at least equivalent to, and often more

than, that to which British and American readers typically have access.

In this analysis, it is the British and American readers who are culturally impoverished, while their publishing industries derive financial benefit from foreign and translation rights.

(Squires, 2007, p. 408)

Squires is talking about books, but much the same could be said of other media: a major study of the cultural practices of people living in Britain found that although educated people tend to pride themselves on having eclectic taste, 'it is not always genuinely a taste for everything' as '[i]t is predominantly Anglophone, British and American forms that are browsed' (Bennett et al., 2009, p. 254).

This reflects a general tendency for consumers to look outside their local media culture only to the extent that this culture fails to fulfil an obvious need. The greatest audiences for BBC World Service radio, for example, have historically been in nations where the only other sources of radio news were monopolistic state broadcasters; when independent media become available locally, World Service audiences tend to fall. In large countries with highly competitive media industries (e.g. France, Germany, Italy and the UK), transnational TV channels may account for as little as 10 per cent of viewing time, but in smaller and post-communist European countries, where national media are comparatively undeveloped, they can account for over 50 per cent of viewing time (Chalaby, 2009, p. 118). And children's preference for 'foreign' (often American) media products has been found to be far stronger in small, linguistically diverse countries like Israel and Switzerland than in large, linguistically unified countries like Germany, in which the national media industries are better able to develop a range of products to compete with those from outside (Drotner, 2001).

However, there is one very notable group of consumers living within the English-language media bloc that appears to perceive a very important lack in the English-language media. This is the group comprising migrants from elsewhere in the world. Studies show that members of minority language communities within majority English communities are often more willing than monolingual English speakers to acquire and consume media from abroad. An interesting example of work in this vein is provided by Liza Hopkins's (2009) research on Turkish-speaking Alevi women living in Australia. Turkish speakers constitute a small linguistic minority in Australia, but Hopkins found that her research participants used the media available to them to maintain contact both with the Turkish-speaking language community overseas and with the English-speaking language community in Australia itself. They maintained relationships with relatives in Turkey and elsewhere through email and webcam, and all were frequent viewers of Turkish-language cable or satellite television channels, yet most watched English-language television programmes on free-to-air Australian television channels as well. Hopkins adds:

> respondents also reported that they listen … to Turkish-language radio, both locally produced and from Turkey, as well as English-language Australian radio. They also read newspapers in both Turkish and English, while some read imported Turkish women's magazines and many watch Turkish DVDs which are borrowed from friends or relatives, purchased in Turkey or hired from local video libraries.
>
> (Hopkins, 2009, pp. 27–8)

Research of this type reveals the complex 'mediascapes' (Appadurai, 1996) in which people now live, and hints at how complicated their linguistic environments have become. The women in Hopkins's study may be members of a linguistic minority community in Australia, but through their use of a range of national and transnational media, they can act both as part of the majority linguistic community and as part of a diasporic Turkish-language community united by webcam and satellite television. In an unconnected study of Turkish-speaking media consumers in London, Asu Aksoy and Kevin Robins (2003) found that the experience of consuming English- and Turkish-language media side by side led these consumers to be more critical of both:

> [The] comparative positioning that migrant audiences find themselves in with respect to the media makes them particularly aware … of the limits of media in terms of being objective mediators of information. As a consequence of their experience of Turkish state media, Turks and Kurds are particularly sensitive to bias and manipulation in the media. 'In general, when you look at the news, they are literally propagating views', said a Kurdish

woman. 'In Turkey the media are extremely controlled. This is so clear. Maybe it's because we are looking at it from afar, from the outside. ...' ... Another participant in the same group then added that 'English media do it more professionally, more unnoticed, in ways we don't understand. In fact, we are influenced by it, but we don't realize. ... Very smooth. The Turkish ones are more blatant' ... The point, then, is that there [is] a generalized scepticism and caution with respect to all media – they are all seen as in some way politically biased.

(Aksoy and Robins, 2003, pp. 37–9)

Thanks to migration, non-English-language media now have an audience within English-speaking countries such as Australia, Britain and the US, and because of technologies such as satellite broadcasting and the internet, they are able to reach those audiences (see Figure 6.6). This trend may lead to the opening up of the English-language bloc whose creation and maintenance was the subject of the preceding sections of this chapter – although it may turn out that this opening up remains limited to members of linguistic minorities. In the next activity you will take a detailed look at what this means in the lives of a particular group of consumers living in the media centre of the Anglophone world: young South Asian American fans of Bollywood films. As you will see, the things these fans say to one another acquire special meaning in relation to texts with which they are familiar (in this case, Bollywood films). This phenomenon is known as **intertextuality**, and it appears to be ubiquitous in modern culture.

Figure 6.6   Bollywood audience in the West

Activity 6.5

Now turn to Reading B: *Reel to real: desi teens' linguistic engagements with Bollywood* by Shalini Shankar. Here, 'desi' refers to people of South Asian origin, regardless of their particular ethnic or national group (Shankar also uses the Indian English adjective 'filmi', which refers to things characteristic of the Indian motion picture industry). Why are Hindi-language movies so important even to those of Shankar's research subjects whose first language is not Hindi?

Comment

Shankar suggests that Bollywood movies enable South Asian teenagers in the US to create a shared culture, not only through viewing together but through engaging in forms of language play such as the creative use of codeswitching (although Shankar suggests that speakers who are only minimally competent in Hindi are more likely to modulate their accents or to code-mix – drop Hindi words and phrases into English sentences than to codeswitch per se). Shankar suggests that these language practices involve a form of intertextuality, as when a Punjabi speaker not only code-shifts from English into Hindi, but affects the 'deep, gravelly, drawling' voice that would be associated with a particular kind of character in Bollywood.

6.8   Conclusion

This chapter has looked at the role played by English in the historical development of several global media, and at the role that the globalisation of those media has played in the development of particular forms of the English language as global prestige dialects. In each medium that we have studied – books, news and the movies – we have found a different story but a similar conclusion: with a few exceptions, media continue to flow from Britain and America to the rest of the Anglophone world, and from the Anglophone world to the rest of the world. This is, of course, a tremendous advantage for cultural producers working in Britain and America.

Take this book, for instance: at the time of writing, it is impossible to know whether it will achieve a 'successful' level of sales. But consider what success will mean for a book like this one: a textbook written in English and benefiting from the distribution network and marketing department of a major British-American publisher, as well as from the reputations both of that publisher and of a well-known British university, could potentially be read in many thousands of copies across many different countries. By comparison, a textbook published in sub-Saharan Africa could never hope to achieve such sales even if its content were identical – and all the more so if it were written in a non-globalised language variety such as Sierra Leone Krio.

On the other hand, we have seen both that English can be effectively used by media producers based outside the Inner Circle of English, and that transnational media industries have developed around languages other than English, even if they do not currently have the same power and wealth. Moreover, our brief look at audiences has shown that the consequences of such a situation for the media consumer are not easy to predict: different people make use of media products in different ways (provided that they can access them, of course).

READING A: Literary translation in current European book markets

Miha Kovač and Rüdiger Wischenbart, with Jennifer Jursitzky and Sabine Kaldonek, and additional research by Julia Coufal

Source: adapted from Kovač, M. et al. (2010) *Diversity Report 2010. Literary Translation in Current European Book Markets. An Analysis of Authors, Languages, and Flows* [online], http://www.wischenbart.com/DiversityReport2010, pp. 7–9, 33–5, 39–44, 51.

Introduction

The goal of this report is to develop a structured overview of a number of contemporary literary authors and their translated works across a representative selection of languages and markets.

As a piece of applied research, this report aims to open minds and pathways to encourage more literary translation, notably at a moment when translation and diversity often tend to be seen, by many market actors, as particularly risky and costly to launch.

The impact (and the limits) of awards

Cultural awards have performed a particularly vigorous expansion over the course of the late 20th century. The primary purpose of prizes and awards in the arts is often assumed to reside in recognizing merit and conferring prestige, but awards also have a range of other impacts, including, notably, increasing promotional opportunities and heightening the visibility of winners and short listees in the media sphere.

For this study, we will look at three national awards. Among the many existing literature awards, the ones chosen serve the purpose of this study best for the following reasons:

- The Man Booker and the Prix Goncourt are two of the highest-profile literary prizes in the world. The decisions reverberate well beyond their national boundaries
- Deutscher Buchpreis, established only in 2005, has set out to replicate for Germany what the Man Booker and the Prix Goncourt have accomplished over decades, i.e., bringing the maximum media attention and market exposure to the winners.

The Man Booker

The Man Booker was successful, over the decades of its existence, in establishing a particularly high impact, in terms of commercial success, promotional appeal, and as a signifier of cultural merit. University courses are based on the Booker Prize and its prize winners, and these authors are given long-term career boosts. The name 'Booker' has become synonymous with success for its winners as well as for success for literary prizes.

Tracking translations of Man Booker winners in all the surveyed markets for the past 10 years, we recognize that all are significantly well represented in translations, in Western Europe and in the usually less represented markets of Central and Southeast Europe.

The label 'Man Booker' seems to work as an effective identifier for enhancing the impact for a writer's perception as the number of available translations demonstrate for Peter Carey, Margaret Atwood, Yann Martell, Aravind Adiga, Hilary Mantel, and Kiran Desai. (The 2010 winner, Howard Jacobson, cannot be taken as a valid example since it is too early to have data on the translations available.)

Le Prix Goncourt

Regarding the Prix Goncourt in the past decade (2000 to 2010), the picture is only slightly different.

Most of the Goncourt winners are regularly and successfully introduced to big Western European markets. Atiq Rahimi and Marie NDiaye perform successfully in Western Europe, and each has had editions published in three Central European markets.

However, we cannot find an author whose career was instantly kick-started all over Europe, as was the case with Aravind Adiga and his 'White Tiger' and Yann Martel and his novel 'Life of Pi' after winning the Man Booker.

Der Deutsche Buchpreis

The German Book Prize (Deutscher Buchpreis), launched in 2005 based on the Man Booker, has not yet helped one of the German winners gain recognition on an international scale.

However the German Book Prize is of high significance for domestic sales and publicity.

Translations and best sellers

To analyze best-seller lists to identify and understand the inherent patterns, developments, and trends that they reflect, a long-term view turned out to be the best approach. Normally, a work first appears in the original language that the author used, and only in subsequent steps is the work then offered in the rights and licenses markets in order to be translated into additional languages for an international readership. Only then, ideally, the work eventually turns out to be successful with the new, expanded readership just as the work was domestically. This process takes at least a few years to evolve.

In the best case, subsequent translations create feedback loops so that every new translation and its readership open wider circles of dissemination, re-enforcing the reputation of a book and its author where it has already an audience. Then, a movie adaptation can create additional impact, and again cross-fertilize the number of book copies sold.

One of the most staggering examples of such a build-up, which was not foreseen by the book's initial success in its domestic market, is the 'Millennium' trilogy of the late Swedish author Stieg Larsson.

Basic patterns of distribution by best-selling authors and languages

Mapping the respective top 10 fiction best sellers of eight main book markets of Western Europe (Austria, France, Germany, Italy, the Netherlands, Spain, Sweden, and the UK) on a monthly basis over three years, from January 2008 to December 2010, we identified 451 different authors who have had a presence at one point among the top 10 on one of these charts. We analysed authors' performances over the past 11 months, between January and November 2010, based on monthly compilations of the top 10 best-seller lists (fiction) of The Bookseller, buchreport/Spiegel Bestsellerliste, El Cultural, Livres Hebdo/Ipsos, Svensk Bokhandel, and a combined top 20 fiction and non-fiction list for Italy provided by Informazioni Editoriali, and of the Netherlands by GfK/CPNB De Bestseller. To assess and compare the impact of an author's books, we attributed points for each month that a book stays in a given market in the top 10 (with 50 points for a #1 rank, 49 for a #2, etc.). This system allows realistic calibration of larger and smaller countries and book markets across Europe.

The leading 20 authors, those with the highest score in impact points, come with a pattern already very familiar from similar surveys that we did earlier:

Table 1 The strongest-performing fiction authors across the top ten best-seller lists in Austria, France, Germany, Italy, the Netherlands, Spain, Sweden, and the UK for the 36-month period of January 2008 to December 2010

	Language	Author	Points	% of Top 20
1	Swedish	Stieg Larsson	7767	24%
2	English	Stephanie Meyer	4394	13%
3	English	Khaled Hosseini	3053	9%
4	English	Dan Brown	2222	7%
5	Spanish	Carlos Ruiz Zafón	1759	5%
6	French	Muriel Barbery	1497	5%
7	Italian	Paolo Giordano	1324	4%
8	English	Ken Follett	1109	3%
9	Italian	Roberto Saviano	1107	3%
10	Swedish	Henning Mankell	916	3%
11	Italian	Andrea Camilleri	890	3%
12	French	Anna Gavalda	874	3%
13	German	Charlotte Roche	846	3%
14	Swedish	Camilla Läckberg	822	3%
15	English	John Grisham	778	2%
16	English	Cecilia Ahern	773	2%
17	English	John Boyne	718	2%
18	English	James Patterson	654	2%
19	Dutch	Jeroen Smit	613	2%
20	French	Marc Levy	611	2%

Only eight out of the strongest 20 titles were written in English, and 12 in other languages, which is a significant deviation from the overall distribution of original languages in translated books. As a rule of thumb, two out of three translated books are from English originals, with German and French well behind at 7 or 8 percent each, and all other languages falling far behind.

In our best-sellers segment, we find a clearly different distribution in languages, with English, of course, in the lead, but totaling less than half, followed by Swedish, Italian, and French.

Distribution among the 20 best
performing authors by languages in %

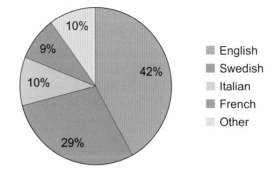

Figure 1 Representation of languages among the 20 best-performing authors

Remarkably, the respective breakdown by languages for all 451 authors represented on the top 10 charts for the surveyed 36 months (2008 to 2010) brings up a more balanced distribution of languages, with English at the origin of only one out of three translations, and the other main original languages represented more evenly.

Table 2 Original language of all surveyed 451 authors from top 10 charts (2008–2010)

Language	Number of authors
EN	159
Other	61
SE	60
FR	52
IT	46
DE	42
SP	31

As a third characteristic pattern, among the top-performing authors, only a very few succeed in having a presence in the top 10 charts of more than just two or three markets.

Altogether, a mere 29 of the 451 authors represented in the top 10 in 2008 to 2010 have such a presence in three or more markets. Thirteen of those write in English, and the remaining 16 in other languages.

Table 3 Breakdown of 29 authors with a presence in the top 10 in three or more markets, by original language of their works

Authors with presence in 3 or more markets	29
Of which EN	13
SE	3
Other	3
FR	3
SP	3
DE	2
IT	2

Conclusions

Obviously, the international markets for translation rights, notably in fiction, do not obey any simple set of rules or forces.

And yet, as our analysis clearly indicates, these markets develop patterns and preferred channels, in which the literary transfers flow with relative ease, while other possible routes in the European reading landscape confront substantial barriers that are difficult to overcome.

We have confirmed, as a trend with great momentum, that the few authors and books at the very top, in terms of sales and recognition, expand their share of the overall reading markets with remarkable vigor.

Those at the top who write in English amount altogether to roughly one third, far below the expected threshold, if the outcries about a globally homogenized best-seller literature flatly dominated by Anglo-Saxon serial authors truthfully corresponded to the facts of the markets. However, the group of strong languages from which an international career can reasonably be started is limited to mostly half a dozen West European idioms, including notably English, French, German, Italian, Spanish, and Swedish. All Asian or African languages, or even those of Central and Southeast Europe, are significantly underrepresented.

READING B: Reel to real: desi teens' linguistic engagements with Bollywood

Shalini Shankar

Source: Shankar, S. (2004) 'Reel to real: desi teens' linguistic engagements with Bollywood', *Pragmatics*, vol. 14, no. 2/3, pp. 317–35.

Introduction

Increasingly, scholars have paid attention to the social life of media in diasporic contexts, especially its role in fostering bonds of community and mediating identity while enabling connections to homeland and other diasporic locales. Often a backgrounded theme, language and the linguistic aspects of media consumption can be an important dimension of this process (Spitulnik 1996). Topics of intertextuality, indexicality, bivalency, and more broadly, identity formation have been sociolinguistically examined in the lives of youth, but seldom with explicit attention to the pervasive role of media in shaping language practices. In this [reading] I explore desi (South Asian American)[1] teens' social and linguistic engagements with 'Bollywood' as well as other types of South Asian diasporic media. Bollywood, the world's most prolific film industry, produces films that are widely viewed in South Asia and beyond. Once a tongue-in-cheek name used by the English language media in India (Ganti 2004), the term Bollywood is now used worldwide to refer to Hindi-language films made in Bombay (renamed Mumbai in 1995). Serving simultaneously as visual culture, a social institution, as well as a linguistic resource for many diasporic youth, Bollywood films have deeply affected the everyday social lives of South Asians in the Subcontinent and worldwide. Even desi teens who may not be fluent in or have limited communicative competence in Hindi – the language of most Bollywood films – nonetheless draw linguistically on this rich and multifaceted medium.

Occupying a prime position in many teenagers' worlds, Bollywood films serve as a linguistic resource alongside various other types of media as well as genres of language. Bauman and Briggs (1992) examine the notion of 'intertextuality' with special regard to genre. Building on work by Bakhtin (1981) and Bourdieu (1991), they argue that various genres of language are not mutually exclusive, but rather overlap with one another. Bollywood-based language practices are no exception; in fact, they epitomize the idea of intertextuality by toggling between spoken dialogue and fantasy-driven narratives set to song and dance. Likewise, teens engage with Bollywood in ways that enable them to move fluidly through different genres of talk, as well as different levels of reflexivity: From the use of Bollywood dialogue in direct as well as reported speech and the narration of their own lives through the stories of film characters, to the deployment of dialogue, film-specific registers, and song lyrics that index a shared sense of aesthetic tastes and communicative competence. [...]

I examine these topics among desi teenagers in two distinct diasporic locales: Queens, NY, and Silicon Valley, CA. [...]

Teen language use

[...] Queens and Silicon Valley are both extremely diverse, linguistically vibrant places. In both Silicon Valley and Queens, a number of teens are bilingual in English and their heritage language. In some cases, this language is Hindi or Urdu, which are morphologically similar but can vary lexically and phonetically, depending on the speaker.[2] Most second-generation teens have not formally studied Hindi. If at least one parent is a first-generation immigrant, however, there is a strong chance this parent may have studied Hindi in India or Urdu in Pakistan.[3] In addition to this bilingualism, teens acquire linguistic skills that reflect a wide range of communicative competencies (including various registers and genres) that are linked to different social identities, activities, and practices (see Romaine 1995; Zentella 1997). [...]

Three types of language practices I observed are code-switching – the process by which speakers alternate between two or more languages in conversation (Auer 1998; Gal 1987; Milroy and Muysken 1995); code-mixing – the use of words and phrases from more than one language during a conversation (Heller 1999); and the use of Indian-accented English (Rampton 1995; see also Chun [2004]). The latter two occurred especially among teens who were less fluent in speaking a particular language variety. [...]

Hindi-language Bollywood films are a prime source from which these communicative means are developed. Many desi teens who did not speak Hindi at home but had a working knowledge of it reported that they picked it up by watching Hindi films. A number of youth largely credit films for facilitating their communicative competence in Hindi/ Urdu. Teens who spoke a language from the Indo-European family – such as Punjabi, Gujarati, or Bengali, among others – often had a quicker and easier time picking up Hindi by watching Hindi films. In contrast, many desi youth who spoke Dravidian languages such as

Tamil, Telugu, Kannada, and Malayalam reported that Hindi was completely unfamiliar sounding and that it bore little resemblance to their heritage language. Some of these teens relied entirely on subtitles to watch, while others reported that their lack of comprehension kept them from enjoying the films at all. [...]

Quoting Bollywood

[...] Although many desi teenagers in Silicon Valley and Queens who watch Hindi movies cannot independently converse in Hindi, they often incorporate humorous passages, romantic dialogues, and song lyrics from Hindi films into their everyday conversational practices. The following discussion explores Bollywood-based talk that occurs during viewing and during other times and places.

During viewing

Vocally interacting with a Bollywood film is not solely a teen phenomenon. Ethnographic research on film viewing in Indian theaters reports that audiences cheer, hiss, and speak to characters on screen (Srinivas 1998). Diasporic film viewing proves to be no different, as particular types of language use are a significant component of group viewings. Whether the viewing is on a VCR or DVD at home, or in a local theater in New York or California, audience members often take vocal liberties that would be frowned upon while viewing Hollywood movies. Such verbal practices occur differently during viewings with peers versus with family, and between boys and girls. Among their peers, kids tend to offer uncensored commentary about who is good looking, make risqué jokes, and sing unabashedly. [...]

When teens watched movies with parents and family, they also verbally interacted with the film, albeit in a more restrained manner. [...]

Outside of viewing contexts

Enjoying Hindi films in the ways discussed above is thus a participatory activity dependent upon linguistic skills and contextual knowledge to generate and appreciate shared viewings. Dramatic dialogue, comedic routines, and romantic lyrics that are consistent with the rest of the film during viewing stand apart as their own *filmi* registers outside of viewing contexts. Indeed, the affect, intonation, and stylized speech that make Bollywood distinctive are immediately recognizable as such to the trained ear. The juxtaposition of such stylized speech interspersed with everyday Northern California or New York City teenage English can be especially stark. Stylized speech, as Coupland (2001) illustrates in his discussion of dialect stylization in radio talk, can be employed in ways that create and cater to a community of listeners that is trained to recognize certain stylized accents and turns of phrase. Likewise, if executed well, a stylized utterance from a Bollywood register can easily create the desired dramatic effect to a receptive audience.

The following is an excerpt from a taped spontaneous conversation during lunch at Green High School during Spring 2001. It features Simran, a girl in her junior year who wore a tape-recorder and clip-on microphone for me for a week, and three boys in her class, Kapil, KB and Uday, all of whom are Punjabi speakers. The conversation begins with Simran and Uday discussing a film they each saw on video with their families over the weekend. Kapil and KB join them, and Simran changes the topic to inform them that she is tape-recording their conversation. […] [4]

Simran: Whatever you're talking is getting recorded. Remember what Shalini told us yesterday?
Kapil: Ooooohhhh! Are you serious?
Simran: It doesn't matter though, 'cause only she's gonna listen to it.
Kapil: [directly into the tape recorder microphone] *Neehiii! Main tera koon kilaun* 'Nooooo! I'm going to murder you/drink your blood!' [in a *filmi* villain register].
            [Simran, Uday, and KB burst out laughing].
Uday: [regarding the tape recorder] It gonna seem like y'all are going crazy, ain't it?
Simran: [laughing, Simran turns to Uday and remarks about Kapil] Doesn't he remind you of that guy [referring to a character in the film she and Uday were discussing earlier]?

In the above conversational excerpt, Kapil employed a *filmi* register that was immediately recognizable to his friends. He created a comedic moment out of being asked to tolerate the tape recorder and masterfully reproduced the affect of an enraged Bollywood character. Rather than using his own voice, he used a deep, gravelly, drawling register associated with a Bollywood villain to create a light and comical response. Moreover, it skillfully conveyed Kapil's irritation about the tape recorder and possible homicidal feelings toward the anthropologist that may have been inappropriate to declare directly. Moving from reel to real, Kapil used this register to create a balance of wit, humor, and annoyance.

Reel flirting is another type of dialogue used in real co-ed [mixed-sex] interactions. Using dialogue and song lyrics indexes particular *filmi* conventions that give this practice several levels of meaning. For example, conversational code-switching can reveal gender dynamics that resonate with romantic stances taken in film. When boys flirt with girls using subtly suggestive phrases of Punjabi or Hindi, drawing on *filmi* conventions, girls can playfully yet demurely refuse to engage in such banter and answer back in English. Girls who reply in English in this way are replicating a pattern of linguistic interaction common to Hindi films, and are indexing themselves as being correct, polite, and pure, partly as a put-down to the rowdy, improper male who code-switches. Yet these same girls comfortably code-switch when gossiping among themselves or speaking with relatives, demonstrating that youth are strategic in their code choices. [...]

Conclusion

Bollywood film, as a medium, creates common ground between youth of disparate religious, national, and linguistic communities, because they not only share such commonalities, but talk about them as well. Indeed, the Bollywood language practices of quoting dialogue, using *filmi* registers for humor and flirting, and engaging with songs and lyrics create a media-based community. Recent Bollywood films that showcase the lives of the South Asian diaspora portray teen subjectivity, to which many strongly relate. Indeed, in the case of a member-driven organization such as the youth center in Queens, Bollywood connects teens from different parts of the diaspora by creating shared frames of reference in conversation. Likewise, Silicon Valley teens of different linguistic backgrounds seek out ways to incorporate aspects of Bollywood into their everyday lives and talk, enabling a shared frame of reference requiring specialized and insider knowledge. With current Bollywood films being increasingly or even entirely set among South Asian diasporic communities, reel life promises to maintain a steady place in the real linguistic and social practices of desi teens.

Notes

[1]   *Desi* is a Hindi word which means 'countryman.' It is increasingly used by South Asians in diasporic locales to refer to one another. Based on the way youth in this [reading] use it, it includes people originally from South Asia who have immigrated to the US from Bangladesh, India, Nepal, Pakistan, Sri Lanka, as well as Africa, the Caribbean, Fiji, and Great Britain. I use the term *desi*

primarily because people tended to use it; I seldom, if ever, heard the term 'South Asian American' in conversation. Even more common than *desi*, however, were specific terms that people used to refer to nationality (such as 'Indian' or 'Pakistani') or to an ethnic, linguistic, or religious group (Gujarati, Tamil, Muslim, etc).

[2]   It is beyond the scope of this paper to discuss in detail the social and ideological significance of Hindi and Urdu in the South Asian context. Hindi is a language taught and spoken in many parts of India, and Urdu is the national language of Pakistan. Both are Indo-European languages, share a morphological structure, and are mutually intelligible. Lexically, Urdu draws on Farsi, and Hindi from Sanskrit, a detail that has increasingly factored into each country's struggle to establish a nationalist identity that distinguishes itself from its neighbor. As such, part of India's nationalist agenda includes replacing Hindi's Urdu borrowings with Sanskrit-based synonyms. This agenda, however, has not been systematically executed in Hindi films, for many of the films' songwriters and composers are Urdu poets. Moreover, in an effort to keep the films intelligible to the masses and have the spoken dialogue reflect lived reality, speakers in films often switch between Hindi and Urdu, much as average speakers in India might.

[3]   Even within India, there is resistance to Hindi as a national language, especially in South India, where people speak Dravidian-based languages rather than the Indo-European varieties spoken in North India.

[4]   […] Elongated sounds are indicated by repeated vowels or consonants [in the transcript]. Contextual notes about speakers and their utterances are indicated with '[ ].'

References for this reading

Auer, J.C.P. (1998) *Code-Switching in conversation*. London: Routledge.

Bakhtin, M. (1981) *The dialogic imagination: Four essays*. Austin: University of Texas Press.

Bauman, R., and C. Briggs (1992) Genre, intertextuality, and social power. *Journal of linguistic anthropology* 2.2: 131–172.

Bourdieu, P. (1991) *Language and symbolic power*. Cambridge, MA: Harvard University Press.

Chun, E.W. (2004) Ideologies of legitimate mockery: Margaret Cho's revoicings of mock Asian. *Pragmatics* 14.2/3: 263–289.

Coupland, N. (2001) Dialect stylization in radio talk. *Language in society* 30.3: 345–375.

Gal, S. (1987) Code-switching and consciousness in the European periphery. *American ethnologist* 14: 637–653.

Ganti, T. (2004) *Bollywood: A guidebook to popular Hindi cinema.* New York: Routledge.

Heller, M. (1999) *Linguistic minorities and modernity: A sociolinguistic ethnography.* New York: Addison Wesley Longman Limited.

Milroy, L., and P. Muysken (eds) (1995) *One speaker, two languages: Cross-disciplinary perspectives on code-switching.* Cambridge: Cambridge University Press.

Rampton, B. (1995) *Crossing: Language and ethnicity among adolescents.* New York: Longman.

Romaine, S. (1995) *Bilingualism.* New York: Blackwell.

Spitulnik, D. (1996) The social circulation of media discourse and the mediation of communities. *Journal of linguistic anthropology* 6.2: 161–187.

Srinivas, L. (1998) Active viewing: An ethnography of the Indian film audience. *Visual anthropology* 11.4: 323–353.

Zentella, A.C. (1997) *Growing up bilingual.* Malden, MA: Blackwell Publishing.

7 Translating into and out of English

Guy Cook

7.1 Introduction

English, however widespread, and however fast its use may be growing, is only one of the many languages in the world. By recent estimates – depending on how one defines a language – there are around 6000 in the world today. Although there are pairs of languages that are sufficiently close to each other for speakers to have some idea of each other's meaning, these 6000 languages are generally mutually incomprehensible. This, as we all know, poses the most fundamental human communication problem of all: that of 'not speaking the same language'. To put it simply, when speaker of Language A meets speaker of Language B, they cannot understand a word the other one says.

Activity 7.1

Allow about 10 minutes

Think of situations where you have been unable to communicate across a language barrier. What ways are there of dealing with this barrier? Which are the most practical ways, which are the most desirable, and why?

Comment

Logically and historically, there are four ways of dealing with this endemic human problem. Speakers must either:

1 abandon the attempt to communicate through language

2 learn the other language (one or both may do this)

3 use a lingua franca (a third language which both know, but is the native language of neither); or

4 use a translator or an interpreter.

Option 1 is undesirable. Absence of communication means no sharing of ideas, no possibility of mutual understanding, and is likely to exacerbate conflict. Option 2 is widespread, but given the sheer number of languages and the impossibility of everyone knowing more than the tiniest fraction, it is also limited. So too, in many circumstances, is Option 3. There is often no universally agreed or available lingua franca, although this (as you have seen in earlier chapters) is changing with the spread of English. In addition, the use of English by speakers of other languages (and their ability to express themselves in ways they would like to in the language) may affect the balance of power, and the degree of influence exerted by different speakers. For these reasons, it is the last option, of translation, which has been the bedrock of communication across language barriers, and continues to be so today. Just imagine how far trade and diplomacy or any other kind of communication would get *without* translation, or how agreements, alliances or treaties could ever be made. In the words of German writer and polymath Johann Wolfgang von Goethe (1749–1832):

> Say what one will of the inadequacy of translation, it remains one of the most important and worthiest concerns in the totality of world affairs.

> (Goethe, 1994, p. 353)

Although we may bemoan human history for its sad catalogue of war, genocide, enslavement and oppression, there is reason to believe that conflicts might have been worse and more frequent without the good offices of translators and interpreters. Translation is simply indispensable to any hope of peace and understanding in a multilingual world or to the everyday task of understanding, at least to some extent, what is said in other languages – and it has played a bigger part than might at first be apparent in the development and use of English. English is the most translated language in the world, as well as the one most frequently translated into, which is why the topic of translation is important in a book about the English language today. In addition, even where those involved speak English well, the decision as to whether to use English as a lingua franca, or to opt for translation, carries important symbolic significance. Choice of language is much more than a mere matter of efficient communication. It is a political and social statement too. If the use of translation and interpreting as a means of surmounting language barriers were to diminish in favour of English, that could have important repercussions for the power relations between speakers of different languages. Translation and interpreting, however, are by no means neutral or unproblematic communication strategies, as will be apparent from the rest of this chapter. As you read, consider the relative merits and demerits of translation as an alternative to the use of English.

The term **translation**, it is worth mentioning at this point, applies to both writing and speech, while the term **interpreting** is reserved for spoken translation.

Activity 7.2

Now turn to Reading A: *What is translation?* by Juliane House, in which House discusses the nature of translation, some differences between written translation and interpreting, the possibilities and limitations of machine translation, and the cultural nature of translation. As you read, make notes about the kinds of situation where written translation might be preferable to spoken interpreting and vice versa, and the kinds of problems which might arise in one but not the other.

Think also about the kinds of problems you might encounter in machine translation, and the reasons for them. (You might like to play around with one of the many internet translation programs – such as Babel Fish or Google translator – to test your hunches. If you know another language well, try translating into it from English or out of it into English, and then judge the results for yourself. If you don't know another language well enough for this, choose any language available on the program, translate something from English into it, then back-translate the results into English, and see what happens.)

Comment

With regard to written translation and spoken interpreting, each brings particular problems and demands of its own. While interpreters need to work fast, to hold things in memory, and to exercise social tact, these skills are not always needed by written translators. Where accuracy is important, the time for reflection in written translation is clearly also important; in addition, written translation provides a *de facto* record of itself. Spoken interpreting, on the other hand, is quicker and allows social interaction, face-to-face contact and moment-by-moment adjustments to the particular situation. With regard to the potential of machine translation, there are clearly many limitations which may well never be overcome. In many ways this relates to House's last points about the importance of cultural difference and context in translation. It can never be a wholly mechanical exercise, but must vary with the needs and background of the human participants.

7.2   Babel and beyond: one language or many?

Figure 7.1   Pieter Brueghel's *The Tower of Babel* of 1563

If we are to believe either contemporary science or the Jewish and
Christian scriptures, this need to cross language barriers has not always
existed. Language evolutionists believe that one original human language
– which they call Proto-World – diverged into many languages as
humans spread out of Africa. The Book of Genesis (11: 1–9) too tells
us of a time when:

> the whole earth was of one language, and of one speech.

and how, when these monolingual early inhabitants of the earth
arrogantly try to build a tower to reach heaven (see Figure 7.1), God
did

> confound their language, that they may not understand one
> another's speech.

Curiously, in this myth, a monolingual world seems to be regarded as a
'good thing', and a multilingual world as a 'bad thing' – a punishment
for sin. Indeed, later in the Christian Bible the disciples of Jesus
suddenly overcome this multilingualism again, without needing either
foreign language lessons or translation:

they were all filled with the Holy Ghost, and began to speak with other tongues, as the Spirit gave them utterance. And there were dwelling at Jerusalem Jews, devout men, out of every nation under heaven. Now when this was noised abroad, the multitude came together, and were confounded, because that every man heard them speak in his own language. And they were all amazed and marvelled, saying one to another, ... And how hear we every man in our own tongue, wherein we were born?

(Acts 2: 4–8)

No need for interpreters here either!

These stories, however, which treat multilingualism as a problem to be remedied, might make us reflect that the variety of human languages is not just a practical obstacle to communication, but a repository of value too. A world with fewer languages, or in which one language dominates as a means of international communication, would be deeply impoverished. The purpose of cross-linguistic communication may not always be the merely utilitarian one of getting things done together. It is also a way to gain understanding of the different worlds associated with different languages – of stepping outside the 'worlds of English', and into the worlds of Ibo, Navaho, Spanish, Tamil, Tibetan, Ukrainian, Urdu, and so on. We have, then, two issues when we talk of translation – practicality and value.

In short, there are advantages to be gained from venturing into another language and exploring how it resembles or differs from one's own. Of our two speakers, the one who learns the other person's language in addition to their own gains more than the one who waits for the other to learn theirs. The translator who has thorough and intimate knowledge of the languages they work with will gain insights and experiences which are denied to those they interpret for. These advantages are not merely personal, to be reaped only by the bilingual individual who develops a knowledge of a language other than their own. Languages themselves may gain from contact, enriching and extending their vocabulary, or allowing foreign ways of using language to influence their own. Paradoxically, the languages most open to such influences may be the 'healthiest' and most dynamic. English, with its legions of borrowed vocabulary, is a good example. Words such as *ad hoc, algebra, ambience, boomerang, bungalow, cafeteria, curry, gong, kosher, kowtow, rendezvous* and *vodka* no longer register in our minds as imports from, respectively, Latin, Arabic, French, Dharug (an extinct Australian language), Bengali, Spanish, Tamil, Malay, Hebrew, Chinese, French and Russian.

Often such words have entered the language – *un*translated – precisely because they denote some idea, cultural practice or object which was not previously available in English – and are thus indicative of openness to new concepts and practices.

Allow about 10 minutes

The spread of global English is discussed in another book in this series: Seargeant and Swann (eds) (2012).

Activity 7.3

Elsewhere in this book, you have read about the exponential growth of English as the language of international communication in global fields such as education, publishing and media. If English continues to expand, do you think the need for translation will disappear? In your view, would the universal use of English as an international lingua franca be beneficial to world affairs and individual lives?

Comment

A world in which formal translation figures less prominently does now seem to be a potential reality – precisely because of the growth of English. Contemporary interpreters into and out of English increasingly find that their clients are less likely to have an absolute need for interpretation. These clients may *prefer* to use interpreters in order to assert their identity, importance and independence; they may appreciate the edge in negotiation which being able to use their own language still provides; they may treasure the thinking time they gain while waiting for a consecutive interpretation; or they may exploit the opportunity to blame the interpreter for anything that goes wrong. Nevertheless, those most likely to have the power and resources to employ interpreters into and out of English in the contemporary world are precisely those – an educated elite – who could increasingly manage perfectly well in English if called upon to do so.

Such a move towards English raises the crucial point of whether speakers of other languages are aiming to use English as an additional language to their own, or to make a transition to its exclusive use. This has been a point of controversy in language-policy debates within historically English-speaking countries, with some Anglophones, such as supporters of the 'English Only' movement in the USA, believing that their country would be better if it were monolingual rather than multilingual. They think, in other words, that US speakers of other languages should simply abandon those languages in favour of English, rather than move back and forth between languages.

Such debates find an echo in different approaches to the teaching of English as a foreign language (Cook, 2010). Some approaches assume that learners' goal should be to operate monolingually in an English-speaking environment, and that the ultimate measure of success is whether their English resembles that of a native speaker. In these approaches, which dominated twentieth-century English-language teaching, any use of translation, whether as an aid to learning or as a skill in itself, was outlawed. Students and teachers were forbidden to translate or make any reference to their own language. Other approaches, both older and more recent, help learners to develop ways, including translation, of relating the two languages, and to see their goal as bilingualism, with a facility to move between the two languages.

Activity 7.4

Allow about 10 minutes

Make a list of situations where you yourself encounter translation in your daily life. If you are a speaker of more than one language, also write down situations in which you have been called upon to translate.

Comment

Although often associated with formal education, the international stages of diplomacy and trade, or the high culture of literature, translation into and out of English is also a part of everyday life, especially in the multicultural, multilingual cities of supposedly Anglophone countries. It is also frequently in evidence in news broadcasts. The simple reason for this is that many speakers of English are – or interact with – speakers of other languages, and English is often part of a multilingual rather than a monolingual environment. A survey conducted in 2000, for example, estimated that 350 languages are spoken by pupils in London schools (Baker and Mohieldeen, 2000). Similar situations pertain in many other 'English-speaking' cities of the Inner Circle – such as Sydney and New York.

This diversity and the constant flow of new arrivals makes translation a necessary and routine part of many people's daily lives. For example, translation happens inevitably in relationships where partners are speakers of different languages; when relatives come to stay, for instance; and in immigrant families where the oldest generation may have less command of English than the youngest (and conversely the youngest less command of the heritage language). It happens socially when visitors come from abroad – translating a restaurant menu is a stock situation. In such a multilingual environment, translation is inevitably also part of school life, whether for parents who do not speak

English, or for newly arrived children. Many primary schools – for example, in London and Cape Town – assign a bilingual 'buddy' to help new arrivals by translating for them in interaction with classmates and teachers. Translation is institutionalised in other local settings too – in courts and hospitals, for example, where interpreter services are provided. Government policy on translation also filters down to a local level. In Wales, a grass-roots campaign led by the Welsh Language Society culminated in the 1993 Welsh Language Act – the first piece of language legislation in the UK – and now all signs and official information in Wales are translated into and out of Welsh. In the European Union, all driving licences have information in nine languages, and food labels commonly list ingredients in several languages.

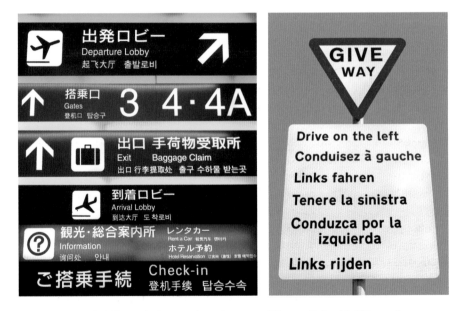

Figure 7.2 Multilingual airport signs in English, Japanese, Chinese and Korean for a range of airport services

Figure 7.3 Multilingual instructions on a sign at a road junction

Given this ubiquity and importance, it is remarkable how marginalised and invisible the act of translation can be, and how it is often taken for granted and perceived as unproblematic. Many English speakers in particular have grown accustomed not only to others having already learnt their language, but also to foreign-language texts being already translated for them as a matter of course – for example, in film subtitling, airport information or menus (see Figures 7.2 and 7.3).

7.3   What does it mean to 'translate'?

Activity 7.5

Allow about
10 minutes

If you know more than one language, think of a brief sentence and translate it. In what ways are both versions the same, and in what ways are they different? Can there ever be such a thing as a perfect or exact translation?

Comment

It is unlikely that two readers will come up with the same example. Not only will different languages be chosen, but even within one language examples will differ. Yet perhaps similar issues will have arisen, whatever the pair of sentences. Take, for example, the following sentence in English and its Italian translation below.

Do you like hip hop?

Ti piace la musica hip hop?

The **equivalence** between the two seems straightforward and unremarkable, but is it actually so? Word for word, the Italian is:

Thee pleases the music hip hop?

It makes *the music* not *you* the subject of the sentence, thus perhaps making *liking* into something which happens to you (being pleased by hip hop), rather than something you actively do (liking hip hop). It has chosen the intimate pronoun *tu*, not the more formal pronoun *Lei*. (The equivalent English distinction – the *thou/you* difference found in Shakespeare, which I have used rather artificially here – although it still persists in some dialects, no longer exists in standard English.) The Italian says *the music* instead of just *music*, and it reverses the order of noun and modifier, making *hip hop music* into *music hip hop*. And what about the term *hip hop* itself? Is it Italian or English, or both, or just international? If we decide it is English, should it be translated too? Would that mean that a new Italian word needs to be invented?

So even in this apparently simple example, there are hidden complications and changes.

The activity and discussion above put paid to the notion that 'translation' is simply about transferring meaning from one language into another. This fallacious but widespread view is reflected in the word's Latin root *translatum*, a form of the verb *transferre*, which means 'to carry across' – also the origin of the English word 'transfer'. On this basis, a translation and an original text are regarded as having the same meaning but in different words. Yet a moment's reflection on almost any two *apparently* meaning-equivalent pieces of language (i.e. an original text and its translation) reveals how problematic this notion is. This is true whether we confine ourselves to 'meaning' (whatever that may mean!), or bring in other elements, such as the sound of words, the shapes of writing or the social function of the words – all of which may be important.

Take, for example, the quotation from Goethe which I used earlier and introduced with the phrase 'in the words of … Goethe'. The words I used were not of course his. What he actually wrote was not:

> Say what one will of the inadequacy of translation, it remains one of the most important and worthiest concerns in the totality of world affairs.

but:

> Denn was man auch von der Unzulänglichkeit des Übersetzens sagen mag, so ist und bleibt es doch eines der wichtigsten und würdigsten Geschäfte in dem allgemeinen Weltverkehr.

> (Goethe, 1994, p. 353)

This raises, as any translation does, enormous problems. The two are in one sense the same, but in another sense completely different. They look different; they sound different; they have no single word in common; they are not even the same length. That is not to say that the English translation does not work. It is a valid translation, in a sense which is difficult to define, but nevertheless real. Bar a few quibbles about alternative wording, someone who speaks German and English would recognise that the first is an effective translation of the second. And a person who knows English but no German, reading this translation, will in a sense know what Goethe said. So there is an equivalence of some kind between translation and original. Yet how to demonstrate the nature of this equivalence has puzzled translation theorists for a long time, and with no satisfactory results.

The causes of the problem are complex. Any piece of language has a number of aspects and exists on a number of levels, all of which may be relevant in translation. Spoken language has a sound; written language has a shape and an appearance; both have grammatical form, component words and an overall semantic meaning referring to a state of affairs in the real (or an imaginary) world. In addition to these formal linguistic characteristics, any piece of actual language use is part of a discourse. It relates to preceding and following utterances, and is spoken or written with a purpose, taking on a pragmatic meaning for those involved in the interaction of which it is a part. To make sense of it, receivers may also need cultural and contextual knowledge which is usually more readily accessible to speakers of the source language than to outsiders, and which may not travel well in translation.

The matching of each and any of these levels presents notorious, well-documented and arguably insurmountable obstacles. This means that as soon as anybody embarks on the task of translating, even between languages which are apparently close to each other, they have to confront the fact that at all levels there are profound differences, that languages do not simply map on to one another in straightforward ways, as though they were encoding some universal 'language of thought' shared by all human beings. These differences range from apparently trivial ones, to those which reflect significant divergences in perception, belief or social organisation.

The problem is most clearly evident at the lexical level. In Russian, for example, there is no single generic word for *cloud*, but only words for types of cloud, such as *tucha* (туча) a dark cloud and *oblako* (облако) a lighter cloud. This means that anyone translating the word *cloud* from English into Russian has to make a choice, to add an interpretation which is not in the original. But it is not that Russian is richer than English, with finer discriminations in its vocabulary. In other cases, Russian has one word where English discriminates between two. Thus, the Russian word *ruka* (рука) denotes the part of the body which stretches from the shoulder to the fingertips – there are no separate words for *arm* and *hand*. Again, this means that the translator (this time into English) has to judge, in each encounter with the word *ruka*, whether it means *hand* or *arm*. There are thus gaps in each language. In Figure 7.4, x shows this gap.

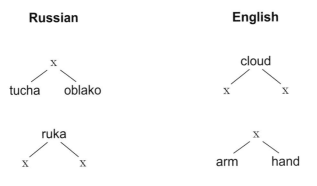

Figure 7.4 Lexical gaps in Russian/English equivalence

This does not mean that the translator cannot find ways around these absences. If necessary, it is possible to say *dark cloud* or *light cloud* in English, or the equivalent of *the palm, fist and fingers* or *from the wrist to the shoulder* in Russian – but this makes the translation longer than the original, which is another kind of non-equivalence. Harder are cases where there is no equivalent word at all, as in the case of the English word *privacy*, which has no equivalent word, and arguably no equivalent concept, in Russian. (Although in dictionaries you will find attempts to give rough synonyms, such as *konfidentsialnost* (конфиденциальность), the word for *confidentiality*, and there are circumlocutionary phrases that are used in international law.) Perhaps this absence reflects different ideas about individuality and individual rights – or perhaps it is merely an accident of the system. In such cases where there is no equivalent, both translators and languages may be disposed to simply lift the foreign word into the target language. English, as already remarked, is full of such lexical borrowings. Often these reflect differences and influences which pertain between the cultures associated with the two languages. Thus, many English borrowings from French are culinary (*hors d'oeuvre*) or literary (*dénouement*). From Italian they are often musical (*operetta*). In the other direction, English words concerning computing (*internet*) and popular culture (*hip hop*) have been adopted in many other languages.

The problem of untranslatability is by no means confined to vocabulary, and there are many grammatical categories which do not find a straightforward equivalent, forcing the translator to make judgements without textual warrant, and to think laterally. Thus (staying with Russian as a source of examples), almost every Russian verb has both a perfective form denoting a completed action, and an imperfective form denoting that the process is ongoing. The Russian equivalent of *to read*, for example, is *chitat* (читать, perfective, to read but not finish) or *prochitat* (прочитать, imperfective, to read to the end). A Russian speaker can therefore differentiate the sentences:

I was reading the book yesterday

and:

I finished the book last week

by using these different forms in the past tense (*chitala* vs *prochitala*), while the English speaker must use different lexical items (*reading* vs *finished*). The Russian speaker is also obliged to make these verbs either feminine (if they are a female speaker) or masculine (if they are male). In the example above they are feminine (*chitala, prochitala*). A male speaker would have to use the masculine form: *chital* or *prochital*. This creates another problem. It means that the translator from English into Russian must always indicate the sex of the speaker, even if there is no evidence in the text.

I am using the term *sex* here to refer to whether the person is male or female, and *gender* to indicate a grammatical difference. In the example of past verb endings the two are the same – a female speaker uses a feminine ending, a male speaker a masculine ending. But this correlation is not always the case. The grammatical gender of nouns may be arbitrary and unrelated to biological sex. Indeed, in Russian the word for dog, *sobaka* (собака), is grammatically feminine, even if the dog is male. So nothing seems to be lost when grammatical gender disappears in the course of translation into English – as it does from many languages – English being an unusual case of a language with minimal use of gender (exceptions being the *he/she* pronouns and the suffix *-ess* as in *lioness*).

Yet even such seemingly superfluous grammatical distinctions as the apparently arbitrary assignation of purely grammatical gender can on occasion be significant. The linguist Roman Jakobson (1959, p. 257) cites the case of the Russian writer Pasternak's collection of poems *My Sister Life* (*Sestra Moya Zhizn* Сестра моя – жизнь) which plays on the fact that the word for *life* in Russian (*zhizn*) is feminine, a dimension which is lost in English, and even more problematic in Czech, where the word for life (*život*) is masculine. More significant than such arcane literary translation conundrums, which however interesting are not commonly encountered in everyday life, are the imbroglios created by those campaigning for non-sexist language, when they try to find equivalents for gender-neutral phrasing in languages where there are more extensive obligatory differences. In French, for example, there are no gender-neutral nouns such as *chairperson* or *fire-fighter*, or genderless third-person plural forms of verbs such as *they went*. (In French *they went* must be either *ils sont allés*, if at least one of *them* is masculine, or *elles sont allées* if all of them are feminine.)

7.4 Linguistic relativity and translation

The lack of fit between languages raises the possibility that – to put it in popular terms – something of the spirit of the original language is lost in translation, that when we say 'the same thing' in another language, it is never in fact the same. In her autobiography *Lost in Translation*, Eva Hoffman describes the feeling of alienation she experienced on changing languages when her family emigrated from Poland to Canada:

Chapter 2 of this book discusses migrant experiences and the role that English and other languages play in present-day migration flows.

Eva?

> The words I learn now don't stand for things in the same unquestioned way they did in my native tongue. 'River' in Polish was a vital sound, energized with the essence of riverhood, of my rivers, of my being immersed in rivers. 'River' in English is cold – a word without an aura. It has no accumulated associations for me, and it does not give off the radiating haze of connotation. It does not evoke.
>
> (Hoffman, 1998, p. 106)

Such ideas relate to what in linguistics is known as 'the **linguistic relativity** hypothesis': the idea that a language determines a unique way of seeing the world (Pavlenko, 2005). Without adopting the strongest version of this hypothesis, which would hold that one language is incapable of representing experience in the same way as another, and completely *determines* the way its speakers think, we might nevertheless want to adopt a weaker view, which holds that a language *disposes* its speakers to think in certain ways. And if we accept this to any degree, then the move from a world where communication across language barriers is effected through translation, to one where it is effected through everyone learning English, inevitably deprives speakers of other languages of the ability to express their own personal, linguistic and cultural world view as fully as they might.

Activity 7.6

Allow about 20 minutes

To what degree do you feel that differences between languages reflect different world views? Consider the following examples.

1   Arabic distinguishes *enti* أَنتِ (= you singular female) and *enta* أَنتَ (= you singular male). English and many other languages have one word (*you*) for both.

2   Spanish (like many languages) uses different second-person pronouns in relationships of familiarity and/or informality (*tú* = singular and *vosotros* = plural, in peninsular Spanish) and relationships which are more distant and formal (*usted* = singular and *ustedes* = plural, in peninsular Spanish). Other forms for *you*, such as *vos*, are also used in other parts of the Spanish-speaking world. Modern standard English has one second-person singular pronoun, *you*.

3   French (like many languages) tends to express liking as something which is done to the beholder: *Mon jardin me plait* ('My garden pleases me'). English tends to express this as something the beholder does: *I like my garden*.

4   In Chinese the terminology describing relatives (the kinship system) makes many distinctions absent in English. Thus, while English has the single words *brother* and *sister*, Chinese must always distinguish between older brother (哥哥 *gege*) and younger brother (弟弟 *didi*), older sister (姐姐 *jiejie*) and younger sister (妹妹 *meimei*). Where English has the terms *aunt* and *uncle*, Chinese distinguishes different types. An aunt, for example, may be a father's sister (姑姑 *gugu*), a father's older brother's wife (伯母 *bomu*), a father's younger brother's wife (婶婶 *shenshen*), a mother's sister (姨母 *yimu*), a mother's brother's wife (舅母 *jiumu*).

5   English speakers say *The sun rises*, but know that the earth turns, and the sun only appears to rise. Other languages also represent the sun as 'rising': *Mae'r haul yn codi* (Welsh); *le soleil se lève* (French).

Comment

There is no conclusive answer to the question in this activity. Do differences in languages reflect different concepts and ways of thinking, or are they just differences of wording? One can interpret the evidence either way, and it is hard to say whether, if there is any connection, it is one of cause and effect. Does a gender difference between second-person pronouns suggest a society which sets more store by differences between the sexes than do languages with one genderless word for 'you'? Does the lack of a polite/intimate second-person pronoun distinction in English reflect a more egalitarian society? Do the sentences in (3) suggest that the French and the English have a fundamentally different view of pleasure? Does Chinese society value the hierarchy of age and lineage more highly than do English-speaking societies? Perhaps these examples can be read as suggesting a degree of linguistic relativity. Note, however, that even when a language is not obliged to express a particular concept, it may still have the capacity to do so. Thus, English speakers can, if necessary, specify the sex of an interlocutor (*you, sir*), express social distance or closeness (*dear friend*), say *my garden gives me pleasure*, distinguish between *paternal aunt* and *maternal aunt*, etc. The last example (5), however, suggests that different ways of saying something may be fairly trivial, perhaps the legacy of a past world view rather than evidence for current thinking. English speakers go on saying *The sun rises* (5), but this does not mean that they still think the sun goes round the earth.

7.5   Translation problems: wordplay and realia

Although translation is conventionally conceived of as a transfer of meaning, a process in which the details of linguistic forms are magically left behind, almost any language-specific detail can be crucial to meaning in certain circumstances. Sound and rhythm may sometimes need to be 'carried across' just as much as meaning. While this is most famously the case in poetry, there are many other genres in which sound may be an integral part of the overall 'message' too, such as the rhythms of rhetoric and liturgy, songs or the sound effects deployed in advertising. How, for example, would one set about translating the famous (and recently revived) advertising slogan for Heinz Baked Beans *Beanz Meanz Heinz* from English into another language in a way which maintains, in addition to its meaning, its three-syllable brevity, its rhyme and its witty substitution of z for s? In such cases, the translator is probably best advised to abandon the attempt and do something which follows the spirit rather than the letter of the original – and indeed this is often done in the 'translation' of English-language advertisements for non-English-speaking markets. In other such genres, such as rhetoric, poetry or prayer, preserving meaning more precisely will be felt to be essential, making the problem much harder.

Such examples remind us that when language refers to itself, it creates particularly insoluble and intransigent translation problems. The most famous example of such reflexivity is the **pun**, in which a random coincidence within one language system is exploited to humorous or other effect.

Word play is discussed in another book in this series: Allington and Mayor (eds) (2012), Chapter 5.

Figure 7.5   Oscar Wilde (1854–1900)

Activity 7.7

Allow about
20 minutes

The title of Oscar Wilde's play *The Importance of Being Earnest* incorporates a pun which plays on the fact that the adjective *earnest* is pronounced, though not spelt, in the same way as the name of one character, *Ernest*. How could one translate this into another language where – even if there is an equivalent name, such as *Ernesto* in Italian, Portuguese and Spanish – there is no similar sounding adjective? If you know a language other than English, think about how you might tackle this problem. Even if you do not come up with a specific answer, you might be able to formulate principles about the kind of solution translators should seek.

Comment

A translator might well decide that the pun on a character's name and the relevant adjective is more important than the name itself, and thus take the liberty of changing it. This has in fact been a common strategy. Thus, translations of the title into French include *L'importance d'être Constant* ('The Importance of Being Constant'), *De l'importance d'être Fidèle* ('On the Importance of Being Faithful') and *Il est important d'être*

Aimé ('It is Important to be Loved'). The adjectives (*Constant, Fidèle, Aimé*) are also French names. A Hungarian translation of the same play applied a similar solution, making it *Szilárdnak kell lenni* ('One must be Szilárd') where *Szilárd* is both a name and an adjective meaning *steadfast, firm*.

A different but no less challenging problem can exist when language refers not to itself but to the real physical world. Although this world is apparently independent of linguistic realisation, it can still cause translation difficulties. Take, for example, the opening line of Shakespeare's Sonnet 18:

Shall I compare thee to a summer's day?

This does not lift easily into a context where the climate of summer is not associated, as it is in England, with welcome warmth and fecundity, but with unwelcome aridity and excessive heat.

The summer sun is at least an aspect of the human environment which is not created by the culture on which it shines. With cultural artefacts (known within translation studies as 'realia') and their significance the situation is more complex. Such artefacts may be both functional and symbolic. Green wellington boots and print headscarves worn by women driving 4x4s in the English countryside are symbols of belonging to a rural upper class, not just items of attire. Any object can, in a given cultural context, take on meaning in this way. Thus, when readers of the original version of the 1960s Russian short story *Fyodor Grye* by Vasily Shukshin are told that a particular character smokes *papirosi* (a cheap cigarette with a cardboard tube and loosely packed rough and cheap tobacco) they would immediately infer that the character is of a particular social and economic group and status. But how is the translator to render this for the English language reader in the 2010s? By a footnote on the significance of this type of cigarette, or by the substitution of an equivalent type of British cigarette from the same period (*Park Lane/Number 6*)? By simply calling it *a cigarette* and letting its significance be lost? None of these strategies is satisfactory – the first as it lengthens and interrupts the text, the second as it introduces an obvious incongruity, and the third as it fails to do justice to the richness of the original.

Such problems are further complicated by the fact that readers in the original language may need explanations too, and the translator should not assume that just because someone is a native reader of a given language they are necessarily fully cognisant of the social and psychological significance of every detail. Indeed, younger Russian readers may neither know nor understand the significance of this particular detail, knowledge of which may be confined to certain periods and age groups. For English, this problem is particularly marked, as many international readers of translations from English do not have, nor otherwise need to have, particular insight into the cultural contexts of English-speaking countries. As English gains ground as an international language, it simultaneously loses an automatic connection to particular cultural contexts.

Translators cope with such problems with different degrees of success and freedom, either by trying to introduce the unfamiliar and culturally alien to readers, or by converting it into something more homely and familiar. Yet clearly there are limits to either strategy. If, for example, a Hindi text concerns the details of Hindu festivals – *Diwali, Durga Puja, Holi,* and so on – it may make little sense to a readership unfamiliar with the festivals if their names are simply lifted into English without explanation. Yet it would clearly be absurd to substitute the English names of holidays from a completely different cultural context, and call them *Thanksgiving, Christmas,* etc. This latter strategy not only misses the role of translation in giving access to other cultures rather than seeing them in terms of our own, but also overlooks the fact that in the contemporary world, cultural boundaries are not straightforward, and ignorance cannot be assumed. Readers of the English translation may well be Hindus themselves.

Freedom of interpretation in the interests of capturing the attention of contemporary audiences, and making difficult texts more accessible to them, is by no means confined to translation. The strategy of making the strange familiar by converting it into something 'nearer home' is not unlike the tactic deployed by theatre and film directors when trying to give an old text contemporary relevance. Baz Luhrmann's film version of *Romeo and Juliet* transposes the tale of the 'star-cross'd lovers' from 'fair Verona' to the gangland of a place reminiscent of contemporary Rio de Janeiro. Michael Almereyda's *Hamlet* has Ophelia wired up with a microphone like a police sting rather than eavesdropped upon by her father and the king. In a sense this is also translation – although intralingual (i.e. within one language) rather than interlingual (i.e. between languages) – terms which, as you will remember, were used by Juliane House in Reading A.

7.6 Discourse and interaction

How are interpreters to deal with differences in cultural conventions in ways which are faithful to what is being said but avoid offence and misunderstanding? There is a joke – possibly based on fact – about an interpreter who was interpreting between a US businessman and the board of a Japanese company. Unaware of cultural differences in humour, the US speaker kept making jokes, which the interpreter faithfully translated, but they were met with silence rather than laughter. Tension began to mount. To defuse the situation, the interpreter resorted to saying in Japanese at the end of each translation, 'That was a joke. He wants you to laugh.' The listeners politely laughed, and the situation was defused.

Intercultural communication in business settings is also discussed in another book in this series: Allington and Mayor (eds) (2012), Chapter 4.

Allow about 10 minutes

Activity 7.8

Do you think the interpreter adopted the best strategy? If not, what do you think they should have done? What are the advantages and disadvantages of spelling out the intention as well as the meaning of what is said?

Comment

Again, there are no easy answers to the problem of cultural differences, although you may have come up with some suggestions. Spoken interaction arguably brings even more problems than written translations, as many of its conventions vary considerably between languages and cultures: the use of first names, physical contact, interruption and turn taking; what personal information it is appropriate to demand; what compliments are appropriate, and when. Tales of misunderstandings are legion. Consider translation between English and Arabic: a language interface fraught with difficulty and potential for misunderstanding, due to differences in conventions and underlying ideas. For example, it is impolite in Arabic discourse to accept a first offer – of a second helping, a drink, a gift, and so on. By convention, the person to whom an offer is made should refuse several times, while the person making the offer should reiterate it until it is accepted. Should the interpreter therefore translate an initial Arabic *no* as *yes*, or an initial English *yes* as a hesitant *no*? Or should they explain the difference?

Differences between the conventions of speech run deeper than such conventional issues. Everyday Arabic is full of expressions which reflect the deeply religious nature of Arab culture: *in-shâ'-llâh* إن شاء الله ('God willing'), *bi mashi at ellah* بمشيئة الله ('by God's will'), *al hamd dallah* الحمد لله ('Thank God!'). These are used in contexts in which most English speakers would use secular expressions (*perhaps, if possible*) or phrases which were once religious but have now lost their original piety (*Thank God*). How is the translator, from Arabic to English or vice versa, to deal with this? Should they use a religious expression (*God willing*) which English speakers now rarely use? Or should they ignore the religious nature of Arabic discourse by secularising through translation?

In late twentieth-century translation theory, the answer generally given to such a question was that the translator should seek communicative or pragmatic equivalence. They should be guided by the communicative effect rather than by the literal meaning, trying to assess how each phrase functions in the interaction (as a hedge, a refusal or an expression of concern) and say what speakers of the target language would say to achieve the same effect – thus avoiding at all costs the entry of anything alien into the target language.

Such a strategy, while it seemed enlightened at the time and a way of distracting attention from the mediation of translation, assumes that cultural differences are ultimately superficial. It can thus become a way of neutralising and ignoring everything that is different about the society whose language is being translated. It would make an Arabic interchange which literally translates as:

How's your health Ali? كيف صحتك يا علي؟ (*kief sahtak ya Ali?*)
Thanks be to God! الحمد لله! (*al hamd dallah!*)

into:

How are you Ali?
Very well, thanks.

Translation theorist Lawrence Venuti (1986, 1995) has distinguished translations which **nativise** (or domesticate) the original, by making it conform to the norms of the language and culture into which it is translated (*Very well, thank you*) and those which **foreignise** it, by making it keep some of the alien characteristics of the original (*Thanks be to God*). Interestingly, this distinction parallels in many ways the older and more familiar one between free translation and a literal word-for-word one, although with more positive evaluation of the literal. Literary translation, however, has often tended to be both free and 'nativising'. For example, Edward FitzGeralds' famous 1859 translation of the Persian poem *The Rubaiyat of Omar Khayyam*, while successful and acclaimed by its English readers, has been authoritatively critiqued for departing from the original at almost every level. While such translations may have merits of their own, they are not the same merits as those of the originals, and should we wish to read translation for insight into alien literature and culture, a less accessible but more faithful translation may have merits of a different kind. On the other hand, a translation whose style is quirky and idiosyncratic as a result of maintaining its foreignness may serve only to keep that work on the margins of the new literature it seeks to enter (Liu, 2007). It appears that translation can never win!

Such problems of cultural difference permeate every level of interaction, from the most everyday examples to matters of worldwide significance. They underline the fact that translation, like any communication through language, is a human affair, and judgements about the best translation must be matters of human judgement in relation to a unique context, and can never be entirely resolved by context-free and people-free rules.

Activity 7.9

Now turn to Reading B: *Reframing conflict in translation* by Mona Baker. In this reading, Baker discusses translation choices in the English subtitles of an Arabic documentary, *Jenin Jenin*. She shows how translation choices serve to 'reframe' the documentary for a predominantly American audience. That is, the translations feed into wider narratives through which this perceived audience is seen to understand the world. As you read the first example ('The Vietnam frame') consider the merits and limitations of the translation.

Baker's second example involves the translation of an Arabic religious term and its political implications ('The secular frame'). As you read, reflect on how vocabulary choices can slant a news report in a particular direction. (For example, the words 'freedom fighter', 'guerilla' and 'terrorist' may all refer to the same person, depending on the allegiance of the reporter.) How, in your view, should the translator cope with loaded vocabulary, especially when there is no straightforward equivalence between a term in the source language and one in the target language? Should lengthy explanations and background information be given? Or would they lengthen the text too much?

Comment

There is no easy answer to these problems and questions. Arguably, there is no such thing as neutral language, and the way we choose to say something always reflects a particular stance. (Indeed, Baker herself is clearly not neutral.) If this is true within one language, then problems can only multiply when equivalence with another enters the equation. The established view is that translators should try to capture both the information and the point of view of the original, and when this is not possible, they have the difficult task of deciding whether the inevitable loss merits extra commentary. In the case of such important issues as misunderstandings between the Arabic- and English-speaking worlds, there is perhaps a particularly good case for extra information and explanation, and the English-language media are often at fault for lifting Arabic words into English without ensuring that readers understand the subtle differences from apparently equivalent words in English.

The following extract from a newspaper report, about translation from English to Arabic during the 2003 invasion of Iraq, illustrates graphically just how badly translation can be handled. To compensate for a lack of translators and interpreters, the invading US troops were issued with:

> a handheld black plastic device the size of an eggbox called a Phrasealator [see Figure 7.6]. Users run a stylus down a series of menus on a screen, pick a phrase in English, touch the line, and the Phrasealator squawks the equivalent in Arabic. The machine lacks elementary social skills. It only covers a handful of situations, such as crowd control, law and order and emergencies. If you want to tell someone to get out of their car slowly or not to be frightened, it's great. If you have to talk to farmers in rural Iraq about intimate details of their lives, families, crops and horticultural needs, and understand what they say back, it's useless.
>
> (Meek, 2003)

Figure 7.6 A phrasealator

The shortcomings of this mechanical device serve to emphasise that translation is of its nature two-way communication, and that a human element is always necessary. This is why, incidentally, despite enormous strides in recent years, automatic translation has not succeeded in replacing the skills of human interpreters and translators, who not only make decisions about linguistic and semantic equivalence (as computers can now do up to a point), but also make social and cultural judgements in particular contexts. In situations of potential antagonism and distrust, such as encounters between soldiers and civilians, these judgements are quintessentially important. This is not to say, of course, that where there is comprehension of what is being said, and insight into different cultures and ideas, concord and compromise automatically follow. As Thomas (1998) points out, clear understanding of another set of values may only deepen antagonism towards them. Indeed, many of the world's worst conflicts have been between those who understand each other only too well. The languages of Urdu and Hindi speakers during the partition of India, or of Croat and Serb speakers after the break-up of Yugoslavia, were so close as not to need interpreters at all. Yet despite such counter examples, and the validity of Thomas's case, it remains true that, in conflict resolution, clear mutual understanding of differences must always be a first stage towards agreement, and that in many cases translation and interpreting have a key role to play.

7.7   Focus on the translator

Awareness of rival alternative translations has a history as long as translation itself. This is no longer, however, merely a continuation of the perennial debate over the relative merits of 'literal' vs 'free' translation, or what constitutes equivalence, on which we have already touched. Contemporary 'translation studies' (a term which has now largely replaced 'translation theory') displays an acute awareness of the ways in which choices between translations can distort what is said or angle it towards one particular point of view.

With this in mind, the focus in recent translation studies has moved towards the process of translat*ing* rather than the product of translat*ion*, together with the person of the translator; and their influence on the communication they mediate has come to the fore. Various theoretical distinctions help to highlight this new emphasis and the way in which it has broken with the established conventional wisdom that the best translator and translation is the one which is least evident. Thus, Lawrence Venuti (1986, 1995) talks of the translator's visibility or invisibility, while Juliane House (1997, 2009) draws a distinction between overt translation, in which the process of translating and its accompanying problems are brought to the attention of those receiving it, and covert translation, in which the act of translating and the person of the translator are kept as much in the background as possible. If accepted, such new emphases might mean that the visible translator comments on problems in translating as and when they arise. However, it is worth observing that while such a move may be advocated by theorists, there is little sign of such development happening in practice. Pause for comment is likely to be unwelcome and even regarded as incompetence. In an article on problems facing court interpreters in Australia, Jieun Lee (2009) reports how a Korean interpreter who attempted to explain a problem to the judge was told to 'just translate'.

Allow about
15 minutes

Activity 7.10

To what extent do you think translators should be in evidence and to what extent do you think they should intervene in, comment on or change what is said? Consider the following three examples, drawing on your own experiences and ideas, as well as what you have read in the chapter so far. Note that there is no commentary for this activity.

1   An interpreter explains to their client that what has just been said is intended as polite even though it may appear rude.

2   A translator of a document containing what they consider to be sexist language changes it into what they consider to be non-sexist language in the translation.

3   A translator tries to make something clearer than the original. For example, the first English translation of Milan Kundera's novel *The Joke* reorganised its to-and-fro chronology in an attempt to clarify the story (Munday, 2001, p. 154).

7.8   Conclusion: the asymmetrical nature of contemporary translation

This chapter began with commentary on the positive role of translation in providing access to other languages and other cultures. If we accept this role as a premise, then languages into which a great deal is translated also gain a great deal from that process. This has certainly been the case with English, which in addition to exerting its own influence around the world, has also been enriched by exposure to a succession of foreign influences mediated by translation.

This notion of mutual enrichment, however, assumes a two-way traffic. In the contemporary world, there is evidence that translation has become a depressingly one-way street. One might argue that the most vital periods in the development of the English language and English-speaking societies have also been periods when they were most open to outside influence. In England, as elsewhere, for example, the Renaissance and the Enlightenment were driven by translation from other languages into English. In the British colonies which became the USA, translations from French philosophy and politics played an important role in inspiring the struggle for independence. Nowadays, however, while ideas continue to travel out from these two English-speaking countries into other languages, very little is coming in. A report presented to a UNESCO conference describes how:

> 55 to 60 % of all book translations are made from a single language, and that is – obviously – English. So English strongly dominates the global market for translations. In terms of a core-periphery model, which is widely used in international relations, one can say that it occupies a sort of *hypercentral position* to borrow a term from Abram de Swaan.
>
> After English, there are two languages that have a *central position*: German and French. Each with a share of about 10% of the global translation market. Both are far behind English, but are clearly ahead of all the other languages. Then – third level – there are 7 or 8 languages that have a *semi-central position*. These are languages that are neither very central on a global level nor very peripheral, having a share of 1 to 3 % of the world market. These are typically languages like Spanish, Italian, and Russian. And, finally – fourth level – there are all the other languages from which less than 1% of the book translations worldwide are made. These languages can be considered to be 'peripheral' in the international translation economy, in spite of the fact that some of these languages have a very large number of speakers – Chinese, Japanese, Arabic. These are among the largest languages in the world, but their role in the translation economy is peripheral as compared to more central languages.
>
> (Heilbron, 2010)

The dominance of English as a language which is translated *from* is also discussed in Chapter 6 of this book.

So, of the world's 6000 languages, we now encounter only a handful through translation into English. The consistent growth of English as an international language brings with it the danger that English speakers have less incentive to enter the cultural territory of other languages. Yet translation is still the major gateway into the cultures and ideas expressed in other languages, and should have a major compensatory role to play in our Anglophone age. By translating only from English, or by making everything foreign conform to the norms of English-speaking culture, we are acting to the detriment of English as well as other languages.

READING A: What is translation?

Juliane House

Source: House, J. (2009) *Translation*, Oxford, Oxford University Press, pp. 3–13.

The nature of translation

Translation is the replacement of an original text with another text.

As such, translation has been regarded as a kind of inferior substitute for the real thing, and it has been likened to the back of a carpet, or a kiss through a handkerchief. But it can also be seen more positively as providing access to ideas and experiences that, although represented at second hand, would otherwise be closed off in an unknown language.

So although translation can be seen as a kind of limitation, it also has the opposite function of overcoming the limitations that particular languages impose on their speakers. Instead of comparing it to such reduced activities as hygienic kissing or laying down a carpet bottom-side up, translation can also be compared to building bridges or extending horizons, metaphors which point to the positive, enabling function of translation. In this sense translation can be seen as a service: it serves a need human beings apparently have to transcend the world to which their own particular languages confine them. Translations mediate between languages, societies, and literatures, and it is through translations that linguistic and cultural barriers may be overcome.

Translation, of its nature, provides access to something, some message, that already exists, and it is always therefore a secondary communication. Normally, a communicative event happens just once. With translation, however, communicative events are reduplicated for people originally prevented from participating in, or appreciating, the original event.

Kinds of translation

Translation is the process of replacing an original text, known as the source text, with a substitute one, known as the **target text**.

The process is usually an **interlingual translation** in that the message in the source language text is rendered as a target text in a different language, and it is in this sense that we have referred to translation so far. But sometimes the term is also used to refer to an **intralingual translation**, a process whereby a text in one variety of the language is reworded into another. This would be the case where the message of a text in, say, Old English is reworked into a text in Modern English, or a text in one dialect or style is reworked into another. And we can also speak of 'translation', when the replacement involves not another language but another, non-linguistic, means of expression, in other words a different semiotic system. In this sense we can say for instance that a poem is 'translated' into a dance or a picture, a novel into an opera or a film. Such transmutations are examples of **intersemiotic translation**.

What all these three processes have in common is that they involve the replacement of one expression of a message or unit of meaningful content by another in a different form.

The term 'translation' is also sometimes used to describe linguistic activities such as summarizing or paraphrasing. Although such activities resemble translation in that they replace a message that already exists, they differ in that they are designed not to reproduce the original as a whole but to reduce it to its essential parts, or adapt it for different groups of people with different needs and expectations. In this [reading] we will be concerned with translation as it is most commonly understood, that is to say as the process of interlingual replacement of one text by another.

[…]

Translation and interpreting

Translation can be written or oral. The written form is known as translation, the oral one is known as **interpreting** […]. In professional conference interpreting, a distinction is usually made between simultaneous and consecutive interpreting. In the former, the act of interpreting is carried out while the speaker is still talking; in the latter, interpreting occurs after the speaker has finished.

In written translation a fixed, permanently available and in principle unlimitedly repeatable text in one language is changed into a text in another language, which can be corrected as often as the translator sees fit. In interpreting, on the other hand, a text is transformed into a new text in another language, which is, as a rule, orally available only once. Since the new text emerges chunk by chunk and does not 'stay' permanently with the interpreter (or the addressees), it is only controllable and correctible by the interpreter to a limited extent. While some steps in interpreting can be regarded as 'automatic' and need little reflective thought, others may be more difficult and take time. This can lead to serious problems, as the interpreter has to listen and interpret at the same time. All this is very different in translating, where the translator can usually read and translate the source text at his or her own pace. Further, the original is available for translation in its entirety, whereas, in simultaneous and consecutive (conference) interpreting, it is produced and presented bit by bit. This is a great challenge for the interpreter who needs to create an ongoing text out of these bits that must eventually form a coherent whole.

Besides conference interpreting in national or international environments, another type of interpreting, known as 'community interpreting' (sometimes also called 'public service interpreting' or 'dialogue interpreting') has recently gained importance. Given increasing international migration and the resulting mixture of linguistic backgrounds, community interpreting fulfils an important mediating function in that it facilitates communication between officials and lay persons who speak different languages. Community interpreting is almost always carried out consecutively (face-to-face or over the phone). It takes place for instance in police or immigration departments, social welfare centres, hospitals, schools or prisons, and is either carried out by untrained 'natural interpreters' such as bilingual relatives and friends, or by professional experts in specialist (legal, medical, etc.) domains. The interpreter has to interpret for both parties, thus switching between both languages. Untrained volunteer community interpreters are often neither neutral nor objective when they interpret for a relative or a friend; rather, they tend to take the side of whoever they are helping out in an institutional context. A type of interpreting which is similar to community interpreting is 'liaison interpreting', but here the interpreting is done between persons of equal status in business and technical meetings.

The distinction between translation (written) and interpreting (oral) is a necessary one – they are very different activities. In written translation, neither author of source texts nor addressees of target texts are usually present so no overt interaction or direct feedback can take place. In the interpreting situation, on the other hand, both author and addressees are usually present, and interaction and feedback may occur. In this [reading], we shall be concerned primarily with the written form, translation, and we shall only occasionally consider the oral form, interpreting.

Human and machine translation

The act of translating can be performed not only by a human being but also by a machine. Machine translation can be fully automatic or semi-automatic. In fully automatic translation, the original text is fed into the computer, and the translation is delivered with no human involvement. So far, fully automatic machine translation can only produce very 'rough' drafts, that is to say quick and dirty first versions, as can be seen in the following (constructed) example of a translation of a Volkswagen annual report:

Original

Die aus den Vorjahren bekannten Probleme im Weltwährungssystem spitzten sich weiter zu. Sie erreichten ihren Höhepunkt, als der Dollarkurs auf 2,28 Mark sank. Dies verursachte eine weitere Verteuerung des deutschen Exports.

Fully automatic machine translation

The from the foreyears known problems in worldcurrencysystem pointed themselves again to. They reached their highpoint as the dollarcourse sank to DM 2.28. This caused a further endearing of German exports.

Such versions can, however, be quite useful, for instance, whenever a human translation is, for whatever reason, simply not available, and whenever highly specialized scientists need to know quickly what a technical article is all about. For such a specialist, a fully automatic translation may be perfectly acceptable even though its wording, as in the above example, can be very clumsy. The specialist's familiarity with the subject in question is likely to disambiguate any oddity in the automatically produced text. If, however, one wants to improve the quality of machine translations, heavy pre- and post-editing by a human translator is still indispensable, and the translation will then become a semi-automatic one. Some translation programs also stop whenever the program cannot, for example, decide which meaning to give to an ambiguous term, and a human translator will make the decision, after which the program carries on.

Further, specific computer programs are available which can help the human translator in three different ways. Firstly, translation software can help the translator solve difficult translation problems by offering lexical help through workstations that provide access to online dictionaries or give grammatical help in the form of conventionally co-occurring patterns of words. Secondly, computers can assist the translator in his or her attempt to retrieve highly routinized and idiomatic target language structures. And thirdly, computers can help human translators by providing encyclopaedic knowledge: they offer search procedures and indicate how to fill knowledge gaps that typically occur with (conceptual and linguistic) problems of terminology.

To improve these different types of machine translation programs, researchers use the findings of studies of translators' thoughts and behaviour. Machines can then imitate these human translation strategies. So there is a kind of 'division of labour' between man and machine in *computer-assisted translation*: computer programs relieve the human translator of boring and time-consuming routine tasks, and give him or her access to different translation reference works thus freeing up the translator for more creative, non-mechanical problem solving and decision making.

It is unlikely that software will ever replace the human translator completely. The dream of a fully competent independent machine translating system is still a long way off. But machine translation in its different forms is certainly here to stay. It is particularly useful if one is interested in regular and predictable translations of highly specific texts, for which the transmission of information is dominant (for example, translating into English Japanese business market reports or Chinese papers in the field of astronomy). The usefulness of machine translation is however much reduced in the case of literary texts and other types of creative writing, which draw heavily on associations and connotative meanings as well as pragmatic and cultural knowledge.

Translation as communication across cultures

Translating is not only a linguistic act, it is also a cultural one, an act of communication across cultures. Translating always involves both language and culture simply because the two cannot really be separated. Language is culturally embedded: it both expresses and shapes cultural reality, and the meanings of linguistic items, be they words or larger segments of text, can only be understood when considered together with the cultural context in which these linguistic items are used. For example, a simple expression such as 'We had dinner' written in a British cultural context cannot be transposed into an Arabic, German, Finnish, or indeed an American English context without considering the different cultural 'meanings' this expression acquires in these different contexts. Since in translation meaning is of overriding importance, it follows that the cultural frame of reference cannot be ignored. In the process of translation, therefore, not only the two languages but also the two cultures come into contact. In this sense, translating is a form of intercultural communication.

But what do we mean when we talk about 'culture' in this context? Culture refers to a group's shared values and conventions which act as mental guidelines for orienting people's thoughts and behaviour. Now it is of course true that we find in any group many different values, beliefs, and behaviours. However, we are interested here in how different cultural habits and views are encapsulated in language and become externalized when communicated to others in the social group. If such communication occurs often enough in a particular social group, it can turn into 'cultural representations' in the minds of group members. Language use and convention, therefore, vitally contribute to social bonding and cultural identity. This conventionalization of meaning through language within a particular culture is of crucial importance for translation: it is precisely these similarities and differences in kind and degree of conventionalization in the source and target cultures which a translator must be aware of when moving a text from one culture to another. In translating a reference to a particular date which is important in a particular culture, for example, it may become necessary to explain the 'meaning' this date has acquired for members of the source culture. Consider for instance a reference to the 4th of July in an American text, the 17th of May in a Norwegian text, the 17th of June in a German text, or the 14th of July in a French one. The 'meaning' which these dates carry is culturally embedded, and cannot be understood in the abstract, divorced from the historical tradition shared by members of a particular culture.

READING B: Reframing conflict in translation

Mona Baker

Source: Baker, M. (2007) 'Reframing conflict in translation', *Social Semiotics*, vol. 17, no. 2, pp. 151–69.

Narratives […] are stories that we come to subscribe to – believe in or at least contemplate as potentially valid – and that therefore shape our behaviour towards other people and the events in which we are embedded. As used here, narratives are not chronologies, not undifferentiated lists of happenings: they are stories that are temporally and causally constituted in such a way as to allow us to make moral decisions and act in the real world. […]

An Arabic documentary entitled *Jenin Jenin* was directed by Mohamed Bakri and released in 2002 following the Israeli attack on the Jenin camp in the Occupied West Bank. The documentary is shot in the Jenin camp in Arabic but is clearly aimed at an international audience: it was subtitled into English, Hebrew, French, Spanish and Italian (Mohamed Bakri, personal communication). The version with English subtitles seems to be aimed predominantly at an American audience, as we will see shortly. The following examples from the documentary demonstrate two attempts at (re)framing that respond to larger narratives circulating beyond the immediate text and cannot be explained by resorting to […] Venuti's foreignizing versus domesticating dichotomy. […]

The Vietnam frame

The first instance of (re)framing activates a narrative framework that seems to have been judged as more effective in the target context. At one point in the documentary, an old Palestinian man expresses his shock at what happened in Jenin and the world's apparent indifference and reluctance to intervene to protect Palestinians. He ends his contribution by saying, literally in Arabic, 'What can I say, by God, by God, our house/home is no longer a house/home'. The subtitle for this frame is 'What can I say? Not even Vietnam was as bad as this' (see Figure [1]).

The decision to replace the original reference to the destruction of Palestinian homes with a reference to Vietnam would traditionally be interpreted in translation studies as an attempt to 'acculturate' the source text, to render it more intelligible to the target audience (in this case envisaged as predominantly American). But this is not a very productive or satisfying explanation. Had this been the primary motivation here, it would have made much more sense to refer to a more recent and hence more salient event, such as 9/11. After all, Vietnam arguably has less resonance among a young American audience than 9/11, and appealing to the memory of the latter is thus more likely to secure the emotional involvement and sympathy of a wider section of American viewers. To appreciate the motivation for this translational choice and its implications, it is necessary to refer to the wider narratives in circulation at that time, in Palestine and internationally.

First, the immediate narrative of what actually happened in the Jenin camp [...] in April 2002 was and continues to be heavily contested [...]. One of the discursive loci of contestation at the time concerned the widespread description of the Jenin event in the English-speaking media as an 'incursion'. Activists in the Solidarity movement insisted that 'incursion' was far too sanitized a description for the full-blown and sustained assault that left the camp in ruins and many people dead. The reference to Vietnam in the above subtitle reframes the event as a war of aggression, rather than a minor raid as the term 'incursion' tends to suggest. Vietnam was certainly no incursion: it is widely perceived as a vicious and bloody war, among large sectors of the American public as well as internationally.

Figure [1] Screen shot from *Jenin Jenin*

Second, one narrative that continues to have considerable currency among Palestinians as well as the growing international solidarity movement in support of Palestinian rights is that America is as responsible for Israeli atrocities as Israel itself – that Israel could not possibly get away with its oppression of Palestinians were it not for the extensive support it receives from the United States. The choice of Vietnam here activates that public narrative. Far from being either foreignizing or domesticating, the choice to evoke the narrative of Vietnam encodes both accommodation to dominance and resistance to it. It accommodates to dominance by opting for a reference (Vietnam) that has resonance for the dominant American audience, rather than one that [...] would have no resonance for that dominant public: Kashmir, for instance, or even Darfur. It encodes resistance by simultaneously framing America as aggressor and signalling that the American audience is complicit in the injustices perpetrated by their government – and can choose to challenge them, just as they did in the case of Vietnam.

The secular frame

Another interesting attempt at reframing the wider Palestinian narrative by recasting aspects of the speech of several Palestinians interviewed in this documentary concerns the treatment of the recurrent word *shaheed*. The standard equivalent for this word in English is *martyr*, but this is problematic for two reasons. First, *shaheed* does not semantically map onto *martyr* in full. In Arabic, *shaheed* is generally used to refer to anyone who is killed violently, especially in war, whether they choose to be involved in that war or not, and irrespective of their religion. It therefore does not have the overtones of militancy and extremism that the term *martyr* has come to acquire in English, in connection with the Arab and Islamic world.[1] Second, *martyr* readily evokes associations of Islamic fundamentalism in this type of context, and using it repeatedly would play into the hands of those who would portray the Middle East conflict as a religious war, fuelled by young deranged Muslims in search of virgins in paradise. The subtitles consistently opt for different equivalents when the word *shaheed* is used by Palestinians interviewed on the documentary, as in the following examples [...]:

Example 1

"لسه بندوّر شهدا من تحت الأرض".

Backtranslation

We are still pulling *martyrs* from underneath the ground.

---

[1] *Martyr* of course has very different associations in other contexts, for instance in the discourse of Christianity.

English subtitle

> We are still pulling *victims* out of the rubble.

Example 2

"متخلفين عقلياً استشهدوا عندنا، معاقين استشهدوا عندنا، أطفال استشهدوا عندنا، نساء استشهدوا عندنا".

Backtranslation

> We have mentally retarded people who have been *martyred*; we have disabled people who have been *martyred*; we have children who have been *martyred*, we have women who have been *martyred*.

English subtitle

> They *killed* some mentally disabled people, children and women in the camp.

The choice of equivalents such as *victims* and *killed* in the above examples (and *corpses* and *dead* in other instances) rather than *martyr* helps to frame the larger Palestinian and Arab narrative in more secular terms.

There are two exceptions in the entire documentary. The first occurs towards the end in a scene involving a young Palestinian girl of about seven or eight years old who had been expressing defiance and determination to survive throughout the documentary. She draws an extended analogy between the Jenin camp and a 'tall, tall towering tree', which 'consists of leaves', with every leaf 'inscribed with the name of a *shaheed*, a *muqawim* [resistance fighter]' (my translation). The subtitles retain the metaphor and the reference to 'martyrs' in this instance, arguably because the innocent-looking, if defiant, young girl does not exactly fit the image of a deranged extremist in pursuit of paradise:

> The camp is like a tall, eminent tree. The tree has leaves, and each leaf of the tree bears the name of a martyr.[2]

---

[2] Note that the subtitles nevertheless tone the image down by omitting 'resistance fighter'.

The second instance in which the term *martyr* is used occurs in the final credits, and is therefore not a 'subtitle'. The documentary starts with the following dedication (reproduced here as is, without correction):

> Dedicated to
> The Executive Producer of 'Jenin'
> IYAD SAMOUDI
> who was murdered at alyamoun
> at the end of the filming by
> Israelian soliders on 23/06/2003
> Mohamed Bakri

The final credits include the following text:

> Executive Producer
> The martyr
> Iyad Samoudi

To sum up, narrative theory allows us to make sense of these apparently conflicting strategies, such as those relating to the choice of equivalents for *shaheed* at different points in the *Jenin Jenin* documentary, as well as ones (like the choice of *Vietnam* above) that are simultaneously foreignizing and domesticating. [...] Dominance and resistance not only shape our behaviour and discursive choices, but [...] they are also always in a relationship of tension. This tension is often played out discursively, and the interplay between the two can produce a range of choices that are difficult to streamline. [... R]ecognizing this interplay between dominance and resistance allows us to elaborate a more complex picture of the positioning of translators and to embed them in concrete political reality.

8 Ideologies of English

Caroline Tagg

8.1 Introduction

Harsh words for BBC over Live 8 stars' swearing

THE BBC was censured yesterday by Ofcom, the media watchdog, after a number of performers used bad language during live coverage of last summer's Live 8 concert.

Madonna, Snoop Dogg, Razorlight and Green Day were among those who swore during the concert from London's Hyde Park last July, which attracted a peak audience of 9.6 million.

No time delay was used for the broadcast and the language, which sparked 400 complaints, was heard by young viewers before the 9pm watershed.

(Sheppard, *The Scotsman*, February 2006)

The complaints over 'swearing' that followed the Live 8 concerts in 2005 illustrate one way in which language is valued, and how people's values shape language use and influence language policy. The concerts were an attempt to bring issues such as debt, trade and poverty in Africa to public awareness prior to their discussion at a summit of world leaders in 2005. Given the gravity of the cause, the fact that 400 people felt it necessary to complain about the words used by some of the celebrities is testament to how strongly people feel about language. This attitude towards swearing finds its expression in the policies adopted to regulate it: measures include censure by the British government's media watchdog 'Ofcom', and the 'watershed' – the period in which adult content can be shown on television, which in Britain begins at 9 p.m. You may be aware of similar regulations in other countries.

We might then ask what prompted Madonna and Snoop Dogg to challenge social and institutional regulations, and conjecture that the answer lies to some extent in their construction of particular public personae – the kind of people who challenge conventions. Swearing (in a public, potentially inappropriate place) is a conscious choice, a facet of the social identities that these musicians wish to convey. (In fact, 'swearing' depends for its effect on disapproving attitudes.) Turning this around, the complaints made about the Live 8 concerts are not simply about how the public feel about the words used, but are bound up with evaluations of the celebrities who use that language and what they stand for. As Chapter 1 points out, language ideologies – the sets of beliefs that people have about language, and the rationalisations they make about its use and status in society (Silverstein, 1979, p. 139) – are never solely about language, but are instead about associations that societies make between particular language uses and various social and moral issues. So, we can glimpse in this example the complex ways in which people's language values interact with:

- their own language use
- their evaluations of other people
- the policies that attempt to regulate language practices.

In this chapter, I explore the above points in relation to the many uses of English in the world today. In particular, I address the following questions:

- First, how do people value English in relation to other languages, and how are certain varieties of English evaluated in relation to other varieties? How do these ideologies play out in complex situations, characterised by competition and conflict, as well as cooperation?
- Second, to what extent do people's attitudes towards English chime with the ideologies that underlie governmental and institutional policies? When and how do people's values diverge from those of policy makers and drive them to contest or subvert policy?

Although these questions can be applied to other languages and to contexts where no English is spoken, the language attitudes of people in diverse world contexts increasingly include how they feel about English. As Chapter 1 (Section 1.1) puts it, 'English – with its global reach, its history rooted in colonialism, its contemporary association with global capitalism, its multiple forms and varieties, and its status as one of the most taught languages around the world – is easily implicated in

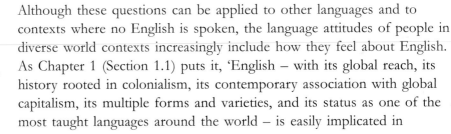

Good !
Quote.
Ref.

manifold political debates, and as such exists as a focus for language policies around the world, in English-dominant countries and elsewhere'.

I start by exploring the values that people attach to varieties of English, before looking critically at the notion of correctness and the extent to which ideas about correctness shape people's views of spoken and written English. I then explore how these values can translate into – or contest – policy, first by revisiting examples from this book and, second, by exploring the debates around grammar teaching in UK schools which arose in the 1990s. I draw attention to the continuing resonance of such debates in the twenty-first century and in other national contexts, looking in particular at Singapore. I conclude by considering how this book is imbued with the values of its authors.

8.2   Exploring language values

Many studies have sought to elicit how people feel about language. An early investigation into this was carried out in 1960 by social psychologist Wallace Lambert and colleagues in Canada. The researchers explored how French and English Canadians reacted to speakers of Canadian French and English, and they did so by pioneering the **matched guise test**. This involves asking people to evaluate the personalities of speakers of different languages (or different varieties of one language) according to the way they read aloud a certain passage. Unbeknownst to participants, the languages or varieties are spoken by the same speakers putting on different 'guises', so that how participants evaluate one speaker in their different guises can be compared. In the 1960 study, participants were asked to rate speakers, on the basis of voice alone, in terms of their general likeability, ambition, dependability, self-confidence, sense of humour, good looks and – surprisingly – their height. They were also asked to state each speaker's most likely profession. It was perhaps to be expected that English Canadians rated other English speakers most highly on favourable traits, but more surprising was the fact that French Canadians also tended to evaluate the English guises positively. The researchers concluded that French Canadians 'may well regard themselves as members of an inferior group' and as such their statements reflect a tendency for minority groups to adopt the 'stereotyped values' of majority groups (Lambert et al., 1960, p. 49). While the 1960 study focused on different languages, subsequent studies have used matched guise tests to elicit attitudes towards varieties of a language, such as English dialects within the British Isles (Ryan and Giles, 1982).

**Allow about
10 minutes**

Activity 8.1

Consider the effectiveness of the matched guise test. How accurately do you feel that it elicits how people actually feel? What does the study tell us about language values?

Comment

Imagine yourself as a participant in a matched guise test responding to recorded voices. The first drawback is that you are only reporting how you feel, and you may (consciously or otherwise) tend towards responses that you feel the researcher wants to hear or that you think put you in the best light. The artificiality of the process may also encourage you to stereotype. Compare the conditions of the test with a natural encounter in a shop or a street. The decontextualised, relatively 'safe' conditions of the test may encourage people towards harsher reactions than they would make to that same speaker's face. In other words, these elicited value positions cannot be assumed to reflect unproblematically how people actually feel.

Attitudes and values

Two terms are often used to describe how people feel about English: language attitudes and language values. According to social psychology research (e.g. Edwards, 1982), what distinguishes **language attitudes** from beliefs or opinions is that the former describes not only what people think and their stated beliefs, but how they feel, and how this disposes them to act. An example of language attitudes thus defined would be the belief that a local dialect uses incorrect forms, coupled with the feeling that its speakers are less intelligent than standard English speakers, resulting in discrimination. 'Attitude' is thus a useful concept, but there are limitations. Can, for example, self-reported accounts of attitudes be relied on? Many studies find that people report not using certain forms which they go on to use in interview. This is one reason why many linguistic studies use the term **language values**. Such research holds that people's stated beliefs and feelings are value positions which are, like other elements of social identity, constructed in the course of social interaction. The value positions

Self-reporting is, for example, discussed in a study on Black Country dialect and identity by Esther Asprey in another book in this series: Seargeant and Swann (eds) (2012), Chapter 5.

> that people report to researchers, for example, are part of their performance as interviewees – how they frame the same phenomena among friends will differ. I therefore use 'values' in this chapter's discussion of how people report to feel about English.

The point that comes through from matched guise studies is that participants are quite happy to evaluate people's personalities through voice alone. As Lambert et al.'s study shows, many judgements about a language or language variety are not in fact about linguistic structures but about people or social groups. That is, reactions to language varieties stimulate sets of beliefs about speakers and social groups, enabling people to make judgements about somebody's character (as well as intelligence, level of education, family background, and so on) based on how they speak. People's responses to different guises will therefore differ, according to the associations they make between the variety and the social group that speaks it. Self-confidence and general likeability are not qualities inherent to a language variety; they are qualities the participants have projected on to imagined speakers, which then become associated with the variety of language spoken by that social group. Since the 1960s, the matched guise test has been used in various contexts (Carranza and Ryan, 1975; Bokhurst and Caleon, 2009), while other studies use questionnaires to elicit language value statements (Lai, 2005; Coupland and Bishop, 2007; Kouega, 2008). Both types of study tend to find that participants are willing and able to judge people's social attributes according to the language variety they speak.

If languages and linguistic features are so readily associated with social groups and their characteristics, the social and policy implications can be serious. Language can become a way of distinguishing between groups. The problem is circular. Linguistic features used by a disadvantaged group in society, such as post-vocalic /r/ (where /r/ is pronounced after vowels as in *car* and *arm*), are often valued negatively by elite groups and eschewed in education and language policies, and it is the language usage of elite groups that tends to be taught in schools and codified in dictionaries. What can then happen is that a linguistic feature (such as post-vocalic /r/) itself becomes associated with such things as a lack of education, which means that if someone uses this feature, they can be classed as uneducated. Milroy and Milroy (1999, p. 77) call this a **linguistic value system**, which reflects and reinforces class, ethnic and gender distinctions in society. If we describe this in

Bourdieu's ideas concerning 'linguistic capital' are discussed in Chapters 1, 2 and 4.

Bourdieuan terms, we can see the linguistic resources – of both elite and disadvantaged groups – as a form of 'capital', which can ultimately be exchanged for 'goods' such as jobs and social status, depending on how the linguistic resources of each group are valued in a particular 'linguistic market'. Of course, far from the neoliberal ideals of a 'free market' (as discussed in Chapter 4), what Milroy and Milroy point out is the extent to which linguistic values are intricately connected with social stratification, and how language can be used as a way of upholding existing social distinctions.

Post-vocalic /r/ is discussed in another book in this series: Seargeant and Swann (eds) (2012), Chapter 7.

My choice of post-vocalic /r/ as an example is not random. The contrasting use of this feature in England and the USA highlights the point that how a linguistic feature is valued can depend on the social status of the people who use it. In Trudgill's (1975) words:

> In England – but not in Ireland or Scotland – accents which pronounce post-vocalic *r* have lower prestige, other things being equal, than those which do not pronounce it. R.P. [Received Pronunciation, a British English accent associated with elite groups across Britain] does not have post-vocalic *r*, and in the minds of some people, at least, the pronunciation of this *r* is associated with speakers who are uneducated or rural, or both. … In many parts of America, on the other hand, the situation is completely reversed. In New York, for example, people who do not pronounce an *r* in *cart* and *car* are often looked down on, and their accent is considered 'bad'. Americans even talk about 'dropping your *r*s' in the same way that British people talk about *h*s.
>
> (Trudgill, 1975, p. 35)

As Trudgill concludes, post-vocalic /r/ is neither good nor bad. How people feel about it depends on its place in a particular linguistic value system.

Allow about 10 minutes

Activity 8.2

What might be the negative implications of the 'linguistic value system' for society, particularly for those people who use features that carry social stigma?

Comment

One implication of the linguistic value system is that how somebody speaks may work to their disadvantage. One area in which accents may be influential is in the attribution of guilt in court. People speaking with non-standard accents may more readily be judged guilty than those who speak prestigious varieties. Mock trials held by John Dixon and colleagues (2002) in the UK, using the matched guise procedure, suggested that speakers of Birmingham's 'Brummie' accent were more likely to be considered guilty than standard British English speakers. 'Brummie' is by most accounts negatively perceived across the UK (Coupland and Bishop, 2007).

Brummie speakers were especially more likely to be found guilty where the crime was armed robbery (because of its association with lower sectors of society) rather than fraud (associated with professional and financial sectors). Dixon et al. suggest that attribution of guilt may occur if testimony in a Brummie accent is deemed less 'assured' and therefore more closely associated with 'shiftiness' or 'related criminal stereotypes' (Dixon et al., 2002, p. 166). Similar places where accent may be the basis for discrimination include education, job interviews and medical consultations.

The nearby Black Country dialect, and the way in which this too tends to be negatively valued, is discussed in another book in this series: Seargeant and Swann (eds) (2012), Chapter 5.

It is, of course, important to recognise that people's value positions may be motivated by complex, varied and shifting factors. Mee-Ling Lai's (2005) study of English, Cantonese and Mandarin in Hong Kong after its handover to China in 1997 is illustrative of this. To elicit language values, Lai collected over 1000 questionnaires from 15–17-year-olds across mainstream schools in Hong Kong, most of whom spoke Cantonese at home (see Figure 8.1). The questionnaire assumed the importance of a distinction between what are known as **integrative** and **instrumental motivations**. An integrative orientation to a language suggests an emotional identification with the social group with which it is associated; an instrumental orientation is motivated by pragmatic reasons, such as wealth, education and job opportunities (Gardner and Lambert, 1972).

The Japanese learners of English discussed in Chapter 1, for example, have integrative reasons for learning English, in that the motivations relate to specific aspects of international or English-speaking culture (Seargeant, 2009, pp. 109–14).

Figure 8.1 Although not the language spoken at home by most people in Hong Kong, English is an official language in Hong Kong, and all road and government signs are bilingual.

In Lai's (2005) study, pupils were asked to rate such statements as those in Activity 8.3 below on a scale from 1 (strongly agree) to 4 (strongly disagree). The following statements focus on English, but similar questions were asked about Cantonese and Mandarin.

Allow about
20 minutes

Activity 8.3

Which of the following statements, quoted from Lai's study (2005, pp. 371, 374), relate to:

(a) the integrative value of English? (the extent to which people in Hong Kong identify with or integrate into an English-speaking community)

(b) its instrumental value? (the extent to which people in Hong Kong perceive that English can be used to further themselves).

1   I would like to speak fluent English because it makes me feel modern and westernized.

2   The use of English is one of the crucial factors which has contributed to the success of Hong Kong's prosperity and development today.

3   To increase the competitiveness of Hong Kong, the English standard of Hong Kong people must be enhanced.

4   As a Hongkonger, I should be able to speak English.

5   English will help me much in getting better opportunities for further studies.

6   English will help me much in getting better career opportunities in the 21st Century.

7   English is highly regarded in Hong Kong society.

8   I like English speakers.

9   A person who speaks fluent English is usually educated, intelligent and well-off.

10   A person who speaks fluent English is usually arrogant, snobbish and show-off.

Comment

Your answers may vary according to how you interpret the above statements. According to Lai, statements 1, 4, 8, 9 and 10 relate to the integrative value of English. The rest (2, 3, 5, 6 and 7) relate to its instrumental value. Note that the social group with which people in Hong Kong wish to integrate is not necessarily an external Anglophone one, but may be an English-speaking Hong Kong community; and that distancing oneself from a group is also included here as related to integrative values.

English was rated more highly than Cantonese and Mandarin for its instrumental value, and more highly for its integrative value than Mandarin. When compared with earlier studies, Lai's findings suggest that the extent to which islanders orientated towards English was shaped by the changing political environment. A study by Herbert Pierson and colleagues (1980), for example, found that Hong Kong secondary school students distrusted the use of English in Hong Kong and as a medium of instruction in schools because they perceived that it threatened their Chinese identity, even though English at that time was the language of prestigious institutions in Hong Kong and valued as the language of international development, science and technology. By the 1990s, this distrust and antagonism seemed to have dissipated; secondary school pupils were found to be strongly motivated towards learning English, and tolerated its use (Pennington and Yue, 1994). Pennington and Yue put these changes down to anticipation of the handover to China and the perception that English was no longer a threat to the islanders' identity as Chinese. However, they also expected that Mandarin would gain in integrative and instrumental value. Instead, it appears that, with its now culturally 'neutral' function as the language of international communication and social mobility, English is perceived as playing a role in the islanders' identity of themselves as 'Hongkongers' (Lai, 2005).

What do these studies reinforce about language values?

- Judgements about language varieties are complex, and people may appear to value different languages or varieties for various reasons.
- People's stated language values are also statements about their own identity: for example, the degree to which they wish to integrate with or distance themselves from other social groups.
- How varieties and practices are valued will vary according to the part of the world an individual lives in, their personal circumstances and their feelings towards other social groups.
- Values can shift with external events, and with changes in the status and perception of social or cultural groups.

8.3   Correctness

In the previous section, I suggested that values attached to a variety of English often reflect evaluations people make about those who speak that variety. According to this argument, linguistic features are coloured in people's minds by the social characteristics of the speech community associated with a particular variety. Where, however, does this argument leave notions of correctness? Can it not be said that some language varieties or practices use correct forms and others do not?

This is *exactly* what is frequently said, but in fact there is no linguistic basis for suggesting that one variety or practice is more 'correct' than another – at least in informal situations and when people are speaking (I shall go on to discuss writing in an educational setting). Of course, it is possible to say that somebody has a particularly wide vocabulary, or that a speaker is more eloquent, clear, creative or expressive than others. It is also generally considered acceptable for teachers to identify and correct 'mistakes' that children or adult language learners may be seen to make. However, the notion that one variety of English is more 'correct' than others must be justified in social, rather than purely linguistic, terms. All English varieties have their own grammatical structures and where these diverge from the 'standard' (the variety which most closely resembles that described in grammar books and used in schools) these are not mistakes or 'sloppiness' but parts of

Standardisation and the 'standard' are discussed in another book in this series: Seargeant and Swann (eds) (2012), Chapters 2 and 5.

(slightly) different systems of grammar: different ways of expressing the same concepts and relations. As Trudgill puts it:

> From a purely linguistic point of view, it makes no sense to talk about 'right' and 'wrong' in language. No one would suggest that French is 'more correct' than English, and there is no reason for treating dialects of the same language in anything other than the same way. No one dialect of English is any more 'right' or 'wrong' than any other.
>
> (Trudgill, 1975, p. 38)

Trudgill's argument is that varieties are considered 'right' or 'wrong' not because of inherent linguistic correctness or incorrectness, but because of the high and low social prestige of their speakers. There is also an ideological factor; that is, the general acceptance among speakers of English – and other languages – that there are linguistically correct or 'standard' versions of a language. This value is one of many typically associated with a 'prescriptive' approach to language use.

8.4 Prescriptivism and the 'Golden Age' of English

Prescriptivism

Proponents of a **prescriptive** approach seek to influence or control the language that others use by prescribing a particular language or language variety, usually on the grounds that it is in some way 'better' – correct, more attractive – than others. The implicit aim is also to inhibit change and preserve older linguistic forms. This approach is often contrasted with what is known as the **descriptive** approach. Modern linguists who adopt a descriptive approach do not consider one variety to be superior to any other, and aim to describe language use rather than judge it.

In this section, I look at two aspects of prescriptivism: the belief in language decline, and the valuing and enforcing of certain language conventions.

A losing battle!

… What I would like to know is, if people like me continue to use the forms of grammar with which we grew up, are we to be perceived as 'wrong' and in need of correction?!

(BBC, 2009)

This appeal (on a BBC online message board devoted to language issues) to 'the forms of grammar with which we grew up' reflects a widely held belief in the idea of language decline. It is tempting to assume a 'Golden Age' of English, and to hold it up as a model of good practice, when 'pure' English was spoken and grammar rules carefully adhered to. But has this Golden Age ever existed?

The fact that people have always complained about declining standards in English suggests not. In recent years, leading retailers have issued statements bemoaning the state of young Britons' literacy levels. For example, Sir Stuart Rose, chairman of Marks & Spencer, suggested that some school-leavers were unfit for work because: 'They cannot do reading. They cannot do arithmetic. They cannot do writing' (quoted in Armitstead, 2009, p. 1). Yet employers made similar complaints about employees throughout the twentieth century. These are evident in the Bullock Report, a 1975 survey on English teaching in the UK, which also identified similar complaints reported in the Newbolt Report (1921), over fifty years previously.

Many allegations about lower standards today come from employers, who maintain that young people joining them from school cannot write grammatically, are poor spellers, and generally express themselves badly. The employers sometimes draw upon past experience for comparisons, but even where they do not there is a strong implication that at one time levels of performance were superior. It is therefore interesting to find in the Newbolt Report … of 1921 observations of a very similar kind. There Messrs Vickers Ltd reported 'great difficulty in obtaining junior clerks who can speak and write English clearly and correctly, especially those aged from 15 to 16 years'. Messrs Lever Bros Ltd said: 'it is a great surprise and disappointment to us to find that our young employees are so hopelessly deficient in their command of English'. Boots Pure Drug Co. remarked: 'teaching of English in the present day schools produces a very limited command of the English language ... Our candidates do not appreciate the value of shades of meaning, and while able to do imaginative composition, show weakness in work which requires accurate description, or careful arrangement of detail'. The last is very close to some of the observations made today, half a century later ...

(Bullock Report, 1975, p. 3)

These complaints suggest that notions of a Golden Age result not from language decline but from the *perception* of decline, given rising social expectations and shifting professional demands. Indeed, it is difficult to find a time when people did not perceive that the best English lay in the past. In 1712, for example, Jonathan Swift's vision of a Golden Age lay in the late 1600s:

The Period wherein the *English* Tongue received most Improvement, I take to commence with the beginning of Queen *Elizabeth's* Reign, and to conclude with the Great Rebellion in Forty Two. ... From the Civil War to this present Time, I am apt to doubt whether the Corruptions in our Language have not at least equalled the Refinements of it ...

(Swift, 1712)

One way in which self-appointed guardians of English through the ages have tried to improve the language is by promoting what appear to be oft-flouted language rules or conventions. Although these were first really enforced in grammars and 'penny manuals' of the nineteenth century, they find their origins in seventeenth-century attempts to forge a national identity for England, at a time when associations between language, literature and nation were first being made in Europe, as discussed in Chapter 5.

Unlike France, Britain never had a language academy. Instead, the prescriptive work that was carried out by official bodies in Europe passed into the hands of private individuals in Britain. These self-appointed and well-meaning grammarians laid down many of the conventions enforced in the nineteenth century and still recognised today (Milroy and Milroy, 1999, p. 28). What is the basis of these rules and why are they so frequently flouted?

Activity 8.4

Can you identify the prescriptive rules or conventions that have been violated in these sentences?

1   'To boldly go where no man has gone before' (Star Trek, on repeated episodes since 1966).

2   'What have you brought that book I don't like being read to out of up for?' (allegedly spoken by a boy tired of being read a certain book at bedtime).

3   'We don't need no education / We don't need no thought control' (lyrics from the 1979 song, 'Another Brick in the Wall' by Pink Floyd).

4   'Asturias is startlingly different to our classic image of Spain' (*The Daily Telegraph*, 11 November 2008).

Comment

Example (1), 'To boldly go where no man has gone before', famously breaks the rule that infinitives, such as *to go*, should not be split by adverbs such as *boldly*. Proscription against split infinitives arises from comparison between English and Latin. In the latter, infinitives formed through word endings rather than *to*, such as *amāre*, cannot be split. Widely used grammars such as William Lily's *A Shorte Introduction of Grammar* (1523) were based on a grammatical model of classical languages, thus ensuring that the grammatical terminology and analytical approach used for codifying and analysing English for the next three hundred years was closely modelled on Latin.

Example (2), 'What have you brought that book I don't like being read to out of up for?', is a humorous take on the rule that one should never end English sentences with prepositions. Originating with John Dryden's (1672) 'Defence of the Epilogue', the rule is also based on the fact that the construction is not possible in Latin. However, prepositions can and do occur at the end of sentences in Germanic languages (and infinitives can be split).

Example (3), the lyrics to Pink Floyd's 1979 song, breaks the convention that, in the words of grammarian Robert Lowth (1710–1787) (see Figure 8.2), 'Two negatives in English destroy one another, or are equivalent to an affirmative'. Lowth's *Short Introduction to English Grammar* (1762) and Murray's *English Grammar* (1795) were perhaps the most influential of eighteenth-century grammars, but there were others. In *The Rudiments of English Grammar* (1761), for example, Joseph Priestley laid down his preference for *difference from* rather than *to*, a rule based on analogy with the verb *differ*, but broken in Example (4). As these examples show, grammar rules were based not only on

Latin (or Greek), but also on analogy with related English words and on logic (the proscription against multiple negatives).

However, these criteria are far from watertight. Analogies can always be found, if one keeps looking: consider *differ **from*** or *similar **to*** (or *smaller **than***). The analogy one chooses to make is ultimately arbitrary, and so too is any rule based on it. Multiple negatives are far from illogical, but are found in other languages (*je **ne** sais **pas***; ***no** quiero **nada*** – 'I don't know' and 'I don't want anything' in French and Spanish, respectively), and in many English dialects. Furthermore, multiple negatives were once used unproblematically as emphatic devices in standard English: Chaucer in *The Canterbury Tales*, for example, said of his Knight that:

> He <u>nevere</u> yet <u>no</u> vileynye <u>ne</u> sayde
> In al his lyf unto no maner wight

> (Geoffrey Chaucer, General Prologue, *The Canterbury Tales* (late 1300s), cited in *Merriam-Webster's Dictionary of English Usage*, 1994, p. 365, underlining added)

The motivations underlying eighteenth-century conventions were not simply linguistic, but social and political, with grammarians often drawing on the usage of the learned elite of the day.

Figure 8.2   Robert Lowth (1710–1787)

What can we say so far about 'correct' English? Our discussion suggests that many rules which were rigorously enforced in the nineteenth century sprang from notions of linguistic correctness laid down by private individuals who faced various motivations and pressures: social, political and personal. The point is that the rules were not always linguistically motivated (and where they were, it was often in relation to Latin, rather than English). The reason that the rules are so often flouted is that they *can* be. English in fact allows speakers to suggest that they don't want *no* education just as it lets them say they don't want *any*. It is social convention that forbids the former.

8.5 The ideology of standards

Our discussion of correctness leads us to consider the existence of an **ideology of standards** – that is, a set of beliefs in the need for an unchanging standard, even where this is not evident in actual language practices. The extent to which eighteenth- and nineteenth-century grammarians actually reduced variation or impeded change is limited. One reason is that while it is clear that, since the advent of printing in Britain, written English can to an extent be standardised and prescribed, at least in public discourse, spoken English cannot. Thomas Sheridan's *A Course of Lectures on Elocution* (1762) was an attempt to extend standardisation to the spoken language but, while his lectures were popular and he spearheaded pressure for a spoken norm, he could not reach sufficient numbers to have an impact on spoken variation (Mugglestone, 2007, pp. 154–8). When, nearly 200 years later, the first Director General of the British Broadcasting Corporation (BBC) decided to use only RP-speaking broadcasters as a model for the nation, the policy hardly succeeded in changing how people spoke. What it did achieve, however, was recognition of 'BBC English' as a correct and authoritative standard (Mugglestone, 2007, p. 167).

Despite the fact that language guardians have far from succeeded in their goal of maintaining the standard, the same ideals of inhibiting change and subduing variety are still valued by many people. The following illustrate several language-related letters sent to the UK's *Daily Telegraph* in 2008:

All my life I have filled in application forms, not filled them out (overweight people fill out their trousers).

(*Letters to the Telegraph*, 22 June 2008)

Your correspondent should not be 'filling in' forms let alone filling them 'out' (Letters, June 22). They should be completed.

(*Letters to the Telegraph*, 29 June 2008)

Standardisation is therefore best seen as a process towards ideals that exists only 'as an idea in the mind rather than a reality' (Milroy and Milroy, 1999, p. 19). If the standard is an abstract set of norms to which actual usage conforms only to varying extents, then the role of language guardians today is largely, as Milroy and Milroy (1999, p. 18) explain, 'to keep the notion of a standard language alive in the public mind'. Recognising that eighteenth-century grammarians instilled an ideology of standards explains continuing prescriptivist practices and evaluative positions towards English in Britain today.

Another implication of the ideology is that the imposition of prescribed norms was extended to Englishes beyond Britain. Standardisation succeeded as an ideology, even where models departed from the British standard. The American standard, for example, was set forth in the 1800s in Noah Webster's dictionary. This included reforms to spelling, so that <u> was dropped from words like *behaviour* and *odour*, and <re> replaced by <er> in *centre* and *theatre*, despite not representing differences in pronunciation.

Webster's dictionary is discussed in another book in this series: Seargeant and Swann (eds) (2012), Chapter 3.

The deliberate implementation of a standard which highlighted departures from British norms shows how language and the ideology of standards are bound up with national identity. In other ex-colonies of Britain, where British administrators taught English to 'a class who may be interpreters between us and the millions whom we govern' (in British politician Lord Macauley's 1835 words), the spread of English from elite usage into the local community inevitably loosened the hold of British conventions. However, what generally happened is that a familiar prescriptivism built up around new sets of local norms, so that we now talk of South East Asian English, for example, or standard Singapore English. These examples highlight the continuing importance of the ideology of standards, and its ultimately unobtainable values:

correctness, absolute authority, complete reduction of variability and a halt to language change.

8.6   Correctness in writing

I have argued so far that there is no entirely linguistic basis for describing varieties of English as either 'right' or 'wrong', and that notions of correctness are socially motivated. This is illustrated by the fact that many language conventions can be traced back to grammarians in eighteenth- and nineteenth-century Britain, who based their conventions on comparisons with Latin, logic, analogy with related English words, and the usage of prestigious contemporary writers. These prescriptive grammarians succeeded in instilling an ideology of standards – a belief in language correctness and purity – which continues to shape ideas about English today. However, the lack of linguistic motivation behind these conventions does not necessarily imply that 'anything goes'. This is true in the general sense that language use is in some respect always normative. People follow norms, whether these are learnt conventions 'imposed' on them by official or external bodies (e.g. the education system), or language practices that emerge within a linguistic community. The point is that no one set of conventions or norms can, in purely linguistic terms, be seen as more or less correct than any other.

A distinction between spoken and written language should also be considered in discussing ideas of correctness. Unlike speaking, writing is not something we easily pick up by ourselves, but is something that we must be taught. What this means is that writing need not always be part and parcel of a person's identity in the way that their speech is (or, at least, it forms a different part of their identity as literate individuals). A child can learn to write following conventions that they do not use when they speak (whether or not they pronounce *three* as /fri:/ or /θri:/, they can learn to spell it with an initial <th>).

Different ways in which children learn the orthography of English and other languages are discussed in another book in this series: Allington and Mayor (eds) (2012), Chapter 3.

Finally, it is arguably more necessary to write in a uniform way. In the 1600s, printing was a pivotal force in the standardisation of English norms, not only because fixed spelling was in the printers' financial interests, but because the production and dissemination of written texts required the clarity that uniformity was seen to engender. However, the following examples show that writing should not always be valued only for correctness and clarity.

Figure 8.3   A shop sign in Taiwan (Curtin, 2009)

The apostrophe (') divides those who berate its misuse (e.g. the *Apostrophe Protection Society*) from those who want it banned (e.g. *Kill the Apostrophe*) and from the majority who remain uncertain over its correct use. In *Eats, Shoots & Leaves: The Zero Tolerance Approach to Punctuation* (2003), a widely popular book at the time, British writer Lynne Truss starts by describing apostrophe misuse:

> "Come inside," it says, "for CD's, VIDEO's, DVD's, and BOOK's."
>
> If this satanic sprinkling of redundant apostrophes causes no little gasp of horror or quickening of the pulse, you should probably put down this book at once.
>
> (Truss, 2003, p. 1)

In this example, and in Melissa Curtin's in Figure 8.3, the apostrophe has been 'incorrectly' inserted before the *s*. However, the apostrophe misuse in *Alway's* does not have to be evaluated as grammatically incorrect. Instead, as Curtin suggests, the sign is interesting when viewed in the context of multilingual Taipei. The use of an English word bestows on the shop attributes associated with English in Taiwan: 'being cosmopolitan, educated, well-to-do, and fashionable' (Curtin, 2009, p. 229). Evaluating whether *Alway's* is grammatically correct is irrelevant to the impact which the sign may have on its Taiwanese audience.

Activity 8.5

Allow about 10 minutes

How would you evaluate the shop sign in Figure 8.4, with its lack of apostrophe, as part of the linguistic landscape of Bangalore, a cosmopolitan multilingual city in southern India, where English is the lingua franca and the language of multinational companies based there?

Figure 8.4 Shop sign in Bangalore, India

Allow about
20 minutes

Activity 8.6

Concerns about correctness unsurprisingly play an important role in assessment. Imagine you were the teacher of the pupil who wrote the following text, and correct it. What features did you focus on, and why?

Ten-year-old boy giving an account of the game of football.

My favorite game is football. It is well none all over the world. It is not just a kids Game it is a Grown up game to. there are lots and lots of teams in Britain. There is Liverpool and Exeter City and York City and West Ham United and Many more team these team meat up and play against each over it. Ends like 3 v 1 and things like that. this is how is how you play. You have a field and up each end of the pitch you have a goal. And the field has lines. thing you got to do is score in the goals. I mean you have to kick a ball in the Net and Goal keeper got to you from doing this.

(cited in Toolan, 2009, pp. 143–4)

Comment

As Michael Toolan points out, there are two main ways in which a text like this can be assessed. We can evaluate, on the one hand, the mechanics of writing: paragraphing, sentence initial capitals, correct spelling; on the other, communicative skills such as clarity, orderliness, accuracy of description, enthusiasm, liveliness. Although a distinction between the two cannot always be assumed, the point is that the first is often the easiest to assess. Counting 'incorrect' spellings is more reliable and less subjective than deciding how lively or engaging a text is – and educational policy often tends to favour such criteria. In actual practice, teachers probably use varying degrees of both. Which approach did you lean towards?

The same, or a similar, point can be made of university students' work. Toolan, a linguistics professor in the UK, is critically aware that, despite his belief in communicative competence, his comments on written work tend nonetheless to focus on correctness:

> But what I particularly noticed ... was the way that my comments frequently focus on the students' *writing* quality (poorly written, well written, gr(ammar)/usage errors, etc.), as if, regardless of what they wrote *about*, or the quality of their insights or arguments, the quality of their own writing was almost always an important criterion.
>
> (Toolan, 2009, p. 146)

My argument is not that grammatical correctness is to be disregarded (and nor is this Toolan's argument). However, a prescriptive approach to written work raises uncomfortable questions given the international students that Anglophone universities now host, and given the gatekeeping role that British and American journals play in regulating academic publishing.

Whose model of correctness is the right one? Should other models and practices be accepted? The issues of power and privilege that tend to determine the answers to these questions are tied up with a language ideology which unquestioningly upholds the value of one, correct version of English. Those involved in assessing written work may do well to consider the extent to which this ideology shapes – and should shape – their assessment practices.

8.7 Language values and policy

So far, I have focused primarily on the first of my questions: how people value English and Englishes in relation to other languages and varieties; and how these play out in situations of competition and conflict. This section looks more closely at examples of the role that language ideologies play in shaping and contesting policy.

Allow about 1 hour

Activity 8.7

Examples of the interaction between language ideology, policy and practice can be found throughout this book. Let's look at one such context: the role of English in education in Malaysia (Chapter 3). Look back through the section on 'A postcolonial case study: Malaysia' (including the reading by Peter Martin) in that chapter, and consider the values which led different groups of people to enforce and challenge the language policies. To what extent did policies shape practices?

Comment

British colonial rulers in Malaysia were torn by two competing value systems along the lines of those discussed in relation to India in Chapter 5. The need for a local elite proficient in English and knowledgeable about European literature and culture to help with administration led to English schools for a minority of children, often those of Malay ruling families. In contrast to this, education in local languages was promoted for others as a way to maintain their lifestyle as productive fishermen and farmers. The government of independent Malaysia saw language as a central part of the nation's identity and unity, a viewpoint affirmed by unrest, and they increasingly focused on the integrative value of Malay. This policy was in turn contested by those who valued Malaysian ethnic and linguistic diversity, and by those who recognised the instrumental values of English in the business community. The subsequent policy reversal in favour of English for some school subjects was accompanied by attempts to change how Malays constructed their national identity, but nonetheless the policy was contested and ultimately halted by people with different linguistic backgrounds united through their opposition to English-medium education. To give an interesting slant on how policy shaped practices, in his reading for Chapter 3, Peter Martin shows how teachers responded to the English-only policy through the practice of using it alongside Malay in the classroom.

As a follow-up, you might like to analyse the development of policy regarding English literature canons in either India, South Africa or Kenya discussed in Chapter 5.

Activity 8.8

In this second case study, the aspect of language under discussion is the teaching in schools of standard grammar. Reading A: *The great grammar crusade*, is taken from Deborah Cameron's 1995 book, *Verbal Hygiene* (a term used by Cameron to refer to all attempts to manipulate or control language). In the reading, Cameron outlines the debate that took place in the UK media shortly after the implementation of the 1988 National Curriculum by the Conservative Party – a right-wing British political party led at the time by Prime Minister Margaret Thatcher and which Cameron refers to here as the 'pro-grammar conservatives'. As you read, consider the following questions:

*   Do you agree with Cameron that a debate about grammar is in fact an argument about other social issues? If so, why are these other issues not directly debated?

*   Can you explain the perception of a link between grammar and social order?

*   Do you feel that Cameron's arguments are valid in your community today?

Comment

I find Cameron's arguments convincing, although it must be borne in mind that hers is not a neutral presentation of events, as reflected in her language: 'the height of the hysteria', 'garnished with scare stories', 'propelled throughout by regular surges of anxiety'. As she argues, debates about language often mask concerns about other social issues because language discrimination does not carry the same social stigma as discrimination on the grounds of colour, gender or physical ability – although in fact, as Halliday et al. (1964, p.165) point out, 'A speaker who is made ashamed of his [*sic*] own language habits suffers a basic injury as a human being: to make anyone, especially a child, feel so ashamed is as indefensible as to make him feel ashamed of the colour of his skin' (quoted in Milroy and Milroy, 1999, p. 84). Prescriptive grammar is ideologically linked to social order, discipline and authority, argues Cameron, by analogy between language structure and social structure, strengthened by the association of grammar with traditional teaching methods which favour drills and rote learning. The success of pro-grammar conservatives was cemented by the fact that their concern over the lack of explicit, disciplined and rule-based teaching tapped into public fears about social control, rising crime and declining family values. This association between correct language use and moral behaviour is one that I still identify today in, for example, the debate surrounding digital English (the English used on the internet and in text messaging). In a study which explored how newspapers reported the use of digital English at the turn of the millennium, Thurlow (2006) found that:

> In addition to being described as **reprehensible, frightening, depraved, infamous, criminal, jarring and abrasive, apocalyptic, execrable, pointless,** and **aberrant,** [digital English] was often held responsible for a number of wider social and educational ills. For example, certain journalists and commentators regarded it as being **inflicted on the innocent public** ..., **creating a whole new culture in the country** ..., **dumbing down the English language** ..., and **lowering standards all round.**
>
> (Thurlow, 2006, p. 677)

Activity 8.9

As Thurlow's views suggest, Cameron's argument has resonance beyond the context in which she wrote. In Reading B: *Reading the 'Singlish debate'*, Anneliese Kramer-Dahl critiques the media construction of a similar 'crisis' discourse in Singapore's *The Straits Times* in the summer of 1999 which forms what Kramer-Dahl calls, elsewhere in the article from which Reading B is taken, 'one long, sprawling macrotext'. Singapore has four official languages and the challenge is to teach in English, which is not always used by pupils outside school. As you read, make a note of similarities and differences between the debates in Singapore and the UK.

Comment

On the surface, the two debates can similarly be described as 'moral panics'. The first most obvious difference is the stimulus for the debate. Although both were initiated by the media, the UK debate was sparked off by proposed curriculum changes, while in Singapore there was no obvious motivation, beyond the importance of English in the repositioning of Singapore in the global economy during the Asian recession. A second difference is the apportioning of blame: while in Britain, linguists were accused of encouraging slipshod approaches to grammar, in Singapore, teachers became the scapegoats. Third, the crisis discourse in Singapore was less of a two-sided debate than the UK's, with participants moving forward together in a discourse 'committed to consensus and closure' and teachers, who may have dissented, not given a voice. The resolution (grammar classes for English teachers) was as authoritarian a solution as in the UK (dismissal of 'permissive' approaches to grammar teaching). In both countries the solutions were at once seen as tackling wider social and economic anxieties while, with the focus on the more manageable topic of grammar, effectively side-stepping them.

8.8 Language values and language research

Evident throughout this chapter is that linguists, such as Cameron and Toolan, also make value judgements about language. In Cameron's words:

> I have undergone a process of professional socialization designed among other things to get rid of 'inappropriate' value judgements. It has worked, up to a point. ... I still find there are things that leap to my eye as if emblazoned in neon. I can choose to suppress the irritation I feel when I see, for example, a sign that reads 'Potatoe's'; I cannot choose not to feel it.
>
> (Cameron, 1995, p. 14)

Cameron's use of the word 'inappropriate' (in scare quotes) is worth considering. Modern linguists tend to distinguish between prescriptive values (those which linguists often associate with non-linguists) and the descriptive approach (that adhered to by modern linguists). However, even linguists claiming to describe what they see cannot be portrayed as value-free; their approach is also the product of particular sets of values, although these may differ from those of the typical non-linguist. In Chapter 1, you read about three world views which shape how linguists research and understand global English:

- the view that English can be a positive resource, also adopted by linguists such as David Crystal (2003), which suggests that the rise of English is inevitable and potentially beneficial
- a critical and overtly ideological 'linguistic imperialist' view, held by linguists such as Robert Phillipson (1992) who describes the spread of English as supported by a global system of trade which disadvantages the poor
- a 'hegemony of English' perspective, which sees English as having attained a powerful ideological and practical position for complex economic, social and political reasons, which can lead to the language playing a role in inequality between people and societies (e.g. Pennycook, 1994; Blommaert, 2010).

The author of Chapter 1 adheres most closely to the last approach which, although critical, recognises the complexity of the situation and the fact that the effect of English depends on how it is used. Which is closest to your point of view?

Allow about 45 minutes

Activity 8.10

As an example, try to identify and describe the values that underlie Reading A by Deborah Cameron in this chapter.

Comment

Some linguists have tended to dismiss what they call the prescriptive views of non-linguists as irrelevant to the study of language. Bloomfield (1944), for example, held what he called 'secondary responses' to language in some contempt and responded with his own dismissive 'tertiary responses'. Cameron's discussion of the moral panic surrounding grammar teaching is driven by her belief that what people think and feel about language is part and parcel of their language use and as such shouldn't be dismissed. Her term 'verbal hygiene' recognises that interfering with language need not be negative or prescriptive; instead, people's love of language (and its speakers) can lead them to intervene in many different ways. This world view shapes her exhortation to linguists that in order to intervene successfully in educational or other language-related matters (which she feels is important), they must engage with, rather than dismiss, how people feel about language.

You may have found this difficult, and you may not have identified the same values. The point of this exercise is rather to appreciate that discussion of English – like any discussion – is never entirely value-free.

8.9   Conclusion

In this chapter, I have revisited the assertion set up at the start of this book that language policy and practice are always based in people's values and beliefs about language. I started by suggesting that many people tend to hold prescriptive views about English. Although linguistically we cannot say that one use or variety of English is better or worse than another, many people do make that judgement, and they do so largely on social grounds. Judgements about language are often indirect judgements about the people who are perceived to speak it (as matched guise tests show). The standard language ideology – the set of ideas that posit a standard variety of English and which condemn variation – can be said to be founded on inequality (the standard is generally spoken by a privileged elite) and it serves as a potential form of discrimination against the less privileged who do not speak it (as we saw with the mock trials in Birmingham). The notion that some varieties are better than others – more correct, more useful, more relevant – shapes attempts to regulate language use. We saw this, for example, with educational policies that require the teaching of standard grammar or of particular languages. Of course, the ways in which Englishes are valued are more complex than this suggests; although they lack prestige, regional varieties of English and other local languages are often valued on other grounds.

Language use can never be value-free (and why should it be?). The important thing is to be aware of the impact our values may have on those around us, and to recognise that attempts to regulate language use are always grounded in a particular way of seeing – and organising – the world.

READING A: The great grammar crusade

Deborah Cameron

Source: Cameron, D. (1995) *Verbal Hygiene*, London, Routledge, pp. 78–115.

In Britain towards the end of the 1980s there was an extraordinary outbreak of public concern about the teaching of English, especially English grammar. At the height of the hysteria, almost every day seemed to bring forth some new and more intemperate manifestation: among those who favoured the public with their views were academics, politicians, columnists and leader writers, novelists, denizens of obscure right-wing think-tanks, union leaders, peers of the realm and – inevitably – Prince Charles [...]. Passions ran high and were slow to subside; between 1987 and 1994 Secretaries of State for Education came and went [...] but grammar remained stubbornly on the political agenda. [...]

In order to understand the furore about grammar, it is necessary to know something about the immediate context for it. Ostensibly it arose as part of a wide-ranging debate about education, precipitated by the planning and subsequent implementation of a piece of legislation in England and Wales, the Education Reform Act of 1988. [...]

The 1988 Education Reform Act is widely regarded as the most radical shift in policy and practice enacted by a British government since the Second World War. The Act accomplished significant change by way of two sets of provisions. First, it introduced a new framework for the management of state schools, weakening or, if a school so wished, even bypassing the control of local education authorities. Second, the Act provided for a National Curriculum which all state school pupils aged from 5 to 16 were required to follow. Official bodies set up under the new law specified what subjects were to be studied and laid down detailed programmes of study for every subject. [...]

[...] The introduction of the new curriculum, and especially of the new tests, attracted opposition from parents and teachers, to which the government at times responded with straightforwardly coercive measures, at other times with a climb-down. [...]

On certain points, however, the conservatives [in the government] did appear to carry both party sentiment and public opinion with them. The most notable such instance was their call for a return to traditional standards, values and methods in the teaching of the English language. That call was couched in a powerful verbal hygiene discourse whose key term was *grammar*. [...]

Moral panic

I am going to suggest that the grammar furore bears more than a passing resemblance to the sort of periodic hysteria cultural historians have labelled 'moral panic' (Cohen 1987). [...]

A moral panic can be said to occur when some social phenomenon or problem is suddenly foregrounded in public discourse and discussed in an obsessive, moralistic and alarmist manner, as if it betokened some imminent catastrophe. In the past hundred years in Europe and America we have had outbreaks of this kind centring on prostitution and 'white slavery', drugs, the 'Jewish problem', juvenile delinquency, venereal disease, immigration, communism, overpopulation, pornography, rock music and pit bull terriers.

[...] To understand cycles of panic, it is necessary to acknowledge that the apparent problem is not always the real one. Behind the facade of legitimate concern about, say, drug abuse, there are usually deeper and less socially acceptable anxieties being expressed in coded terms. [...]

In the light of all this, it might be thought that grammar is a very unpromising candidate for triggering moral panic, remote as it is from the staple themes of sex and drugs and rock and roll. And yet the fact is that in the case we are concerned with here, grammar *did* bring forth an extraordinary surge of passion [...]. And if we keep in mind that moral panics are highly coded affairs, this becomes less surprising: for questions of language can readily become a code for issues of race, class and culture. [...]

The grammar 'panic': a brief history

The first stage in a panic is the discovery of a 'problem'. In this case, the problem can be stated as follows: because of English teachers' wilful neglect of grammar, children were leaving school illiterate and undisciplined. The 'permissive' teachers became the main scapegoats, along with the linguistic and educational theorists who had brainwashed them with half-baked theories and trendy left-wing nonsense. [...]

In 1987 the Thatcher government initiated the planning of a National Curriculum. The procedure used throughout the planning process was to set up working groups to make recommendations for each subject area; there would be an English working group to draft the curriculum for this crucial 'core' subject. But before this group set to work, the then Secretary of State for Education, Kenneth Baker, had already taken the unusual step of announcing the formation of a separate committee under Sir John Kingman, whose brief was specifically to enquire into the teaching of the English language in schools. [...]

[...] The Kingman committee's report was published in 1988 (DES 1988). The report's conclusions were not to pro-grammar conservatives' liking, and the Secretary of State himself was also conspicuously unenthusiastic about them. Nevertheless, the planning process continued along the lines that had been established at the outset. The English working party (which would deal with literature and drama as well as language) was duly convened under the chairmanship of Brian Cox, and its report appeared not long afterwards (DES 1989). The Cox Report was even less satisfactory to right-wingers than the Kingman Report; and their dissatisfaction (the reasons for which will be explained below) ensured that what should have been the end of the controversy – the official publication of the working party's conclusions – was actually only the beginning of a protracted and bitter struggle. [...]

Essentially there were three connected points of controversy. One was whether grammar should be formally taught at all. [... M]ost schools in Britain had abandoned traditional grammar lessons based on rote-learning and drilling as they adopted more 'progressive' and 'pupil-centred' teaching methods, partly [...] for ideological reasons, but mainly because of research findings suggesting traditional methods were not effective, and that grammar-teaching itself was of questionable value. At the time, these conclusions and the associated changes in practice had been endorsed by governmental committees of inquiry; conservatives in the 1980s, however, wanted traditional grammar and traditional methods restored.

The second point of controversy was what kind of grammatical model to adopt – a prescriptive one based on Latin paradigms and expressed as a set of commandments, or a descriptive one based on linguists' analyses of how people actually use English? Whereas linguists and the so-called 'educational establishment' favoured the latter alternative, conservatives favoured the former, which was more in line with their views on the third and most controversial point, namely, the purpose for which grammar was to be taught. For conservatives, the object of the exercise was to ensure that pupils would learn to use standard

English correctly. In framing this objective they were motivated not only by positive attitudes to the national language, but also by prejudice against non-standard English; and they took it as obvious common sense that if you wish to eradicate non-standard English and replace it with standard English, the way to do this is to teach standard grammatical rules explicitly. (Conversely, they assumed that ignorance of standard English was rife *because* schools had ceased to teach grammar formally.) Expert opinion, while not disputing that everyone should be able to use the standard language, maintained that formal grammar teaching had little effect on actual language use; it further maintained that teaching standard English and/or grammar need not, and should not, entail intolerance for other varieties.

With expert and pro-grammar conservative opinion so polarized on these crucial issues, it is not surprising that the Kingman and Cox committees were unable to satisfy both sides; but as appointees of a radical right-wing government they might have been expected to be more sympathetic to the pro-grammar faction. Their recommendations showed, however, that they had been influenced significantly by expert evidence. Although both committees made a point of endorsing the importance of standard English and the usefulness of teaching language structure explicitly (thus challenging the views of many education professionals, particularly those at the 'progressive' end of the spectrum), neither report endorsed a return to traditional models and methods of grammar teaching or condoned intolerance of dialect variation. […]

The unfolding debate about English teaching was presented to the public liberally garnished with scare stories about falling standards among pupils and ideological subversion among teachers. […]

When other interested parties entered the debate, they did so on terms which had already been established: anyone who dissented from pro-grammar conservatism was forced on to the defensive. The most significant group of dissenters, not surprisingly, were English teachers themselves. But because of the form media coverage of the issue had taken, namely a barrage of scare stories in which the ludicrous notions of these professionals were held responsible for widespread near illiteracy, contributions from anyone with either specialist knowledge or direct experience had effectively been discredited before they were even made.

So effective were the media and the pro-grammar conservatives in keeping up the steady flow of horror stories and complaints that the years between 1988 and 1992 were virtually a state of linguistic emergency. The issue of grammar was not laid to rest by the passing of the Education Reform Act, but continued to be a rallying point for attempts to whip up anxiety about language, literacy and educational standards. And in time these attempts began to have the desired effect. [...]

What the pro-grammar Right, assisted by the media, accomplished with these ideas and images over a period of several years was a steady movement towards more and more authoritarian views of what English teaching should be, sustained by increasingly authoritarian decision-making procedures, which in turn were legitimated by increasingly vitriolic attacks on the English teaching profession. And this movement was propelled throughout by regular surges of anxiety, comparable in intensity to the anxiety that is usually provoked by such staples of moral panic as crime and drugs. [...]

But if the debate on grammar was a case of moral panic, one crucial question remains to be asked: what was the panic really about? What buried anxieties, what threatening social changes could have caused English grammar to inspire such strong emotions? [...]

Grammar as moral metaphor: the roots of panic

[...]

> The overthrow of grammar coincided with the acceptance of the equivalent of creative writing in social behaviour. As nice points of grammar were mockingly dismissed as pedantic and irrelevant, so was punctiliousness in such matters as honesty, responsibility, property, gratitude, apology and so on.
>
> (John Rae ['The decline and fall of English grammar'], *Observer*, 7 February 1982)

> If you allow standards to slip to the stage where good English is no better than bad English, where people turn up filthy at school ... all these things tend to cause people to have no standards at

all, and once you lose standards then there's no imperative to stay out of crime.

(Norman Tebbit [British politician], Radio 4, 1985)

[...] In each of these utterances there is a characteristic slippage between linguistic and moral terms. [...] Ignorance or defiance of grammatical rules is equated with anti-social or criminal behaviour. Grammar needs to be taught, we gather, less to inculcate the norms of polite usage than to encourage respect for persons and property, to keep people clean and law-abiding, to build their 'character' and discourage indiscipline or 'sloppiness'. [...]

The otherwise baffling observations of pro-grammar conservatives become intelligible if we hypothesize a systematic analogy between the structure of language and the structure of society. More specifically, [...] conservatives use 'grammar' as the metaphorical correlate for a cluster of related political and moral terms: *order, tradition, authority, hierarchy* and *rules*. In the ideological world that conservatives inhabit, these terms are not only positive, they define the conditions for any civil society, while their opposites – *disorder, change, fragmentation, anarchy* and *lawlessness* – signify the breakdown of social relations. A panic about grammar is therefore interpretable as the metaphorical expression of persistent conservative fears that we are losing the values that underpin civilization and sliding into chaos. [...]

During the twentieth century, however, some elements of the ancient metaphorical code have been challenged by a powerful competing discourse. The 'enemy within' is linguistic science, which preserves a notion of grammar as ordered, hierarchical and rule-governed, but dispenses with tradition and authority as necessary components of its meaning. Linguistics has introduced a new definition of grammar as 'descriptive not prescriptive', in which the rules are underwritten not by traditional authority but by internalized native speaker competence.

For conservatives this is a major blow. Tradition and authority are crucial to their concept of social order, and if the language/society analogy is to hold (which of course it does not for linguists), they must also remain central in the definition of grammar. Because of this consideration, pro-grammar conservatives in the 1980s debate were obliged to fight on two fronts simultaneously. Not only were they forced to defend grammar itself, they were also compelled to defend a particular concept of grammar – traditional prescriptive grammar – against the dangerous 'new orthodoxy' of descriptive linguistics. [...]

The moral of the story ...

[...] It is important to recognize that the conservative argument played on widespread fears and desires. Just about every parent wants a better life for their children, and a campaign to persuade parents that trendy left-wing teachers were denying children opportunity by fostering illiteracy and indiscipline had more rather than less resonance in the chilly economic climate most school leavers were facing by the late 1980s. [...]

The pro-grammar conservative argument about grammar succeeded in appealing to a broad constituency, not only because it symbolically expressed powerful fears and desires to do with moral and social order, but also and importantly because it resonated with common-sense assumptions about *language*. It spoke to the belief almost everyone has that language-using is a normative practice, properly subject to judgements of correctness and value; that in the words of *Today* newspaper, 'some kinds of English really are more worthwhile than others'. [...] And this is an important reason why conservatives can so easily manipulate grammar as a political symbol: if the only way of talking about value in language is the one elaborated by right-wing authoritarians, then their prescriptive metalanguage and their moral terms are almost bound to dominate people's thinking on the subject.

Verbal hygiene and social or moral hygiene are interconnected; to argue about language is indirectly to argue about extra-linguistic values. The links which pro-grammar conservatives made between language and moral values were doubtless irrational and mystificatory. But it is just as mystificatory to suppose that issues of language can be stripped of any evaluative dimension. Where linguistic science insists on trying to do this, it diverges from the concerns of most language-users. To be sure, in many areas of linguistic scholarship this will be a matter of indifference: that the ordinary speaker has no interest in complex phonological processes should not preclude scholarly investigation of them, for example. But in socially oriented linguistics – and in the making of public policy about language – it cannot be a matter of indifference.

References for this reading

Cohen, S. (1987) *Folk Devils and Moral Panics: the Creation of Mods and Rockers* (new edn), Oxford: Basil Blackwell.

DES (1988) Report of the Committee of Inquiry into the teaching of the English language [the Kingman Report], London: HMSO.

DES (1989) *English for Ages 5–16* [the Report of the National Curriculum English Working Group chaired by Professor Brian Cox], London: DES.

READING B: Reading the 'Singlish debate'

Anneliese Kramer-Dahl

Source: Kramer-Dahl, A. (2003) 'Reading the "Singlish debate": construction of a crisis of language standards and language teaching in Singapore', *Journal of Language, Identity, and Education*, vol. 2, no. 3, pp. 159–90.

One is hard-pressed to pin down any one concrete event as the stimulus for all the discursive activity that unfolded in the Singapore media between late June and mid-September 1999. Not that this is highly unusual; in fact, in analogous debates in other contexts where the language curriculum has become an ideological battleground, the argument for a crisis also may be rather thin ([…] Freebody, 1997). However, the event triggering a rhetoric of crisis is usually at least something as tangible as the release of new statistics indicating a decline or, more often but viewed as equally alarming, a lack of improvement in the linguistic performance of the school population ([…] e.g., Freebody's account of the media debate triggered by the release of flat-line literacy test figures in Australia in 1997). In the Singapore context, on the other hand, this was not the case. […]

In this analysis of the way the media reported the debate, […] I will review the various reports, editorials, and readers' letters published in the one high-quality local daily, *The Straits Times,* during the crucial period between late June and mid-September 1999, as semantically of a piece, as forming part of the same larger debate about falling standards. […]

The Singapore media text about falling standards overall exemplifies the logic of crisis discourse […]: the early news stories focus on outlining the problem and progressively specifying it further and spelling out its effects:

- 'Worrying signs ahead for English' ('Worrying Signs ahead for English', June 3 1999, p. 41)

[...]

- 'We need to beware of falling standards in the use of the language' ('English: Get Serious', August 8 1999, p. 38)
- 'If the less-educated half of our people end up learning to speak only Singlish, they will suffer economically and socially' ('Singlish "a Handicap We Do Not Wish on Singaporeans"', August 15 1999, p. 26)

[...]

This is then promptly followed by the recursive naming of scapegoats, some more persistently blamed in subsequent articles than others. [... R]esponsibility for the problem was initially apportioned to Singapore media productions epitomized in the lead character of the then most popular local television sitcom, Phua Chu Kang, and his brand of Singlish: 'Blame it on Phua Chu Kang' (July 27 1999, p. 35). 'See lah! Causing trouble again!' (July 28 1999, p. 1). Not only were these suggestions themselves often tongue-in-cheek, but we find them swiftly questioned and critiqued in a string of letters and editorials defending the show. To quote just two:

- 'Don't heap blame on Singlish speaking PCK [Phua Chu Kang]' (July 31 1999, p. 69)
- 'Blaming the media amounts only to finding a scapegoat for our failure to inculcate the right values in our youth' ('How Kids Turn Out', 1999).

At this point the macrotext may appear to be unfolding in the form of an argument with the various microtexts taking different positions on the responsibility of the media and what they ought to do, hence sustaining difference. However, this openness, this dissent, is short-lived because it is embedded within a larger text that is committed to consensus and closure. Not that the competing views are reconciled, but the to-and-fro between Phua Chu Kang and Singlish-on-television bashing and defending eventually made room to pinpoint what seemed the more serious, 'real' culprits, foremost English teachers and what happens in their classrooms. And here, there seemed to be consensus

— It's the teachers' fault!
Argument manipulated by the media —

among the various participants in the unfolding chain of texts about how things ought to be.

This new stage slowly set in with two articles shifting the focus to the scene of teaching: 'Banish PCK? No, Just Teach English Better' (July 28 1999, p. 1) and 'Teachers Give up Speaking Good English' (July 28 1999, p. 1). They followed a rather tangential, anecdotal comment a language expert made at a *Sunday Straits Times* roundtable discussion. To underscore 'the tremendous obstacles' teachers in neighborhood schools are up against, she related the following experience:

> At symposiums, I've heard teachers say that they found themselves having to code-switch to Singapore colloquial English or Singlish in the neighborhood secondary schools, because otherwise your students just speak to you in Hokkien and say that you are *cheem* (deep) and don't understand you. The teachers said that it is not that they don't want to speak good English, but that their students don't understand when they speak in full sentences.
>
> ('Teacher, English Is Too Cheem, Speak Singlish', July 25 1999, pp. 36–37)

But the newspaper went far beyond merely quoting this comment as it was passed, rather innocently and inconsequentially (it seemed) in the course of the extended roundtable discussion; the comment was catapulted into prominence when the newspaper drew on it for the catchy headline, 'Teacher, English is too cheem, speak Singlish', highlighting it as a pull quote and recirculating the linguist's experience in several follow-up articles and editorials. Swiftly and probably unwittingly, she achieved the status of someone authorized to speak on behalf of teachers and what happens in their classrooms. Hence few were surprised when, three days later, a spate of articles and letters to the forum page had turned what she clearly had framed as hearsay into an established fact of Singaporean classroom life:

> My concern stems … from the fact that some teachers have indicated that they have given up speaking good English to their students altogether. … As a parent, I am shocked that instead of

[handwritten: (This is a blame game but highlights anxieties over Singlish)]

being standard bearers for our children, some of our teachers have actually thrown in the towel.

('Surprised with Singlish Usage', July 27 1999, p. 42)

I reckon that 80 to 90 per cent of them write substandard English riddled with grammatical errors which even Primary 6 children should be aware of if they had been taught English correctly.

('Teachers Give Up Speaking Good English', July 28 1999, p. 46)

And this time, unlike in the case of the scapegoating of Phua Chu Kang and the media at large, alternative voices enabling debate and sharpening differences of viewpoint remained unheard. No other teachers or educational experts rushed to defend the anecdote the language expert cited, even though her comment could have provided an easy opening to talk in a more informed way about what bidialectal negotiation looks like in local neighborhood classrooms and the complex functions it can perform for classroom management and knowledge transmission. For instance, many educational linguists elsewhere would consider the switch to Singlish in situations such as the one highlighted during the roundtable, where teachers annotate key concepts or statements for students who have limited English resources, a creative and effective communicative act of 'linguistic and academic brokerage' on the part of the teacher, as well as being a pragmatic compromise with the local 'use English, not mother tongue' institutional rule (Lin, 1996, p. 70 [...]). Yet, none of this well-documented research made its way into the local public discourse.

[handwritten: (why not like bilingualism?)]

Interestingly, when it seemed that teachers' views were finally made known in an article prominently but misleadingly subtitled, 'Teachers' reactions' ('Glad to Upgrade', 1999), they had no control over their representation. They were not authorized to speak directly. Instead, the authority to offer teachers' opinions and classroom experiences was given to higher level school representatives, school principals, and heads of English departments. And they resorted to vague, generalized but mutually supporting statements. Their 'other' presentations, heavily modulated by means of us/them distancing strategies and apologetic gestures, readily complied with the popular verdict on their teachers' negligent ways with language in class:

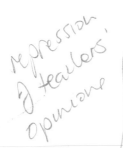
[handwritten: Repression of teachers' opinions]

[...]

Blame the teachers again

- 'The problem is a big one. Some of the school teachers don't speak good English themselves because grammar was either not taught or not emphasised when they were students' (principal of a neighborhood school).
- 'Some of the teachers are being stretched too much and this is hurting them' (a principal 'who spoke on condition of anonymity').
- 'Singapore's teachers have welcomed proposed courses to improve their English, but have asked not to be overburdened with training' (general secretary of teachers' union).

More than that, as is evident from the preceding comments, not only did the school officials position their teachers guilty as charged, but by portraying them consistently as a 'wary' and 'overstretched' group, they went on to mobilize more general anxieties about their lack of knowledge, judgment, and ability to cope with work pressure.

Thus, halfway into the crisis narrative, the source of the problem of English-language standards has clearly shifted from television, which valorizes the use of Singlish, to teachers and teaching, which do so. One editorial, through its title, 'After PCK', signaling that a new stage in popular thinking about the issue has evidently been reached, put it as follows:

Don't blame it on the media

> Critics ask: how can students learn proper English, when they are surrounded by Singlish and even the national television company produces programmes in it? That is a genuine concern, but the debate in English standards must move beyond that. For the reality is that while language environment is important, language teaching is even more so. ... So we should be looking at the way English has been taught over the years.
>
> ('Blame it on Phua Chu Kang', July 27 1999, p. 35)

Assessing the narrative pattern as it has unfolded midway into our macrotext, Cameron's (1995) general crisis scenario is clearly evident. We can see the media piling up 'more and more scare stories,' which gradually fuel 'a disproportionate sense of crisis.' This, in turn, she tells

↑ struggle created by the media ?

us, prepares the way for the last stage, the provision of 'more and more authoritarian 'solutions' (p. 93). That tour-de-force resolutions from above are a common ingredient of falling-standards discourse has been well documented in analyses of many of its contemporary manifestations (see particularly Cameron's [1995] *[see Reading A of this chapter]* and Carter's [1996] analyses of the implementation of the National Curriculum in the United Kingdom), but what sets the Singaporean case apart from those elsewhere is the decisiveness and expediency of these interventionist measures, as well as the fact that they were construed as being willingly taken on board, even actively supported, by those concerned [...]. Phua Chu Kang's broken English problem was swiftly contained through a much-publicized gesture from the very top. Within a few days after the Senior Minister Lee Kuan Yew in his National Day dinner speech had drawn attention to the problem, warning 'not to popularise Singlish' and 'not to use it in our television sitcoms' ('Singlish "a Handicap"' [...]), the Television Corporation of Singapore was quoted to have decided, independent, as it stressed, of 'Senior Minister Lee's call, ... [that] the use of Singlish in its local programmes will be checked and toned down' ('TCS to Tone Down', 1999). A week later, in what one editorialist lauded as 'a masterful stroke, the best possible win–win situation,' the prime minister proudly announced in his National Day rally speech that Phua Chu Kang, the sitcom character, would be attending English classes 'to avoid his bazaar [*sic*] English becoming taken as the norm by impressionable Singaporeans' and thus turning him into 'a role model [the average Singaporean] can sympathise with in his struggle to master the language' ('Bazaar Get Better', 1999).

At this stage, ironically, through a recursive move, an almost absurd parallelism was established between Phua Chu Kang and the more 'real,' widely agreed-on prime offenders, negligent English teachers, who had seemingly renounced their traditional responsibility. For them grammar classes became the proposed solution as well. At first glance, one may find the sense of power attributed to grammar lessons here dangerously oversimplified. But one needs to bear in mind that learning in grammar classes in their classic form [...] involves more than acquiring a body of facts (Hasan, 1996). On the surface level pupils will learn the norms of language use, or in the case of teachers-as-pupils, the rules of how to teach the norms of language use; at a deeper level both sorts of pupils will also learn the value of conformity, docility, and discipline in Foucault's sense. After all, 'the so-called rules of normative grammar are rules that have to be accepted *by fiat*, usually nonnegotiable, allowing for 'very limited ways of answering a "why" question' (p. 389).

That the grammar lessons for both Phua Chu Kang and English teachers are as much projects of moral regulation as linguistic regulation is clear when we examine their intended outcomes. Like Phua Chu Kang, through grammar lessons teachers were to become fine exemplars, disciplined to accept the negative value placed on the local vernacular and to 'lead the way to better English standards in the country' ('Teachers to Go for English Upgrading', July 25 1999, p. 1).

And the parallels did not stop there: they even included specifics such as the way the errant linguistic citizens were told about their impending return to pupilhood. The directive to attend grammar classes was communicated from the top down, with most English teachers finding out about it from the Sunday morning newspaper: 'Teachers to Go for English Upgrading', it announced on the front page, stating that 'the Education Ministry plans to send 8,000 teachers for English language courses' (July 25 1999, p. 1). What softened its force, however, and made it less an act of coercion than one of consent, was the fact that in the same text and others around it was repeatedly emphasized that 'English language teachers had told the ministry that they wanted this grammar course' and that 'Singapore's teachers have welcomed proposed courses to improve their English.' Evidently the teachers had accepted the popular judgment of themselves as lacking in their ability to exemplify competent linguistic and pedagogic subjects and had a strong desire to compensate for that which they lacked.

Thus, by the time the narrative had reached its final stage, apparent consensus existed among all its participants. Along the way they had jointly constructed an ideological perspective on what the 'real' problem was and who carried 'real' responsibility for it. Even though the resolution of difference was brought about through authoritative intervention, it had nonetheless, in line with the ideology underpinning narrative organization, been reached unproblematically, 'in an uncontentious mode' (Kress, 1989, p. 12).

References for this reading

Cameron, D. (1995). *Verbal Hygiene*. London: Routledge.

Carter, R. (1996). Politics and knowledge about language: The LINC project. In R. Hasan & G. Williams (Eds.), *Literacy in Society* (pp. 1–28). London: Longman.

Freebody, P. (1997). Assessment as communal versus punitive practice: Six new literacy crises for Australia. *Literacy and Numeracy Studies*, *7*, 5–18.

Hasan, R. (1996). Literacy, everyday talk and society. In R. Hasan & G. Williams (Eds.), *Literacy in Society* (pp. 377–424). London: Longman.

Kress, G. (1989). Texture and meaning. In R. Andrews (Ed.), *Narrative and Argument* (pp. 9–21). Milton Keynes, England: Open University Press.

Lin, A. M. Y. (1996). Bilingualism or linguistic segregation? Symbolic domination, resistance and code-switching in Hong Kong schools. *Linguistics and Education*, *8*, 49–84.

Afterword: Imagining the future of English

Philip Seargeant

Introduction

In the novel *Riddley Walker*, Russell Hoban envisages England in a remote future, many years after a nuclear holocaust. Civilisation has regressed to the state of a second Iron Age, and the English that the characters use – and in which the novel is narrated – has been worn down and lost its shape:

> I dont think it makes no diffrents where you start the telling of a thing. You never know where it begun realy. No moren you know where you begun your oan self. You myt know the place and day and time of day when you ben beartht. You myt even know the place and day and time when you ben got. That dont mean nothing tho. You stil dont know where you begun.
>
> (Hoban, 2002 [1980], p. 8)

Hoban's purpose in imagining the future of English is an artistic one. He uses the imagined language as part of the paraphernalia of the society he is creating: and the 'broken down' nature of his version of English metonymically reflects the post-apocalyptic circumstances in which his community of characters lives (Hoban, 2002 [1980], p. 225). It is still recognisably English, but its form and shape have altered, just as the society that speaks it has.

Speculating on the future of English is not just the preserve of fiction writers, of course. It is also a popular pastime for those concerned with real life. In fact, a fascination with the future of English often seems an inevitable corollary of discussions about the development and current nature of the language. Given the changes that have occurred to English over the centuries – given the diversity that has resulted from its spread, and the transformations produced by the influence of technology and the shifts and swings in social structures – asking what this phenomenon which is so fundamental to so many people's lives will look like in the years to come is a compelling question; and it is one that receives a great deal of attention.

As with all divination projects, however, the results of such speculation are usually rather shaky. The future has a habit of confounding even the most informed guesswork, and this is as true of speculation about English as it is of anything else. This is not to say that there's no benefit to be had from addressing the question. Even if it is highly unlikely that today's conjecture will match tomorrow's reality, there are still two interesting reasons for entertaining this line of thought and for examining the predictions that people make. The first is that the way people envisage the future of English relates closely to the concerns they have about the language in the here and now; the second is that language policy – which has been a central theme throughout this book – is itself a process of attempting to control the future of the language.

In this Afterword I consider what it is that speculation around this topic can indicate about current attitudes towards English. My contention, in other words, is that predictions about the future are in great part evaluations about the present; and that we can therefore use a discussion of the ongoing development of English as an insightful means of reviewing the present-day politics of the language as it features in societies around the globe.

Predicting the future of English

Allow about 40 minutes

Activity

Let us start by looking at the opinions presented in two books, published in 2010, about the phenomenon of global English. Read the extracts below, both of which outline aspects of a possible future for the language. Extract 1 is from Robert McCrum's *Globish: How the English Language Became the World's Language*. ('Globish' is the term McCrum uses for English as a lingua franca.) Extract 2 is from Nicholas Ostler's *The Last Lingua Franca*, in which he discusses English's current global role within the context of other lingua francas throughout history. Consider how the opinions of the two writers differ. Which do you find the most convincing, and how do they relate to the themes and ideas you have looked at in the course of this book?

Extract 1

The enemies of English culture will criticize its guile and greed, but the outcome is beyond question. In the first decade of the twenty-first century English-speaking people and their culture are more widespread in numbers and influence than any civilization the world has ever seen. Globish, a world dialect, will be less a language and more a means to an end. It will continue to enfranchise millions who lack the benefits of a formal education into a global economy and provide a means of communication that will, for the most part, leave local languages unscathed. Globish might seem to have imperial roots, but it is not imperious. It derives its character from a language that has always been hospitable to change, from the roots up.

(McCrum, 2010, p. 257)

Extract 2

In the medium term, probably by the middle of this century, and possibly earlier ..., a global lingua-franca will no longer be needed. Language technology will take care of interpreting and translation, and foreign-language learning will become an unnecessary chore, except for specialists and enthusiasts. Active communication with speakers of other languages will no more require a special skill than is currently needed to read a foreign text in translation, or to follow the subtitles of a foreign-language video.

This will not happen immediately, but the importance of English is likely to be downgraded anyway as the relative political and economic power of non-English-using states increases. It is often assumed that power politics and the global competition among great states will naturally be reflected linguistically. Hence if English is doomed to pass with the predominance of the USA, then it must, it is presumed, be followed by some other common language. The choice falls most obviously on Chinese, since this is already the world language with most mother tongue speakers, and on current trends the Chinese economy is growing to be the largest in the world.

(Ostler, 2010, pp. 281, 283)

Comment

In Chapter 4, John Gray also discusses McCrum's book, and the way in which McCrum ascribes power to the English language itself rather than to its users and policy makers.

Robert McCrum's attitude to the future of English is a mixture of the positive and the slightly triumphalist. Earlier in his book he writes that during the 1980s the status of English had risen to a position of international dominance, but that its future was far from certain. With the end of the Cold War, however, and with the expansion of global capitalism and the information technology revolution, its spread gained an extra impetus so that now, he suggests, barring a nuclear winter or seismic economic crisis, it has a secure international role for the foreseeable future.

Also noticeable in McCrum's account is his attitude to the idea that English is a threat to other languages. He rejects the notion that this is something which happens frequently or habitually, and downplays the implications of English's imperial past. In other words, he takes a rather anodyne view of political issues relating to the language – which is in stark contrast to many of the approaches we have looked at in this book.

Nicholas Ostler offers a rather different opinion about the future of the language in the excerpt from his book. His conclusion is that English will go the way of other lingua francas; that is, shifts in geopolitical power will undermine its status, just as they did for the other great international languages of history. As the USA, the UK and Australia lose their economic supremacy in the world, challenged in particular by China and India, so other strategies for global communication will become more popular. Ultimately, however, Ostler thinks that it will be technology rather than politics that decides the linguistic future of the world, with advances in 'language technology' (especially machine translation) at some stage superseding the need for a global lingua franca completely.

The questions most often asked about the future of English – some of which are featured in the extracts above – can be summarised as follows:

- Will English remain as the dominant global language, or will its position be challenged by competitors such as Chinese or Spanish?

- Will minority languages survive in areas in which English is assuming a dominant role?
- Will native-speaker norms continue to dictate standards around the world, or will non-native norms become more important?
- Will English split into mutually incomprehensible languages, just as Latin did at the end of the Roman Empire?
- Will standards of English 'degenerate' due to its worldwide spread and the influence of technology?

We have touched on all these topics, in one way or another, during the course of this book, and have considered how the issues they raise relate to the current state of English. In reformulating them as queries about the future, however – in asking, for example, not only how English is affecting local languages around the world, but what its effect will be in twenty or fifty years' time – we venture into different epistemic territory. We move from conclusions based on what we can observe from the data around us to those based on what we can predict from our understanding of how things have developed in the past.

There have been a number of attempts at formulating such predictions. At the end of the 1990s, for example, three significant books were published – all within a year of each other – examining the current state of English within a global context, and commentating either explicitly or implicitly on the likely future of the language. David Crystal, in his *English as a Global Language* (1997), was of the opinion that by the end of the twentieth century English had spread to such a degree that it had gained an independence from the broad planning initiatives of individual societies, and for this reason he could conceive of nothing that was likely to stop its continued expansion as a global lingua franca. Tom McArthur, in *The English Languages* (1998), focused his attention on the processes of variation produced by the worldwide spread of English, and concluded that it was likely eventually to splinter into a 'family of languages'. And David Graddol, in *The Future of English?* (1997), looked to contemporary trends in the development of the language for an indication of its future development, and suggested that it may well be the case that English's dominant position will wane within a few decades, leading to (or caused by) the emergence of new hierarchies of global languages. A decade and a half after the publication of these books, and all these different futures are still possible. English still operates as the pre-eminent language of international communication; it still exists in many different national and regional varieties, each with its own linguistic and cultural identity; and there is still debate about how

For a more recent account of David Crystal's views on English as a global language, see another book in this series: Seargeant and Swann (eds) (2012), Chapter 4.

the rise of languages spoken in other emerging world powers will alter the global linguistic map.

As we have seen in the course of this current book, over the last two decades, and in the years since Crystal, McArthur and Graddol's books were written, a great deal of scholarly attention has focused on the nature of English around the world and the roles it plays in diverse global contexts. As Crystal (2006) points out, however, one of the problems of predicting the future is that there are no historical precedents for a language achieving this sort of status. Latin's 'global' reach existed in an era in which the known world was a good deal more compact than it is now, and so this doesn't provide a particularly useful comparison. There are, however, a few things one can do to forecast a likely future for the language, at least at a very general level. One can, for example, make conjectural estimates about the number of speakers of the language in the coming decades, based on an analysis of population growth trends. This is the technique that Graddol (1997, 2010) has employed, predicting the future population sizes of nations where English presently has a particular role, and in this way estimating the number of speakers in given areas in the years to come. One seemingly clear conclusion based on this method is that the number of non-native speakers of English will continue to grow at a far quicker rate than that of native speakers. As such, it is likely that speakers in countries such as India, which is predicted to have the largest population in the world by 2030, will have a significant influence on the future of English (Graddol, 2010).

Another predictive technique is to look at how things have developed in the past, to see what appears to have caused these developments, and then postulate that if certain similar events occur in the future (particular countries continue to exercise or consolidate global power, particular political systems continue to dominate, etc.), this or that would be the consequence for language practices. As we have seen, it has almost invariably been issues of power which have lain behind the spread of English to date, and as such, issues of power will likely also lie behind the future of the language. Following this line of reasoning, and assuming that China continues to develop as an economic superpower, it is extremely likely that China's linguistic and cultural practices will rise in value around the world, and thus the future of English will in part be determined by the future of Chinese. However, whether this means that Chinese will come to rival or replace English as the pre-eminent international language depends in part on the decisions made by language planners and educationalists in China about how the two languages are promoted and regulated. At present, the population of China is learning English in unprecedented numbers – estimates suggest that there are more English learners in China than there are native speakers of English the world over (Gu, 2009, p. 28), and thus it is not impossible to envisage a future in which English continues to be promoted as a global lingua franca (given the resources, such as the extensive scientific literature, already available in it), despite no longer being the native language of the current economic superpowers. A scenario such as this brings us to a further element in our enquiry into the future of the language: the extent to which this future can be shaped or manipulated by policy initiatives.

Regulation

A key point about language policy is that it is always future-oriented, and it attempts to master forthcoming scenarios by regulating or engineering the elements and circumstances which contribute to them. In other words, language policies respond to present-day concerns about the state of a language or its role in society in order to alter or control the causes of these concerns in the future. For example, those who wish to implement language rights legislation to ensure the future vitality of the linguistic ecosystem do so because they worry about the effects that the spread of majority languages are presently having on the well-being of minority languages. As we have seen, however, language policies do not necessarily always achieve the results they aim for. In Malaysia, for example, over the last few decades the government has swung back and forth between policies advocating English or Malay as the medium of instruction in schools, and each time the effects of these policies have generated a great deal of critical reaction from sectors of society.

The issue of language rights is discussed in Chapter 1 of this book.

The topic of language policy in Malaysia is discussed in Chapter 3 of this book.

Conclusion

In summary then, what can we say that the future holds for the English language? Without being able to give detailed or extensive answers to the questions listed above, we can nevertheless give a good account of the factors and processes that are likely to decide these details. In response to the question of whether English will remain as the dominant global language, this is an issue that will probably be determined by shifts in global geopolitical power and by the choices made by those speech communities who gain economic and political ascendancy. It is worth adding, however, that it is not necessarily the case that English's current position as pre-eminent international lingua franca will be challenged only if another language or group of languages replaces it in this role. If recent trends towards linguistic pluralism continue – trends such as those seen in political movements for the protection and promotion of vernacular languages in education, and in the way that digital technologies such as the internet are now facilitating rather than constraining linguistic diversity – English's dominance may well give way to a future less in thrall to a single 'global language'.

Moving to the question of the continued relevance of native-speaker norms and the legitimacy of what have traditionally been referred to as 'non-standard' usages (and sometimes considered as 'impaired' or 'broken' versions of the language), it seems likely that this issue will be decided by those communities which have the authority to promulgate their own preferences in this matter. Here again, therefore, political and cultural power will be a major factor. As to the question of whether English will split into a collection of mutually incomprehensible languages, in many ways this has already happened with the emergence of mixed languages, such as Singlish, and English-based creoles, such as Jamaican Patois. This does not mean, however, that a variety with global reach does not or cannot co-exist alongside these 'local' varieties; nor does it mean that these different varieties will all have the same social status. As we have seen, the issue of what counts as 'English' is, and will likely continue to be, a site for political debate.

For a discussion of the 'ideology of standards' that surrounds English, see Chapter 8 of this book.

To give much more of a detailed mapping than this of the future of English is probably futile. In many ways, language is such an intrinsic part of the human experience that to predict the future of English – or of any other widely spoken language – necessitates predicting the future of global society itself. All we do know for certain is that it will continue to evolve, and that while policy and planning regulation may try to guide this evolution, ultimately it is the diversity of human society which will shape the future of English, just as it has shaped its past.

References

ABC Premium News (2009) 'Writers, publishers to fight cheap books', 15 July, Australian Broadcasting Corporation.

Adsera, A. and. Pytlikova, M. (2010) *The Role of Language in International Migration: Evidence from OECD Countries 1985–2006* (Research Report), Princeton University and IZA and Aarhus University, CCP and CIM.

Aksoy, A. and Robins, K. (2003) 'The enlargement of meaning: social demand in a transnational context', *International Communication Gazette*, vol. 65, no. 4/5, pp. 365–88.

Allington, D. and Mayor, B. (eds) (2012) *Communicating in English: Talk, Text, Technology*, Abingdon, Routledge/Milton Keynes, The Open University.

Appadurai, A. (1996) *Modernity at Large: Cultural Dimensions of Globalisation*, Minneapolis, MN and London, University of Minnesota Press.

Armitstead, L. (2009) 'Sir Stuart Rose: schools are not providing workers with the right skills', *The Daily Telegraph*, 24 November; also available online at http://www.telegraph.co.uk/education/educationnews/6638699/Sir-Stuart-Rose-Schools-are-not-providing-workers-with-the-right-skills.html (Accessed 6 December 2011).

Armstrong, K. (2007) *The Bible: A Biography*, London, Atlantic Books.

Au, A. Y. W., Garey, J. G., Bermas, N. and Chan, M. M (1998) 'The relationship between acculturation and job satisfaction among Chinese immigrants in the New York city restaurant business', *International Journal of Hospitality Management*, vol. 17, no. 1, pp. 11–21.

Australian Bureau of Statistics (2011) *Population Clock* [online], http://www.abs.gov.au/ausstats/abs%40.nsf/94713ad445ff1425ca25682000192af2/1647509ef7e25faaca2568a900154b63?OpenDocument (Accessed 31 January 2011).

Australian Government (2010) Australian Education International. *Research Snapshot, February 2010* [online], http://aei.gov.au/AEI/PublicationsAndResearch/Snapshots/2010022610_pdf.pdf (Accessed 28 January 2011).

Baker, P. and Mohieldeen, Y. (2000) 'The languages of London's schoolchildren' in Baker, P. and Eversley, J. (eds) *Multilingual Capital: The Languages of London's Schoolchildren*, London, Corporation of London.

Bamgboṣe, A. (2009) 'A recurring decimal: English in language policy and planning' in Kachru, B. B., Kachru, Y. and Nelson, C. L. (eds) *The Handbook of World Englishes*, Oxford, Blackwell.

BBC (2009) *Word of Mouth*, BBC Radio 4, 29 October; previously available online at http://www.bbc.co.uk/dna/mbtoday/html/NF2766781?thread=7036251 (Accessed 8 March 2010).

BBC News (2011) *Factfile: Global Migration* [online], http://news.bbc.co.uk/1/shared/spl/hi/world/04/migration/html/migration_boom.stm (Accessed 20 April 2011).

BBC News: Africa (2011) 'Rwanda profile', BBC News [online], http://www.bbc.co.uk/news/world-africa-14093240 (Accessed 6 December 2011).

Belot, M. and Ederveen, S. (2011) 'Cultural and institutional barriers in migration between OECD countries', *Journal of Population Economics* [online], Original Paper, pp. 1–29, http://dx.doi.org/10.1007/s00148-011-0356-x.

Bennett, T., Savage, M., Bortolaia Silva, E., Warde, A., Gayo-Cal, M. and Wright, D. (2009) *Culture, Class, Distinction*, London and New York, Routledge.

Ben-Rafael, E. (2009) 'A sociological approach to the study of linguistic landscapes' in Shohamy, E. and Gorter, D. (eds) *Linguistic Landscape: Expanding the Scenery*, New York and Abingdon, Routledge.

Berger, J. (1972) *Ways of Seeing*, London, BBC/Penguin.

Biko, S. (1979) *I Write What I Like*, London, Heinemann.

Blackledge, A. and Creese, A. (2010) *Multilingualism: A Critical Approach*, London, Continuum.

Blommaert, J. (2010) *The Sociolinguistics of Globalisation*, Cambridge, Cambridge University Press.

Bloomfield, L. (1944) 'Secondary and tertiary responses to language', *Language*, vol. 20, no. 2, pp. 45–55.

Bokhurst, W. D. and Caleon, I. S. (2009) 'The language attitudes of bilingual youth in Singapore', *Journal of Multilingual and Multicultural Development*, vol. 30, no. 3, pp. 235–51.

Bourdieu, P. (1984) *Distinction: A Social Critique of the Judgment of Taste* (trans. R. Nice), Harvard, MA, Harvard University Press.

Bourdieu, P. (1991) *Language and Symbolic Power* (trans. G. Raymond and M. Adamson; ed. J. B. Thompson), Cambridge, Polity.

Breidbach, S. (2003) 'Plurilingualism, democratic citizenship in Europe and the role of English', Language Policy Division DG IV – Directorate of School, Out-of-School and Higher Education, Strasbourg, Council of Europe.

British Council (2009) *Annual Report 2008–09: Building Trust and Understanding Worldwide*, London, British Council.

British Council (2010) *Annual Report 2009–10: Working for the UK Where It Matters*, London, British Council.

Brouillette, S. (2007) 'South Asian literature and global publishing', *Wasafiri*, vol, 22, no. 3, pp. 34–8.

Browne, J. (2010) *Securing a Sustainable Future for Higher Education: An Independent Review of Higher Education Funding and Student Finance* [online], http://www.independent.gov.uk/browne-report (Accessed 19 December 2010).

Brutt-Griffler, J. (2002) *World English: A Study of its Development*, Clevedon, Multilingual Matters.

Bryman, A. E. (2004) *The Disneyization of Society*, London, Sage.

Bullock Report (1975) *A Language for Life*, Report of the Committee of Enquiry appointed by the Secretary of State for Education and Science under the chairmanship of Sir Alan Bullock FBA, London, HMSO.

Businessweek (2000) *Bollywood vs. Hollywood* [online], http://www.businessweek.com/magazine/content/02_48/b3810019.htm (Accessed 24 September 2010).

Cameron, D. (1995) *Verbal Hygiene*, London, Routledge.

Canagarajah, S. (2006) 'Changing communicative needs, revised assessment objectives: testing English as an international language', *Language Assessment Quarterly*, vol. 3, no. 3, pp. 229–42.

Carr, B. (2009) 'Low prices open fresh chapter for readers', *The Australian*, 15 July, p. 5.

Carranza, M. A. and Ryan, E. B. (1975) 'Evaluative reactions of bilingual Anglo and Mexican American adolescents towards speakers of English and Spanish', *International Journal of the Sociology of Language,* vol. 6, pp. 83–104.

Carrió-Pastor, M. L. (2009) 'Cultural diversity in content and language integrated learning (CLIL)' in Carrió-Pastor, M. L. (ed.) *Content and Language Integrated Learning: Cultural Diversity*, Bern, Peter Lang.

Casanova, P. (2004) *The World Republic of Letters* (trans. M. B. DeBevoise), Cambridge, MA, Harvard University Press.

Chalaby, J. K. (2009) *Transnational Television in Europe: Reconfiguring Global Communications Networks*, London, I. B. Tauris.

Chaucer, G., *The Canterbury Tales*, available through Project Gutenberg: http://www.gutenberg.org/ebooks/23722 (Accessed 6 December 2011).

Citizenship and Immigration Canada (2011) *The Citizenship Test* [online], http://www.cic.gc.ca/english/citizenship/cit-test.asp (Accessed 1 June 2011).

CJGTC (Prime Minister's Commission on Japan's Goals in the Twenty-First Century) (2000) *The Frontier Within: Individual Empowerment and Better Governance in the New Millennium* [online], Tokyo, CJGTC, http://www.kantei.go.jp/jp/21century/report/pdfs/index.html (Accessed 29 November 2011).

Coleman, J. (2006) 'English-medium teaching in European higher education', *Language Teaching*, vol. 39, no. 1, pp. 1–14.

Cook, G. (2010) *Translation in Language Teaching: An Argument for Reassessment*, Oxford, Oxford University Press

Coullie, J. and Gibbon, T. (1996) 'Saints and sinners in the canonisation of African literature: a reply to Bernth Lindfors', *Alternation*, vol. 3, no. 1, pp. 15–21.

Coupland, N. and Bishop, H. (2007) 'Ideologised values for British accents', *Journal of Sociolinguistics*, vol. 11, no. 1, pp. 74–93.

Crystal, D. (1997) *English as a Global Language*, Cambridge, Cambridge University Press.

Crystal, D. (1999) 'The death of language', *Prospect*, November, pp. 56–9.

Crystal, D. (2003) *English as a Global Language* (2nd edn), Cambridge, Cambridge University Press.

Crystal, D. (2006) 'English worldwide' in Hogg, F. and Denison, D. (eds) *A History of the English Language*, Cambridge, Cambridge University Press.

Crystal, D. (2012) 'A global language' in Seargeant, P. and Swann, J. (eds) *English in the World: History, Diversity, Change*, Abingdon, Routledge/Milton Keynes, The Open University.

Curtin, M. L. (2009) 'Languages on display: indexical signs, identities and the linguistic landscape of Taipei' in Shohamy, E. and Gorter, D. (eds) *Linguistic Landscape: Expanding the Scenery*, New York, Routledge.

Curtis, M. (2003) *Web of Deceit. Britain's Real Role in the World*, London, Vintage.

Daily Telegraph (2008) 'Asturias is startlingly different to our classic image of Spain', 11 November; also available online at http://www.telegraph.co.uk/sponsored/travel/spanish_tourist_board/asturias/3441235/Asturias-is-startlingly-different-to-our-classic-image-of-Spain.html (Accessed 6 December 2011).

Damrosch, D., Melas, N. and Buthelezi, M. (eds) (2009) *The Princeton Sourcebook in Comparative Literature*, Princeton, NJ, Princeton University Press.

Davies, J. (1994) *Broadcasting and the BBC in Wales*, Cardiff, University of Wales Press.

Davis, C. (2005) 'The politics of postcolonial publishing: Oxford University Press's Three Crowns Series 1962–1976', *Book History*, vol. 8, pp. 227–44.

De Santis, L. and Ugarriza, D. (1995) 'Potential for intergenerational conflict in Cuban and Haitian immigrant families', *Archives of Psychiatric Nursing*, vol. IX, no. 6, pp. 354–64.

Desai, J. and Dudrah, R. (2008) 'The essential Bollywood' in Dudrah, R. and Desai, J. (eds) *The Bollywood Reader*, Maidenhead, Open University Press/McGraw-Hill Education.

Dixon, J. A, Mahoney, B. and Cocks, R. (2002) 'Accents of guilt? Effects of regional accent, race, and crime type on attributions of guilt', *Journal of Language and Social Psychology*, vol. 21, no. 2, pp. 162–8.

Dobson, M. (1992) *The Making of the National Poet: Shakespeare, Adaptation and Authorship, 1660–1769*, Oxford, Oxford University Press.

Drotner, K. (2001) 'Global media through youthful eyes' in Livingstone, S. M. and Bovill, M. (eds) *Children and Their Changing Media Environment: A European Comparative Study*, Mahwah, NJ and London, Lawrence Erlbaum.

Dudrah, R. K. (2006) *Bollywood: Sociology Goes to the Movies*, New Delhi, Thousand Oaks and London, Sage.

Economist Intelligence Unit (EIU) (2011) [online], http://www.eiu.com (Accessed 6 June 2011).

Educational Testing Service (ETS) (2011) *About the TOEIC® Speaking and Writing Tests* [online], http://www.ets.org/toeic/test_takers/speaking_writing/about (Accessed 6 December 2011).

Edwards, J. (1982) 'Language attitudes and their implications among English speakers' in Ryan, E. B. and Giles, H. (eds) *Attitudes towards Language Variation: Social and Applied Contexts*, London, Edward Arnold.

Epstein, G. and Gang, I. (2010) *Migration and Culture*, Discussion Paper No. 5123, Bonn, IZA Institute for the Study of Labour.

Escarpit, R. (1966) *The Book Revolution*, London/Toronto/Wellington/Sydney, George G. Harrap & Co. and Paris, United Nations Educational, Scientific and Cultural Organization (UNESCO).

Ethnologue (2009) *Ethnologue: Languages of the World* (ed. M. P. Lewis) (16th edn), Dallas, TX, SIL International; online version available at: http://www.ethnologue.com/ (Accessed 6 September 2011).

Euromonitor International (2010) The Benefits of the English Language for Individuals and Societies: Quantitative Indicators from Cameroon, Nigeria, Rwanda, Bangladesh and Pakistan: A Custom Report Compiled by Euromonitor International for the British Council [online], http://www.teachingenglish.org.uk/sites/teacheng/files/Euromonitor%20Report%20A4.pdf (Accessed 7 December 2011).

Ferguson, G. (2006) *Language Planning and Education*, Edinburgh, Edinburgh University Press.

Foo, B. and Richards, C. (2004) 'English in Malaysia', *RELC Journal*, vol. 35, pp. 229–40.

Foucault, M. (1977) *Discipline and Punish*, Harmondsworth, Penguin.

Foucault, M. (1998) *The History of Sexuality, Vol. 1: The Will to Knowledge*, Harmondsworth, Penguin.

García, O. (2009) *Bilingual Education in the 21st Century: A Global Perspective*, Chichester, Wiley-Blackwell.

Gardner, R. C. and Lambert, W. E. (1972) *Attitudes and Motivation in Second Language Learning*, Rowley, MA, Newbury House.

Gill, S. K. (n.d.) 'Language and cultural identity: balancing national and international needs in public universities in Malaysia', ICHE conference presentation final draft [online], http://www.intconfhighered.org/Saran-Malaysia-ICHE%20Conf%20presentation%20final%20draft.doc (Accessed 6 February 2011).

Goethe, J. W. von (1994) Werke, Kommentare und Register. Band 12: Kunst und Literatur. Zwöflte, durchgesehene Auflage. München, C.H.Beck'sche Verlagsbuchhandlung (Oscar Beck).

Goffman, E. (1979) *Gender Advertisements*, London, Macmillan.

Gooch, L. (2009) 'In Malaysia, English ban raises fear for future', *The New York Times*, 9 July [online], http://www.nytimes.com/2009/07/10/world/asia/10iht-malay.html?scp=1&sq=In%20malaysia,%20english%20ban%20raises%20fears%20for%20future&st=cse (Accessed 3 September 2011).

Gopal, S. and Sen, B. (2008) 'Inside and out: song and dance in Bollywood cinema' in Dudrah, R. and Desai, J. (eds) *The Bollywood Reader*, Maidenhead, Open University Press/McGraw-Hill Education.

Graddol, D. (1997) *The Future of English?*, London, British Council.

Graddol, D. (2010) *English Next India*, London, British Council.

Gramsci, A. (1971) *Selections from the Prison Notebooks of Antonio Gramsci* (trans. and ed. Q. Hoare and G. N. Smith), London, Lawrence & Wishart.

Gray, J. (2002) 'The global coursebook in English language teaching' in Block, D. and Cameron, D. (eds) *Globalization and Language Teaching*, London, Routledge.

Gray, J. (2010a) 'The branding of English and the culture of the new capitalism: representations of the world of work in English language textbooks', *Applied Linguistics*, vol. 31, no. 5, pp. 714–33.

Gray, J. (2010b) *The Construction of English: Culture, Consumerism and Promotion in the ELT Global Coursebook*, Basingstoke, Palgrave Macmillan.

Grin, F. (2001) 'English as economic value: facts and fallacies', *World Englishes*, vol. 20, no. 1, pp. 65–78.

Grundy, P., Benson, P. and Skutnabb-Kangas, T. (1998) 'Introduction', *Language Sciences*, vol. 20, no. 1, pp. 1–3.

Gu, M. (2009) *The Discursive Construction of Second Language Learners' Motivation*, Bern, Peter Lang.

Halliday, M. A. K, McIntosh, A. and Strevens, P. (1964) *The Linguistic Sciences and Language Teaching*, London, Longman.

Hamlet, film, directed by Michael Almereyda. USA, double A films, Miramax, 2000.

Hanisch, C. (1970) 'The personal is political' in Firestone, S. and Koedt, A. (eds) *Notes from the Second Year: Women's Liberation*, New York, Radical Feminism.

Haque, R. (2002) *Migrants in the UK: A Descriptive Analysis of their Characteristics and Labour Market Performance, Based on the Labour Force Survey*, London, Department for Work and Pensions.

Harding, J., Clarke, A. and Chappell, A. (2007) *Family Matters: Intergenerational Conflict in the Somali Community*, London, London Metropolitan University.

Harpham, G. (2002) *Language Alone: The Critical Fetish of Modernity*, New York, Routledge.

Harvey, D. (2005) *A Brief History of Neoliberalism*, Oxford, Oxford University Press.

Hashim, A. (2009) 'Not plain sailing: Malaysia's language choice in policy and education' in Lim, L. and Low, E.-L. (eds) *Multilingual, Globalizing Asia: Implications for Policy and Education*, *AILA Review*, vol. 22, pp. 36–51.

Heilbron, J. (2010) 'Structure and dynamics of the world system of translation', UNESCO International Symposium *Translation and Cultural Mediation*, 22–23 February. Available online at johan.heilbron@planet.nl http://portal.unesco.org/culture/en/files/40619/12684038723Heilbron.pdf/ Heilbron.pdf (Accessed 10 October 2010).

Heller, M. (2002) 'Globalization and the commodification of bilingualism in Canada' in Block, D. and Cameron, D. (eds) *Globalization and Language Teaching*, London, Routledge.

Hernandez-Marin, E., Seth, M. and Ziegler, T. (2010) 'Density functional theory study of the electron paramagnetic resonance parameters and the magnetic circular dichroism spectrum for model compounds of dimethyl sulfoxide reductase', *Inorganic Chemistry,* Article ASAP Publication Date (Web), 21 January.

Hewings, A., Lillis, T. and Vladimirou, D. (2010) 'Who's citing whose writings? A corpus-based study of citations as interpersonal resource in English medium national and English medium international journals', *English for Academic Purposes*, vol. 9, no. 2, pp. 102–15.

Hincks, R. (2010) 'Speaking rate and information content in English lingua franca oral presentations', *English for Specific Purposes*, vol. 29, pp. 4–18.

Hoban, R. (2002 [1980]) *Riddley Walker*, London, Bloomsbury.

Hoffman, E. (1998) *Lost in Translation: A Life in a New Language*, London, Vintage.

Holland, T. (2010) 'The week in books: poetry pamphlets, a plea to the Chancellor and Updike honoured', *The Guardian (Guardian Review)*, 19 June, p. 5.

Hopkins, L. (2009) 'Citizenship and global broadcasting: constructing national, transnational, and post-national identities', *Journal of Media and Cultural Studies*, vol. 23, no. 1, pp. 19–32.

House, J. (1997) *Translation Quality Assessment: A Model Revisited*, Tübingen, Gunter Narr.

House, J. (2009) *Translation*, Oxford, Oxford University Press.

Hultgren, A. (n.d.) 'Reconciling essentialist and constructionist theories of language and foreign language proficiency: the case of English at Nordic universities', unpublished manuscript.

It Started in Naples, film, directed by Melville Shavelson. USA, Paramount Pictures, 1960.

Jakobson, R. (1959) 'Linguistic aspects of translation' in Brower, R. A. (ed.) *On Translation*, Cambridge, MA, Harvard University Press.

Jenkins, J. (2006) 'The spread of EIL: a testing time for testers', *ELT Journal*, vol. 60, no. 1, pp. 42–50.

Johnson, D. (1996) *Shakespeare and South Africa*, Oxford, Clarendon.

Kachru, B. (1985) 'Standards, codification and sociolinguistic realism: the English language in the outer circle' in Quirk, R. and Widdowson, H. G. (eds) *English in the World*, Cambridge, Cambridge University Press.

Kachru, B. (1992) 'Teaching world Englishes' in Kachru, B. (ed.) *The Other Tongue: English Across Cultures* (2nd edn), Urbana and Chicago, IL, University of Illinois Press.

Kachru, B. (1988) 'The sacred cows of English', *English Today*, vol. 4, no. 4, pp. 3–8.

Kachru, B. (ed.) (1982) *The Other Tongue: English across Cultures*, Urbana, IL, University of Illinois Press.

Kerswill, P. (2006) 'Migration and language' in Mattheier, K., Ammon, U. and Trudgill, P. (eds) *Sociolinguistics/Soziolinguistik. An International Handbook of the Science of Language and Society* (2nd edn), Vol. 3, Berlin, De Gruyter.

Kouega, J. P. (2008) 'Minority language use in Cameroon and educated indigenes' attitudes to their languages', *International Journal of Social Language*, vol. 189, pp. 85–113.

Kovač, M. (2002) 'The state of affairs in post-communist Central and Eastern European book industries', *Publishing Research Quarterly*, vol. 18, no. 3, pp. 43–53.

Krauss, M. (1992) 'The world's languages in crisis', *Language*, vol. 68, pp. 4–10.

Kress, G. and van Leeuwen, T. (1996) *Reading Images: The Grammar of Visual Design*, London, Routledge.

Lai, M.-L. (2005) 'Language attitudes of the first postcolonial generation in Hong Kong secondary schools', *Language in Society*, vol. 34, no. 3, pp. 363–88.

Lambert, W. E, Hodgson, R. C., Gardner, R. C. and Fillenbaum, S. (1960) 'Evaluational reactions to spoken languages', *Journal of Abnormal and Social Psychology*, vol. 60, no. 1, pp. 44–51.

Larkin, B. (2004) 'Degraded images, distorted sounds: Nigerian video and the infrastructure of piracy', *Public Culture*, vol. 16, no. 2, pp. 289–314.

Lee, J. (2009) 'Interpreting inexplicit language during courtroom examination', *Applied Linguistics*, vol. 30, no. 1, pp. 93–115.

Letters to the Telegraph (2008) 22 June [online], http://www.telegraph.co.uk/comment/letters/3559761/Letters-to-the-Telegraph.html (Accessed 6 December 2011).

Letters to the Telegraph (2008) 29 June [online], http://www.telegraph.co.uk/comment/letters/3559995/Letters-to-The-Telegraph.html (Accessed 6 December 2011).

Leung, C. and Lewkowicz, J. (2006) 'Expanding horizons and unresolved conundrums: language testing and assessment', *TESOL Quarterly*, vol. 40, no. 1, pp. 211–34.

Lillis, T. and Curry, M. J. (2010) *Academic Writing in a Global Context: The Politics and Practices of Publishing in English*, Abingdon, Routledge.

Lindfors, B. (1996a) 'African literature teaching in South African University English departments', *Alternation*, vol. 3, no. 1, pp. 5–14.

Lindfors, B. (1996b) 'Interrogating the interrogators: a reply to Coullie and Gibbon', *Alternation*, vol. 3, no. 1, pp. 22–9.

Linn, A. R. (2010) 'Can parallelism save Norwegian from extinction?', *Multilingua*, vol. 29, no. 3/4, pp. 289–305.

Liu, Y. (2007) 'Towards "representational justice" in translation practice' in Munday, J. (ed.) *Translation as Intervention*, London, Routledge.

Living in Bondage, film, directed by Chris Obi Rapu. Nigeria, 1992.

Lobato, R. (2010) 'Creative industries and informal economies: lessons from Nollywood', *International Journal of Cultural Studies*, vol. 13, no. 4, pp. 337–54.

Macauley, T. B. (1835) Minute on Indian Education, speech given in 1835; see, for example, http://www.columbia.edu/itc/mealac/pritchett/00generallinks/macaulay/txt_minute_education_1835.html (Accessed 14 December 2011).

Mackiewicz, W. (2002) 'Plurilingualism in the European knowledge society', speech delivered at the conference on Lingue e Produzione del Sapere, organised by the Swiss Academy of Humanities and Social Sciences at the Università della Svizerra Italiana on 14 June, [online], http://www.google.co.uk/search?sourceid=navclient&aq=0h&oq=p&ie=UTF-8&rlz=1T4ADBR_enGB328GB328&q=plurilingualism (Accessed 30 March 2010).

Mahathir, M. (1999) *A New Deal for Asia*, Petaling Jaya, Selangor, Pelandok Publications.

Mannheim, K. (1936) *Ideology and Utopia: An Introduction to the Sociology of Knowledge*, London, Routledge & Kegan Paul.

Martin, J. R. (1985) *Factual Writing: Exploring and Challenging Social Reality*, Oxford, Oxford University Press.

Martin, J. R., Christie, F. and Rothery, J. (1987) 'Social processes in education' in Reid, I. (ed.) *The Place of Genre in Learning*, Victoria, Deakin University Press.

Martin-Jones, M. (2000) 'Enterprising women: multilingual literacies in the construction of new identities' in Martin-Jones, M. and Jones, K. (eds) *Multilingual Literacies: Reading and Writing Different Worlds*, Amsterdam, John Benjamins.

Marx, K. (1998 [1845]) *The German Ideology: Including Theses on Feuerbach and Introduction to The Critique of Political Economy*, Amherst, Prometheus Books.

May, S. (2009) 'Language rights' in Coupland, N. and Jaworski, A. (eds) *The New Sociolinguistics Reader*, Hounslow, Palgrave Macmillan.

Mayhew, A. (1938) *Education in the Colonial Empire*, London, Longmans, Green.

McArthur, T. (1998) *The English Languages*, Cambridge, Cambridge University Press.

McCallen, B. (1990) *English in Eastern Europe. Special Report No. 2057*, London, The Economist Intelligence Unit.

McCrum, R. (2010) *Globish: How the English Language Became the World's Language*, London, Viking.

McElhinny, B. (2007) 'Introduction: language, gender and economies in global transitions: provocative and provoking questions about how gender is articulated' in McElhinny, B. S. (ed.) *Words, Worlds and Material Girls: Language, Gender and Globalisation*, Berlin, Mouton de Gruyter.

McNamara, T. (2008) 'The socio-political and power dimensions of tests' in Shohamy, E. and Hornberger, N. H. (eds) *Encyclopedia of Language and Education. Volume 7: Language Testing and Assessment* (2nd edn), New York, Springer.

McNamara, T. and Shohamy, E. (2008) 'Viewpoint: language tests and human rights', *International Journal of Applied Linguistics*, vol. 18, no. 1, pp. 89–95.

Meek, J. (2003) 'Speaking a different language – but we've got the Phrasealator', *The Guardian*, 31 March, [online] http://www.guardian.co.uk/world/2003/mar/31/iraq.jamesmeek (Accessed 14 December 2011).

Melvern, L. (2000) *A People Betrayed: The Role of the West in Rwanda's Genocide*, London, Zed Books.

Mercer, N. with contributions from D. Barnes (2007) 'English as a classroom language' in Mercer, N., Swann, J. and Mayor, B. (eds) *Learning English*, Abingdon, Routledge/Milton Keynes, The Open University.

Merriam-Webster's Dictionary of English Usage (1994) Springfield, MA, Merriam-Webster Inc.

Miller, E. (2010) 'Agency in the making: adult immigrants' accounts of language learning and work', *TESOL Quarterly*, vol. 44, no. 3, pp. 465–87.

Milroy, J. and Milroy, L. (1999) *Authority in Language: Investigating Standard English* (3rd edn), London, Routledge.

Minett, A. J. (2009) 'Reproduction, resistance and supranational language management: a critical discourse analysis of the role of Soros-funded English language programs in the building of open societies', PhD thesis, Indiana University of Pennsylvania, USA.

Monsoon Wedding, film, directed by Mira Nair. India/USA, Mirabai Films, 2001.

Moyer, M. G. and Martín Rojo, L. (2007) 'Language, migration and citizenship: new challenges in the regulation of bilingualism' in Heller, M. (ed.) *Bilingualism: A Social Approach*, New York, Palgrave Macmillan.

Mugglestone, L. (2007) 'Accent as social symbol' in Graddol, D., Leith, D., Swann, J., Rhys, M. and Gillen, J. (eds) *Changing English*, London, Routledge.

Munday, J. (2001) *Introducing Translation Studies: Theories and Applications*, London, Routledge.

Munshi, K. and Rosenzweig, M. (2006) 'Traditional institutions meet the modern world: caste, gender and schooling choice in a globalizing economy', *American Economic Review*, vol. 96, no. 4, pp. 1225–52.

Mutloatse, M. (1980) *Forced Landing*, Johannesburg, Ravan Press.

Nettle, D. and Romaine, S. (2000) *Vanishing Voices: The Extinction of the World's Languages*, Oxford, Oxford University Press.

Newbolt Report (1921) *The Teaching of English in England*, London, HMSO.

Newell, S. (2000) *Ghanaian Popular Fiction: 'Thrilling Discoveries in Conjugal Life' & Other Tales*, Oxford, James Currey.

Newell, S. (2002) *Literary Culture in Colonial Ghana: 'How to Play the Game of Life'*, Manchester, Manchester University Press.

Ngũgĩ wa Thiong'o (1986) *Decolonising the Mind*, London, James Currey.

Niño-Murcia, M. (2003) '"English is like the dollar": hard currency ideology and the status of English in Peru', *World Englishes*, vol. 22, no. 2, pp. 121–42.

Norton, B. (2000) *Identity and Language Learning: Gender, Ethnicity and Educational Change*, London, Longman.

Okoye, C. (2007) 'Looking at ourselves in our mirror: agency, counter-discourse, and the Nigerian video film', *Film International*, vol. 5, no. 4, pp. 20–9.

Ostler, N. (2010) *The Last Lingua Franca*, London, Allen Lane.

Palmer, S. and Jumiran, A. (2008) *Project to Improve English in Rural Schools (PIERS): Final Report*, Jelebu Pertang Negri Sembilan: Centre for British Teachers (CFBT), Malaysia.

Park, J. K. (2009) '"English Fever" in South Korea: its history and symptoms', *English Today*, vol. 25, no. 1, pp. 50–7.

Pavlenko, A. (2005) 'Bilingualism and thought' in de Groot, A. and Kroll, J. (eds) *Handbook of Bilingualism: Psycholinguistic Approaches*, New York, Oxford University Press.

Pax, S. (2002) *Where is Raed?* [online], http://dear_raed.blogspot.com/2002_12_01_archive.html (Accessed 30 June 2011).

Pennington, M. and Yue, F. (1994) 'English and Chinese in Hong Kong: pre-1997 attitudes', *World Englishes*, vol. 13, no. 1, pp. 1–20.

Pennycook, A. (1994) *The Cultural Politics of English as an International Language*, Harlow, Longman.

Pennycook, A. (1994) *The Cultural Politics of English as an International Language*, London/New York, Longman.

Phillipson, R. (1992) *Linguistic Imperialism*, Oxford, Oxford University Press.

Phillipson, R. (1998) 'Globalizing English: are linguistic human rights an alternative to linguistic imperialism?', *Language Sciences*, vol. 20, no. 1, pp. 101–12.

Pierson, H., Fu, G. S. and Lee, S. Y. (1980) 'An analysis of the relationship between language attitudes and English attainment of secondary school students in Hong Kong', *Language Learning*, vol. 30, no. 2, pp. 289–316.

Pool, H. (2007) 'Question time: ex-BBC reporter Rageh Omaar, 39, on the "Scud Stud" label, switching to Al-Jazeera, and why he's fallen in love with Iran', *The Guardian, G2*, 15 February, p. 21.

Potter, S. J. (2008) 'Who listened when London called? Reactions to the BBC Empire Service in Canada, Australia, and New Zealand, 1932–1939', *Historical Journal of Film, Radio, and Television*, vol. 28, no. 4, pp. 475–87.

Prime Minister's Office (2008) *English – The World's Language*, Prime Minister's speech, 17 January 2008 [online], http://webarchive.nationalarchives.gov.uk/+/www.number10.gov.uk/Page14289 (Accessed 31 May 2011).

Quirk, R. (1990) 'Language varieties and standard language', *English Today*, vol. 6, no. 1, pp. 3–10.

Rai, A. (2009) *Untimely Bollywood: Globalisation and India's New Media Assemblage*, Durham, NC and London, Duke University Press.

Rappa, A. L. and Wee, L. (2006) *Language Policy and Modernity in Southeast Asia*, New York, Springer.

Rassool, N. (1997) 'Fractured or flexible identities? Life histories of "black" migrant women in Britain' in Mirza, H. S. (ed.) *British Black Feminism: A Reader*, London, Routledge.

Rassool, N. (2000) 'Contested and contesting identities: minority languages vs. the teaching of "world" languages within the global cultural economy', *Journal of Multilingualism and Multicultural Education*, vol. 21, no. 6, pp. 386–98.

Rassool, N. (2004) 'Sustaining linguistic diversity within the global cultural economy: issues of language rights and linguistic opportunities', *Comparative Education*, vol. 40, no. 2, pp. 199–214.

Ritzer, G. (1996) *The McDonaldization of Society: An Investigation into the Changing Character of Contemporary Social Life*, Thousand Oaks, CA, Pine Forge Press.

Romeo and Juliet, film, directed by Baz Luhrmann. USA, Bazmark Films, Twentieth Century Fox, 1996.

Ryan, E. B. and Giles, H. (eds) (1982) *Attitudes towards Language Variation: Social and Applied Contexts*, London, Edward Arnold.

Sakr, N (2005) 'Maverick or model? Al-Jazeera's impact on Arab satellite television' in Chalaby, J. K. (ed.) *Transnational Television Worldwide: Towards a New Media Order*, London, I. B. Tauris.

Seargeant, P. (2009) *The Idea of English in Japan: Ideology and the Evolution of a Global Language*, Bristol, Multilingual Matters.

Seargeant, P. and Erling, E. J. (2011) 'The discourse of "English as a language for international development": policy assumptions and practical challenges' in Coleman, H. (ed.) *Dreams and Realities: Developing Countries and the English Language*, London, British Council.

Seargeant, P. and Swann, J. (eds) (2012) *English in the World: History, Diversity, Change*, Abingdon, Routledge/Milton Keynes, The Open University.

Searle, J. R. (1996) *The Construction of Social Reality*, London, Penguin.

Sheppard, F. (2006) 'Harsh words for BBC over Live 8 stars' swearing', *The Scotsman*, 21 February; also available online at http://news.scotsman.com/live8/Harsh-words-for-BBC-over.2752753.jp (Accessed 6 December 2011).

Shohamy, E. (2008) 'Introduction' in Shohamy, E. and Hornberger, N. H. (eds) *Encyclopedia of Language and Education. Volume 7: Language Testing and Assessment* (2nd edn), New York, Springer.

Shohamy, E. and Gorter, D. (eds) (2009) *Linguistic Landscapes in the City*, Clevedon, Multilingual Matters.

Siiner, M. (2010) 'Hangovers of globalization: a case study of laissez-faire language policy in Denmark', *Language Problems and Language Planning*, vol. 34, no. 1, pp. 43–62.

Silverstein, M. (1979) 'Language structure and linguistic ideology' in Clyne, P. R., Hanks, W. F. and Hofbauer, C. L. (eds) *The Elements: A Parasession on Linguistic Units and Levels*, Chicago, IL, University of Chicago, Chicago Linguistic Society.

Skutnabb-Kangas, T. (2000) *Linguistic Genocide in Education – Or World-Wide Diversity and Human Rights?*, Mahwah, NJ, Lawrence Erlbaum.

Skutnabb-Kangas, T., Maffi, L. and Harmon, D. (2003) *Sharing a World of Difference: The Earth's Linguistic, Cultural and Biological Diversity*, Paris, UNESCO.

Smith, S. (2011) 'Rwanda in six scenes', *London Review of Books*, vol. 33, no. 6, pp. 3–8.

Squires, C. (2007) 'The global market 1970–2000: consumers' in Eliot, S. and Rose, J. A. (eds) *Companion to the History of the Book*, Oxford, Blackwell.

Straubhaar, J. D. and Duarte, L. G. (2005) 'Adapting US transnational television channels to a complex world: from cultural imperialism to localisation to hybridisation' in Chalaby, J. (ed.) *Transnational Television Worldwide: Towards a New Media Order*, London, I. B. Tauris.

Sutherland, J. (2002) 'Linguicide: the death of language', *The Independent*, 10 March [online], http://www.independent.co.uk/news/science/linguicide-the-death-of-language-653646.html (Accessed 31 May 2011).

Swales, J. M. (1990) *Genre Analysis: English in Academic and Research Settings*, Cambridge, Cambridge University Press.

Swann, P. (2000) 'The British culture industries and the mythology of the American market: cultural policy and cultural exports in the 1940s and 1990s', *Cinema Journal*, vol. 39, no. 4, pp. 27–42.

Swift, J. (1712) 'A proposal for correcting, improving, and ascertaining the English tongue' [online], http://classiclit.about.com/library/bl-etexts/jswift/bl-jswift-propcor.htm (Accessed 6 December 2011).

Tackey, N., Casebourne, J., Aston, J., Ritchie, H., Sinclair, A., Tyers, C., Hurstfield, J., Willison, R. and Page, R. (2006) *Barriers to Employment for Pakistanis and Bangladeshis in Britain: A Report of Research Carried Out by the Institute for Employment Studies on Behalf of the Department for Work and Pensions*, Research Report DWPRR 360, Leeds, Department for Work and Pensions.

Taylor, G. (1990) *Reinventing Shakespeare: A Cultural History from the Restoration to the Present*, London, Hogarth.

Tharu, S. (1991) 'The arrangement of an alliance: English and the making of Indian literatures' in Joshi, S. (ed.) *Rethinking English: Essays in Literature, Language, History*, Delhi, Trianka.

The Publishers Association (2010) *PA Statistics Yearbook 2009*, London, The Publishers Association.

The Talented Mr Ripley, film, directed by Anthony Minghella. USA, Paramount Pictures/Miramax, 1999.

The University of Nottingham Ningbo (n.d.) *Study with Us: Undergraduate Course A to Z* [online], http://www.nottingham.edu.cn/en/study/a-z.aspx (Accessed 3 September 2011).

The World Bank (2009) *Doing Business Report 2010: Reforming through Difficult Times*, The International Bank for Reconstruction and Development/The World Bank [online], http://go.worldbank.org/DC5JETJPR0 (Accessed 11 April 2011).

Thomas, D. (1999) 'Culture, ideology and educational change: the case of English language teachers in Slovakia', unpublished PhD thesis, Institute of Education, University of London.

Thomas, S. (1998) 'Translation as intercultural conflict' in Hunston, S. (ed.) *Language at Work*, Clevedon, Multilingual Matters.

Thomas-Hope, E. (2002) 'Skilled labor migration from developing countries: study on the Caribbean region', *International Migration Papers 50*, *International Migration Programme*, Geneva, International Labour Office.

Thompson, J. (2005) *Books in the Digital Age: The Transformation of Academic and Higher Education Publishing in Britain and the United States*, Cambridge, Polity.

Thurlow, C. (2006) 'From statistical panic to moral panic: the metadiscursive construction and popular exaggeration of new media language in the print media', *Journal of Computer-Mediated Communication*, vol. 11, pp. 667–701.

Tollefson, J. W. (1989) *Alien Winds: The Re-education of America's Indochinese Refugees*, New York, Praeger.

Toolan, M. (2009) 'Assessing students' writing: just more grubby verbal hygiene?' in Toolan, M. (ed.) *Language Teaching: Integrational Linguistic Approaches*, London, Routledge.

Torkington, K. (2008) *Exploring the Linguistic Landscape: The Case of the 'Golden Triangle' in the Algarve*, Portugal, Paper from the Lancaster Postgraduate Conference in Linguistics and Language Teaching, vol. 3, pp. 122–45.

Trivedi, H. (1993) *Colonial Transactions: English Literature and India*, Calcutta, Papyrus.

Trudgill, P. (1975) *Accent, Dialect and the School*, London, Edward Arnold.

Truss, L. (2003) *Eats, Shoots & Leaves: The Zero Tolerance Approach to Punctuation*, London, Profile Books.

UK Council for International Student Affairs (2010) *International Students in the UK: Facts, Figures – and Fiction* [online], http://www.ukcisa.org.uk/files/pdf/about/international_education_facts_figures.pdf (Accessed 31 January 2011).

UNESCO (1996) *Universal Declaration on Linguistic Rights*, Paris, UNESCO; available at http://www.unesco.org/cpp/uk/declarations/linguistic.pdf (Accessed 29 November 2011).

United Nations Development Programme (UNDP) (2009) *Human Development Report 2009 Overcoming Barriers: Human Mobility and Development*, New York, UNDP.

Universities Australia (2009) Media Releases 2009: *Study Highlights Diverse, Long-Term Benefits of International Education* [online], http://www.universitiesaustralia.edu.au/page/media-centre/2009-media-releases/benefits-of-international-education/ (Accessed 7 September 2011).

Velthuijs, M. (2000) *Frog and the Stranger* (English-Bengali edition), (trans. K. Datta), London, Milet Publishing.

Venuti, L. (1986) 'The translator's invisibility', *Criticism*, vol. 28, pp. 197–212.

Venuti, L. (1995) *The Translator's Invisibility: A History of Translation*, London, Routledge.

Viswanathan, G. (1989) *Masks of Conquest: Literary Study and British Rule in India*, London, Faber.

von Schlegel, A. W. (1846 [1815]) *A Course of Lectures on Dramatic Art and Literature* (trans. J. Black), London, Henry G. Bohn.

Wagnleitner, R. (1994) *Coca-Colonization and the Cold War*, Chapel Hill, NC, University of North Carolina Press.

Watson, K. (1982) 'Colonialism and educational development' in Watson K. (ed.) *Education in the Third World*, London, Croom Helm.

Waxman, P. (2000) 'The impact of English language proficiency on the adjustment of recently arrived Iraqi, Bosnian and Afghan refugees in Sydney', *Prospect*, vol. 15, no. 1, pp. 4–22.

Wayland, S. (2009) 'Religious change and the renaissance elegy', *English Literary Renaissance,* vol. 39, no. 3, pp. 429–59.

Webby, E. (2006) 'Colonial writers and readers' in Webby, E. (ed.) *The Cambridge Companion to Australian Literature*, Cambridge, Cambridge University Press.

Wei, L. (1994) *Three Generations, Two Languages, One Family: Language Choice and Language Shift in a Chinese Community in Britain*, Clevedon, Multilingual Matters.

Wei, L. (2011) 'Moment analysis and translanguaging space: discursive construction of identities by multilingual Chinese youth in Britain', *Journal of Pragmatics*, vol. 43, no. 5, pp. 1222–35.

Wickramasekera, P. (2002) *Asian Labour Migration: Issues and Challenges in an Era of Globalization*, International Migration Papers 57, Geneva, International Labour Office.

Widdowson, H. (1994) 'The ownership of English', *TESOL Quarterly*, vol. 28, no. 2, pp. 377–89.

Wiesemes, R. (2009) 'Developing theories of practices in CLIL: CLIL as post method pedagogies?' in Ruiz De Zarobe, Y. and Jimenez Catlan, R. M. (eds)

Content and Language Integrated Learning: Evidence from Research in Europe, Clevedon, Multilingual Matters.

Willan, B. (1984) *Sol Plaatje: South African Nationalist, 1876–1932*, London, Heinemann.

Williams, R. (1983) *Keywords: A Vocabulary of Culture and Society*, London, Fontana.

Wong, L. (1991) 'The Vietnamese Chinese speech community' in Alladina, S. and Edwards, V. (eds) *Multilingualism in the British Isles*, Vol. 2, London, Longman.

Woolard, K. (1998) 'Introduction: language ideology as a field of inquiry' in Schieffelin, B., Woolard, K. and Kroskrity, P. (eds) *Language Ideologies*, Oxford, Oxford University Press.

Yasin, Sopia Md., Marsh, D., Ong, E. T. and Lai, Y. Y. (2009) 'Learners' perceptions towards the teaching of science through English in Malaysia: a quantitative analysis', *International CLIL Research Journal*, vol. 1, no. 2, pp. 54–69.

Acknowledgements

Grateful acknowledgement is made to the following sources:

Text

Page 10: Sutherland, J. (2002), Linguicide: the death of a langauge, *The Independent*, 10 March. Copyright © independent.co.uk; page 33: Prendergast, C. (2008) '"We live and learn": English and ambivalence in a new capitalist state', *Globalisation, Societies and Education*, vol. 6, no. 1, pp. 89–100. Copyright © 2008 Taylor & Francis Ltd, http://www.informaworld.com, reprinted by permission of the publisher; page 39: Blommeart, J. (2010) *The Sociolinguistics of Globalization*, Cambridge University Press. Copyright © 2010 Jan Blommaert. Published by Cambridge University Press, reproduced with permission; page 57: 'Your language abilities' taken from The Citizenship Test, www.cic.gc.ca, Citizenship and Immigration Canada; pages 58–9: US Citizenship and Immigration Services, 'Scoring guidelines for the U.S. naturalization test', www.uscis.gov, U.S Department of Homeland Security; page 79: Piller, I. and Takahashi, K. (2010) 'At the intersection of gender, language and transnationalism' in Coupland, N. (ed.) *The Handbook of Langauge and Globalization*, Wiley-Blackwell. Copyright © 2010 Blackwell Publishing Ltd. Reproduced with permission of Blackwell Publishing Ltd; page 84: Hult, F. M. (2009) 'Language ecology and linguistic landscape analysis', in Shohamy, E., and Gorter, D. (eds), *Lingusitic Landscape: Expanding the Scenery*, Routledge. Copyright © 2009 Taylor and Francis; page 121: Lin, A.M.Y. and Martin, P.W. (2005) '"Safe" language practices in two rural schools in Malaysia: tensions between policy and practice', *Decolonisation, Globalisation: Langauge-in-Education Policy and Practice*, Multilingual Matters Ltd. Copyright © 2005 Angel M.Y. Lin and Peter W. Martin. Reproduced by permission of the publisher; page 164: This paper is by Professor Eddie Williams, and features in the publication *Dreams and Realities: Developing Countries and the English Language* (British Council, 2011), which is available online at http://www.teachingenglish.org.uk/transform/books/dreams-realities-developing-countries-english-language or for print copies from www.bebc.co.uk; page 171: Pegrum, M. (2004) 'Selling English: advertising and the discourses of ELT', *English Today 77*, vol. 20, no. 1, January 2004. Copyright © 2004 Cambridge University Press, reproduced with permission; page 207: Rajan, R.S. (2001) 'Writing in English in India, again' and 'Dealing with anxieties', *The Hindu*, www.hindu.com. Reproduced by permission of the author; page 214: Saussy,

of Ann Hewings; page 109: © University of Cape Town 2011. All rights reserved; page 110: © University of València; page 145: © REUTERS/ Tobias Schwarz; page 153 (top): Taken from http://www.ets.org/toefl/; page 153 (bottom): Taken from http://www.ielts.org/default.aspx; page 180: © Historical image collection by Bildagentur-online / Alamy; page 183: © Neil McAllister / Alamy; page 188: © The British Library. 247/3 (3); page 198: © Carrie Craig; page 201: © Mark Peters/Getty Images; page 207: © AFP/Getty Images; page 219: Permission granted, however publisher unable to supply an image. © Spectrum Books (Nig) Ltd & Tony Marinho; page 227 (left): Tandoh, Ike K.F. (2003) *Oforiwaa: The Tempations of an Innocent Girl*, Kumasi: King Bazooka Publications; page 227 (right) Assan, A. (1978) *Christmas in the City*, Macmillan Education Ltd. Copyright © Macmillan Publishers Ltd. Reproduced with permission; page 231: © AFP/Getty Images; page 238: © Mirabai films; page 243: © RichardBaker / Alamy; page 266 (left): © Juergen Sack / iStockphoto 15 credits; page 266 (right): © Peter Burnett / iStockphoto; page 275: © Archive Pics / Alamy; page 282: © Reuters/ CORBIS; page 293: © Arab Film Distribution; page 304: © dbimages / Alamy; page 311: © Classic Image / Alamy; page 315: © Melissa L. Curtin; page 316: © Caroline Tagg.

Illustrations

page 187: Taken from http://en.wikipedia.org.

Tables

page 147: Pinon, R. and Haydon, J. (2010) 'English language quantitative indicators: Cameroon, Nigeria, Rwanda, Bangladesh and Pakistan', A custom report compiled by Euromonitor International for the British Council, Euromonitor International. Copyright © 2010 Euromonitor International.

Every effort has been made to contact copyright holders. If any have inadvertently been overlooked the publishers will be pleased to make the necessary arrangements at the first opportunity.

Index